George MacDonald:
Victorian Mythmaker

George MacDonald: Victorian Mythmaker

Rolland Hein

Star Song
PUBLISHING GROUP
Nashville, Tennessee

Star Song Publishing Group, a division of Jubilee Communications, Inc.
2325 Crestmoor, Nashville, Tennessee 37215.
Printed in the United States of America.

First Printing, May 1993

Library of Congress Cataloging-in-Publication Data

Hein, Rolland.
    George MacDonald: Victorian mythmaker / by Rolland Hein.—1st ed.
        p. cm.
    ISBN 1-56233-046-2
    1. MacDonald, George, 1824–1895. 2. Authors, Scottish—19th
century—Biography. 3. Myth in literature. I. Title.
PR4968.H45 1993
823'.8—dc20   93-19639
    [B]   CIP

1 2 3 4 5 6 7 8 9 10 — 99 98 97 96 95 94 93

As if the story of a house
Were told, or ever could be . . .
—E. A. Robinson

If to myself—"God sometimes interferes"—
I said, my faith at once would be struck blind.
I see him all in all, the lifing mind,
Or nowhere in the vacant miles and years.
—George MacDonald

Contents

Acknowledgments

I am pleased to have been awarded the 1989 Clyde S. Kilby Research Grant for this biography. My work has grown out of my interest in the writings of George MacDonald over many years. Clyde S. Kilby, of precious memory, introduced me to MacDonald's writings thirty-five years ago. He established the Wade Collection, which is housed at Wheaton College and which contains, among other authors, a collection of MacDonald's books and criticism.

I am deeply grateful for the help of a number of people. Barbara McClatchey gave the manuscript careful attention and offered valuable advice, Lyle Dorsett offered counsel, my daughter Christine responded helpfully to various chapters, and my son Steven did photography copy work. I am especially appreciative for the advice and encouragement offered by Jill Baumgaertner and Frederick Buechner, who read the manuscript in its final form.

I feel sincere appreciation toward Wheaton College for granting me a sabbatical leave to do research, a reduced teaching load for one semester so that I could concentrate on my writing, and financial help for securing copies of manuscripts, articles, and letters. I wish to thank the family of G. W. Aldeen for establishing the fund from which I was granted money to secure these materials. The staff at The Beinecke Rare Book and Manuscript Library was especially cooperative in making available to me the large collection of George MacDonald family letters reposited with them. I wish to thank The Beinecke Rare Book and Manuscript Library, Yale University; The Houghton Library, Harvard University; the Huntington Library; and the Trustees of the National Library of Scotland for granting me permission to quote from numerous letters. The British Library and the Brown University Library both helped make available to me the several manuscripts of *Lilith*.

I am also grateful to many people at other libraries and institutions who have made an invaluable contribution to the accuracy of my work by patiently answering my inquiries and making available to me by mail copies of letters and newspaper articles: Aberdeen University Library, American Antiquarian Society, Boston Public Library, Brander Library (Huntly, Scotland), Brooklyn Public Library, Butler University Library, Carnegie Library of Pittsburgh, Commonwealth of Massachusetts State Library, District of Columbia Public Library, Duke University Library, Enoch Pratt Free Library, Fraser-Hickson Institute of Montreal, Forbes Library, Hartford *Courant,* Historical Society of Delaware, Historical Society of Western Pennsylvania, Houghton Library of Harvard University, Kansas State Historical Society, Lawrence Public Library, Library of Congress, Milton S. Eisenhower Library at Johns Hopkins University, National Library of Canada, Ohio Historical Society, Newark Public Library, New York Historical Society, Pollard Library, Princeton University Library, Royal Commission on Historical Manuscripts, Springfield City Library, University Library of Colorado at Boulder, William L. Clements Library at the University of Michigan, and Wilmington Library.

Freda Levson, great-niece of George MacDonald, has been of especial help and encouragement. I also wish to express thanks to Roger Phillips, former research librarian at Wheaton College, for his assistance, and to Lynette (Bashaw) Hull, my student assistant, for help in researching MacDonald's American tour. Michael Nicholls, of Spurgeon's College, London, graciously made available to me his extensive research contained in his thesis "Ministerial Training in London 1830–1890." John Creasey, of Dr. Williams's Library in London, was helpful in researching references to MacDonald in Highbury College files. Michael Page, of King's College, London, made clear MacDonald's association with that institution. Professor Giorgia Spina of the Universita Degli Studi di Genova was a helpful correspondent on many matters relating to the MacDonalds' residence in Italy. And I will always recall with fond gratitude the gracious hospitality and help that Peiro and

Laura De Angeli of the Civica Biblioteca Internazionale di Bordighera extended to me during my visit to Italy. The depiction of Casa Coraggio at the early part of this century, contained among the illustrations, is from them.

Preface

Writing to James T. Fields in 1879, George MacDonald firmly refused to release materials for the writing of a biography. "I have refused such a request again and again," he explained, "because I dislike the thing so much—partly on personal grounds, partly on principle. A man should keep his shell till he gets his coffin instead—and for my part I trust the outer life of one who has written a good many volumes tending to reveal most that is worth knowing of his inner life, will be forgotten in this world after he has left it." He added as an afterthought: "If anything is left after a hundred years, accompanied by a desire to know, *then* is soon enough."[1] One hundred years have passed; the story of this Scots man of letters needs to be fully told.

MacDonald's eldest son, Greville, chose not to honor his father's wish to wait one hundred years before writing an account of his life. He undertook to commemorate the centenary of his father's birth by publishing in 1924 *George MacDonald and his Wife*,[2] an account of his parents' lives. Eight years later he presented more material in his *Reminiscences of a Specialist*[3] (Greville was a throat surgeon). Greville's work is not impartial, and careful research shows it is not completely reliable; nevertheless, anyone interested in his father's life owes him a great debt for preserving a body of anecdote and detail that would otherwise have been lost.

Recently, various biographies have appeared from smaller trade publishers building on Greville's foundation.[4] The strengths and weaknesses of these notwithstanding, none of the authors has adequately researched the large collection of autographed letters by MacDonald, his wife Louisa, and several of their children, that is reposited at The Beinecke Rare Book and Manuscript Library on the Yale University campus. These uncatalogued letters—some cross-written and most with elaborate marginal notes, written in crimped handwritings to save space (and hence postage), and faded with age—abundantly repay the student's patience in sorting out the true facts and details of the family's life. There are as well smaller collections of MacDonald's letters in other libraries, such as the National Library of Scotland, The Houghton Library, the Huntington Library, the Aberdeen University Library, and the University Library of Colorado at Boulder.

Muriel Hutton, who spent considerable time with the Beinecke collection before her death, complained about the "patent deficiencies" and " 'inexplicable dumb show' of misrepresentation" in the biographical and critical writings on MacDonald.[5] This biographer agrees and undertakes as much as possible to correct this situation. This work is based on a careful reading of the available letters and other available materials, together with a consideration of what may be judiciously inferred about MacDonald's life from each of his writings. As he himself remarked, his more than fifty volumes do indeed reveal a great amount concerning his inner life. The story of how intricately his thoughts are related to the facts of his outer life and how he struggled to live out his ideals is a story worth telling.

Foreword

When I was a child, an aunt gave me an illustrated edition of *At the Back of the North Wind.* Probably because I found its three hundred and fifty-odd pages a rather long row to hoe, I didn't get very far into it, but it left me with the impression of a somehow snug, silvery, magical world that I carried around in the back of my head for long afterward. I remembered the stable loft where Diamond slept—the sweet-smelling hay and the chomping of the horses down below, the howling of the north wind, the little skylight through which he watched the stars when he couldn't sleep. But I was lured away by the somehow more rakish, faster-moving Oz books, which were and remain to this day my particular favorites, and by Dr. Doolittle and the Andrew Lang fairy tale collections, with their gorgeous cloth bindings stamped in gold and richly dyed to match each title as it came along: *The Crimson Fairy Book, The Olive Fairy Book, The Lilac Fairy Book,* or whichever ones I found on the glassed-in shelves of my grandparents' library in Pittsburgh, Pennsylvania. I was lured away too by the books of the great E. Nesbit, especially the ones that had magic in them, and, among those, especially her masterpiece, *The Enchanted Castle,* where the garden statues come alive at night. When the one of Phoebus Apollo goes swimming under the moon, "rings of liquid silver spread across the lake, widening and widening, from the spot where the white joined hands of the Sun-god had struck the water as he dived." I lost track of George MacDonald among all these flashier riches, and it wasn't, I think, until my seminary days in the mid-1950s that I found my way back to him again.

Like so many others both before me and since, I have C. S. Lewis's little anthology of quotations from MacDonald's work to thank for it. Until then I had thought of MacDonald, insofar as I had thought of him at all, as a writer exclusively of children's books, but from Lewis's introduction I discovered not only that he had written a great deal of both fiction and nonfiction for grown-ups, but that all of it was deeply imbued by his Christian faith. Lewis wrote of him as his "master" and said that his debt to the three volumes of *Unspoken Sermons* in particular was "almost as great as one man can owe to another." He called attention to MacDonald's gift for somehow conveying above all else a sense of *holiness* and went on to say, "I know hardly any other writer who seems to be closer, or more continually close, to the Spirit of Christ Himself." It was words like these that started me reading him again, and I have been reading him off and on ever since with my interest regalvanized by the semester I taught at Wheaton College in Illinois several years ago. There I not only found my way to the extraordinary Wade Collection with its hoard of MacDonald rarities, but also became the friend and admirer of an English department colleague named Rolland Hein, who probably has a more extensive command of the life and works of George MacDonald than anyone else in the galaxy. It was Dr. Hein who put me on to *The Diary of an Old Soul* whose daily entries have often proved almost eerily pertinent to what has been going on in my own life that day (on this soggy, chill Vermont January 22, for instance, I find "Do thou, my God, my spirit's weather control; / And as I do not gloom though the day be dun, / Let me not gloom when earth-born vapors roll / Across the infinite zenith of my soul."). When I asked him what MacDonald novel he would recommend, he suggested *Thomas Wingfold, Curate,* in which I found several passages that I have returned to many times since, especially one which (since for some reason Lewis doesn't include it in his anthology) I want to quote here in full. Responding to a man named Polwarth, who has just asked him if he is thinking of giving up his curacy, Wingfold replies:

> I have almost forgotten I ever thought of such a thing. What-
> ever energies I may or may not have, I know one thing for
> certain: that I could not devote them to anything else I should
> think entirely worth doing. Indeed, nothing else seems inter-

esting enough, nothing to repay the labor, but the telling of
my fellow men about the one man who is the truth, and to
know whom is the life. Even if there be no hereafter, I would
live my time believing in a grand thing that ought to be true
if it is not. No facts can take the place of truths; and if these
be not truths, then is the loftiest part of our nature a waste.
Let me hold by the better than the actual, and fall into nothingness off the same precipice with Jesus and John and Paul
and a thousand more, who were lovely in their lives, and with
their death make even the nothingness into which they have
passed like the garden of the Lord. I will go farther, Polwarth,
and say I would rather die forevermore believing as Jesus believed, than live forevermore believing as those that deny him.
If there be no God, I feel assured that this existence is and
could be but a chaos of contradictions whence can emerge
nothing worthy to be called a truth, nothing worth living for.

MacDonald was extremely popular in his prime. Between
1851 and 1897 he wrote over fifty books—novels, plays, essays,
sermons, poems, fairy tales, not to mention two fantasies for
adults (*Phantastes,* 1858, and *Lilith,* 1895) that elude the usual
categories. They won him a large and devoted following on both
sides of the Atlantic. Lewis Carroll was a great friend and gave him
the manuscript of the first *Alice* to try out on his children, who
loved it. John Ruskin, Charles Kingsley, Lord Tennyson, Matthew
Arnold, and many others scarcely less exalted were among his close
associates and admirers. When he came to the United States for
a highly successful lecture tour in 1872, Emerson, Longfellow,
Whittier, Phillips Brooks, Oliver Wendell Holmes, Bret Harte,
and Mark Twain were among the native luminaries who paid him
homage, and Dr. Hein tells us how in New York City a large Fifth
Avenue church tried unsuccessfully to entice him to become its
pastor by offering him what was for its time the almost unheard-of
salary of $20,000 a year. A Chicago reporter wrote of his "Christ-
like countenance," and wherever he went people flocked to him
as prophet, seer, saint, all in one.

In addition to this period of triumphant success, however, his life was continually shadowed by tragedy, beginning with the death of his mother when he was a child of eight. After a brief period as the minister of a dissenting chapel in Arundel, he was charged with heresy and the taint of German theology and forced to resign what turned out to be his one and only pulpit. His lungs were diseased and his poverty at times so extreme that his family occasionally faced literal starvation. Tuberculosis killed two of his brothers, two half-sisters and his mother-in-law by the time he was thirty-five and then started to ravage his children, including his beloved firstborn, Lily, who played Christiana to her father's Mr. Greatheart in their amateur theatricals and died in his arms at the age of thirty-nine. There must have been many times when the world seemed to him the same "chaos of contradictions whence can emerge nothing worthy to be called a truth, nothing worth living for" that Thomas Wingfold so eloquently describes. Yet to the extent that we can judge of such private and interior matters from the outside, he never let go that "grand thing that ought to be true if it is not" or at least in spite of everything remained somehow lovely in his life to the end of it.

To examine his long life as tirelessly and exhaustively and conscientiously as Rolland Hein has examined it must have required an almost overwhelming amount of work and years of time. In addition to everything else, one thinks of the labor involved simply in poring through those mountains of hitherto unresearched letters that he describes in his introduction—cross-written to save on postage, faded with age, presumably in many cases all but indecipherable. Yet without such patient and loving labor, we might never have seen, for instance, the letter that MacDonald sent Lily on what proved to be her last birthday. "It is so much easier to write romance," he said, "where you cannot easily lie, than to say the commonest things where you may go wrong any moment. . . . I can only tell you I love you with true heart fervently. . . . I don't thank you for coming to us, for you could not help it, but the whole universe is 'tented' with love, and you hold one of the corners of the great love-canopy for your mother and me. . . . Darling, I wish you life eternal. I daresay birthdays will still be sparks in its glory. May I one day see that mould in God out of which you came." In addition to such treasures as that, we can be deeply grateful to Dr. Hein also for his particular sensitivity to the profound role that religious faith played in MacDonald's life and for the erudition and insightfulness with which he has examined Mac-Donald's work in light of it.

Toward the end of his days, plagued by eczema and insomnia, MacDonald's mind began to fail him. Little by little he gave up reading and writing and spoke less and less, until finally he became almost entirely silent and sank into a five-year period that his son and early biographer Greville MacDonald describes as "his long vigil" during which he had "the heart-rending air of waiting for something—far off or nearby—[that] never left him." There is a haunting photograph of him taken on the occasion of his golden wedding anniversary in 1901, which occurred during this time. The white-bearded old man sits in a wheelchair with a cloak or blanket around his back and over his knees. In what could be a nurse's cap and cape, a woman with one hand on the arm of his chair and the other on his right shoulder leans a little toward him with an air of deep solicitude. The old man is looking away from her and off to one side of whoever is taking the picture. His eyes—"still blue as a child's" Greville tells us—are gazing intensely and uncertainly at heaven only knows what.

Not even Rolland Hein, who knows and has enriched us with so much about him, can tell us what "the grand old saint," as a young friend called him, was gazing at, gazing *for*. We can only pray that in the end it proved well worth all the long years he had spent waiting for it.

—FREDERICK BUECHNER

Introduction

In 1853, George MacDonald wrote his father, who was deeply distressed because his son was not "getting on" well as a pastor: "The life, thoughts, deeds, aims, beliefs of Jesus have to be fresh expounded every age, for all the depth of eternity lies in them, and they have to be seen into more profoundly every new era of the world's spiritual history. Else the new men needing higher things than the former saw in Christ . . . must of necessity refuse him. . . . For my part I think . . . I can help such."[1] Determined and energetic, with something of a Messiah complex, he left his church to begin his career as a would-be prophet to his age. He became one of the most prolific of Victorian writers.

Over the next forty-five years he wrote indefatigibly in a wide variety of genres from poetry to sermons, excelling in mythopoeia.[2] He and his friend Lewis Carroll are perhaps the two finest writers of children's literature in the nineteenth century. Stephen Prickett refers to him as "one of the greatest of the [Victorian] period's myth-makers."[3] Such writers as G. K. Chesterton, C. S. Lewis, and W. H. Auden have generously praised his achievements, and key images in T. S. Eliot's later poetry appear to spring from MacDonald's fantasies.[4] His gift of creating an atmosphere blending holiness with an aura of mystery initiated the renaissance of the writing of fantasy with a Christian flavor that comes to noted expression in the work of Charles Williams, J. R. R. Tolkien, and C. S. Lewis.[5]

His art provoked diverse critical assessments in his time. Deeply religious, he doggedly defied orthodoxy and public opinion alike in the service of his vision. In his many writings[6] he placed within his visions of the ideally lived Christian life combative attacks upon all religious attitudes and practices he believed were false. Some felt his insistences were largely irrelevant to contemporary issues; others were offended by his attacks on Christian doctrines they held dear, and yet others openly scoffed at his insistence in assuming Milton-like the burden of justifying the ways of God to man.[7] On the other hand, a large popular following developed, especially in America, that felt the vision of Christianity embodied in the novels placed him among the foremost of Christian teachers.

He continues today to appeal to diverse audiences. Interest in him, if modest, is widespread. Some scholars believe MacDonald's fantasies may be contemplated quite apart from Christian doctrinal considerations and appreciate their purely literary stature and Jungian patterns.[8] Among Christians, the theological ideas that once condemned him as a heretic among the Victorians now have wide currency; indeed, they have nearly won the day.[9] His vision of people as being essentially spiritual beings with primary obligations to the moral nature of the world of spirit, while highly controversial in the culture at large, wins strongly appreciative affirmation among many. Louis MacNeice observes that "what is unique in MacDonald is his passionately spiritual attitude to the universe and his prolific invention of symbols to embody it."[10] In this he is mythic. His vision of spiritual reality fuses his work in fantasy, the novel, and theology into a unified whole.

Northrop Frye sees MacDonald as important in the tradition of sentimental romance that includes such writers as Edmund Spenser, William Morris, and J. R. R. Tolkien, a tradition in which he places Sir Walter Scott.[11] As a Scots poet and novelist, MacDonald stands readily compared to Scott, as well as to Robert Burns. While MacDonald lacks Scott's interest in history and Burns's lyrical and satirical gifts, his strength—his vision of the eternal within the temporal—appreciably excels that of his fellow countrymen. Both Scott and Burns manifest a certain interest in the spiritual aspects of life—Burns more than Scott—but neither treat spiritual dimensions as integral to our humanity as MacDonald does. The dominant metaphor he develops in *Lilith*—that the spiritual world is one of "seven dimensions," a world wherein lies the "one home" for all people—provides a fit figure to crown his life's work, for in all his writings he sees the world of the spirit as essential to the very nature of man.

Not considered an evangelical in his day, MacDonald can be most satisfyingly classified with such contemporary Broad Churchmen as A. J. Scott, principal of Owens College, Manchester, and Frederick Denison Maurice, the controversial Anglican theologian. He joined with them in opposing many prevalent views of the nature of God, the Atonement, and hell, but at the same time maintaining a strongly pietist stance.

His effect was larger than theirs because, while they worked by means of expository statement and pulpit oratory, he created a large body of imaginative literature that was widely read and admired. Eric Rabkin believes his fantasies offer "true consolation for all ages from the rigors of contemporary religious doctrines."[12] Because his novels were distributed in abundance throughout the English-speaking world, he probably did as much as any single individual to modify in the mind of the typical lay Christian the harsher aspects of the image of God derived from popular versions of the theologies of such figures as John Calvin and Jonathan Edwards.

He was important to the church of his own day because he spoke to so many who were on the verge of being disaffected from religious faith. He presented Christianity as an issue centered in the spirit of man, not his intellect. While taking a stern attitude toward all unrighteousness, he at the same time assured them a loving God was everywhere working for their spiritual welfare, so that the mundane events of their lives had great potential to contribute to their inner growth. To discern the divine purpose was the essence of moral and spiritual wisdom, and actively to obey God's will was essential to becoming truly human.

He was most concerned with the patterns of the ideal human that he saw existing within the hearts of people. He explained to William Mount-Temple that his purpose in his books was "to make them true to the real and not the spoilt humanity. Why should I spend my labour on what one can have too much of without any labour! I will try to show what we might be, may be, must be, shall be—and something of the struggle to gain it.''[13] And his good characters are his most successfully drawn. Whereas most novelists would attest that evil characters are easier to draw than good ones, MacDonald's experience was, interestingly, the opposite. Although he did not escape a morally prissy quality in some, the majority of his good characters seem plausibly human and attractive.

His writings appealed to what many laity felt were their true religious instincts. Their deep longings after the ideal were satisfied. Contemporary disputes concerning the impact on Christian faith of the latest scientific theories seemed irrelevant to spiritual concerns. MacDonald presented the Christian not as being opposed to the true nature of the world but rather as being opposed to spiritual dullness. Nature itself, and the very tenor of events in ordinary lives, were mysteriously on the Christian's side. Truth would triumph; error die. By comparison, much that came from church leaders as respectable theological thinking seemed but jargon-ridden philistinism that quibbled over matters irrelevant to daily life, raised constant alarm, and spoke nothing to the human spirit.

Many in the intellectual community, of course, did not agree. Science was discrediting the supernatural; biblical revelation was increasingly attacked as untrustworthy. Traditional foundation tenets of the Christian faith were assailed. MacDonald's insistences seemed largely irrelevant to the demands of the day; they were hopelessly idealist, repetitive, and tiresome. His attacks on what he considered to be unchristian attitudes within the church seemed to many as misplaced energy, unnecessarily contentious, and his lofty idealism quite beyond the reach of ordinary people. Hostile critics averred his appreciable creative talents were being put to the service of a wishful vision that did not square with the hard realities of life.

Just as MacDonald's voice was a singular one in his time, so it is today. He presents a model of humankind dismissed by most but radically affirmed by some. It is generally assumed that people are beings consisting of bodies and minds. The spirit, if acknowledged at all, seems unrelated to practical living and hence of little moment. But MacDonald's writings present people as beings whose spirits, or "deeper selves," are their most important component.[14] A person is not whole or complete until the spirit awakes within; further, the nature of any given individual's life beyond death has entirely to do with the quality of spiritual life.

He insisted that at birth the spirit is asleep and that nothing is more important in life than its awakening. Yet circumstances and incidents appropriate to its awakening and growth may to the unaided mind seem absurd. For instance, pain and suffering may seem to the mind to teach nothing more significant than that pain and suffering are uncomfortable, but they may be indispensable to awakening the spirit and teaching it virtue. If suffering is beneficial to a person, as the church has historically affirmed, it is because suffering affects first the spirit, then the mind.

Some sects have arisen recently that tend to take a shallow view of the nature of the spiritual aspects of people and to separate faith from righteousness. Consider for example events during the eighties in the realm of television evangelism. Among Christians dissatisfied with such inadequacies, there is a certain contemporary resurgence of interest in MacDonald as a theological teacher. His voice calls his followers to develop a faith that accounts more adequately for human experience.

MacDonald believed that when a person's spirit is flourishing, all aspects of human experience assume different dimensions. Since he was not one to teach to others what he himself was not experiencing, he was preoccupied with how his own spirit could be awake and growing and how the experiences of his own life might nurture it. This biography undertakes to tell the story of how he acquired his own spiritual perspectives, how the circumstances that befell him shaped his convictions, what nature those convictions assumed, and how he presented them in his writings.

ONE

In a Green Field

It is better to be a child in a green field than a knight of many orders in a state ceremonial. —Orts

An understanding of George MacDonald's childhood in the far north of Scotland, together with his Scottish ancestry, go far in helping one to understand the man. His lively imaginative energies, not unlike those among his ancestors, were stimulated early by Gaelic myths and Old Testament stories. His delight in the Scottish countryside issued in his later insistence that the grace of God is constantly offered to people through nature and experience. Although considered unconventional by many in his day, his later religious convictions were nevertheless rooted in the deeply held Calvinism of his family, especially that of his father and grandmother. They combined in their personalities a stern sense of justice with an enveloping love, a paradox consistently prominent both in his attitudes and in his image of God.

The vivid imaginations and love of narrative that characterized the ancient Scots offered a rich background for MacDonald's own. Clan Donald, the largest of the Highland clans, inhabited the Western Isles and the territories by the western sea in the extreme northwest of Scotland. Gaelic in language, ceremonies, and traditions, the clan bore the name MacDonald with great dignity and pride. It, as well as the clans in general, highly honored the office of bard, or oral poet. Poetic improvisations were not uncommon in daily life, and even some of the clan decrees were issued in verse. The rich mythopoeia of ancient Erin, such as the tales of Cuchullin and Deirdre, enriched the imaginations of all the clansmen.

MacDonald's clan history, however, intermingled the stark and violent with the idyllic. He was descended from the MacDonalds of Glencoe. The infamous massacre of Glencoe was, therefore, a stark reality in their family history. When, in 1691, all the Highland chiefs were ordered to declare their allegiance to William and Mary, MacDonald of Glencoe put off doing so until the deadline was past. The clan, however, did give the oath, knowing that failure to do so would give the authorities excuse to attempt to exterminate them as rebels. A party of Campbell soldiers loyal to the English throne arrived. The MacDonald chieftain, feeling he had duly complied, received them and regaled them for several days. Then, in the middle of a winter's night, the soldiers arose to massacre men, women, and children indiscriminately, with only a few escaping.

Nor was Glencoe the only political fray that colored the family history. In the famous attempts of the Jacobites to regain the throne from the Hanovers in the eighteenth century, the members of the Clan Donald were fiercely loyal to the Stuart pretenders. George MacDonald's great-grandfather, a Catholic, served as piper—an honored position—to the forces of Bonnie Prince Charles and barely escaped the defeat at Culloden with his life. The forces of Clan Ranald, another of MacDonald's hereditary families, were decimated in that battle.

In January 1746, just prior to the defeat at Culloden of Bonnie Prince Charles, George MacDonald's grandfather, Charles Edward (named after the Young Pretender), was born. He was among those who, whether from conviction or from prudence, later became Protestant. The defeat of the Roman Catholic pretender to the throne influenced many to do likewise, since the House of Hanover was Protestant. The Established Church of Scotland had been Presbyterian since 1690.

Apparently an ambitious man, George MacDonald's grandfather rose from the position of clerk to become proprietor of a bleaching business in Huntly, George MacDonald's birthplace, and later he became the banker there as well. In 1778, he married Isobel Robertson, a woman of independent thought and of conviction so stern it became legendary. Of their nine children, four sons and one daughter lived to maturity. William established a profitable brewery along the banks of the Bogie River, and the remaining three inherited the bleaching business.

These three—Charles, George, and James—leased in 1821 a quantity of land just southeast of Huntly from the Duke of Gordon, the local landowner and proprietor of nearby Huntly Castle. They used the land for bleach fields and also for raising cows; whey from the curdled milk was necessary for the bleaching process. Conscientiously, the three brothers tried to conduct their business according to Christian principles. Years later, in 1872, when the novelist was touring America, an American woman recalled her mother telling how, as one of the workers in their thread factory, she attended the weekly prayer meetings that the MacDonald brothers held for their workers from seven to eight o'clock in the evenings.

Charles, however, fell into disgrace. Apparently his father's favorite, he had inherited the largest portion of the bleaching business, and this position allowed him to become, like his father before him, the local banker. He was accused of mismanaging funds his customers entrusted to him. One of George MacDonald's early memories was of visiting on a Sunday morning with his grandmother, who lived in the house on Duke Street adjacent to the one in which he was born. A strange man intruded without knocking, bolted the door, and held an extended conference with her before fleeing. Unknown to him at the time, it was his errant uncle. Charles escaped prison only by fleeing to America, leaving his wife behind. He died in New York in 1836.

The remaining brothers, George and James, became responsible for his debts—over six thousand pounds—and paid them in full over a period of several years. The financial burden on the family was considerable and explains the financial hardship of the family during much of George MacDonald's life. Charles's mother, concluding that it was her son's violin lessons that had allowed Satan a toehold in his life, committed his instrument to the flames.

Although her husband was an elder in the local parish church, Isobel found fault with the minister's lack of zeal and took her children to the nearby "missionar' kirk," whose energetically proclaimed religious certainties were more to her taste. Apparently she was responsible for admitting to the family a strong evangelical spirit. As an aged woman she was a legendary figure in the village, each day walking to her sons' farm accompanied by her servant, who carried a camp stool for her mistress to rest on. She died at the age of ninety-two in 1848.

During her long life Isobel saw both the rise and the decline of the family prosperity. Her son George, George MacDonald's father, bore much of the burden of the decline. In 1822, during the more prosperous times of his early manhood, he married Helen MacKay, whose brother was a Gaelic scholar and friend of Sir Walter Scott. A woman noted for her beauty and poise, she possessed a good education for a woman of her time. For his bride George MacDonald, Sr., built a house in Huntly, on Duke Street, immediately adjacent to his mother's. There their first son, Charles, was born in 1823. The following year, on December 10, 1824, George MacDonald was born. The building stands today, bearing a plaque commemorating the event.

The land previously leased from the Duke of Gordon, however, offered an excellent wooded building site, and there George MacDonald, Sr., and his brother James decided to erect a home for both their families to live together. They built a plain rectangular structure in typical Scottish style, of granite and mortar, with walls some thirty inches thick. The milk processing rooms, together with the family kitchen and the servants' quarters, were in the basement, the family living space on the primary floor, and the sleeping rooms above. First known as Bleachfield Cottage, it later was referred to simply as The Farm. It is known today as Greenkirtle, and, although privately owned, is under the aegis of the Scottish Historical Society. Here four more boys were born to George and Helen MacDonald: James, in 1826; Alexander, in 1827; John MacKay, in 1829; and John Hill, in 1831.

George MacDonald, Sr., and his brother James took their growing families to The Farm in 1826. The family prosperity, however, soon began to decline. The Industrial Revolution was bringing many changes to Britain; the textile industry was among those most radically affected by a series of inventions and the introduction of chemicals that revolutionized the processing of cloth. In the huge cities the factory system developed. As these changes appeared in the Glasgow textile mills, the MacDonalds' family business became obsolete. They converted their mills to process flour from potatoes, only to be devastated by the potato blight of 1846–1848. They then changed to the grinding of oats. The resulting diminishment of income and the continuing burden of paying off the remainder of the debts incurred through their brother Charles's absconding explain why George MacDonald, Sr., was later unable to do more financially to help his sons get started in life.

Nor was lack of money his only heartache. After having borne him six boys, Helen died of tuberculosis in 1832, when her son George was eight years old. A boy with a great emotional dependency, he was deeply affected by his mother's death.[1] His father did his best to fill his emotional needs and be both father and mother to all his sons. MacDonald always revered him for it, and years later wrote:

> Whole-hearted is my worship of the man
> From whom my earthly history began.[2]

One of George and Helen's boys, John MacKay, died in infancy; a second, James, died when he was eight years of age. An aunt of George's, Christina MacDonald, came to keep the home and help her nephew raise his boys until his marriage to Margaret McColl in 1839. Margaret, the daughter of an Episcopalian minister, was a strong and loving mother to the large family. Three daughters were born to this second marriage: Isabella, in 1841; Louisa, in 1843; and Jane, in 1846. "She has my love and the love of us all, for she has been our mother in truth," George Mac-Donald remarked to his father when she was ill in 1849.[3] A woman of grace and stamina, she lived until her one hundred second year, 1910, five years longer than her novelist stepson.

George's father was a faithful member and deacon of the local independent chapel, commonly referred to as the missionar' kirk, as opposed to the Huntly Parish Church (Presbyterian), and there the family worshiped regularly. Rev. John Hill was pastor when MacDonald was growing up, a man so much admired by the family that they named MacDonald's young brother after him. The young George took churchgoing very seriously, and much that he heard left indelible impressions on his mind but not always just as the adults expected. Once he heard a sermon on the Christian's hope of one day becoming a pillar in the house of God, and he found the prospect so dismal he experienced actual pain. On another occasion, in response to his hearing of the doctrine of election, he said he did not want God to love him if he did not love everybody.

Isobel Robertson MacDonald, who had been responsible for the family's joining the dissenters, was a woman of intense conviction and narrow views. But, incongruously, she combined an extremely severe demeanor with a great capacity for love. Her grandson George was not only deeply impressed with her character, but he also as an adult bore the impress of this mold. He too was a person of paradoxical extremes. On the one hand, he was a stern, self-disciplined Scot, who took cold baths in the mornings for his health, pulled his own teeth when they abscessed, and raised his eleven children to be, above all things, righteous. On the other hand, he was almost desperately dependent on his wife for love and support (as he had been on his father as a child); he placed utmost value on cultivating for himself an attitude of child-like trust in God and advocating it for others; and his children prized no memory of their childhood, which was happy, so highly as that of their father's profusely loving forgiveness when they confessed to a wrong.

His frequent swings of mood also reflect this duality. He experienced periods of euphoria when his energies seemed superhuman. He romped with his children and enthusiastically shaped for them imaginative worlds in Faerie. His favorite pastime was to play parlor charades with family and friends, excelling in mimicry himself and laughing with unfeigned delight at the efforts of others. He dreamed of future ages when God would shape for humankind worlds that beggar the imagination. But this aspect of his character was balanced by periods of depression and a sense of defeat, in which his mind seemed to him paralyzed, and he would wrestle with his God, who seemed to have vacated the universe. Migraine headaches were frequent.

In his fiction some of his most vivid and believable characters paradoxically possess the same duality he saw as a child in his grandmother and experienced in himself. Grizzie, the aged housekeeper in *Warlock O' Glenwarlock,* is a good example. Perhaps his most imaginatively gripping presentation of this type is Grandmother Falconer in *Robert Falconer* (Chapter 10), of whom he remarked: "Frivolity . . . was in her eyes a vice; loud laughter almost a crime; cards, and *novelles,* as she called them, were such in her estimation, as to be beyond my powers of characterization. Her commonest injunction was, 'Noo be *dooce,'*—that is *sober.* But her extreme severity of tone and manner was a facade to prevent the "ebullition of a feeling which she could not otherwise control, and which she was ashamed to manifest"[4]: a large-hearted love. MacDonald himself came to reject her narrow dogmatism, but he stood in awe of the personality type.

Many of the scenes and situations in his novels are also imaginative reworkings of actual places and occurrences in Huntly. For instance, in *Robert Falconer,* Robert's seeing Mary St. John suddenly appearing on a short stair, having come through a door that connected two houses, recalls the MacDonalds' closely connected houses on Duke Street (the grandmother's with the one in which MacDonald was born). The abandoned factory in the novel recalls the MacDonalds' own.

But it is a mistake to read the novels with too keen a biographical eye. In all his Scottish stories MacDonald's vivid imagination extensively reworked and embellished materials from his past. Duncan MacPhail, the bagpiping grandfather in *Malcolm,* continually relives in his imagination the outrage of the Campbell massacre, his very life's energies sustained by his faith that God is a god of vengeance who will yet repay the Campbells for their treachery. His insistence that his native Gaelic, being the very language of nature, does not need to be learned, provides a comic version of MacDonald's own love of the language and the idyllic past he saw it to symbolize.

MacDonald's strongest impressions from his past came from its religious realities. In such novels as *Alec Forbes of Howglen,* he presents the "muckle kirk," or the Scottish Presbyterian Church, as highbrow and spiritually ineffectual, and the missionar' kirk as being gripped with fanaticism. The latter term, one of contempt, was attached to the local dissenters by the populace because they advocated the sending out of missionaries. He gave a disparaging picture of both churches but showed each group, despite its shortcomings, as capable of having a positive effect on an earnest soul.

The persistence with which MacDonald's imagination kept returning to such scenes reveals how deeply his childhood religious experiences among the Scottish dissenters shaped his adult mind. "I wonder if one will ever be able to understand the worship of his childhood—that revering upward look which must have been founded on a reality, however much after experience may have shown the supposed grounds of reverence to be untenable," he mused later with helpful self-revelation.[5] As an adult he came to feel that many of the doctrines he learned as a child were seriously deficient, but he also believed that his personal relationship to God, secured within that context, was the basic reality of his life. His father's mediation of Christianity to him made the difference.

Like his mother, George's father also had seemingly contradictory personality traits. The reverses and domestic hardships that befell him were absorbed by his sanguine and magnanimous disposition. He was an austere and spirited Calvinist of great personal strength and fortitude but the rare sort that combined piety with good humor, being wisely tolerant of human foibles. When in 1825 his tubercular leg had to be amputated, he refused to take the customary whisky to deaden the pain and watched the operation by means of a mirror in stoical silence. His amputated leg having been buried in a churchyard beyond the Bogie River, he joked that he was the only man who could stand with one leg on each side of the local stream. Life was a momentous and difficult affair, but he affirmed it with zest, enjoyed people, and loved his family.

The effect on George MacDonald of his father's character and approach to life was profound. George gave his father respectful obedience as a child, maintained a constant and open-hearted correspondence with him from the time he left home until his father's sudden death in 1858, and modeled many of the fatherly characters of his fiction on him. David Elginbrod, in the novel by that name, is the most vivid.

Further, as an adult he drew on his image of his father to form his image of God. The scrupulous conscientiousness with which he served God derived from his youthful efforts to please his father. Inasmuch as MacDonald is important among those thinkers of the nineteenth century who are responsible for replacing the widespread popular image of God as absolute tyrant with that of loving Father, the extent of the influence of his father's life is awesome.

The land around MacDonald's boyhood home was gently rolling, with the spires of Aberdeen some forty miles to the east, coastal fishing villages lying somewhat closer to the north, and the black-green Highlands with the royal blue lochs to the west. Huntly was a village of modest size, with thatched cottages and a gathering of slated, two-story houses around the town square, situated somewhat to the north of Bleachfield Cottage. Just north of it sat the crumbling castle of the House of Gordon. When approaching the village on the Aberdeen Road from the southeast, a traveler crossed a stone bridge spanning the Bogie River and noticed perhaps first a thatched mill with an open waterwheel and next the gaunt and forbidding square block parish kirk, standing with not even a tree near it.[6]

One of MacDonald's earliest memories was seeing the funeral cortege of one of the dukes of Gordon. The somber funeral pomp made an extraordinary impression on his infant mind, and no doubt was in part responsible for his preoccupation as an adult with death. The castle ruins, where he played as a child, established his deep fascination for castles and great country houses.

The "little grey town" of Huntly itself also offered him memorable experience. It was flooded in 1829, when MacDonald was five, the river rising to sweep away the wooden bridge that spanned it. Flood scenes in his novels, such as in *Alec Forbes of Howglen,* are among his most vivid. Also, after school he frequented the local pub, overhearing the bonhomous Gaelic conversations of the local shepherds and crofters. Such experiences deepened his love for the native dialects; his later ability to transcribe them accurately is one of the noted strengths of his Scottish novels.

His abounding energies notwithstanding, he had a delicate constitution and was frequently ill, especially with pleurisy, for which he was duly bled. His health prompted his father to send him during many of his summers to the home of his uncle, George MacKay, living in Portsoy on the sea, where he was urged to bathe in the ocean and drink the seawater. "Aunt makes me drink the water but I am very unwilling to do it," he wrote to his father when he was eleven.[7] The family also vacationed at times in the coastal towns of Cullen and Cabrach, and Cullen became the model for Portlossie in *Malcolm* and *The Marquis of Lossie.*

Letters from Portsoy to his father from the summers of 1833 and 1834, written with painstaking neatness in an elongated, slanting hand, were frank and intimate. He described the adventures of living by the sea, riding out in the pilot boat to meet schooners docked offshore, and hoping to master the art of swimming. Making a friend of a Swedish sea captain, he learned from him how to make and rig boats.

One summer, when a teenager, the love of the sea so overwhelmed him that he announced to his father: "I must tell you that the sea is my delight and I wish to go to it as soon as possible." He was certain, whatever else he may have intended in his former "childhood," that now he "could apply to nothing else to your or my own satisfaction, but would be continually wishing and longing to be at sea. . . . I hope that you will not use your parental authority to prevent me, as you undoubtedly can. . . . O let me, dear father, for I could not be happy at anything else."[8] How his father handled this request is not clear, but inasmuch as MacDonald later asserted he never asked his father for anything but what he granted it, it is safe to conclude that his father did not issue a peremptory denial.

His relationship to his father was open and frank, and he was eager to please him. Once he recounted to him how he artfully avoided taking gin offered by a congenial hostess, and so "I got away and did not break any of the rules of the temperance society."[9] His scrupulous rejection shows his conscientious adherence to the principles of the local dissenters. Encouraged by his crusading grandmother, at thirteen he became the first president of the Huntly Juvenile Temperance Society. At its semimonthly meetings in his father's factory, he spoke with energetic conviction on the evils of drink. The group was jubilant when in 1841 a local whisky shop closed its doors.

As an adult MacDonald's recollections of his childhood were replete with memories of his father's care, love, and discipline. His love of story, fed by the Gaelic and Celtic myths that were a part of his cultural heritage, was strengthened within him by his father's attempts to retell the stories from both the Old and New Testaments in a manner that captured his children's imaginations. Reminiscing in a letter to his father in 1853, shortly after the death of his brother Alec, MacDonald recalled "running with him [Alec] through the long grass on a warm summer night, trying to catch the corn scraich, till recalled by you and reprimanded for trampling down the grass. And the well too! from which on hot noon-days I so often fetched you a jug of cold water when you came into the house hot and thirsty."[10] Such memories gave him a sense of both security and pleasure. As an adult he was quick to admit that his experiences of his earthly father shaped his perceptions of the nature of the heavenly one.

God, as MacDonald came to envision him, is a pervading presence, manifesting himself in both nature and dreams to the attentive person. One of his many vivid childhood dreams was of the ceiling of his room containing sun, moon, and stars. The impression was so deep that years later he kept the ceiling of his study painted with depictions of these heavenly bodies. The childhood pleasures he received from nature and dreams left such an impression that he generally believed that whatever lessons may be acquired from them should be honored above those that could be acquired from abstract formulations of truth. His childhood experiences with the latter were through the many tedious encounters with the Westminster Shorter Catechism that his formal schooling afforded him.

Formulated in 1647, the Shorter Catechism is a document that answers quite thoroughly to the Westminster Confession of Faith. The epitome of abstract theology, it was to his childhood mind as dry as summer's dust. Every Scottish schoolboy learned it by rote and was expected to give on demand any of a long series of precisely worded responses to specific doctrinal questions. The frequent references to it in MacDonald's writings reflect the many hours he spent with it as a child and the manner in which it remained a constant point of reference for him as an adult.

The Shorter Catechism was distasteful to him in part because he later came to embrace different theological convictions, but more directly because it represented an approach to truth that he felt was deadening to the human spirit. A knowledge of its affirmations is helpful, therefore, to understanding MacDonald the man.

With its beginning—that "man's chief end is to glorify God,

and to enjoy him forever"—he had no quarrel. The catechism proceeded, however, to define God abstractly as a coalescence of attributes, to affirm his decrees whereby he "hath foreordained whatsoever comes to pass," to relate God's work in Creation and Adam's disobedience in the Fall, and to insist that the consequences of Adam's acts pass on all men so that "all mankind by their fall lost communion with God, are under his wrath and curse, and so made liable to all the miseries in this life, to death itself, and to the pains of hell forever."

It taught that God, "out of his mere good pleasure from all eternity, elected some to everlasting life" and entered into a covenant of grace to redeem them through the sacrifice of Christ. The elect are made partakers of "the redemption purchased by Christ" through the Holy Spirit's bestowing on them an effectual calling and effecting faith within them. They have the righteousness of Christ imputed to them, are adopted into the family of God, and through sanctification are "renewed in the whole man after the image of God." At their death their souls are "made perfect in holiness and do immediately pass into glory," while their bodies "await the resurrection."

The framers then presented the Ten Commandments as the revealed will of God, which it is the duty of everyone to obey, giving special stress to the need to keep the Sabbath holy. They considered the nature of the sacraments of Baptism and the Lord's Supper in careful conformity with the principles of Reformed theology and concluded with an analysis of the Lord's Prayer.

While MacDonald never lost respect for this theology when he saw it producing a genuine righteousness within the lives of its adherents, he came to feel that such formulations served mainly to crush the spirits of genuinely sensitive people. "For my part," he writes in *Alec Forbes of Howglen,* "I wish the spiritual engineers who constructed it [the Shorter Catechism] had, after laying the grandest foundation stone that truth could afford them, glorified God by going no further. Certainly many a man would have enjoyed Him sooner, if it had not been for their work."[11]

TWO

The Borders of Fairyland

He saw the whole world golden through the stained-glass windows of his imagination. . . . Alec felt as if he had got to the borders of fairy-land, and something was going to happen. A door would open and admit him into the secret of the world. —Alec Forbes of Howglen

George MacDonald's education was highly disciplined and intensely religious. From it came his extreme conscientiousness and his preoccupation with religious realities. His need to earn the finances for his schooling seems to have given him a spirit of independence and enhanced his resourcefulness, and these traits, combined with the deeply emotional side of his nature, prompted him to an early questioning of some of the more stern tenets of his Calvinist background.

His family sent him to the local school for dissenters, known as the "adventure" school, as opposed to the more respectable parish school. Rock fights between groups of boys from each school, such as those recounted in *Ranald Bannerman's Boyhood*, were not uncommon. In the parish school the master was appointed by the presbytery; whereas, in the adventure school, the master was appointed by the parents of the scholars. Both were licentiates of the established church.

MacDonald's first teacher was a notoriously severe Highlander, the Rev. Colin Stuart, whose liberal wielding of the taws— a leather strap slit into strips at the end—may have been responsible, at least in part, for the death of George's eight-year-old brother James. In his schoolroom, which was an old handloom weaver's shed, he taught the Shorter Catechism with a vengeance. Once, when nineteen of his boys failed to master a section of the catechism to his satisfaction, he locked them all in the schoolroom on a Saturday.

When he forgot to let them out, they escaped by a window. On Monday he vented his wrath by flogging them each so severely that his strap was covered with blood. He later had to send it out to be cleaned.[1] MacDonald imaginatively reworks this incident in *Alec Forbes of Howglen*. When Alec and some of his young companions are kept in on a Saturday morning for not having sufficiently mastered the assigned portion of the Shorter Catechism, little Annie escapes through a window to bring them a loaf of bread. The outraged master, Murdock Malison, soundly thrashes them when he discovers their escapade. But he too, like Grandmother Falconer, fits the stereotype of the strict demeanor that hides a potential for love, and later in the novel the potential is realized. Conscience-stricken for having crippled a boy by punishing him, he begins to serve the boy to make atonement and comes to love him. They die together as Malison attempts to rescue the boy from raging floodwaters. MacDonald moralizes: "When we love truly, all oppression of past sin will be swept away. Love is the final atonement."[2] The idea is often presented in the novels.

When after a time Stuart left the school, the dissenters chose Rev. Alexander Millar to take his place. Stuart went to Wales, where, interestingly, he met and married one of MacDonald's aunts, and they subsequently emigrated to Australia. Perhaps the parents were more careful this time to choose a schoolmaster less harsh, for the new teacher was a more humane and sensitive man. He looked favorably on young George, who was already writing compositions in verse, and became to him a friend and companion as well as teacher. He even allowed him on occasions to help with the teaching. MacDonald's deeply held convictions on the importance of a teacher's being sensitive to the nature and particular stage of development of his pupils, convictions which he expatiates on in his earlier novels, sprang from his experiences.

The same understanding of religious realities that permeated George MacDonald's childhood characterized his education at King's College, Aberdeen, where he enrolled in 1840. Then sixteen, he left his family home and rural environs to begin life in the austere and solemnly beautiful "Silver City by the Sea," so nicknamed because of its gleaming array of majestic granite buildings. It was for him a big metropolis opening out onto the wider world, with the ships in its port offering the most ready means of travel to the south of Britain. MacDonald wrote that Alec Forbes, who similarly went off to college in that novel, saw "the whole world golden through the stained-glass windows of his imagination." Whatever promise the world may at that time have seemed to offer, however, he always saw it as inferior to the rural Aberdeenshire of his youth. The hills and lakes of home had in his mind a potential to nurture spiritual growth into a stalwart Christian maturity that he never tired of describing in his writings.

At King's he was exposed to a rigorous Christian humanist education substantially buttressed by Reformed theology. During their four years of study students were known as bajans, semis, tertians, and magistrands respectively. They were expected to be proficient in Latin upon entrance and gained proficiency in Greek and Hebrew during the bajan year, with students reading widely in Hesiod, Homer, Theocritus, and the Old Testament. The concentration of the semi year was on geometry, the tertian year on the teachings of Aristotle, and the magistrand year on a variety of the sciences, including astronomy, as well as geography and music. On the Sabbath all students gave their entire attention to Christian worship and study, with the Heidelberg Catechism being their chief authority.[3]

Student life, lived largely according to rules elaborated in the mid-seventeenth century, was carefully regulated. The school year opened at the beginning of November, thereby allowing students from rural areas to finish harvest before assuming their studies, and ran through June. Students arose at 5:00 A.M. to don their gowns and academic hats for the day, respectfully uncovering their heads each time they approached a teacher. On a typical day they attended a lecture, repeated and discussed it in the presence of the teachers who fielded their questions, and then gave a full account of the day's lesson to their individually assigned mentors each evening. They were expected to retire at nine, after Bible reading and prayer. Disputations were held on Saturdays. Special duties and privileges were accorded to the bursars—students too poor to pay for their education—having been admitted to the college by virtue of their performance in the "competitions," or established examinations.

George MacDonald entered this competition in the fall of 1840. His father, burdened with his own brother's debts and struggling to maintain a teetering family business, was unable to support his son at college, however earnestly he may have desired to do so. To prepare for his examinations by refining his knowledge of Latin, MacDonald had enrolled during the summer of 1840 in the Aulton Grammar School in Aberdeen—the school the young Byron had attended some forty-five years earlier. Then, taking twelfth place in the competition, he was awarded an annual bursary of fourteen pounds, sufficient to meet his basic expenses, with some small additional help from home for books and food. "Our potatoes and meal are both almost done. Be so good as to send a fresh supply as soon as convenient," he wrote his father in 1841.[4]

He was at King's College from the fall of 1840 until the spring of 1845, missing the 1842–1843 session, evidently for financial reasons. His interests at first lay in the natural sciences, and, making high marks in chemistry and what today we term physics, he determined to study medicine. Lack of sufficient money to study under the best doctors of the time, however, curbed his inclinations, while his interest steadily increased in the study of literature and language. He had long been writing verse, and he had developed a deep fascination with folk ballads. Further, the study of literature fed his natural curiosity concerning life and his sensitivity to the tenor of human experience. The romantic spirit, now well established in Britain some twenty years after the deaths of Shelley and Byron, answered to longings deeply felt in his heart. When he discovered the poetry and *Marchen,* or fairy tales, of the German Romantics, in which there was considerable interest among the literati of his day, he knew he had found for himself the most satisfying of academic pursuits.

He lived with his older brother Charles in the corner house of Owen Street where it met Broad Street, not far from the Blackfriars Congregational Church. Charles was already established in business in Aberdeen.[5] They both attended Blackfriars, which held services both Sunday morning and afternoon, and even became good friends with the minister, the Rev. John Kennedy. He was an evangelical Calvinist who demonstrated a concern for the poor and spoke out on social issues. But MacDonald, while he appreciated aspects of Kennedy's message, did not join the church, as did Charles and their friends. He was already taking exception in his mind to the evangelicalism that was so strong throughout Britain. His brother and others of his friends were genuinely concerned about his spiritual state.

His chief problem was that he felt a growing consternation over the doctrines of election and the eternal punishment of the damned. The famous "Ten Years' Conflict" was then at its height in the Church of Scotland, and in 1843 about a third of the members and ministers seceded and formed the Free Church of Scotland. While the main issue was whether members of a local church could have a say in the choice of their minister, there was also abroad the doctrine of universal redemption, with ministers being expelled and churches disendowed because of it. His emotions sided with the universalists, yet he was not yet ready to break away from his theological heritage.

Blackfriars Church, however, had a large social ministry to children of the street, and MacDonald was sympathetic. He would later exhibit in his novels a similar application of the gospel. Having come himself from a family beset with financial hardship, his sympathies were readily with the poverty stricken in Aberdeen. Not unlike the poet Robert Burns, he had been impressed by the dignity of the common man—an impression that never left him—and he sympathized with the needs of the working people. When the Chartist Movement, a popular attempt to win voting rights and better representation in Parliament for the working classes, held a rally in Aberdeen in October 1841, MacDonald described the occasion to his father:[6]

> I saw a most splendid procession today of the chartists going out to meet Fergus O'Connor. There were about two thousand of them in the procession and taking all who accompanied them, there might have been fifteen thousand on the streets. There were several different bands of music, and banners and mottoes innumerable. There were a coach, which happened to be coming up and three open carriages which went out to meet O'Connor, two with four horses and one with six horses in which was the chap himself—a pretty good looking man, but not a good figure—tall and stout.

O'Connor was a famous popular leader. MacDonald's interest in the working poor combines here with his love of pageantry. But such interests were comparatively incidental during his college days; he mainly concentrated on his studies.

When the time came in 1842, however, for him to enter his tertian term, he did not enroll. Evidently the family fortune was so low his father could not spare the little money needed to supplement the college scholarship. Most scholars from rural areas would work on the farms for the summer months in order to maintain themselves at college during the term. This is the case with MacDonald's scholar-hero in his long poem written some few years later, "The Hidden Life." MacDonald's health, however, was too fragile for him to follow this accustomed course; he secured a teaching post instead.

His love of books and his aptitude for teaching to his credit, he found a position as teacher of arithmetic at the Aberdeen Central Academy, run by Thomas Merton, from February to November 1843. Merton later recommended him as having "conducted the class with which he was intrusted with great spirit and skill." He found him to be "a young man of good intents, of amiable disposition, and active habits." MacDonald also tutored individual students in Latin and Greek. He found such satisfaction in teaching that he determined to be a tutor upon his graduation in 1845. He had a sheaf of testimonials from satisfied parents, together with one from Merton, to help him secure such a position.[7]

George MacDonald returned to his studies at King's College in the autumn of 1843. He was a young man beset with contradictions. On the one hand he was often dreamy and preoccupied, with an apparent unconcern for his scholastic standing, but on the other he was a careful thinker, pondering issues and following positions to their ultimate conclusions. He had a love of Scottish sartorial finery, such as tartan plaids and kilts (which the British had outlawed for a period in the eighteenth century due to the prevalent Scottish opposition to the Hanoverian regime), but his spirit was singularly free from pretentiousness or airs of self-importance.

He was unconcerned about the opinions of others. Although he was often withdrawn and thoughtful, he had a reputation for imaginative resourcefulness in playing the then-popular parlor game of charades, and he was an enthusiastic debater and active member of the debating society. Periods of illness sometimes incapacitated him, but he was athletic and agile. He later told his son Greville that as a youth he had been able to place two chairs back to back and jump over them from a standing positon and that as a young man he could lift two twenty-eight pound weights, one in each hand, up to the level of his head.

He took especial delight in walking along the sandy Aberdeen shoreline known as the "links." On one occasion, he and a friend, James Maconochie, went together to watch the progress of a storm as it agitated the waters and sent waves to break against the beach. Later, Maconochie confided with his sister his concern for MacDonald's sanity, for, he said, MacDonald "walked backwards and forwards on the sands amid the howling winds and the beating spray with the waves coming up to our feet and all the time went on addressing the sea and the waves and the storm."[8]

His friend Robert Troup described him as "studious, quiet, sensitive, imaginative, frank, open, speaking freely what he thought. His love of truth was intense, only equalled by his scorn of meanness, his purity, and his moral courage. So I found him when I became acquainted with him [in 1844]. . . . So I have found him ever since."[9] Years later, in 1865, when MacDonald was applying for the Chair of Rhetoric and Belles Lettres at the University of Edinburgh, he solicited a testimonial from one of his classmates at King's, William D. Geddes, who was then on the faculty of the University of Aberdeen. Happy to help his friend, Geddes complied. In the testimonial, he reminisced:

> Though you did not mix much with the students at college and indeed hardly cared to descend into the ordinary arena of emulation, your fellow students were not unaware of the talents which you possessed. I remember distinctly the universal impression regarding you, that you were master of powers which you had not put to the full measure of proof, but which were touched to fine issues and destined to yield great things. I have no doubt that those talents were even then richly employed by you in excursions of your own through walks of thought of your own choosing, the fruits of which were soon to appear in so large measure.[10]

Geddes's statement conveys an impression of independence and self-sufficiency; MacDonald must have spent considerable time by himself.

He was a man of strong emotions, often possessed of moods, alternating between periods of exhilaration and euphoria on the one hand and melancholy and depression on the other. But in whatever mood he found himself, he did not generally allow his mind to capitulate to his feelings, indulging in raw emotion for its own sake. His Scottish sternness and sense of decorum were expressed in rugged self-discipline. The result was that his emotional energy tended to stimulate his mind, so that throughout his life his best writings were achieved at times of strong feeling.

He wrote an appreciable quantity of poetry throughout his lifetime but especially during his college days. His first published poem, titled "David," appeared in the *Congregational Magazine* for January 1846. His cousin Helen MacKay, whose family lived nearby, seemed to understand his nature more than any other. When she lent him a sympathetic ear, he shared much of his early verse with her. She was the daughter of MacDonald's mother's brother, an officer who fought at Waterloo. This friendship with his pretty relative enlivened his stay in Aberdeen. He may have fallen in love with her, but they could not have been often together. In 1840, the same year that MacDonald came to Aberdeen, she enrolled in a finishing school in London, and in 1844 she married a brother of MacDonald's future wife. They nevertheless maintained a correspondence sparked with banter and gentle teasing that continued throughout their lives; she outlived him by six years.

MacDonald received a master of arts degree from King's in April 1845. His training had given him a good foundation in the liberal arts, since he had done considerable work in both science and literature, and he decided to become a tutor. This was a somewhat less imposing vocation than becoming a doctor, which had been his first intention, but it was an attractive calling for someone who had fallen in love with books and now nurtured an aspiration to become a man of letters. His desire to stay in Scotland, however, must have been strong. The scholar-hero in his early poem "The Hidden Life" also chooses a rural and secluded life after he has received his education:

> At length, when he had gained the master's right—
> By custom sacred from of old—to sit
> With covered head before the awful rank
> Of Black-gowned senators; and each of those,
> Proud of the scholar, was ready at a word
> To speed him onward to what goal he would,
> He took his books, his well-worn cap and gown,
> And, leaving with a sigh the ancient walls,
> Crowned with their crown of stone, unchanging gray
> In all the blandishments of youthful spring,
> Chose for his world the lone ancestral farm.

As much as MacDonald may have wished to return to the family farm, his delicate health rendered such a course impractical, and his education had prepared him for a more intellectual life. Teaching seemed the ready choice.

Having secured testimonials from his previous employer, Thomas Merton, and from the parents of those children whom he had taught during the hiatus in his college career, he proceeded to look for a tutoring positon. His father had a friend among the clergy who had risen to become a popular preacher in London, the Rev. John Morrison. The large Trevor Chapel in Brompton had been recently built to accommodate his flourishing evangelical congregation. When Morrison learned of the young MacDonald's desires, he found him a position as a tutor to the children of a prosperous merchant family in his nonconformist congregation, the Radermachers. They lived in Fulham, a section of west London along the banks of the Thames.

London must have seemed an immense distance from his home in Huntly, and it certainly took strength of resolve for Mac-Donald to leave his Scottish countryside, with its hauntingly beautiful glens and lochs and its peaceful landscapes, for big city life, to say nothing of being so far from his father with his now-growing second family. Nevertheless, he left his ancestral lands and went by sea to take residence in the bustling center of the British Empire five hundred miles to the south.

THREE

A Glorious Light

I think faith can never have a greater victory than when it will trust even in the midst of darkness and doubt and temptation. —MacDonald to Louisa

The period from 1845 through 1853—that is, from MacDonald's leaving Aberdeen to his going to Manchester—was crucial in shaping his spiritual life. It marked the transition from his early immersion in more conventional Christian attitudes to the characteristic exceptions to them he took during his adult life and ministry. His later inveighing against the "moral vulgarity of theory," the "injustice toward God," and the "tyranny of stupid logic over childlike intuitions,"[1] which he saw as prevalent in the evangelicalism of his time, grew out of his encounters with these religious aberrations. He was not long in London before he had a yet fuller encounter with these realities, and he began to feel a spiritual revulsion toward them. As he moved through his tutorship, seminary training, apprentice preaching, and then his association with the congregation in Arundel, each experience made its distinct contribution to his spiritual maturation.

The evangelical milieu at mid-century presents a mixed picture. The Great Revival of Wesley and Whitefield during the eighteenth century issued (in addition to the establishment of the Methodist Church) in the spirit of evangelicalism which steadily spread through both the established and nonconformist churches. On a Sunday in 1851 (when MacDonald was minister at the Trinity Congregational Church in Arundel), a national census taken of all worshipers showed that roughly nine million people, or about half of the population, was in church. Between two and three million of these were evangelicals. By 1853, *The Edinburgh Review* computed that of the 17,000 clergymen in the Church of England, 6,500 were evangelicals, 7,000 High Churchmen, and 3,500 Broad Churchmen.[2]

Evangelical influence, therefore, for both good and ill, had permeated all of British society. The zeal generated by the gospel that Wesley and Whitefield preached to secure the eternal destiny of individuals had become a crusade for the forms and facades of a legalistic morality. No doubt evangelicals were responsible for greatly enhancing the social consciousness of the century and for doing what they could to alleviate the deplorable living conditions of the working class. Their infiltration into British politics did much to make the Victorian Age more serious, honest, and highly principled than was the eighteenth century. But the need politicians felt to profess morality also opened the door to greater cant and hypocrisy.

Further, evangelicals embraced economic gain as the just reward for righteous living. They were much concerned with "getting on"—a phrase MacDonald came quickly to hate—and generally felt that Providence made manifest its approval of virtue by bestowing monetary gain. Salvation was a prudent deal negotiated with the Deity. Determined that their society be outwardly and legalistically moral, they worked indefatigably on behalf of laws forbidding commercial activities of any kind on Sunday and crusaded against social vices, such as prostitution and gambling. They frowned on card playing and theater going, and their homes were generally free from novels and fairy tales.[3]

When MacDonald, an earnest young Scot, first came to London, he found himself deeply immersed in this evangelical world. Around him was a thriving city of great contrasts. Squalid poverty in the slum areas was juxtaposed with the conspicuous opulence of the well-to-do. Between these two extremes lay the flourishing world of the London merchant class. At first it appeared to be Christian. Newly arrived, filled with awe, and determined to do well, he tried to find a place in this world. But he soon came to perceive that these people were decidedly more impressed with the value of the British pound for materialist ends than with the value of biblical precepts for spiritual ones. These people were patently self-preoccupied and ambitious, obsessed with getting on.

The Rev. Morrison lost no time in enlisting the young tutor into his congregation: "On Friday last week Dr. Morrison sent me a letter by messenger who waited for an answer saying that he wished to propose me as a member that evening but did not like to do so without a line from me to say yes. I consented, but with fear and trembling," MacDonald wrote his father.[4] He was reading Bunyan at the time, trying to perfect his Christian experience in terms of *Pilgrim's Progress*. The prescriptions advocated by the tinker-turned-preacher from Bedford were widely accepted as the pattern to follow. Bunyan's agonizings over whether he was among the elect had their effect: "I do think I am a Christian although one of the weakest. . . . My greatest difficulty always is, How do I know that my faith is of a lasting kind and such as will produce fruits? . . . My error seems to be always searching for faith in place of contemplating the truths of the gospel which are such as produce faith and confidence."

Earnest and intense by nature, he was given to introspection, and he entertained a strong sense of the ideal. "Pray that I may not be that hateful thing—a lukewarm Christian," he pleaded. Such halfheartedness he saw as springing from a diminished sense of any need for redemption. "I think God is leading me slowly on to know more of him—What I most need is a deep sense of sinfulness, and the evil of it—I think the want of this must be very much the reason why so many Christians are careless and lukewarm."[5] But while aspects of his experience harmonized with Bunyan's views, it was not long before he began to take issue with Bunyan's theology: "I see Bunyan holds the opinion that the righteousness of Christ is imputed by God previous to faith, which is only a sign that this righteousness has been imputed—I cannot agree at all with this view."[6] The doctrine of imputed righteousness was soon to become the object of his special opposition.

On the whole, he appreciated Morrison's early expressions of kindness and help, and he got on tolerably well with his employers, the Radermachers. Aware that he had been chosen from among several applicants for the position of their tutor, he felt grateful. Radermacher visited his classroom shortly after his arrival, pronounced himself pleased, and presented him with a "beautiful pipe," which MacDonald began smoking a good deal: "When I am well it is a great enjoyment to me," he told his father. The image of a smoking son, however, gave his father little enjoyment, and when he asked his son please to give it up, MacDonald obliged him without rancor.

As the months went by, however, certain difficulties in MacDonald's situation began to try his temper and patience. "The worst bother is ill brought up noisy children—especially the younger ones who scream frightfully—two girls like Bella and Louisa." Although he conceded, "One ought to give up thinking of little things which do not quite suit one's idea of propriety."[7] When two of the boys under his charge, twelve-year-old twins, showed "some concern about religion," he was given "much pleasure, and I pray God they may be kept of him." Nevertheless, their ignorance was exasperating: "one of them . . . asked me, when reading the New Testament if Jesus Christ wasn't crucified four times—and another of them nearly two years older thought he was so twice."[8]

By March 1846 he was beginning to consider other pursuits but was uncertain what these should be. After patient consideration he decided the following spring to enter a seminary and begin preparing for the ministry. He thought it best not to do so, however, until the commencement of the session in the fall of 1848.

Among the reasons he gave his father for his willingness to consider staying another year at the Radermachers' was that he wished his "opinions and feelings and motives to solidify more," and also "I wish to lay in a good stock of clothes, if I can, which will make expenses much less at College." Then, interestingly, he gave a third reason for delay: he was stoically determined to become a better person, and his present hardships were instrumental to that end. "I am . . . a little unwilling to give up the continual trials of my temper which I have here—not that I like them, but I cannot help regarding them as very good exercise—although I so often fail in overcoming my temper."[9] He was taking to heart St. Paul's admonition to "glory in trials," and thus he was determined neither to avoid hardship nor capitulate to it. The conviction that the suffering and hardship that came his way in the course of duty provided a goad to virtue was one he strongly adhered to throughout his life, allowing it to shape many of his decisions.

He therefore accepted certain inconveniences, such as studying in an unheated room through the winter. The Radermachers were the more pleased with their employee, seeing the savings his determination netted them. The temperature of his room notwithstanding, he read avidly. In addition to his love of literature and his interest in religious thought, he tried to keep abreast of recent publications in biology and geology. He recommended to his father with enthusiasm, confident they would give him "much pleasure and satisfaction," a "recent publication of Darwin's account of a voyage around the world" and "Dr. Page Smith's work on geology."[10] During this period when advances in these sciences were beginning to raise alarm in the religious world, MacDonald's positive interest in them is a good indication of the openness of his mind and the eclecticism of his spirit; that he felt free to make uninhibited recommendation of them to his father indicates a good deal about the latter's attitudes as well.

Although he had very little money, he was trying to build a library, being very careful what he purchased. "With not much of a stretch beyond 2 [pounds] I have bought Hall's *Works,* 6 vols., Sismond's *History of the Literature of the South of Europe,* 2 vols., Coleridge's *Poems,* 3 vols., and Campbell's book which you recommended to me."[11] The latter had to do with church history and government, two areas that were not of foremost interest to him, but he purchased and read the book to oblige his father. He openly lamented his comparative lack of interest in history and church government. "I would rather be of no sect than a sectarian, which I fear most good men are in a greater or less degree, however unwilling they may be to acknowledge it to themselves. . . . I wish however our churches were liker the primitive ones in more than the mere theory of government."[12] Church polity was very much on Scottish minds at the time, the Free Church of Scotland having been formed in 1843.

What is most striking about this phase of MacDonald's life is the manner in which his personal experience of the presence and teachings of Christ became his solid center. Here he took his stand and found strength of conviction and clarity of insight to assume independent religious stands. As he came to find himself morally distanced from the attitudes of the contemporary dissenting church, and having been momentarily confused at King's, he turned with desperation to study firsthand the teachings of Christ. Had he found in them support for the religious climate that was increasingly becoming to him morally repugnant, he would no doubt have defected from Christianity, but he found in the Gospels teachings that poignantly exposed and condemned the self-centeredness and worldliness that surrounded him. He was spiritually exhilarated. The more he studied them, the more excited he became by the aptness of Christ's teachings to the human predicament and the more he perceived that they were being seriously overlooked by the majority of professing Christians.

In the spring of 1847 he had a distinctly deepening Christian experience. Since the crucial letter that marks this change is only a fragment, with the initial page missing, it is impossible to date it with certainty, but the contents would place it between January and April. He exclaimed to his father: "What should I be now without religion! With nothing here to make me happy besides, with health bad enough to make me generally feel miserable, though nothing is seriously the matter with me—Yet I am able I trust to thank God for all these, for thus I hope he has led me to find the joy of being—the real existence." Coleridge, whose poetry he had been reading, insists in "Dejection: An Ode" that true joy comes alone from God and only to those who are pure in heart. Perhaps this is his source of reference. In any case, he felt the experiencing of joy to be the mark of God's favor. "Although I have not yet experienced much real continuous joy—from sin, difficulties, anxiety, and forgetfulness, I seem to see a glorious light before me, into the fullness of which glory I trust he will lead me." His sense of quest toward a glorious destiny—a prominent motif in his future fantasies and fairy stories—became at this time an integral and sustaining element in his personal experience.

This vision of glory occurred to him from his intense and private study of the Bible. "I love my Bible more—I am always finding out something new in it—I seem to have had everything to learn over again from the beginning—All my teaching in youth seems useless to me—I must get it all from the Bible again." Scripture now seemed to stand over against many of the teachings of his past, rather than in conjunction with them. It was the teachings of Christ in the Gospels that spoke with a power that kindled his excitement. "I have of late seen more of the necessity of studying Christ's character, and I am in the habit of reading the Gospels every day—That seems the only thing that helps me to overcome my temper, and be patient. This seems to give a ground work for the exhortations of the Epistles to build upon. If the gospel of Jesus be not true, I can only pray my maker to annihilate me, for nothing else is worth living for—and if that be true, everything in the universe is glorious, except sin." This granting of primacy to the teachings of Christ, rather than seeing them on a par with the teachings of the Epistles—an attitude that he maintains in all his writings—was the result of his personal search of Scripture. His conclusions come prior to his entering seminary and in contrast to the doctrinal system in which he had been trained, which tended to grant primacy to the teachings of Paul.

His general understanding of doctrines having to do with the believer's personal experience, however, was at this time quite in line with what he had been taught from childhood. This is plain from this same letter fragment, a long one, in which he analyzed his present spiritual state to his father:

> But everything else is insignificant—even God's most beautiful works—when we look at the only-injured dying for the only-injuring. It does often seem to me too glorious to be true—And yet I have had little sorrow for sin. . . . But these seem to me very important and principal parts of sanctification—which God's Spirit will I trust go on to teach me. I am told to believe in my Redeemer, who has already paid the ransom, whether I understand it properly or not. He is exalted to give repentance and the remission of sins. I look upon repentance as a work including everything else in religion. The first part of repentance is turning to God by prayer for direction—The last act is the last struggle against an evil thought—the last effort to trust in Him, the last feeling of sorrow for wrongdoing, perhaps the last thought of gratitude for His unspeakable goodness—which last thought will never never come.

Although his thought on the nature of initial Christian experiences did not inspire him at this time to praise God, his later thinking on these matters most certainly would.

The foundation for praise was, however, already well laid. He exclaimed:

> Religion must pervade everything—absorb everything into itself. To the perfectly holy mind, everything is religious. It seems to glorify everything (yet how cold is my heart while I write). One of my greatest difficulties in consenting to think of religion was that I thought I should have to give up my beautiful thoughts and my love for the things God has made.

These fears were a legacy from the Christianity of his childhood, with its stern negations of many aspects of normal human experience.

> But I find that the happiness springing from all things not in themselves sinful is much increased by religion. God is the God of the Beautiful—Religion the love of the Beautiful, and

Heaven the home of the Beautiful—Nature is tenfold brighter in the Sun of Righteousness, and my love of Nature is more intense since I became a Christian, if indeed I am one—God has not given such thoughts and forbidden me enjoy them.[13]

These convictions grew to pervade his thinking and issued in the spirit of praise characteristic of his later work.

FOUR

An Affectionate Cousin

*But he had now arrived at that season when, in the order of
things, a man is compelled to have at least a glimmer of the
life which consists in sharing life with another. . . . And the
love between man and woman arising from a difference deep
in the heart of God, and essential to the very being of each—
for by no words can I express my scorn of the evil fancy that
the distinction between them is solely or even primarily
physical—is one of His most powerful forces for blasting the
wall of separation, and the first step towards the universal
harmony, of twain making one.* —Malcolm

Whatever annoyances MacDonald's tutoring of incorrigible
children may have offered him, the loneliness he must have felt as
a young Scot in the great city was lightened by his introduction
into the James Powell household. Their oldest boy, Alexander,
had married Helen MacKay, MacDonald's cousin, in 1844. She
was quick to introduce the eligible young bachelor to the six Powell daughters and two sons. (Powell's wife, now an invalid, had
borne him thirteen children, but only eight lived to adulthood.)[1]
Their home, named The Limes, was situated in Upper Clapton
in north central London. It was a stately house of Georgian design, with grounds large enough to include a meticulously kept
rose garden and ample stables filled with horses for the children
to ride.

Their faith was staunchly nonconformist, their attitudes rig-
idly evangelical. Being a devout Protestant upper-middle-class

family, they held to well-defined values, strict propriety, and strong discipline. A premium was placed on effort and accomplishment. The source of the family's prosperity was a thriving business in leather trading. James Powell, unquestionably the center of authority in the home, was a man of many interests. In addition to spending much time with his business, he was apt in gardening, carpentry, and book binding. He also played the violin, and musical gatherings in his home were not uncommon—religious and classical music, that is; no dancing was allowed.

The family shared in contemporary evangelical attitudes toward theater. All play-acting was forbidden, although parlor charades were permitted, a pastime in which MacDonald took considerable delight. He was also beginning to attend the theater at the time, an activity that would hardly have met with Powell's approval. Evidently, Powell was not told.

Of the six sisters Louisa quickly attracted MacDonald's attention. Two years MacDonald's senior, she had been born on November 5, 1822. A demure girl given to self-deprecation, she was slight of build, with a waist that was the envy of all her sisters. Later, her children were to be most fond of her "wonderful" blue eyes, and MacDonald's preoccupation with eye imagery in his writings no doubt sprang from his fascination with Louisa's. With a disposition at once lighthearted and deeply conscientious, she had a keen sense of the ridiculous behind all pretension, whether in dress, manner, or religion. The third daughter among the six, she was expected to meet the Victorian ideal of femininity: to be graceful, exemplary in manners, adept in music, and properly deficient before men in her ability to think.

MacDonald soon became a regular visitor at The Limes. Himself uncomfortable with the prevalent attitudes toward women in his society, he undertook to raise the self-confidence of the Powell girls and generally to teach them. Louisa's younger sister Angela, thought by the family to be unable to learn because of her difficulty in spelling, provided MacDonald with a particular challenge, and he undertook to see how much she could be taught. He surprised everyone with his success. The experience served to establish his growing convictions both on the capacity of women and also on the nature of education. He was becoming convinced that an appeal to the imagination was the readiest way to induce a pupil to learn. His reading of his favorite poems to the girls—from Wordsworth, Coleridge, and the early Browning—most aroused their interest and broadened their horizons.

His early interest in Louisa soon blossomed into a regular correspondence. In his first extant letter to her he signed himself "Your affectionate cousin(?)," evidently unsure whether his connection with the family through Helen gave him full right to claim the relationship. However, this complimentary closing, minus the question mark, became his accustomed one in the many letters that followed, until he added a "very" in 1848, with "dear" becoming "dearest."

He had taken to sewing upon his arrival at the Radermachers in an effort to get the most wear possible from his meager wardrobe, and sewing had become a pleasant pastime for him. His first letter to Louisa was prompted by his having inadvertently carried away her thimble. He also enclosed some of his poetry, hoping it would meet with sufficient favor for her to enter it in her scrapbook. Penned across the back of an early letter dated July 20, 1846, in a hand undoubtedly Louisa's, are the words "My dearest dearest. An overgrown baby with manners like a bear." She evidently was not greatly impressed with his finesse. Her use of the image of a bear when referring to her husband in correspondence years afterward suggests she found the metaphor an apt depiction. That it did not become a nickname underscores the fact that her dominant attitude toward him was one of respect and even awe, rather than playfulness.

In the beginning their relationship seems to have been predominately one of willing teacher and eager student, spiritual mentor and novitiate. Louisa, who was given all her life to feelings of insecurity, held MacDonald in awe for his spiritual intensity and his preoccupation with his relationship to God. She felt she must be religiously cold and indifferent by comparison, and she told him so, together with expressing an agonizing desire to change. He saw in her the same spiritual turmoil that he had known and believed he could help her by sharing his recent spiritual discoveries. He counseled her: "You promise in your last note to try to strive. A fear is upon me that you have tried and tried earnestly and tried again, since writing that, and have failed, or seemed to fail, and have become discouraged and are again ready to tell me it is no use. It might well seem to us often to be no use, if we had not hope of help from above. But God wants to have us back to himself, and he will help us." Their relationship to God was plainly the most important aspect in each of their lives. "I wish I could think to you the thoughts of encouragement which I could give you," he continued, paralleling her experience with his own. "How often has it seemed to me as if it was no use trying, and how often have I been helped to go on. . . . my difficulties are of the same nature as yours—those which a heart far from God must feel, even when the hand of the Heavenly Father is leading it back to himself, as I trust He is with me—It seems a wonder that he can bear with one." In interesting contrast to many religious counselors he did not take recourse to prescriptions of the church, nor even to Scripture, but rather to his personal experience. His inner reality was consistently his touchstone for religious truth.

Central to his experience was his perception of the humanity of Christ. He continued: "In all temptations and trials the readiest help is to try to pray to God for help and to think of the Man Christ Jesus." Then he began to generalize:

What is it that is the principal cause of everyone's unhappiness who is not a Christian? It is the want of enough to love. We are made for love—and in vain we strive to pour forth the streams of our affection by the narrow channels which the world can give—and well is it if stagnated in our hearts they turn not to bitterness. Now the religion of Jesus Christ is intended to bring us back to our real natural condition—for all the world is in an unnatural state. This will give us that to love which alone can satisfy our loving—which alone, as we climb each successive height, can show us another yet higher and farther off—so that as our powers of loving expand in an infinite progression (not to infinitude) the object of loving grows—not with it—but ever beyond it, in all those glories which excite our love and satisfy it, yet make it long for more.

His genuine excitement in his emerging vision is evident, a vision that stands in compelling contrast to the predominately negative tone of much contemporary evangelical thought concerning the nature of the world. He concluded with a self-indictment characteristic of his romantic sense of the importance of the emotions: "Strange that the intellect can thus contemplate truth and my heart be yet so cold towards it. But God is our hope—That He may lead you to Himself is the prayer of your ever affectionate cousin George.[2]

His careful delineation of spiritual experience arose from lessons learned and anticipation of further ones to master. His was not the pompous and condescending language of a self-assured religious adviser who saw spiritual remedies in terms of easily adduced formulae but rather well-earned advice gleaned directly from personal experience. His advice was based on the perception that people were made to love God and one another and that earnestly trying to love opened for people a yet greater capacity to do so.

Not that the letters between them were dominated by these types of concerns; far from it. Both were eager to confide the events of their everyday lives, be solicitous of the other's health, and anticipate, as lovers will, their next meeting. They shared with each other descriptions of nature. Louisa wrote from Hastings by the sea, where the family often spent time:

Here I am my dearest friend, encamped on a stone with a bit of a rock for my desk, the sea blue and green sparkling in the bright sun, before now that same bright sun over my head and the softest most refreshing breeze blowing round me. I have just been paying a most delightful visit to the sands and beach below the waters though I certainly did not stay there long enough to find out whether I should like to live always with Undine and Neptune.[3]

MacDonald closed one of his letters with: "The sun is low—and the drops on the needle of a fir-tree before my window, are sparkling so beautifully." In another he composed in verse an answer to one of her questions:

> The mysterious night
> When but a light of the low horned moon
> Looks o'er the rest of a peaked cloudy night
>   Edging it with a glory—fading soon
> And few pale stars are mid the cloud rifts strewn
> And the low wind is running to and fro,
>   Like a forsaken child, that knows not where to go—
> Oh! to have the silence of such a night
> Around us once more![4]

It is difficult to imagine the question to which this was a proper answer, but his romantic spirit with its love of a moon-blanched natural scene is evident enough.

Their interest in nature was prompted by deeper considerations than may at first appear. MacDonald was becoming thoroughly convinced that the Christian should take a faith-filled, imaginative view of nature in order to see God in it and rejoice. His readings in the German Romantics and in Wordsworth and Coleridge were influencing him. He asked Louisa: "Tell me again about everything round about you—Every expression the beautiful face of nature puts on—And tell me too about the world within your own soul—that living world—without which the world without would be but a lifelessness. Think of God in the beautiful things round about you. They are the expressions of God's face or as, in Faust, the garment whereby we see the Deity."[5]

It was not only nature around them that was a means of grace. They saw their relationship of love as being preeminently so, filled with a divine potential to enrich their spiritual lives. In the enraptured language of love MacDonald exclaimed to Louisa:

> You and I love, but who created love? Let us ask him to purify our love to make it stronger and more real and more self-denying. I want to love you for ever—so that although there is no marrying or giving in marriage in heaven we may keep each other there as the best beloved. It is to heaven I look as the place where I shall have most enjoyment in you—both from my perfection and yours. Oh Lousia is it not true that our life here is a growing into life, and our death a being born— our true birth. . . . And in our life together . . . when the cloud is over my head, I may see the light shining from your face, and when darkness is around you, you may see the lights on mine, and thus, we shall take courage. But we can only expect to have this light within us and on our faces—we can only expect to be a blessing to each other by doing that which is right—and striving against those principles of evil which if allowed to work their own work would make us hate each other.[6]

The letter is prophetic in that they seem continually throughout their lives together to see life and each other in these terms: The foundation for the life to come is laid firmly in this life, and a person's relation to their mate can lead directly to a higher heaven or a deeper hell. Clearly MacDonald felt God had so created people that their sexuality is intimately related to their spirituality. These ideas anticipate many scenes from the novels and fantasies.

MacDonald's thinking affirms a precious value to all aspects of human experience, insisting that there is a way of meeting God in every facet of life. It stands in the tradition of Dante, whose love of Beatrice led him out of his spiritual foundering in "the middle way" to the heights of Paradise.[7] This is an appreciably distinct vision of the nature of Christian thought and experience from what MacDonald generally encountered at Highbury College, where he enrolled in the autumn of 1848.

In the spring of 1848, he resigned his tutorship in Fulham and traveled north to visit his father, whom he had not seen for three years. There were momentous reasons for the trip. He had made two decisions concerning his future that he felt he must discuss with him face to face. The one was to enter training for the nonconformist ministry; the second was to seek the consent of Louisa, and that of her father, for her to become his wife. Further, he now had two small sisters from his father's second wife with whom he wanted to become acquainted. During the past three years his spirit had often yearned for his Scottish home, and he returned there with joy. In the sharper air of the northern countryside he found much to strengthen his spirit, as he renewed acquaintances, visited childhood haunts, and, above all, had long and intimate conversations with his closest adviser, his father.

Returning in the autumn, he enrolled as a theological student in Highbury College, located in Highbury Park, in north central London. Once he was situated he wrote a formal letter to James Powell. He began, "I feel considerable embarrassment in writing to you, and the only way I can get over it is to come to the point at once," crossed it out, and began again in a yet more formal tone:

> *The continued improvement of Mrs. Powell's health, of which I need not say I am glad to hear, encourages me to write to you on a subject about which I have communicated with you before. Will you permit me to visit your daughter Louisa, with the hope of one day making her my wife? My expectations as far as the things of this world are concerned are none of the greatest and I need say nothing of them, as you can judge of them more accurately than I can. However you may regard my request, I*

beg you will forgive me, if my present note is at all deficient in propriety, and be assured if so that it is the result of ignorance—which I hope you will excuse.

> *I am, my dear sir*
> *Yours most truly,*
> *George MacDonald*[8]

He was delighted to be duly accepted. They were not married, however, until MacDonald had completed his seminary training and had secured for himself a church.

FIVE

Certainly Not Highbury

When souls like Robert's have been ill-taught about God, the true God will not let them gaze too long upon the Moloch which men have set up to represent him. He will turn away their minds from that which men call him, and fill them with some of his own lovely thoughts or works such as may by degrees prepare the way for a vision of the Father.—Robert Falconer

"If I do go, I should like to go to Homerton to Dr. Pye-Smith—certainly not to Highbury," MacDonald wrote his father in the spring of 1847. But to Highbury Seminary he went. Just why he finally chose Highbury over Homerton is not entirely clear. The aged John Pye-Smith was then president of Homerton, a sister Congregational college, where during the past fifty years he had established a wide reputation for combining a fervent and genuine Christian piety with very high academic achievement, and MacDonald desired this combination for himself.

He suspected that Highbury was a coldly intellectual school, without a warm sense of fellowship in the gospel of Christ. But some of his closer friends from King's were there, such as Robert Troup and Robert Spence, and he had also met and established a close friendship with some other students. Of the many schools that were training Congregational ministers at the time, Highbury was the largest. Although it was comparatively young, it too had established a strong academic reputation.

Since the time of the Restoration, the Congregationalists had maintained a well-educated ministry. Denied admittance into the established universities of England by laws passed under Charles II to crush independence of religious thought in Britain, dissenters had been quick to establish and maintain their own schools. The first of these were clandestinely founded, but in the eighteenth century under Queen Anne such schools received an accepted place in English education. Some historians believe these institutions provided in their day the finest education in England. In attending Highbury MacDonald was undoubtedly exposed to a more rigorous and demanding curriculum than would have been the case had he attended one of the prestigious Anglican colleges. The latter was not a consideration for him, however, inasmuch as he was deeply entrenched in the dissenting tradition.

MacDonald's family had been active in the "Disruption of 1843" on the side of the Free Church of Scotland, which broke from the Established Church (Presbyterian) over matters of church polity and patronage. In England the sect most nearly in line with the Scottish Free Church was the Congregationalists. They embraced a Calvinist theology imbued with an evangelical spirit. They earned the term *Congregationalists* by their emphasis on the right of each local church to maintain political autonomy and exercise full authority to administer the sacraments. They were, therefore, entirely independent from the doctrines, polity, and discipline of the Church of England and were sometimes referred to simply as independents, or, of course, by the blanket term *nonconformists*. In the course of MacDonald's spiritual odyssey, he joined the Church of England some twenty years later, but in 1848 he was far from ready for such a move.

His experiences at Highbury, however, began the process that led to the change. He did not mind the demanding daily schedule, and he welcomed the challenge from the breadth and heft of the curriculum. The schedule, although rigorous and rigid, was somewhat less demanding than what he had known at King's. Students arose at 6:00 A.M. (7:00 A.M. in winter), attended family prayers at 8:00 A.M. and 8:00 P.M., took their meals at 8:30 A.M., 1:00

P.M., and 8:30 P.M., and attended classes from 9:00 A.M. to 1:00 P.M., and from 3:00 P.M. to 5:00 P.M.

They were provided with the printed texts of the lectures before classes. The lectures tended to be thoroughly rationalist analyses of all conceivable facets of sacred truth, translated into pure abstractions by the mentor's philosophical cast of mind and structured in the form of detailed outlines. Subpoints proliferated like funguses. Class sessions were devoted to the professor's explanation and illustration of his materials and to his examining the students on the prior day's work. Thursday evenings were devoted to preaching exercises, each student practicing on his peers.[1]

Theological studies composed only a part of the curriculum of Highbury, being the concern of the latter two years of a five-year course. Because the Congregationalists were determined to provide their churches with a learned ministry, the emphasis of the first three years was on liberal classical studies, philology, and mathematics. During their five-year tenure, students were expected to become proficient in the Greek and Latin classics, together with European biblical scholarship, and to read the Bible fluently in its original languages. A typical student, therefore, would have a command of six languages: Latin, Greek (both classical and Koine), Hebrew, German, French, and English.

MacDonald, having acquired a strong Christian humanist education at King's, demonstrated his proficencies in philology in entrance examinations and was permitted to concentrate on the theological studies, so that he completed his work in two years. This was a highly unusual feat. Indeed, academically he held a position of eminence among his peers, so that he tutored fellow students needing help and even taught a course in chemistry.

Only three professors were teaching at Highbury while he was there: Ebenezer Henderson, a Hebraist; William Smith, a classicist; and John Godwin, principal and professor of theology and New Testament exegesis. The first two were notoriously dull pedagogues, but Godwin was exceedingly popular. The influence of Godwin on MacDonald was strong, both because MacDonald admired him and because he would within a few years marry one of Louisa's sisters. He was able to instill within his students a love of the Greek language and an appreciation for finer shades of meaning in the Greek New Testament. MacDonald was one of his most successful students in this regard for he had throughout his life a thorough fascination for the biblical text in Greek. He once told Louisa, "I would be sorry to lose one of Mr. Godwin's lectures, or rather conversations, even for the pleasure of seeing you."[2]

Some in the denomination questioned Godwin's orthodoxy for he was known for more generous interpretations of questionable Scripture passages than those entertained by his colleagues and he had a reputation for contriving subtle and ingenious arguments. In general he was an Arminian among Calvinists.[3] In 1862, a theological watchdog brought nine charges of heresy against him arising from his lectures. The governing council of the college exonerated him but reduced his teaching responsibilities to that of philosophy only.

MacDonald was admitted to Highbury on September 6, 1848. Together with a group of applicants, he met with the admissions committee to be examined. Instead of reading a sermon of his own composition, as applicants were expected to do, he read a portion of an essay he had written on how best to promote a spirit of piety in the student body. The committee, deeming it satisfactory evidence of his potential, admitted him to the customary three-month probationary period upon his agreeing to observe the rules of the college by duly signing the rule book. He came with letters of recommendation from Rev. John Hill, minister of the Congregational Church at Huntly; Rev. John Morrison, MacDonald's London pastor; and Rev. Robert Spence, of Liverpool.[4]

A lover of books, MacDonald studied with pleasure, but he was dismayed at the prevalence of a brittle religious mentality that assumed truth to be completely propositional and that a thorough and meticulous rationalist handling of theological ideas could apprehend it all. Such an intellectual atmosphere was stifling. Not that he did not feel at home with logic and argument; he did. He was adept at debate and enjoyed a keen-minded analysis of an issue. But increasingly he came to feel that reason unassisted by imaginative explorations was not only completely inadequate but also unaware of its inadequacies.

His sensibility instinctively preferred the imaginative encounters with truth that he had in the presence of literature and art: "Oh I have two such pieces to read to you—One of Tennyson's *Poems*—and the other a translation from Jean Paul Richter—oh! oh! oh! The last is—I hardly know what to call it—They were both to me worth hundreds of sermons—of some kinds at least" he confided to Louisa.[5] Poetry and story inspired his spirit. In another letter he shared his enthusiasm for romantic painting: "What a strange picture of Turner's I saw yesterday at the Exhibition—a rainbow over a stormy sea, ships far and near, boats, and a buoy—I could make nothing of it at first. Only by degrees I awoke to the Truth and wonder of it."[6] Joseph Turner's controversial paintings were currently being championed by the critic John Ruskin (later to become a close friend of MacDonald's).

His love of the arts, the roots of which had been laid in childhood by his love of his father's stories and the ballads of the Highlands, had budded during his days at King's College when he first discovered the large body of German Romantic literature. The reference to Richter indicates this interest was now coming into full bloom. His letters to this time contain no indication that it had been any more than a pleasant pastime to him until now when his spirit, choked by pedantry and abstract reworkings of sacred revelation, cried out for those intuitive encounters with truth that art afforded. His reaction to Highbury was not unlike that of Wordsworth to the atmosphere of Cambridge fifty years earlier: arid academic exercises lacked "the living voice / To carry meaning to the natural heart; / To tell us what is passion, what is truth. . . ."[7]

In his readings of imaginative literature MacDonald had known many moments of spiritual confrontation that his intuition had told him were with Truth itself. Now the contrast between these approaches to truth—that of art and that of rational abstraction—struck him forcibly. But unlike so many Victorians who as young people found themselves in similar quandaries, MacDonald never jettisoned his faith. Rather, out of the clash between the purportedly religious and the seemingly secular, his spirit moved steadily to achieve a unified vision.

German folktales should receive some of the credit for the steady strengthening of MacDonald's religious views. Louisa's playful reference to Undine in her letter quoted in the last chapter—in which she described the seashore at Hastings—and MacDonald's excitement over a tale of Jean Paul Richter reveal some of the stories he was reading at the time. In an essay written near the end of his career MacDonald referred to *Undine* as a perfect fairy tale, the ideal for all who aspire to create this genre.[8] Evidently this deftly told story by the little-known germanized Frenchman Baron de la Motte Fouque was MacDonald's lifelong favorite. A look at its contents quickly suggests why it so fascinated him.

The story concerns the life of Undine, a water sprite who becomes a human and aspires to possess a soul as other humans do. Raised as the foster daughter of a pious old fisherman and his wife, she falls in love with a knight. Dramatic conflict derives from the knight's vacillating love for Undine and for his fair lady Bertalda. His marriage to Undine notwithstanding, his love for Bertalda finally triumphs. But Undine, because of her loving acts to both of them, together with the sorrow and suffering her growing knowledge of her situation yields her, comes to receive within herself her chief desire—a true soul. The story affirms the principle that "everything is blessed to him in whom a true soul dwells." How people may develop "true souls" may certainly describe the motivating principle behind MacDonald's long writing career.

The method of instruction present in these German tales is remarkably different from that of the Puritan allegories, of which John Bunyan's *Pilgrim's Progress* is the most famous example. The insights offered by the Puritan allegories seem imposed deductively on life, whereas in the fairy tales the religious and moral significances seem to emerge from the very nature of things. But these tales no less than the Puritan allegories possess a strong pietist strain. The ultimately benign character of Faerie is due to the pervading presence of God, and man's redemption in Christ is often affirmed. Further, the elements of the ideal world of the fairy tale are imaginative depictions not infrequently inspired by Christian eschatology and biblical visions of the world to come.

All these characteristics anticipate many aspects of MacDonald's fantasies. His immersion in such fantasy literature as a young student, allowed to work on his consciousness for some ten years, would issue in his early attempt at the genre, *Phantastes,* in some respects perhaps the most significant of all his writings. But understanding the chief ideas of this body of German literature also helps us more keenly to appreciate some of MacDonald's remarks occurring in his letters during his student days. In one letter, for instance, after having translated for Louisa Goethe's little love poem "Nahe der Geliebten," he asks her to "write to me about the sea and the sky and all those never ceasing beauties, ever changing yet still the same which are common to all men like those great truths the sense of which make a man feel great too—those truths ever the same yet ever presenting new aspects of beauty, different to different minds, different to the same mind at different times— yet ever in essence one and the same."[9] This assertion of the dynamic nature of things with which the mind of man interacts to perceive universal truths reflects the German spirit of romanticism with singular directness.

The truths that came to him through his study of poetry, fantasy, art, and nature itself seemed to come from a higher, more universal order than those that came from mere rationalist inquiry, though they did not necessarily contradict the latter. In fact, he saw that these truths coincided with those found in some theological propositions, provided the latter were taken out of the realm of dead abstractions and clothed in individual, living images. But such perceptions were not generally welcomed at Highbury, where the dominant mentality tended to question the worth of all light, entertaining literature and art. Excited about his convictions, he confronted his colleagues with them. One of them seemed "wakening up to truth and reality," he told Louisa. "I think he is on the way to improve very much." But soon finding himself deeply embroiled in arguments, he told Louisa he resolved to be less vocal on these subjects: "Believe me, darling, I have not much changed any of my opinions, but I have learned a little more to hold them with gentleness as towards those who are very loud about what they cannot understand so well as I do—perhaps I have learned to make excuses for them too."[10]

These clashes taught him clearly that those individuals who truly appreciate the imaginative arts are in a minority in a predominately philistine world. Like the poet Keats writing in *Endymion*, he must have lamented "the inhuman dearth of noble natures" and that in the very place where he had expected to find them, the community of aspiring leaders of the church. He did, however, discover some few kindred spirits in whose friendship he took delight. James and Greville Matheson, brothers who lived with their large family in nearby Islington, shared MacDonald's interest in the German fairy tales and in poetry. MacDonald soon became a frequent guest in their home. He came to esteem Greville above all his peers as a person and thinker. A few years later, when MacDonald was in his pastorate, he sent Greville successive portions of his first long poem, *Within and Without,* and carefully considered his criticisms.

Another kindred spirit who was to become a close friend and help was Alexander John Scott. MacDonald began attending his public lectures during his seminary days and became fervently interested, both in Scott's views of literature and in Scott as a person. It is difficult to say much about Scott, as he was not a writer, but his influence on MacDonald's thinking was perhaps larger than that of any other single individual. A fellow Scotsman twenty years MacDonald's senior, Scott had been licensed to preach in the Church of Scotland by the presbytery of Paisley. Having gone down to London, he became what today would be termed a charismatic preacher, his sermons precipitating speaking in tongues and

prophesying in the church, although he himself tended to minimize these manifestations. He came to the place in his thinking
in which he was no longer able to subscribe to the Westminster
Confession, objecting especially to its assured pronouncements
concerning the "elect" and its use of the term *sabbath* for Sunday.
The presbytery at Paisley indicted him for heresy, and his license
was revoked.

A student of literature as well as theology, Scott secured the
Chair of English Language and Literature in University College,
London. With a manner characterized by lucidity, force of presentation, and beauty of expression, he established a wide reputation
as a masterly lecturer. As MacDonald came under his influence
he felt him to be a man speaking with a special unction from
God, and he was thrilled with the integration of his faith with
his views on English poetry. Scott's lectures were the model that
inspired MacDonald later to launch his career as a lecturer on
literature.

Scott's influence and example also enabled MacDonald to recognize even more clearly the shortcomings of sectarianism. In a
poetic tribute to Scott written later MacDonald suggested the very
important role Scott played in his spiritual maturation. In the
poem MacDonald presented himself as in a dream approaching a
temple door. When he entered, he heard a great chorus of separate
voices "together tossed / As if they sought some harmony to find /
Which they knew once." But they seemed unable to blend into
one harmonious song, so that they "were but single rimes / By
single bells through Sabbath morning sent, / That have no
thought of harmony or chimes." It was to MacDonald all "hope-
ful confusion" until he heard Scott's voice, "Truth's herald, walking the untuned roar, / Calm and distinct, powerful and sweet
and fine," and was enlightened.[11] The poem suggests the spiritual
dilemma MacDonald felt as a student confronting the history of
conflicting Christian theologies. Each contained some attractive
notes of truth, but together they failed to achieve a great harmony
because of the undue importance each placed on its sectarian

distinctives. Then, coming under Scott's influence, he was enabled to achieve an integrating vision, and life again seemed whole and good.

In Scott's teachings he found expression of those larger and more universal principles that he was coming to believe should be the primary convictions among all Christian peoples. Among these were the verities that God is the Creator and Father of all mankind, his disposition toward all nations from eternity past is one of forgiveness and steadfast love, and he will judge all peoples with justice and without partiality. God's purpose in working with man is to bring to himself by grace all those who seek a deep, self-consuming relationship with him that they may in a true sense be righteous people. The momentousness of these realities should make evident how comparatively insignificant are all dividing sectarian considerations. Scott's teachings and example, therefore, greatly inspired and buoyed MacDonald in spirit during his Highbury days, in spite of the general atmosphere of the seminary. Later, when MacDonald himself would come into conflict with his fellow Congregationalists, he would find in Scott a staunch friend and supporter.

His revulsion to the prevailing attitudes notwithstanding, MacDonald held a position of honor at Highbury. Godwin as principal took a special liking to him, and although on the one hand he "censured" him for his soft-spoken preaching style, he did much to encourage him. He appointed him senior to his class in the fall of 1849, a position of honor and influence. Since he brought to the school from his education at King's College a special interest in chemistry, the school purchased and gave to him sufficient chemical apparatus to enable him to give lectures and conduct experiments, which he did with zest.[12] Later he told his father that, should he fail to secure a position in the ministry, he could be sure of securing one in chemistry.

Louisa responded to his enthusiasm for his experiments in a playful tone that nevertheless gives some indication of his sense of the potential residing in chemical discoveries:

> I am so glad dearest George that you are really going to begin
> the wonders of your cabalistic art—I hope at least you discover
> the Rosicrucian secret of prolonging life. . . . I shall not be
> afraid of the magic of your bottles and crucibles and liquids
> and essences and shall only be too delighted to be admitted
> into your mystic chamber or laboratory sometimes.[13]

MacDonald's probing curiosity was ever trying to unlock the mysteries of life, whether by chemistry, physics, or theology. His interests ranged far, seemingly not having the same sense of inhibition in the presence of the unknown that generally characterized conservative Christians of his day. His knowledge of the biochemistry of his day was appreciable, as well as of various fields of medicine, especially as they had to do with dreams and visions.[14]

Nor is this the only indication of his roving spirit. Since the deepening spiritual experience he had in the spring of 1847, the person and teachings of Christ were central to his thinking. He was increasingly zealous to further a sense of the reality of Christ the *man,* who came to show people the way to the Father, as opposed to the abstract theological presentations of Christ that were coming from the pulpits. He began, therefore, to look with some favor on the Unitarians, wondering if their view of the person of Christ did not do greater justice to the Son of Man, which designation was, after all, Christ's favorite one for himself. Unitarianism was fairly strong during the period. A majority of the old Presbyterian congregations were Unitarian in creed by 1830, and by 1851, the Unitarian sect had two hundred twenty-nine places of worship throughout England and Wales. They represented a blend of deism and evangelicalism, with many accepting miracles and plenary inspiration, differing mainly from more orthodox Christians in their conviction that the Scriptures did not teach the Trinity.[15]

That MacDonald had an ongoing respect for them is evident in a letter he wrote to his father in 1853:[16]

> The first thing is to know Jesus as a man, and any theory about
> him that makes less of him as a man with the foolish notion

of exalting his divinity—I refuse at once. Far rather would I be such a Unitarian as Dr. Channing than such a Christian as by far the greater number of those that talk about his Divinity are. The former truly believed in Christ—believed in Him far more than the so-called orthodox.

This conviction was evidently growing on him during the summer of 1849. He wrote Louisa, asking what her opinion of him would be were he to turn Unitarian. She responded with confused amazement:

> How shall I answer your question about that dreadful word— I scarcely know what to say—I am glad you did not see me reading your letter this morning you might have thought me very silly, happily I was alone in the garden when I had it. Oh dear George, how could you ask me such a question, you know so well yourself why it would give me pain to think of any one I had the least interest in, being a Unitarian. I feel afraid almost to write the word now.—But it cannot be—you tell me not to be frightened and yet I could not help feeling such dread and fear as I scarcely knew before. I am afraid to answer your question because it will seem to imply a more fervent love to Jesus Christ than I perhaps have, but surely if I have the least desire for my own or another's salvation, how can I help being sorry that they should not know of the only *sacrifice* for sin, of our divine Saviour suffering the Just *for* the unjust, that the blood of the Son of God might cleanse us from sin. But, dear George, I cannot write learnedly on such questions.[17]

Certainly Louisa's earnest and unyielding orthodoxy had a deterring effect. Then too while he was no doubt serious in his question to her, his deeper loyalties were still with the Congregationalists, even though he was deeply concerned for their seeming inability to feel the momentous faith they professed.

The disparity between herself and her beloved weighed at times on Louisa. Given to feelings of unworthiness and occasionally to depressive moods, she agonized over her supposed deficiencies. Apparently at times MacDonald attempted to expand her horizons more rapidly than she was prepared to accept. At one point in their courtship she was near despair at something he had said:

> If I cannot appreciate and love your enthusiasm for all that is high, holy and beautiful, for all that is above the common ideas of the *multitude* most truly you must feel unhappy at the prospect before you and [have] thought of [my] being a hindrance—a *fear* oh! the thought is what I cannot bear. What a terrible word that is, what a monster I must be—You say "deliver you from this bondage"—how can I—oh! what very terrible words for you [to] use to me—I could write no more just now, but have been trying to ask God to help me to be meek and humble—You have helped me much already but oh do not let anything of all that has passed between us—beautiful as it has been to me make you feel obliged to live with one whose temper he would lead a life of *bondage*. I cannot bear the idea.[18]

Although it is conceivable that MacDonald had used the term *bondage* to refer to the possibility of their relationship becoming a burden to him, it is far more likely that he was referring to the effect of her depression on herself, and she had misunderstood his intention; however that might be, one may be sure he was quick to clarify his meaning. He was in truth already much dependent on her, and this dependency grew steadily through the years. Their love gave him opportunity to express the deep emotional side of his nature. What he desired from her was understanding of his feelings and sympathy with his longings; these depended on a degree of emotional and intellectual maturity that she had yet to achieve.

The experiences of life would soon help Louisa. Her timid nature felt an unusual horror in the contemplation of death, and during the period of their engagement death struck close to her. In July of 1849 her Aunt Sarah and her cousin Alexander's wife Charlotte died in the same house within twenty-four hours of each other. She was deeply moved by both the coincidence and the loss, but greater heartache soon followed.

The slow death of her mother, long an invalid, served to help Louisa become more mature. In late September 1849 the family took the worsening Mrs. Powell to Lynmouth, Devonshire, in the hopes that the climate would work some salutary effects on her. Apparently it did for a time. When Powell joined them by boat, he was overjoyed to see his wife improved. "It was a truly beautiful picture to see them meeting and their tears of chastened love, thankfulness, and something too like fear," Louisa wrote MacDonald.[19]

But the respite from her steadily deteriorating condition was short-lived. The following April, while MacDonald was temporarily occupying a pulpit in Whitehaven, Cumbria, her periods of hemorrhaging from the lungs, now alarmingly frequent, could not be effectively stopped, although two doctors in attendance did all within their ingenuity to stem them. She was laid on a board in bed to ensure that her chest would not bend in the slightest; ice packs were kept on her chest and cold cloths on her head; she feebly spelled out her limited messages with her fingers. Louisa, who with her sisters took turns watching by the bed around the clock, pleaded with MacDonald to return from Whitehaven, even though it meant his asking the congregation there to release him from his commitment to them. He did, knowing that his precipitate leaving precluded the possibility of his receiving a call from them to be their pastor. Louisa's cry prevailed: "You are the only one of her children that has not seen her. . . . I fear you will not see her alive."[20] Apparently he did not; the family was devastated by her passing. "I never felt the *use* of religion, of love and trust in God, so much before," the grieving Louisa confessed.[21]

SIX

Too Quiet to Please

*Not only . . . has each man his individual relation to God,
but each man has his peculiar relation to God. He is to God
a peculiar being, made after his own fashion, and that of no
one else. Hence he can worship God as no man else can
worship Him.* —"The New Name," Unspoken Sermons,
Series One

Strong as the emphasis on the academic life at Highbury was,
the chief goal of the school was to produce effective pulpiteers and
pastors. Therefore, it made earnest efforts to secure opportunities
"in the field" for young aspirants to the ministry to practice their
preaching and be initiated into pastoral duties. Churches were in
general not eager to have an initiate, and such opportunities were
not as plentiful as the school wished.

MacDonald was eager for such work, both because he wanted
to develop his personal ministry to people and because he needed
the money, some debts from his Aberdeen education still lingering. He did succeed in raising a little money by having his father
ship some farm produce to the Radermachers' with the arrangement that he keep the money himself, but other help from home
was meager. During his seminary days, however, he was singularly
fortunate in his number of preaching opportunities.

In the spring of 1849 an indication came from a church in
the ancient and beautiful city of Cork, in southwestern Ireland,
that they would be willing to receive a student apprentice for the
summer, and Godwin offered the opportunity to MacDonald.
The actual invitation was slow in coming, and MacDonald temporarily dismissed the possibility by conjecturing that only his

expenses would be paid anyway. Nevertheless, the invitation did come and he went. It proved to be a good experience. He was able to write some sermons that were gratifying to him, to work on his pulpit manner, and to enjoy the lush Irish countryside, flourishing in rich green under the "soft" rains for which western Ireland is famous. He lodged with the church's deacons, one of whom owned a livery, and was privileged to indulge his love of horseback riding.

One day he rode east as far as St. Declan's, site of one of Ireland's round towers, this one rising ninety feet above the ruins of an early Christian monastery. The wells there were considered holy, as was a holy stone "said to be floated from Rome." He was bemused to observe the "poor Catholics" creeping under the stone in hopes of being relieved of their rheumatism, while others knelt "on the graves and by the wells, and by the stone counting their beads, and washing themselves—Some of them very respectable looking country people."[1] On another occasion he could have seen Queen Victoria, had he made the effort. He was struck with the contrast between English disdain for the Irish people and Irish loyalty to the throne. "I didn't see her," he told his father, "for I am no worshipper of royalty, and had no intention of going to look at her. . . . I believe there was no great enthusiasm among the lower classes—how could there be!—but she was received with every possible demonstration of loyalty—a great deal more (show I mean) than I was pleased with considering the state of the country—except for the good it may do the people afterwards."[2] As a young Scot, MacDonald could hardly be expected to stand in awe of Victoria, a Hanoverian, his ancestors having been loyal to the Stuarts.

While he enjoyed his Irish summer, he did begin to have some misgivings about his suitability for the ministry. "I often fear I won't do for a minister," he confessed to his father, "but God will guide me as will be best for me—and what is of more consequence, best for the accomplishment of his plans."[3] This sense of a different destiny from that of the traditional pastorate grew during the years immediately ahead. It arose in part from the criticisms he received concerning his manner of preaching and in part from his unwillingness simply to please his hearers by presenting scriptural teachings in harmony with their denominational understanding.

When MacDonald returned to Highbury, Godwin told his protege that his manner of preaching was at once too informal, too intellectual, and too poetic. Worse yet, he was too uncertain about his doctrines. The practical-minded Godwin felt that the average person in the pews favored a dignified presentation of un-disturbing evangelical cliches; MacDonald felt that a great many doctrinal certainties were less firm in conscientious minds. God-win wanted rhetorical polish; MacDonald was striving for a sim-ple, unartificial manner.

MacDonald is admired by his readers today precisely because he possessed a sensitivity that was offended by coarse and cliche-ridden handlings of sacred truths and a mind that delved to un-cover underlying realities and present them afresh. As to his pulpit manner he apparently had an ideal in mind that was more deriva-tive of Scott than of Godwin, one that made for effective presenta-tion when later as a mature speaker he perfected it. His ideal emphasized naturalness, in which the attention of the audience was held by strength of personality and earnestness of tone. As a preacher he was inclined to refer to personal experience and to re-veal his struggles with the understanding of a text rather than con-fidently to affirm more traditional interpretations. The sort of sermons he was giving may be found in any of a number of his novels, such as *Annals of a Quiet Neighborhood*. His manner an-noyed some while gratifying others. Almost all accounts of his later lectures, such as those he gave in America in 1872–1873, praise him for his ability to hold an audience in rapt attention for extended periods of time, although they often characterized his manner as unorthodox.

As was his habit he soon confided his problem to his father: "Perhaps my manner is too quiet to please dissenters commonly. However, I must not do violence to the nature God has given me, and put anything on. I think, if people will try, I can make them understand me—if they won't, I have no desire to be understood. I can't do their part of the work."[4] But when his father read his letter, his sympathies tended to lie with the confused laity. Taking a different view of the matter, he expressed his fatherly indignation:

> "Do violence to our nature"! What if you had been born with *duck feet* like your maternal grandmother? Or have been gifted with the *Higgenbotham* of a *Dutchman* . . . all of which might have been rectified by doing "a little violence to your nature." . . . and why not suppose that your very quietness may be somewhat of an infirmity as a public speaker and seeing that in the country a little animation tends to arrest the attention or prevent some from sleeping or in the estimation of many gives a zest to what may independently be excellent, why should not some violence be done to one's nature.[5]

This fatherly lecture is compelling in its energetic directness, the homey force of its logic, and its evident parental concern for how his son was being perceived. MacDonald especially prized this intriguing mixture of tight reasoning, candid forthrightness, and salty humor in his father, for he knew it sprang from fatherly love and wisdom.

MacDonald had further opportunity to improve his pulpit manner the following spring when he responded to a five-week opening at Whitehaven, a small seaport town on the edge of the beautiful Lake District in Cumbria. Reluctant to miss A. J. Scott's lectures, he secured Louisa's promise to attend them and take notes for him in his absence. Louisa was dismayed in the lecture hall:

> I felt 2 or 3 times as if I should have cried because I could not follow him—really I do think it is rather too strong meat for such as I.[6]

Nevertheless, she pluckily did her best.

Meanwhile MacDonald was enthralled by the beauties of the sea and the fells, or low mountains, with the tarns and lakes for which the area is justly famous. Not far away were the regions in which Wordsworth lived, experiencing his mystical encounters with nature. As it happened, the aged and venerable poet, living at Rydal Mount, died on April 23 that year. MacDonald never met him, but he no doubt seized such opportunities as his pastoral duties afforded him to trek over the fells and around the idyllic lakes, perhaps with some of Wordsworth's poems in mind. His wanderings reinforced his convictions that the power of natural scenes was the power of the grace of God directly resident in nature everywhere.

The people of Whitehaven responded to him, and the congregation began to grow. So absorbed was he with his work and his wanderings that he neglected for some time to write his father, who "was really wondering with no little wonderment" why no letters were forthcoming. But he partly suspected the reason for the hiatus: "I am sure you will get mountains not far off made ready to your mind so that you will not need to manufacture them in your own poetic fancy."[7]

At this time, however, Mrs. Powell's final illness and death occurred. It brought his promising situation to an abrupt conclusion, and MacDonald found himself back in London, on the eve of completing his seminary work, with no immediate prospect of another opening. Upon certifying the completion of his courses, the officials at Highbury expressed their hope that he would soon find "a suitable sphere of ministerial labor." MacDonald did not take a degree there because he already had a master's degree from King's.[8]

SEVEN

"Warstling" On

Please do not address me as Rev. It is many long years since I dropped that always to me unpleasant title.—MacDonald to Mr. Grundy

Manchester was a possibility. Not only were his brothers Charles and Alex established there, but now his brother John also had found a position as tutor in the vicinity. Charles, assuming the prerogatives of elder brother, insisted that George come north, assuring both him and their father that he would use his influence to secure a promising middle-class church where he would have strong prospects of "getting on." George's father wrote, hoping, "when you get to Manchester some suitable opening may occur in the kind providence of God."[1]

So MacDonald began planning to go to Manchester, at least to survey the possibilities. But he did so with little relish, not wanting to convey any impression that "getting on" was part of his motivation in being a pastor. Circumstances, however, became unfavorable for going north. Charles's wife was having periods of blood spitting, and her doctor advised that Alex should quit his lodgings with them and find independent quarters; it was an inopportune time to visit there. Further, MacDonald felt little attraction to the industrial complexes of the north, their smoke-laden air promising to be uncongenial to his asthma. Besides, Manchester was far from Louisa. Moreover, he had recommendations to his credit and felt it not unreasonable to expect that an opening would soon occur closer to London.

Wanting to reassure his father, he wrote to him, indicating that he was enclosing a copy of a recommendation he had received while preaching in Salisbury. Inadvertently, however, he forgot to enclose the promised document. His father's response illustrates something more of the playful side of his nature:

> I received your letter I think on Saturday but as for the enclosed letter of which you speak I do not see one expression in it calculated to do you any credit! You stare do you?—Know then, if you don't know already, that there really was no enclosure and how could I see anything good therein? The only thing for me is to set my "clairvoyance" agoing and read it within the folds of your coat pocket. Here then is contents revealed—"Salisbury, June 1850. Sir. You are a stupid dunce of a fellow and not fit to instruct sensible well-informed people such as we are. So you may go about your business and teach the A B C to the half savage and half clad highlanders of Scotland of whom I believe you are a worthy descendant . . ." Now, is not mesmerism a wonderful invention when it can pry into your pockets and make such discoveries![2]

Whether MacDonald corrected the oversight and sent the disputed document later correspondence does not reveal. However, he soon had an invitation to speak at Brighton, the very place where the Powells had been living since Mrs. Powell's death. The church there was mixed in its response to him: some were enthusiastic and strongly urged him to consider coming to them; others were cool. MacDonald did not pursue the matter, feeling the need for a unanimous call. Then an invitation came from the Trinity Congregational Church in Arundel, Sussex. He visited and preached for them, the invitation was renewed, and he was soon confident that he had found his first pastorate.

Arundel was a quiet little village directly south of London, almost within sight of the Atlantic. Situated on the southern slope of a rather steep hill, the Arun River at its base runs lazily through the graceful arches of an ancient stone bridge, of which MacDonald was to become particularly fond. Immediately on the east side of the village was a massive, sprawling castle—frequently renovated through the centuries—belonging to the Duke of Norfolk. To the northwest, immediately atop the hill, was an ornate cathedral, stately but curiously topped with a disproportionately small steeple. Halfway up the hill, on Tarrant Street, stood the square, stark brick church housing MacDonald's congregation. Its undistinguished architecture reflected the general distrust among the Congregationalists of adornment and art.

To the north lay the gently rolling hills of Sussex, over which MacDonald loved to walk. Somewhat later, when writing to cheer his adolescent half-sister Bella, then dying of consumption, he compared Sussex to the terrain of Scotland dear to both of them:

> How much I should like to spend a winter at home again, a snowy winter, with great heaps and wreaths of snow, and sometimes the wild storm howling in the chimneys and against the windows and down at the kitchen door. And how much I should love to spend one long summer day in June, lying on the grass before the house, and looking up into the deep sky with large white clouds in it. . . . It would be delightful if I could go to sleep here some night, and waken there. . . . Everything looks so different here. Behind the town there are a number of hills, or rather braes, very low hills, but with sweet short grass, on which such numbers of fallow deer are feeding. Here and there are plantations of fine trees, very large some of them; and down in one of the hollows rises and runs a very clear stream of water, most wonderfully clear, clearer than the Bogie, and so nice to drink in the hot days. . . . The fields grow much richer crops than with you, and there are many more trees growing about the fields; but it is not such a beautiful country to my mind nearly as the one I left.[3]

Arundel was not Huntly, but it was in many ways a pleasant and promising place for the young minister, fresh out of seminary, to begin his ministry. He was pleased with the prospect. The inviting natural terrain promised many opportunities to perceive the grace of God flowing through nature itself, and the people seemed receptive to the prospect of his ministry. He was, nevertheless, somewhat apprehensive. "I hope to be happier than I have ever been, if I am once settled," he wrote his father. "My only trouble is the almost continual feeling that I shall not be able to provide sermons for my people."[4] The writing of sermons loomed large as a demanding task. He preferred writing religious poetry. When he, or at times Louisa, would copy a sermon and send it to his father, he would include poems as well, some quite lengthy. The poem "Light," which he was working on during this time, runs to some three hundred lines.

His father was not unappreciative of the poems but plainly preferred the sermons. In a note to Louisa dated November 4, 1850, George's father thanked her for "the trouble you took upon yourself, to transcribe a poem of such a length merely for my gratification. Had I thought you would have had so much work at the job I would not have asked to put you to so much trouble, but seeing it is accomplished, I beg again to thank you very kindly for your pains." Poetry writing was for MacDonald a passion, although few seemed to value his work. One of the reasons Arundel was attractive to him was that its small church and quieter surroundings seemed to promise him at least some time to pursue his love of verse.

Whether Arundel would become MacDonald's home for long depended considerably on the approval of James Powell; after all, his daughter would live there. Following the death of his invalid wife the prior spring, he had removed his family temporarily to Powis Place in Brighton, a fashionable resort on the coast some twenty-five miles to the east of Arundel. Although now a gentleman of seventy years, neither his energies nor his authority were diminishing—he traveled daily to his business in London—and his blessing on the plans of his future son-in-law was crucial.

An aloof and austere Victorian father, he was held in awe by everyone; even his silences inspired fear. When MacDonald returned in 1849 from his sojourn in Cork, he had grown a full beard. It was in part a gesture of rebellion, although he may not have consciously recognized it as such. On his first visit to the Powells, he was in the drawing room with some of the daughters when the elder Powell entered. When he saw the beard, Powell turned without a word of greeting and left the room. Beards were heathenish affairs. MacDonald left the room as well—to shave himself clean. Only later, when Louisa's hand was secured, did he exercise his independence and grow back the full beard, which was to distinguish his appearance throughout his life. But at this time the prospective father-in-law's Victorian authority and evangelical sentiments held sway.

As regards Arundel, Powell had expressed himself willing, provided the entire situation met with his approval, to secure and furnish lodgings for the couple when married. MacDonald could hardly have contemplated marriage at this time without this provision. Consequently, on a Sunday in August, after due announcement and preparation, the august Powell appeared with Louisa and a retinue of her sisters, to attend MacDonald's services and to advise him on securing lodgings. Afterward he indicated he was inclined to bestow his blessing, and Louisa was very pleased:

> Papa spoke so kindly about us at Leamington he told them all about the house and how he had advised you—he told them also about the "elegant bracelet" you had given me. I was pleased.[5]

Clearly, Powell felt the time was opportune to grant his favor. When he returned to Brighton, he wrote, giving his fatherly advice. His manner in the following letter gives considerable indication of his personality and indicates something of his stern evangelical emphasis on decorum. After expressing perfunctory appreciation for MacDonald's "professional services," he gave his critique:

> There is however one thing in your service I think you may amend. In my earlier life if I had been asked what I thought of your reading the scriptures I should have given an answer of approval because you avoided monotony by given [sic] the emphasis natural to the various speakers in the narrative parts of scripture, but the remarks of my late illustrious friend S. T.

Coleridge on this subject has [sic] so modified my opinion on this point that what I should then have admired I now deprecate. . . . I wish I could give you a tithe of his eloquent words, but his meaning was that in reading the scriptures it never should be forgotten whose scriptures they are, and that while monotony is avoided the oracular nature and divine source should never be forgotten—that the words of our Saviour in particular should be delivered with great deliberation, and that everything which might bear the appearance of flippancy should be shunned.

I might my Dear Sir if I had time very gently hint only that some of these remarks were applicable to the Dissenting pulpit but as I have not time to go roundabout I will at once say that I think you read too fast and without the consideration . . . that it should be more as the Oracles of God, than the opinions of man.[6]

MacDonald probably sighed with relief that Powell did not have more time. Powell's contact with Coleridge was through his physician son by his first wife, who was among those who attempted to moderate Coleridge's intake of opium around 1816. He knew that MacDonald's esteem of Coleridge was very high, and no doubt used the reference to the poet to strengthen his authority. That Powell was solicitous of MacDonald's manner is evident enough, desiring that it be more formal and sedate. But MacDonald was more concerned with communicating the scriptures to his hearers with expression and verve, feeling that the primary object in reading scripture was to convey a sense of the reality of the text for everyday situations, rather than an impression of pompous formality. He quietly continued to use his natural manner in public reading.

The majority of the Arundel flock, seeing more to commend than to criticize in their prospective pastor, assembled at an official business meeting on October 3, 1850, and voted to extend him a "call." Fifty-seven voted positively; five abstained on the grounds they had not heard him. How it was that these five members were at the business meeting but not at the services of the last several weeks is unexplained. They may have composed the nucleus of the opposition that was soon to grow. At any rate the salary was fixed at one hundred fifty pounds per year,[7] a figure that quite satisfied him: "I might go very far indeed without finding so good a plan" he wrote to his father. [8]

Determined to have the people like him, and to develop a ministry among the "poor and unwell," he energetically set about a demanding schedule for a beginning pastor. He undertook to conduct a prayer meeting every Monday evening and to present a lecture each Thursday evening, in which he enlarged on and clarified his last Sunday's sermon. He also undertook to hold Bible classes on these same evenings, one for young men and the other for young women. But he took most seriously his preparation for the pulpit, finding it difficult to compose a new sermon for each Sunday. His ambitious plans, however, were soon interrupted.

In early November, Louisa left London by train to visit her aunts in Leamington, a village to the north. Opening a letter from her fiancée after comfortably situating herself on the train, she was shocked with the news that a severe cough had issued in a pronounced hemorrhaging from his lungs. This was, of course, an ominous indication of tuberculosis, the disease—in those days incurable—that plagued the family. Horrified, Louisa disembarked at her first opportunity and returned to her father; she must go to MacDonald at once. Exercising the evangelical penchant to read circumstances and events in terms of divine messages, Powell considered this may well be an indication she was never to marry him. She, rather, chose to read the event in precisely opposite terms: she should marry him immediately and nurse him back to health.

Propriety, however—that ultimate consideration for the Victorian mind—was the final interpreter of the will of God. For a young woman to leave home and nurse her male friend before they were duly married by appropriate ceremony was simply improper. MacDonald was confined to bed and nursed by a woman of the congregation whose mature age rendered her acceptable for the task. He lay patiently on his back, the proper number of leeches faithfully fulfilling their blood-letting office on his chest. Although it was perilous for MacDonald to travel, Powell sponsored his trip to an eminent London physician, Dr. Williams, an authority on tuberculosis. The doctor rendered a careful opinion that the lungs were indeed affected; MacDonald was ordered not to preach for at least two months. Thus the Arundel church discovered almost immediately after issuing a call to this promising young seminarian that they had an invalid pastor to support and were obliged to make do with pulpit substitutes.

MacDonald spent two weeks at The Limes, but he did not think it well to continue with the Powells. He was not the only invalid in the house: a sister of the late Mrs. Powell was recuperating there as well, having come to London for an operation for breast cancer, and he thought it best to secure other lodgings. His maternal aunt, Mary Spence, living at Newport on the Isle of Wight—an easy distance to the west of Arundel—was willing to open her home to her nephew, and he went to convalesce with her.

Then he faced the task of writing his anxious father. "I feel very doubtful whether I shall preach much longer," he told him frankly. "I feel if I were to begin again now, it would bring back the attack." If he recovered, he was not intending to stay long in the ministry. The exertions of the pastoral routine, undertaken with great energy, made too large demands on his weak constitution. MacDonald was confident he had done his duty and professed to his father that he was unafraid in the presence of death. Yet he feared his father might not understand, and he knew as well that he faced the possibility of dying. He ventured the hope, "Perhaps such attacks might come and go, and one yet *warstle* [Scotticism for wrestle] on for some years." Then he assured him:

> But I have no *idol of chance* as many called Christians seem to have. All will be well with me. I know you would give me the best you could—my heart's desire if you could—and I know

God is better than you, and it was Christ himself that taught us to call him Father. If I were to die tomorrow, I would thank God for what I have had, for he has blessed me very abundantly—I could say "I have lived."

He seems to have had no inclination to quarrel with his lot; on the contrary, he found cause for praise: "such a mingling of glorious gifts, along with much mental discomfort, has been mine, and the last the greatest blessing of all. I mean the mental trouble."[9]

The "mental trouble" probably refers to his periods of despondency and suggests that his illness had at least in part a psychological cause. Subconsciously, he was rebelling against the demands of his new position, although he was mentally making a herculean effort to discipline himself and shoulder his burdens. The exertion, prompted by his extreme conscientiousness, may have combined with his distaste for his tasks to precipitate the bleeding. Part of his thankfulness for his despondency might have been because it was out of such moods that he composed his best poetry. Undoubtedly his desire was to become a poet. During the two months of his convalescence he wrote with amazing energy and considerable skill, composing a dramatic poem of over forty-five hundred lines, which he titled *Within and Without*. It is replete with evidence of MacDonald's state of mind at the time.

The poem is the story of Julian, a young man who undergoes great agonies in search of a satisfying relationship to God. Curiously plotted and melodramatic, the poem is nevertheless noteworthy in that it presents the first literary announcement, in technically respectable lines, of some of MacDonald's foundation beliefs.

As the poem opens, Julian, a monk in a monastery agonizes over his deep need to discover God as his personal father. The crass atmosphere of the monastery, with its rationalist preoccupations and empty rituals (shades of Highbury), cannot satisfy this quest. Despairing, Julian escapes, marries, and fathers a child. He becomes estranged from his wife Lilia, however, because of his depressed and morbid state brought on by his search. Finally, he realizes his true spiritual problem: instead of allowing Lilia and her love to be a means of the grace of God to him, he had sunk into an obsession with his quest and had become spiritually paralyzed with self-concern.

He comes to realize he should have given himself to Lilia in open and unrestrained love, allowing the grace that would flow through such a conscientious abandonment to marital love to assuage his need. The ideas on women underscored in the poem depict the views MacDonald had formed prior to his marriage and consistently held: Woman was given by God to man, not to be a possession over which he exercised tyrannical control, and certainly not to be a plaything, but rather to be a partner in receiving the grace of life. These ideas are forward-looking, given the Victorian context in which they were formed.

Julian, Lilia, and their child Lily all having died in the course of the strained actions of the plot, the poem ends with Julian's being reunited with them in a celestial world. Julian's final insight is that God had been with him throughout his quest; although he had felt estranged from God, he was all the while enveloped by God's presence and loving care:

> And thou wast with me all the time, my God,
> Even as now! I was not far from thee.
> Thy spirit spoke in all my wants and fears,
> And hopes and longings. Thou art all in all.
> I am not mine, but thine.

These themes, ubiquitous in MacDonald's many writings, are thus unequivocally announced in his first imaginative work: The presence of God pervades all of experience; there is nowhere where he is not. The very sense of alienation from God that the questing soul feels is necessary, preceding the bliss of spiritual union with him, just as thirst precedes the satisfaction of a drink. Since the normal course of life is permeated with grace, life should be lived fully. To assume that the spiritual level of experience is achieved by denying the physical aspects of life—as Julian's monastic beginnings suggest—rather than by earnestly and sincerely honoring them, is to mistake the true nature of grace.

In spite of the fact that *Within and Without* suffers from what today seems an incredible plot, MacDonald produced an impressively long poem of respectable quality in a two-month period, while recuperating from a serious malady. Emotionally highstrung, his mounting indignation over the pervasive religious crassness—a mentality that he now was beginning to detect in his church at Arundel—contributed to his physical breakdown, but at the same time resulted in a fury of artistic endeavor. Emotions that on one level had earlier prompted him to grow a beard now issued on another level in a work of art.

His experience was destined to demonstrate, through painful experience over the next two years, what he already knew in part: His ideas, together with his artistic sensibility, removed him too far from the tolerances of understanding and sympathy of the average dissenting congregation. "There are none," he wrote his father concerning his congregation, "I could call society for me."[10]

MacDonald's doctor felt he was well enough to return to his pulpit ministry on the third Sunday in January 1851, and gradually resume his pastoral responsibilities. For him, however, as for his hero Julian, "lowness of spirits" was a lingering malady.

EIGHT

Necessary to Each Other

May you ever be more and more necessary to each other, and ever more and more competent to supply the necessity.—MacDonald to Flora Powell, before her marriage to Joshua Sing

It is popular today to question the nature of the family in Victorian society, emphasizing discrepancies between the ideal of the happy family unit and the reality of men who kept mistresses and frequented prostitutes and of women who were enslaved to childbearing. Certainly these realities were part of the total picture. But the classic ideal of family life realized in many homes was also a part of that picture. Family life was highly structured, with the father the ultimate authority, the mother the emotional center, and the children dutiful recipients of parental instruction.

From the beginning of their lives together George and Louisa MacDonald worked hard to shape their lives according to this ideal. Their many letters record their joys and sorrows, their judgments and prejudices, their frequent struggles and occasional triumphs. Reading them reveals how their growing strength of feeling each for the other resulted in a seemingly indestructible bond of unity. The loss they would feel at the many deaths that were to come was the more poignant because of their solidarity and sensitive dependence on each other.

No sooner was he well enough to return to his pastoral duties than MacDonald determined to marry as soon as possible. He felt he could no longer live without Louisa Powell. His father received the announcement with no little amazement: "Really you are a *chap* of some *pluck* after all to speak of getting married when you seem by past accounts to require more the aid of some *old gran-nyma* of a nurse than to come under obligations to provide for and cherish a wife," he teased. He continued with gentle needling: "I therefore am led to gather that a considerable portion of your ailments was sickness—*oil* sickness and love sickness from which I trust you will be ultimately delivered." But he was also sincerely apprehensive lest his son's exhilaration in love temporarily mask the true state of his health: "But seriously, let me know how you stand out and don't calculate by the amount of liveliness of spirit you may have gained that your bodily strength is correspondingly improved."[1]

Having to take the cod-liver oil his doctor prescribed was one of MacDonald's deepest aversions; hence, his father's allusion to "oil sickness." He felt it made him ill, and indeed he may have been allergic to it. But lovesick he was, greatly desiring that Louisa be with him. In his earnest concern that nothing stand between him and his prospective bride, he told her he had written and sent to Helen Powell in years past several poems, which he had bound together in little pocket-sized books, and asked her to secure them from Helen.

Louisa was hesitant because Helen tended to intimidate her, and she would rather MacDonald had secured them himself. He no doubt would have, except that Helen was in London at the time, and he was not. Finding herself forced either to undertake the task or be left with an uneasy curiosity, she determined to confront her sister-in-law, asking her to give the books to her father. Louisa had always resented Helen's air of superiority, feeling that she flaunted her greater beauty. On a former occasion, however, Louisa had opposed both her and Charles MacDonald when they loudly criticized MacDonald's going to Cork, and she could do so again. Helen reluctantly agreed to yield the books, after teasing she had committed some of the poems to the fire, as they were "for no eyes but her own." Louisa, nevertheless, was relieved and satisfied, not only to have retrieved the poems but also to sense that Helen after all respected her for her pluck. She told MacDonald afterward that the task was "much easier" than she expected.[2]

Powell, however, did not quickly give his permission for the marriage. He must first approve the lodgings, then furnishings must be supplied. George and Louisa were confident they could arrange all in time for a March 1 wedding, but Powell talked of the necessity of waiting until May. Dismayed, Louisa sought her older sister Charlotte to intercede with her father, while MacDonald was so bold as to express chagrin in a letter to Powell. Finally, Powell acceded. The greatly relieved Louisa described to George her father's altered manner: "Last night he put his arm round my neck and at bedtime walked me up-stairs in that way into his room and first showed me your letter, then told me in the kindest way that all his objections were removed and that he would now do all in his power to help us."[3]

Consequently, February was filled with a flurry of activities. Now consistently amiable, Powell approved a house MacDonald chose and proceeded to furnish it handsomely, including carpets in all rooms upstairs as well as down and appropriate draperies throughout. After much discussion on who should marry them, they asked Godwin to do the honors, settled on a March 8 ceremony, and secured the needed certificate. Louisa chose their servant carefully from among country girls, as "they do not expect so much wage and are generally more thorough" than city ones. Mr. Hounsom, the church deacon from whom the house was rented, congenially extended to them a month's free rent, and MacDonald moved into the freshly furnished house the last week in February, impatiently awaiting his bride.

The marriage ceremony was held at a quaint old meeting-house in Hackney known as The Old Gravel Pits, formerly the place of worship for some of the Powell family. As Godwin was not able to perform the rite, the Rev. John Davies conducted the service on March 8, 1851. Powell, however, was not present, ostensibly being in Bristol on business. More plausibly, he feared that he would be unable to control his emotions—another indication of the overriding importance of propriety and restraint to the nineteenth-century British gentleman. Propriety also had its direct place in MacDonald's father's blessing: "May the Lord bless and direct you both. I trust she will prove a help meet who will draw her half of the yoke with steadiness and propriety, and may you not leave too much for her to do."[4] After a short honeymoon in Leamington they took up life together in earnest as pastor and wife.

Life for the newly wedded couple in their pleasantly furnished hired lodgings appears to have been bustling and happy. MacDonald's friend from his student days, Robert Troup, paid them a brief visit that summer, attending at the same time the Great Exhibition in London. He professed to be impressed with the joy they seemed to possess.[5] Besides keeping the home, Louisa entered into the life of the church with zest and undertook very earnestly to share her husband's responsibilities and interests. His depression of spirits was lightened. The writing of sermons did not continue to be quite the onerous task it was at first, and he found growing satisfaction in getting to know the people of the village, particularly the poor and disadvantaged.

Occasional opportunities to see his brothers, with whom he felt strong emotional ties, also lightened the burden of the pastorate. John, who was now a tutor near Manchester, had graduated from King's College with distinction before his twenty-first birthday and was MacDonald's favorite. Of a dreamy, imaginative nature, John was intensely interested in poetry, writing a good deal of it and sharing it with his brother. Alec, the more stable of the two, was well established in a mercantile business in Manchester. Although less of a practicing poet, he was no less interested in the craft. Whenever the brothers were together, they fell into deep discussions concerning their poetry.

Charles, the oldest of the brothers, stood somewhat apart from the other three. Also living in Manchester, he moved in the world of business and finance, and George did not especially admire his financial ambitions and adventures. The perennial desire of the middle class to rise in the world of trade and affluence never elicited MacDonald's approval. Charles seems to have had something of the daring of his namesake uncle who had been forced to flee to America twenty years earlier to avoid jail for his irregular banking practices. Charles also seems to have been too liberal in his financial advice to his brothers.

James Powell often brought his daughters for extended weekends, and Angela, who felt a special bond with MacDonald because of his teaching help, regularly came to stay with them when Louisa was in her first confinement. Even MacDonald's father was implored to visit, and seemingly planned to make the trip, but evidently was too reluctant to leave Scotland. Frequent visits were also exchanged with the Mathesons, who lived in London. That these days were memorable is evident from the imaginative reworking MacDonald would give them a decade later in his novel *Annals of a Quiet Neighborhood*.

Early in the summer following their marriage, MacDonald was ordained to the Christian ministry. The authority of a Congregational minister to administer the sacraments was not complete until the local church ordained him. The service was held in June, with MacDonald's favorite professor from Highbury, John Godwin, presiding. It proved a very significant occasion for Godwin, inasmuch as he, then a widower, met Louisa's sister Charlotte, who had come to help with the guests. Two years later MacDonald would have the honor of marrying them.

MacDonald did not allow his involvement in the life of the church to abate his other interests. The burst of poetic inspiration he had felt during the prior winter continued. Having discovered the mystical and intensely visionary poetry of the German poet writing under the pen name Novalis, he undertook to translate a selection of his devotional poems into acceptable English verse. Indeed, MacDonald found in Novalis compelling expression of some ideas that he strongly held: that nature is a universal metaphor of the spirit, a "garment of God"; that the spirit of virtue and the spirit of poetry are one and the same; and that true poetry is itself a means whereby people may participate in the higher spiritual world. The influence of Novalis's thought is most strongly present in MacDonald's first adult fantasy, *Phantastes,* which he would write a few years later.

Novalis wrote his "spiritual songs" just prior to his premature death at age twenty-nine, at a time when his deep trust in God and his mystical sense of the presence of Christ were especially strong. MacDonald translated twelve of these poems, had them privately printed and bound, and he and Louisa distributed them among their friends as gifts for Christmas in 1851. They also penned and designed a little album of the poems of their close poet friend Greville Matheson.

Shortly after Christmas, on January 4, 1852, Louisa delivered their first child, whom they named Lilia Scott. Lilia was the name of the heroine in *Within and Without;* Scott was for A. J. Scott, now principal of Owens College in Manchester. "She is a much larger child than I had expected—and seems to have a very good pair of lungs. . . . I think she is rather a pretty baby too—certainly prettier than I had expected, or her momma either," the new father boasted when he announced the glad news to his father.[6] She was destined to be an extraordinary child, giving her parents considerable delight. Within four months MacDonald again expressed his paternal delight: "Our little child is almost drowned or devoured . . . with kindness and admiration. She is such a happy laughing strong and loving little thing."[7]

NINE

Trouble

*The things God says to you come in mostly at the back door,
and what others say, at the front.* —MacDonald to
Georgina Cowper-Temple, January 26, 1880

Not all went well, however, in 1852. Reverses came in Mac-
Donald's personal and professional life, but out of the pain and
disappointment he gained a strengthened sense of direction toward the career that would eventually emerge.

In March MacDonald's brother Alec came to visit, and it was
painfully evident that he was ailing. He too endured hemorrhaging from the lungs and had periods of excessive perspiration. More
staid and reserved by nature than his brothers, he had been deeply
in love with a girl from Manchester, Hannah Robertson, and he
had mastered his shyness sufficiently to ask her to marry him.
Now, with consumption evident, her father had intervened to dis-
courage their relationship, and the engagement was canceled.
Both ill and lovelorn, Alec was greatly depressed in spirits. Soon
after his visit to Arundel, he left Manchester to return to Huntly,
where his health steadily declined.

MacDonald was also increasingly aware that all was not well
in the church. Some of the more prosperous members were taking
alarm at their young pastor's insistence that Christian people exhibit those attitudes the Bible commends as "fruits of the Spirit,"
that they be active in their expressions of compassion and sympathy for those outside the church, and that they cease to shape their
lives by the attitudes and ambitions of the world. His vision of
God as a Heavenly Father whose love is as a burning fire and whose
intention is to save his followers from their sins, rather than simply

from hell, made them uncomfortable. Further, they began to sense that MacDonald's conviction of the universal presence of sacramental grace was different from the general tenor of teaching within the Congregational Church. The biblical statements themselves they could hardly openly oppose, so they had to find some means of deflecting attention from themselves to their pastor. They began to make clear to him that they preferred more "doctrinal" sermons, meaning thereby to shift the focus of attention away from the quality of their lives to more abstract probings. They would have been more pleased with clearer assurances that they were among God's elect.

The presence of opposition challenged MacDonald to redouble his efforts. He preached a sermon in which he affirmed that Christians in general were "far too anxious to be definite, and have finished, well-polished systems, forgetting that the more perfect a theory about the infinite the surer it is to be wrong—the more impossible it is to be right." The evident reason why no system of thought could be "right," in any exclusive sectarian sense, was simply that the mind was capable of containing it. The truth concerning God and his ways, being infinite, necessarily stood outside the capacity of the finite human mind fully to grasp. If the mind could grasp it all, humans would be equal to God.

With an air of exasperation he wrote his father: "I firmly believe people have hitherto been a great deal too much taken up about doctrine and far too little about practice. The word doctrine, as used in the bible means *teaching of duty* not *theory.*" He had little esteem for attempts to achieve doctrinal preciseness in areas in which scripture itself is vague. "I am neither Arminian nor Calvinist," he affirmed. "To no system could I subscribe."[1]

But this was an understanding of the nature of Christian truth that not all in his congregation were prepared to accept. Many much preferred doctrinally precise sermons, feeling no guilt at wanting to be "right" intellectually. Among these was Deacon Hounsom, the MacDonalds' landlord. Wishing to be free from obligation to him, and considering that their family was growing, the MacDonalds began to look for somewhat larger living quarters. The objectors, however, who were the ruling minority in the church, sought an opportunity to pressure them into looking for another pastorate rather than simply another dwelling. They met with MacDonald to announce with deep regret that due to financial exigencies the church could no longer pay him his one-hundred-fifty-pound annual salary.

MacDonald, however, was unwilling to be deterred from his course. After all, many in the congregation were deeply moved by what he was preaching and were thoroughly supportive even to the extent of being solicitous of the MacDonalds' daily needs and comforts. Readily willing to make sacrifice for the sake of his service to God, he replied that his family would try to live on less. The church was true to its word and paid him a reduced salary of 56.16 pounds for the final half-year of his ministry.

In July 1852, when he took a short respite from his pastoral duties to be in Brighton, lending moral support to a pastor friend who was in somewhat deeper difficulties with his congregation than MacDonald yet was with his, a church meeting was conducted in his absence. The proceedings were recounted to Louisa by Mr. Bull, a member sympathetic to MacDonald. The meeting took place on July 5; twenty members were present. Bull, anxious that the MacDonalds stay, proposed a resolution expressive of attachment and affection for them, and several agreed. But someone objected to a recent sermon MacDonald had preached in which he had enlarged on the concept of "sympathy," contending that their young pastor had simply gone too far in defining the concept.

Dwelling on the nature of human sympathy and drawing an analogy from the human to the divine was a movement characteristic of MacDonald's mind. It suggested that if the mature Christian consciousness would condemn to hell no one who had not had a fair hearing of the gospel and made a clear-sighted choice for or against it, neither would God, for it can hardly be argued that humankind is capable of being more compassionate or more just than God. He was formulating at this time his version of universalism, which he held throughout the rest of his life and to which he gave definitive imaginative expression in the 1890s in *Lilith:* that is, that in eternity all people, after experiencing the consequences of those sins for which they had not found forgiveness while on earth, will be afforded a vision of God as he exists in the full beauty of his truth and will be given opportunity to decide for or against him. To decide positively is to begin to become a righteous being. The justice of God demands that each soul be given a clear-sighted choice—a privilege few on earth enjoy. Further, he affirmed that it was impossible that any purged soul could see God as he is and not desire him. He also expressed his hope that the animal kingdom would as well experience redemption.

Bull told members Allen, Broadbridge, and Hounsom, who were the most unhappy, that they should, in the interest of biblical prescription and church unity, make specific in writing precisely what their objections were to these and any other of MacDonald's ideas. An attempt might then be made to reconcile their differences. Backbiting should stop. The group eventually agreed on a statement in which they expressed their respect, but warned that, unless he altered the content of his preaching, serious consequences would follow. They also suggested that he give attention to his style, trying to make his material less intellectual and more accessible to common people.

Among themselves, several were sure they knew the root difficulty: he was affected by German theology. MacDonald's private printing of the translations of the poems of Novalis was probably the only solid evidence to them that he had any knowledge of German thought whatsoever. But German higher criticism, with its attack on the biblical text, was currently affecting the intellectual circles of Britain. Suspicions were rife. To the uneducated mind it was all one: any deviations from what to them was "sound doctrine" was properly to be condemned by the label "German."

Understandably disheartened when given the news, Mac-Donald began to wonder if his first pastorate might come to an untimely end. But, one by one, people began to tell him how much they appreciated his ministry, finding it spiritually profitable. It became quite apparent to him that the unhappiness resided in a comparative few. Writing to his father, he apologized for being preoccupied with his problems and told him that, while some "very unteachable" members were giving him annoyance, many others were expressing appreciation and support. "However," he affirmed, "if God put the means at any time in my power, I mean to take another mode of helping men, and no longer stand in this position towards them, in which they regard you more as *their* servant than as Christ's. Of course, till then, he means me to labour as I am, and I am more than content, I hope."[2] He was determined to stay at Arundel so long as he was convinced that his presence was doing some sincere Christian people good, but once he felt released from his obligations there, he clearly intended to adopt another form of Christian ministry than the pastorate. Serving people for God was one thing; having them treat him as the world treated servants was another.

How it was that only twenty members of the congregation were present at the business meeting remains unexplained. Possibly MacDonald's most loyal friends and supporters were only peripherally connected with the church itself. Perhaps they already had been disillusioned by the quality of the lives of the more socially prominent members who ruled the church and, having given up the official church organization as a hypocritical affair, were not present for its deliberations. MacDonald's ministry would characteristically appeal to the otherwise disaffected.

The original call, however, did contain fifty-seven signatures, so the church evidently had a larger functioning business nucleus when he came than it had two years later. If one effect of MacDonald's preaching was to increase the awareness of some members of the deviation of their fellow members' from true Christian conduct and attitude, they may have simply chosen not to attend a business meeting conducted by those very members. Mac-Donald's strongly proclaimed attitude that God takes care of those who trust in him and brings good out of evil may have influenced them not to fight. Nevertheless, it may be argued that the loyalty of his supporters at Arundel was "softer" than he had supposed.

An acquaintance with two new friends helped somewhat to compensate MacDonald for these reversals. A nearby minister, Rev. Caleb Morris, who had gone through a similar falling out with this church, began preaching in his home with some success. He extended a sympathetic ear to his neighbor at Arundel, and MacDonald found in him a sensibility that answered to his own. He told his father:

> He is almost the only minister of standing whom I respect intellectually morally and spiritually. People think he has gone down, because he has taken to teaching in his own house instead of preaching on Sundays. He thinks he has risen, and I agree with him. . . . O for a few that really wanted to learn, to be earnest divine men—partakers of the divine nature—in one word *Christians*. What a hidden meaning—hidden to most that use it—lies in that word.[3]

Another "earnest divine" man whom MacDonald came to know at this time was a friend of his brother John, Henry Cecil, who taught with John at Sheffield Academy. He saw some poetry MacDonald had sent to John and was profoundly impressed. A close friendship followed that lasted many years. John, an aspiring poet himself, deferred to his brother in both poetic theory and practice and urged him to send as much of his work as he could. MacDonald obliged, with a sense of satisfaction. He was greatly delighted when both John and Cecil came to spend the Christmas season of 1852 at Arundel; those days were an oasis in his otherwise increasingly bleak situation.

But great sadness soon followed. At the end of March news came from Huntly that Alec had died. Both George and John had taken a somewhat protective attitude toward Alec; perhaps they felt he was less adept than they at making his way in the world. During the last year the pathos of his steadily declining health was increased by his deeply felt disappointment in love. Now he was gone. MacDonald's letter to his father is among the many moving letters of condolence he was to write through his lifetime:

> Of him we need never say he *was,* for what he was he is now only expanded, enlarged and glorified. He needed no change, only development. . . . Let the body go beautiful to the grave, entire as the seed of a new body, which keeps the beauty of the old, and only parts with the weakness and imperfections. Surely God that clothes the fields now with the wild flowers risen fresh from their winter-graves, will keep Alec's beauty in his remembrance and not let a manifestation of himself, as every human form is, so full of the true simple noble and pure, be forgotten. We shall recognize it again. I thank you too for what you say about the suffering of death, but though I do fear that sometimes, I should fear more if I thought God would not lay on me every pain that was necessary for me to attain to the perfection he has made me for.[4]

MacDonald's stepmother had insisted that Alec's face not be given cosmetic treatment in death but that it appear in its natural state. MacDonald also felt that an attempt to conceal the effects of suffering was ill-conceived. Suffering works spiritual maturity. The unnatural, not the natural, is the truly ugly.

The principle that suffering brings spiritual maturity was now being worked out in his experience. Although he was feeling the pain of his brother's death, mounting tensions within the church, the hardship of trying to live on a slashed salary, and the uncertainty of his future course, he was, to his delight, not depressed. He felt an inner strength and joy, the like of which he had not formerly known. "I grow younger and happier," he told his father, alluding to Swedenborg's saying that in heaven the angels are always growing younger. "I see an outlet now from miseries of the mind, unknown to any which form portions of my earliest recollections, and have grown with my growth, but which by and by

I shall quite outgrow. . . . Oh I know a little now and only a little what Christ's deep sayings mean about becoming like a child, about leaving all for him, about service and truth and love." He was discovering relief from anxiety in an utter abandonment of his affairs to God.

"God is our loving true self-forgetting friend," he continued. "All delight, all hope and beauty are in God. God is—therefore *to be* is blessed." He even became bold to give his father some advice: "My dear and honoured father—if I might say so to you—will you think me presumptuous if I say—leave the epistles and ponder *the Gospel*—the story about Christ. Infinitely are the epistles mistaken because the Gospels are not understood." He was more convinced than ever that the Christian people he knew were in such a state because Christian theologians had minimized Christ's own teachings and ignored his spirit. They had tried to expound Paul while overlooking the very base on which Paul stood.

> Because Christ is not understood and felt in the heart—because the readers of the Epistles too often possess nothing of that sympathy with Christ's thought and feelings and desires which moved and glorified the writers of the Epistles, they cannot receive from them the true impression. The Epistles are very different from the Apostles' preaching. The Gospels form the sum and substance of the apostle's teaching, and preaching. The Epistles are mostly written for a peculiar end and aim and are not intended as expositions of the central truth in general forms. Hear the words of Christ.[5]

He had discovered the absolute centrality of Christ to the Christian life earlier during the deepening spiritual experience that took place when he was a tutor in Fulham. Now the hardships he was undergoing drove him into a fuller realization of the resources of grace available in Christ. His esteem of the Gospels over the Epistles was perhaps due in part to the fact that the systematic doctrinal systems that were increasingly becoming distasteful to him were constructed from texts taken mainly from the Epistles.

But now in a deeper sense he was finding in the arena of experience that the truths at the core of Christianity lay in Christ's teachings themselves. He closed the above letter with: "The rational mode to me is just what Christ says: 'Leave meat and drink to God—seek the kingdom of God and his righteousness.' Ah there is a grand world to come of Truth and Love and Blessedness and God."

Meanwhile, Louisa, sympathizing deeply with her husband's plight, tried to compensate for their reduced salary by advertising to take in girl pupils. No prospects applied. But her sister Carrie came to stay with them—Louisa was again expecting—and the board she paid helped them through. It may have been Powell's way of offering encouragement by indirectly providing financial support to his son-in-law.

Another encouragement also came: MacDonald's lengthy article on Browning's extended poem "Christmas Eve," which had been published in 1850, was accepted for publication in the May issue of *The Christian Spectator*. The fact that MacDonald was impressed with Browning's poem—which commends the worship of dissenters over that of other Christian groups but sees some good in all and discerns love as the all-important element in Christianity—also helps to define the state of his thinking at this time. Getting an article published in such a widely circulated publication must have lent fuel to his hopes of gaining a greater portion of his livelihood from his pen.

Then in early March a letter came from Charles, one that gave MacDonald and Louisa a happier day than they had had for some time. Charles urged his brother to come to Manchester, even if they had to stay for a time in his home. He knew, he said, of a chapel that would soon need a pastor; other opportunities were certain to present themselves. MacDonald accepted with gratitude, he and Louisa both agreeing that Manchester seemed to be the place to go. He was not eager to take another church, but the greatly admired A. J. Scott, now principal of Owens College, was also in Manchester. Some opportunity for teaching might occur through him.

A letter also came from his old teacher, Godwin, now soon to be his brother-in-law, inviting them to visit him in London for a period of rest and "recreation." Having heard of MacDonald's relationship with his church, Godwin felt he could give his former pupil some timely advice that would salvage his threatened career. But MacDonald was not especially anxious to be in Godwin's company at this time, having to explain in detail his situation to his former teacher and feel his displeasure. Much as he had profited in the past from Godwin's teaching, he felt he did not need more of it now.

So he declined the offer, assuring him that "it is recreation enough to be delivered from relationships that are a burden and weariness." He also told him that they were so financially pressed that he must try to find other work immediately, perhaps in teaching, for he acknowledged: "I know my ways of thinking are so very different from those of any churches, that it is very doubtful whether I shall even find a church already formed that will choose me." Then he mused with some asperity, "If one should, I shall hold my self in readiness to be turned out very soon."

Nevertheless, he felt no diminishment in his call to minister to people. "Preaching is my work, and preach I will somehow or other." Increasingly, his experience of the biblical promises of grace gave him much to share with others. "That which is gradually bringing to my mind a great eternal peace and hope I will try to give to others—but it is and must be very different from what is commonly accounted religious teaching."[6] Increasingly he felt the best course was to venture out completely by faith, rent a room in a public place, and begin teaching any who would come sincerely wanting to learn. He was beginning to see clearly that his destiny was to be a religious teacher with a message quite distinct from that of most others.

He submitted the inevitable resignation from his pastoral duties at Arundel in May 1853. His staying as long as he did was less out of desperation to retain an income than out of a sense that his staying was accomplishing good in the hearts of some. When the time came that he saw his remaining was to effect a split in the church, he resigned.

The reasons for MacDonald's apparent unsuccess in the pastoral ministry are certainly more deep and varied than the charge of heretical teaching that some in his congregation so handily laid on him. His pulpit ministry demanded on the part of his hearers a willingness to think and attempt to obey; this they were unprepared to give. He took an idealist view of human experience in general, with an emphasis on the necessity for the Christian to realize goodness in everyday life, to which the most powerful members of the church were unresponsive. Such a congregation would have had a strong expectation that their pastor would conform to the generally held concept of what a dissenting pastor should be. But MacDonald was quite disillusioned with the stereotype, feeling that for the truth's sake he must take exception to it.

He was committed to communicating to his hearers his vision of truth as explicitly as possible and affecting their lives for the sake of goodness as thoroughly as possible. Some did respond; others did not. To his father he commented:

> Mr. Godwin says I want a place with a number of young men. He says they can't understand me in Arundel; but I know that some of all classes do understand me, and I am happy not to be understood by those that do not understand me. Where the earnest heart is wanting, be a man deacon or high priest, he cannot understand grand, simple divine things. Some say I talk foolishness, others go away with their hearts burning within them.[7]

Another factor contributing to his unsuccess was his unequivocal desire to be a man of letters. He loved poetry and was writing so much of it during these years that his father early on had kindly but firmly advised: "I would have you to give over pursuing the fruitless game of poetry and apply yourself to the preaching of the gospel and the instruction of your people. A nervous temperament and a poetical imagination are too much for a frail clay tabernacle, as witness poor hypochondriac Cowper."[8] Even had MacDonald agreed with his father, which obviously he did not, he could hardly have curbed for long this side of his nature. The talent that he had for writing had to be developed, but it would be some time before he would discover that his truest imaginative talents lay in writing fairy tales.

TEN

Finding Something More

*For surely the working of some help in the world is the chief
hold that one has upon the world. To live only for what one
can get out of the world is but to lead the lowest kind of life—
the existence of a mere parasite.*—Lilith, Manuscript A

The years immediately ahead were MacDonald's most difficult. His disillusionment with his denomination, now almost
complete, was nevertheless painful. He sensed that friends who
tried to understand him really did not. He felt called to a mission,
but the means to accomplish it seemed ever to elude him.

On a hot July day in 1853, MacDonald, newly arrived in
Manchester, attended the graduation ceremony of Owens College.
After the granting of degrees, known as the "distribution of
prizes," he mustered courage to send his card to the president,
A. J. Scott. Scott courteously responded, remembered the former
seminary student and his wife from his London days, and kindly
inquired as to their welfare. MacDonald was so elated by the meeting that he relayed in his daily letter to Louisa their conversation:

"Are you in Manchester long?" he asked.

"For only a fortnight now," MacDonald answered. "But I
hope to get here permanently, for my heterodoxy has driven me
out, and I have nothing to do."

The kindly Scott took a stronger interest in his guest. "Will
you come and see me tomorrow evening, about six or seven?"

"With great pleasure," MacDonald affirmed.[1]

Scott was careful in the promised meeting not to be more

encouraging than realism allowed. His mind was filled with the memory of his own clashes with Presbyterian authorities, the heated exchanges during his trial for heresy, and the subsequent embarrassments of his defrocking. He gave MacDonald a sympathetic ear; his very personality emitted a sense of understanding and strength. Greatly buoyed, MacDonald exclaimed to Lousia: "How delightful it is to hear Mr. Scott talk so gently so strongly—confirming so purely whatever I said—and making it stronger—with things I had not thought of—And he told me of his own trials—and his father's distress . . . and was most brotherly and simple and human to me—and therefore divine."[2]

But Scott's ability to help was limited. Some tutorial opportunities at the college might open; occasionally students needed extra help to maintain a college level of studies, and some would pay well for it. He promised to introduce MacDonald to his faculty; he could do little more.

MacDonald therefore turned to his second contact, one suggested by Godwin. Eager to keep his former student in the fold of Congregationalism, Godwin had urged MacDonald to see Dr. Halley, the aged Congregationalist minister of the Cavendish Street Chapel in Manchester, whose authority was respected throughout the area, in the hopes he could place MacDonald in a church. Halley offered opportunities to preach in two churches, but MacDonald had little enthusiasm for these prospects. He was thoroughly disillusioned not only with the Congregationalists, but with the established church in general. "I feel more and more that I shall never be happy or well in health so long as I try to get on with this sect. It makes me so wretched. It really seems more hollow here than ever," he confided to his wife.[3]

Increasingly he felt that his best course of action—since he did want to continue preaching—was to hire a public room and see if he could attract an audience of people who sincerely wanted spiritual help. He felt especially called to impart his understanding of Christian truth to the young people of his generation. He explained his conviction to his father:

> The life thoughts deeds aims beliefs of Jesus have to be fresh
> expounded every age, for all the depth of eternity lies in them,
> and they have to be seen into more profoundly every new year
> of the world's spiritual history. Else the new men needing
> higher things than the former saw in Christ, and being taught
> that that was all by those who know the words only and more
> external explanation, must of necessity refuse him, except they
> be strong sighted enough to see for themselves without the
> aid of Teachers.[4]

He was convinced that Christian truth must be rethought and
freshly applied in every period of the history of the world and that
his understanding of truth was especially relevant to his own.

Apparently, he hoped that among these "few young men"
he might be able to number his brother Charles. MacDonald had
been warmly welcomed to their lodgings on Radnor Street, and
Charles expressed himself as genuinely interested in his brother's
ministry and desirous to help attract a group of receptive followers.
His wife Jane did all she could to make her brother-in-law feel at
home: "I lay in bed a long time this morning and read. Jane
brought up my breakfast," he told Louisa.[5] He was reading
Charles Kingsley's recently published novel *Hypatia* at the time
and was delighted with it. One of the founders of the Christian
Socialist movement, Kingsley presented an understanding of human nature and an awakened social conscience that appealed to
MacDonald.

Feeling that Manchester held reasonable promise for the development of his ministry, but without having secured any definite means for providing a living for himself and his family,
MacDonald returned southward to his wife and daughter. Almost
immediately thereafter, Louisa gave birth to Mary Josephine, their
second child. On an early morning's walk on the day of her birth,
July 23, MacDonald discovered a lark's nest and long held the
event in his memory as a sign of blessing on the occasion as well
as on their contemplated venture.

Concerning another family event, however, MacDonald had

mixed feelings. Godwin, a widower, had fallen in love with Louisa's sister, Charlotte, and the wedding was set for August 4. MacDonald was asked to perform the ceremony. Although he had greatly admired Godwin during his student days, he had since found him a burdensome acquaintance. Godwin was overbearing in trying to keep him within the fold of Congregationalism. Openly solicitous of his former student's welfare, Godwin was too liberal in giving him advice—advice MacDonald simply perceived as obtuse. With Godwin as his brother-in-law, clashes with him would be hard to avoid.

In short, Godwin felt that MacDonald should be more willing to preach what the people wanted to hear. Feeling now was the time to help as much as he could, Godwin visited the MacDonalds in Arundel in late spring. After he returned he sent MacDonald a package containing two volumes of Bradley's model sermons and explained: "In looking over your books, I could see very few that appeared to me likely to be of much service to you, in respect to your chief work." He counseled that, while he did not expect MacDonald to use them as exact models, they should illustrate to him "how, to a large class of persons, the exhibition of Christian truth may be made interesting and impressive."[6]

Few gestures could have exasperated MacDonald more. He saw his library as his greatest material possession and had most carefully spent what little money he could manage only on volumes he had carefully selected. A few years earlier he had defended to his father his taste in books, explaining: "Seeing I never read a book without knowing something about it first, you may be sure I never buy a book, except I have just reasons for believing it a pearl and not paste."[7] The sort of thing Godwin sent seemed to him exceedingly pasty.

In contrast to their feelings concerning Godwin, both he and Louisa held Charlotte in warmest esteem. Being Powell's eldest child from his second wife, she occupied the position of mediator between the rest of the family and the august father, fulfilling her office with aplomb. She was a colorful and energetic woman, active in such evangelical organizations as The Society for Converting Roman Catholics. MacDonald had little difficulty in containing his enthusiasm for that activity, but he felt warmly toward her and especially admired her beautifully pure soprano voice.

As Victorian society was free of local card shops advertising cards with ready-made sentiments for all occasions, people wrote their own letters for birthdays and anniversaries. MacDonald's birthday letter to Charlotte, written January 14, 1853, eloquently attests to his genuine feelings for her. It also shows MacDonald's ability to talk naturally and compellingly with an individual about a personal relationship to God.

> I trust you are a year nearer to God, and this is the only true ground of congratulation. To be one with Him is the only Human perfection—to be becoming one with Him, the only true Human History. There is a story of every human soul, wrought out in secret between God and that soul, and everlasting blessedness is the last page of the History where God and that soul are coming nearer, if indeed there be any close to the history. . . . This is your end, though it may not be clear in prospect to you always. May every year bring you nearer to God and nearer to men, make you love all men more and more, and be more and more beloved of the many friends who already love you. May you ever seek to please Christ, and be anxious that God should honour you—This last is a wonderful saying—one of Christ's. How absent are all excludings from his words—how near does he draw us to the Father's heart! There is nothing to be learnt but from him.

Charlotte and Godwin were married on August 4, 1853. Louisa, being as yet unable to travel because of her confinement, stayed at Arundel with the infant Mary Josephine, while Lily accompanied her father to The Limes. Lily even took her share of attention during the ceremony. MacDonald explained to his wife: "They say she called papa two or three times in the chapel. I did not hear her but several of the wedding company did. . . . Lily looked so sweet though so poorly in the pretty white dress and bonnet which they sewed for her."[8] Lily's complexion was pale because she was having difficulty teething, but her childish chattering delighted them all.

MacDonald made earnest efforts to see the newly formed union in the best light. Earlier he had told Louisa concerning Godwin: "We are very unlike, and the meeting of the unlike, even with the kindest feelings, is unpleasant to one of my nature."[9] But in the years ahead, Christian charity (exercised, one suspects, by both parties) prevailed, so that outward relations, at least, between the brothers-in-law were cordial enough.

The wedding was not the only event in MacDonald's family life at this time that he had difficulty seeing congenially. His adventuresome brother John had taken a position as tutor in a boy's school in Moscow and was ready to sail. MacDonald stayed in London to see him off on August 10. It was a difficult event for him; he felt an especially close bond with John not only because he was his younger brother but also because he believed John had a poetic talent superior to his own.

He then returned to Arundel where he and Louisa completed the arrangements for their move. Not having secured independent lodgings in Manchester as yet, they packed their furnishings for storage and shipped them by barge to London, where Powell found room for them in his warehouses. Louisa, severely disappointed that her new piano must be sold, was somewhat heartened when her father promised her another as soon as they were again in a suitable place.

ELEVEN

For the Truth's Sake

Jesus lived a grand simple life in poverty and love. Why should not I?—MacDonald to his father, June 3, 1853

Doing without their furnishings soon proved a comparatively minor sorrow indeed. Difficulty followed difficulty, but each reversal seemed to instill more solidly in MacDonald the conviction that each experience could teach them some spiritual lesson. He was adamant in refusing the slightest compromise of his personal integrity, regardless of how dire their plight. From one source or another money came for their needs.

Since they had no money to secure independent lodging in Manchester, and no immediate prospect of steady income, George and Louisa had no choice but to live apart for a time. Taking advantage of the hospitality of relatives, MacDonald stayed with Charles and Jane, while Louisa and the children, after spending a few weeks at The Limes, went in October to reside with Alec and Helen Powell, now living in Liverpool. Flora Powell, who had married Joshua Sing (destined to become quite well-to-do), also lived in that neighboring industrial metropolis. Everyone concerned tried to make the best of a difficult situation.

Then word came that the post of librarian and clerk at Owen's College was open, and MacDonald was invited to apply. Elated, he did so but with trepidation. "The chief difficulty would be my inexperience in book-keeping," he told his father, and he knew that many others were applying. The one-hundred-pound salary that the post offered would make him less dependent on preaching as a sole means of support. Another cause for encouragement came from a London publisher, who agreed to publish a volume of his poems, taking all the risk and promising MacDonald half the profits. So he gave himself earnestly to studying bookkeeping in the mornings and correcting poems in the afternoons, his hopes running high that he would soon have sufficient money coming in to provide for his family.

Such hopes were soon dashed. The librarianship went to another—a disappointment that affected him deeply—and the London publisher, after reading MacDonald's poems more closely, reneged on his agreement. This latter circumstance affected him less sorely. He explained to his father:

> I am sorry to say—sorry because it will disappoint you, for it affects me very little, that my publisher has disappointed me; and, having accepted my poems on the testimony of others, now on reading the first instalment of them himself, draws back and wishes to be clear of the engagement, which he certainly shall be. . . . I am thankful to God for the pleasure the expected publication gave me, and so helped to keep my spirits up. Now I am able to let it go. A better time will come, if it be desirable at all, and a better publisher, for this is not a man of much note. Indeed I had scrupled about letting him have it, as he was not a first-rate publisher, but on second thoughts, I believed I ought not to let the opportunity slip. Now I am content.[1]

He was, therefore, reduced to doing irregular pulpit supply work among the Congregationalists through the fall, an occupation that paid little. Engagements in Liverpool allowed him to go between there and Manchester, Louisa remaining with the Powells. He told her: "We are going through the hard time now, without which never man was worth much in himself, and consequently could never be worth much in the world—I mean for its salvation. May He keep me from being a time-server, and so I and mine will pass through the world honorably and receive the *well done* at the end."[2] He was imperturbable in his conviction that patience in adversity would have beneficial spiritual effects.

But as the fall wore on, a sense of the awkwardness of their situation increased. Each felt keenly the difficulty of being dependent on others for their daily shelter. Nevertheless, MacDonald continued to interpret their trials in terms of God's efforts to refine their spirits: "It is a very good thing for us to be parted sometimes—It makes us think more, both more truly about each other, and less interruptedly about our GOD." He saw the Spirit of God resident in every aspect of what was befalling him. "He is Truth, and all that we can see [that is] beautiful and true is in Him and we were taught by Him to see it. Perhaps it is a very bad want of faith in him to doubt whether he means what we see." Things must be taken at their face value and not explained as though they were otherwise. "But he knows too that it is impossible for us to be good all at once, or to be good at all without him. So we must seek him." Prompted by his hardships to reexamine his theological convictions, he became the more convinced of the dynamics of growth: "We may however say to ourselves—one day these souls of ours will blossom into the full sunshine. When all that is desirable in the commonness of daily love, and all we long for of wonder and mystery and the look of Christmas time will be joined in one, and we shall walk as in a wondrous dream yet with [a greater] sense of reality than our most waking joy now gives us."[3] This vision is already anticipatory of the conclusion of such fantasies as "The Golden Key" and *Lilith*.

As these convictions grew so did his determination to avoid lapsing into any dogmatic attitudes. There was a contemporary movement in Congregationalism toward becoming a more unified denomination instead of simply a federation of independent chapels.[4] One result was a strengthening of the sectarian spirit. Not only did MacDonald abhor this, but he saw the danger of his adopting a type of sectarian spirit toward his growing convictions, together with a spirit of opposition toward his detractors.

> A true Revival is springing up, and kept down I suppose in other quarters besides Arundel by those who cry most for it.

> But our great danger is of acting or feeling as a party. I wish
> to ignore and forget all opposition and be in a condition in
> which I can do my work for the Truth's sake without any refer-
> ence to others as opposing my teaching. We ought never to
> wish to overcome because we are the fighters. Never feel—there
> is my Truth—the hardest lesson to learn.

Through the years ahead, he was always very careful not to allow
his followers to become another sect.

Further, he perceived that the nearer the individual comes to
incarnating truth in his life the more imminent and perilous are
the spiritual temptations that attend each stage.

> Every higher stage of Truth brings with it its own Temptation
> like that in the Wilderness and if one overcomes not in that,
> he overcomes not at all. The struggle may be hard. I would I
> could be full of the struggle, and then I should of the victory.
> But Jesus overcame in the truest spiritual fight. So shall we
> overcome, too. Our God will surely help us to attain to that
> which he himself loves most.

He saw all his resources in God, not in himself apart from God;
hence, the distinction between his thinking and that of the humanist. He concluded:

> Oh dearest, whatever you may feel about our homeless condi-
> tion at present, I hope it has helped to teach your husband
> some things. Pray for him that he may not forget them, but
> that he may be all God's, and then let God give him what he
> will. We may wait a little for a home here, for all the universe
> is ours, and all time and the very thought of God himself.[5]

What God gave him for the time was a continuing series of
dashed expectations. A group of seemingly progressively thinking
Christians had banded together for the purpose of starting a new
church in Manchester, under the temporary leadership of a Dr.
Davidson. Charles entertained high hopes that this would be his
brother's golden opportunity. The group wished to establish a

broad doctrinal framework for their church, in which they would require only that their pastor believe in "the Divinity of Christ and in the atonement." "I don't mean Maurice's theory, nor Pye Smith's, nor Bushnell's—but that a man acknowledge Christ as the source of Life," MacDonald approvingly quoted Davidson,[6] and he again felt his hopes rise.

However, he soon found himself opposed by certain members of this new group—just why is not clear—and this prospect also ended in disappointment. Nor was this his only difficulty. After spending Christmas of 1853 with the Powells of Liverpool, he returned to his lodgings with Charles and came down with a combination of a bad cold and an ulcerated tooth. Confined to bed, his sinuses blocked and his jaw pounding, he was prevented for a time from responding to the commitments he had made for pulpit supply.

Further depressed and longing for Louisa and their children, he determined to look for lodgings for them all as soon as he was able, no matter if their present supply of money would soon be depleted by the rent.

> If we could just get enough food to keep *us* alive and the children quite happy, I would rather be half-starved together, than well-fed asunder. . . . It is rather a sad time for us to begin house-keeping with our little means. . . . But if we are doing right, it is all the same to the rich God whether we begin with ten pounds or a thousand. *Appearances* are nothing, if *realities* are on our side.[7]

Through Scott they finally located independent lodgings so they could be together again as a family. Mrs. Scott's sister, Miss Ker, was in possession of Alderley Cross, a farmhouse at Alderley, some fifteen miles from Manchester. It was presently empty, and she offered it to the MacDonalds rent free. Elated, MacDonald explained to his father: "It is a delightful spot—the house—an old farm-house—everything in a very primitive fashion but made comfortable by means of her [Miss Ker's] things. There is a piano and books and everything."[8]

Their trials, however, were not over. Before occupying their new quarters they went as a family to Birkenhead, a port lying westward across the mouth of the Mersey River from Liverpool, where MacDonald was to preach. While there, MacDonald was stricken with another attack of hemorrhaging from the lungs. He was put promptly to bed and obliged to accept the extended hospitality of the Rawlins family, with whom they were staying in Liverpool. The stresses of his situation no doubt were responsible for bringing on the attack.

But the attendant doctor minimized the seriousness of the threat, telling his patient he had simply to resign himself to being a person of delicate health. By the middle of March, MacDonald was well enough to move to Alderley Cross and, although he failed to win another librarianship, having his family together again in commodious quarters was immensely gratifying. An added boon was the clean country air, especially important to him after the industrial atmosphere of Manchester. But the greatest source of pleasure was enjoying, with Louisa, their girls: "The youngest is such a happy laughing thing, very different from the grave elder sister, though she has lively enough fits of play, too." Mary's full head of ebony hair earned her the nickname "blackie"; playing with them, MacDonald entered imaginatively into their childhood world with much pleasure.

This situation was, however, temporary; Miss Ker's rights to the property were to end the last of March. Could his father receive them for a time? he wondered in a letter to him. The last twenty years had seen a fury of railroad building in Britain, and rail transportation, thanks to an act of Parliament passed some ten years earlier that had fixed a ceiling on passenger rates, was not expensive. The tracks now went directly to Huntly. In fact, the railroad right-of-way had severed the old farmstead, and an engine house was built so near that MacDonald was horrified to hear of "the profanation" of his old home. "Will there be steam engines whistling there all day long? and all night long? Surely you ought to have good compensation for that . . . honestly I mean, not extortionally, as has been done in many cases."[9] The coming of rail transportation was, however, of large benefit and meant that his beloved north would be from this time on much more easily accessible. He was very anxious for his father to meet his growing family; this time, while he was regaining his strength might be an appropriate time to make the visit.

They decided to postpone going to Huntly, however, when more solid prospects for establishing a home in the Manchester area began to appear. Louisa, who had for some time thought she could contribute to the family finances by taking in pupils, now finally had the promise of one: a niece of Miss Rawlins was willing to receive her instruction. Further, an old friend from Highbury days, Arthur Francis, needed lodgings and was willing to negotiate his room and board with them. Together with these sources of income, Louisa's father pledged himself to pay the rent for new lodgings, if necessary, until MacDonald was self-sufficient. The possibility of MacDonald's giving formal instruction in literature in their home also occurred to them, provided they could find a suitable dwelling.

Studying literature had become fashionable of late among middle-class people, especially women, who wanted to "improve their minds" by being helped to understand the English literary heritage. The formal study of English literature during the middle of the nineteenth century had not yet come into its own as an academic discipline; it was not accorded the same respectability as the study of the classics. The knowledge of the English literary past was self-acquired by the "well-bred" person. Literature was especially valued because it presented imaginative embodiments of moral truths, and this fact formed a large part of MacDonald's interest. Attendees at lectures would presumably subscribe to a series for a stipulated amount.

With these possibilities in mind, and with his health reestablished with the coming of spring, MacDonald looked earnestly for a suitable vacant home. He was successful in finding one at No. 3 Camp Terrace, in Lower Broughton, a "large and in some respects handsome" house, "quite respectable and open," but "not so fashionable as it once was." Powell pledged himself to pay whatever portion of the thirty-five-pound annual rent might be needed, and George's father sent a cask of provisions from The Farm. One room was suitable for public lecturing and preaching, and MacDonald began to prepare a series of lectures on English literature with the hopes of attracting some young ladies as students. His career in public lecturing grew from this beginning.

He soon developed the practice of speaking without a written script. Years later, he told his daughter Winnie that he wrote a lecture once and read it three times. The third time he thought, "What a humbug I am—I am supposed to be feeling all this and I don't one bit." He determined then never to write another. His conviction that it was important to feel the realities of what he spoke at the moment is another indication of his romantic sensibility.

These early successes in establishing themselves as a family in new environs were all causes for thanksgiving. He wrote his father,

> We have wanted for nothing yet. I was possessed by an angry evil thought yesterday, and went out of the room to get rid of it. Coming up stairs to my study, the moon shone bright in the high heavens, and the conviction arose within me that God cared for his children. Has he really, I thought, put that shining thing up there to light up this round earth, and will he not minister to my wants?[10]

The moon always carried a special significance for him, often as a symbol of the providence of God, as a reading of his fantasies shows.

MacDonald's love of the natural found another notable expression this spring: he again grew a beard. When his father seemed amused and somewhat indignant, he defended his action with vigor. "I feel nearer to nature, yes, seriously, nearer to God's intent when he made man in his own image," he affirmed. He was willing to yield only slightly to the custom of his day for shaving; he removed the hair on his upper lip. But he was firm in his resolve:

> Having been an advocate for it from my boyhood, I hope ere I die, when my hair is as grey or white as this paper, and when no one will dare to call me affected for whose opinion I care a rush, to wear it all just as God meant it to be, and as men wore it before some fops began, as fops always do, to imitate women, from which the custom spread with the help of law to sensible men; who are not sensible in this, that they almost deify custom, and treat an offence against her almost as severely as an offence against the law of the Maker, tho' one may be keeping the one more really by breaking the other.[11]

His donning of a full beard—a feature which distinguished his appearance for the remainder of his life—coincided with his breaking with the Congregationalists. The desire to be bearded, which he had had from his childhood, gained some impetus from the advice of his doctor, who felt that a full complement of whiskers might help protect his nasal passages from abrupt changes in air temperature and thus reduce the risk of hemorrhaging. But the tone of his statement shows a state of mind that was quite ready to defy any custom. From the numerous contemporary depictions of Victorian men as bearded, beards might be considered quite the vogue of the day, but not so. The rising middle class looked on them as barbaric, in England certainly, and yet moreso in Scotland. MacDonald had to defend himself to both his father and his father-in-law, but neither persisted in his remonstration. Powell, who had formerly refused to have anything to do with a bearded prospective son-in-law, increasingly respected MacDonald for his spiritual earnestness and capitulated to the reality of his wearing a beard.

While MacDonald saw himself completely as a servant of men, he meant to serve on his own terms and felt the need to be free from their whims and opinions in order to serve them truly. He must work according to his own understanding of servanthood; he could no longer bow to the arrogance of those who saw the clergy as merely servants submissive to their whims.

A group he felt he could serve in a true manner had now formed. Several young men committed themselves to renting a public room among the shops on Renshaw Street, contributing to MacDonald's support as they could. "I was never so happy all my life," he told his father, "and have the prospect of increase of happiness too. I have been today looking after the advertising of my preaching in my new place. Next Sunday evening I begin the realization of a long cherished wish—to have a place of my own to preach in which I should be unshackled in my teaching. This I now possess. May God be with me." He now had to answer to no one else but God. "No one can turn me out of this. It will be taken and the agreement signed in my name. If any one does not like what I say, he can go away and welcome, but not all can turn me away. I call them together, not they me."[12]

As the weeks passed, however, the hoped-for growth was minimal. A faithful nucleus were quite convinced of the truth of his teachings and were loyal. But most people who attended out of curiosity, although they may have felt a certain agreement with what he was saying, were unwilling to depart from their pattern of participation in the established churches. Income from this effort was indeed meager.

Some money, however, was forthcoming from other sources. *The Christian Spectator* began showing an increased interest in his contributions, and his early fictional sketches, such as "The Broken Swords," began to appear. "My object [in the story] was principally to show that the most external manifestations of manhood are dependent on a right condition of heart," he explained to his proud father.[13] More immediately profitable was his attempt to give a series of lectures in his home. (From this beginning grew in time the Ladies College of Manchester.)

Drawing on his background in both physics and literature,

which he had steadily developed since his King's College days, he worked up a number of lectures in both fields and announced them. "They seem to have awakened a great interest in those who attend," he reported to his father. "I have about 25 regular attendants, who have paid or have to pay 1.1 [pounds] each—so that 25.5 [pounds] for twelve lectures is pretty well for a beginning."[14] He quickly counted on the prospect of continuing this practice. Together with earning some money from occasional tutoring opportunities secured from his contacts with Owens College, he was again able to support his family.

And the family continued to grow. On September 16, 1854, Caroline Grace came to join her two sisters. Christmas of 1854 found the entire family in London with the Powells. When MacDonald returned to Manchester, Louisa and the children stayed at The Limes for an extended visit.

MacDonald, thinking to increase his income by finding a larger market in the journals and magazines of the day, had also made a trip to London that autumn. Seventeen shillings took him there and back by train. While there, he attended an address by Frederick Denison Maurice, newly appointed principal of the Working Men's College. A popular Broad Church theologian and founder of the Christian Socialist movement, Maurice was currently receiving much attention because of his public quarrel with Dr. R. W. Jelf, principal of King's College in London. Jelf had dismissed him from the faculty at King's because his *Theological Essays,* published in 1853, rejected the doctrine that the punishment of the wicked was eternal. Much public sentiment was sympathetic with Maurice, who was perceived as championing the love of God.[15] MacDonald keenly followed the controversy and was impressed by Maurice, who would soon become a close friend and appreciable influence in MacDonald's life. In a few years, when MacDonald began writing novels, he came out on the side of Maurice.

Despite the dire poverty in which the MacDonalds lived throughout 1854, two examples illustrate his commitment to complete honesty. In need of the remainder of his library in London, he had asked Charlotte to have his books sent, stipulating that he would pay for the cartage. As it was close to his birthday, Charlotte sent him the books, offering the cost of transportation as a birthday gift. MacDonald responded: "I wish I could say what I think without hurting your kind loving heart. I will try. . . . it was such a business transaction, so plainly understood, and ratified between us, and the amount even to you so large, and useful, that you must permit me to remain your willing debtor still to the amount of 6.10 [pounds], to be paid at the unbusiness-like time of 'when you can.'" Then he added, lest she misunderstand: "Do not think me proud in wishing to owe you this money. I am hardly more than honest in it."[16] Although it would in all probability be a considerable while before he would have the money to pay her, he insisted on doing so eventually.

The second instance comes from a letter to Alphaeus Smith, a friend from Arundel who wrote asking MacDonald's advice on certain personal matters. After giving his specific advice, MacDonald counseled:

> Keep your heart and conscience and hands clean, dear friend, and be ready to lose all, wife and life, rather than act ignobly, unrighteously in the smallest matter—you will not misunderstand me. It is an easy thing to be as honest as society requires of one, but it is not easy to be pure, to be in what are counted better things thoroughly, divinely upright—May God teach me in this.[17]

MacDonald was as committed to complete uprightness in human relationships as was humanly possible.

TWELVE

A Summer of Stark Contrasts

How little are we our own! Existence is decreed us; love and
suffering are appointed us. We may resist, we may modify;
but we cannot help loving, and we cannot help dying. . . .
Great in goodness, yea absolutely good, God must be, to have
a right to make us—to compel our existence, and decree its
laws!—What's Mine's Mine

The new year, 1855, would be a better one. Lecturing from
his home proved to be a successful venture, and before the year
was over MacDonald added engagements to lecture at the newly
forming Ladies College as well. He handled such diverse subjects
as Shakespeare, the "modern poets," natural philosophy, and
mathematics. In addition, he took several smaller boys into his
home for tutoring. He was again busy, and he was happy.

Then, a great boon came. Longman's of London agreed to
publish *Within and Without,* and it appeared in April. After several
disappointments with publishers of lesser stature, this was a solid
triumph. "They take all the risk—I half the profits. I have now
got the right publishers, and it is a very advantageous agreement
for an unknown author," he told his father.[1]

Taking Lily with him, MacDonald made a trip to London
shortly after the appearance of his poem, to find mixed reactions
to it among his relatives. His proud father-in-law was reading it
when MacDonald walked in. "He reads it at breakfast and at tea
time, with the tears running down his face," Carrie affirmed. Godwin, who did not like poetry, spoke disparagingly when he was

out of MacDonald's hearing: "Mr. MacDonald is not happy in the choice of his subject, at least for this world." But he admitted, "I'm at a loss to know just what end he had in view in writing it."[2]

The general sense of satisfaction MacDonald now felt in being a published author bolstered his desire to make a trip back home to Scotland. It was, in fact, much on his mind; he had been gone for seven years. Early in 1855 he said that he doubted he could get through another year without again seeing his father. Further, his father had not yet seen Louisa, to say nothing of Lilia, Mary, and Grace. Then news came that his sister Bella was spitting blood, and the doctor was grave about her condition; she was failing rapidly. George's father, anxious to see for the first time Louisa and the children, had nevertheless a great anxiety that the excitement of their visit would further endanger Bella's life. Not knowing how to express his concern in a letter for Louisa's eyes, he wrote to Charles, expressing his dilemma and asking him to explain the risks of the entire family coming at this time. This, together with the simple fact that there was not sufficient money for the entire family to go, forced them to make the difficult decision: MacDonald should go alone.

At 11:00 P.M. on July 2, he was sitting at an "old fashioned mahogany table of the commercial room of a second rate but respectable hotel" in Edinburgh, beginning to compose the first of the many letters he would write to Louisa during this trip. The train from Manchester had arrived early in the evening, and he and a traveling companion had taken advantage of the time to stroll through the streets of one of the quaintest of European cities, one that he had not yet seen. At the end of Cannongate Street they stood in front of the colorful Palace of Holyrood House, its high projecting windows suggesting to MacDonald all the "beautiful women and grand men who may have met by means of them at night." But he was most struck by the squalid living conditions of the people along Cannongate and Cowgate Streets:

Oh such houses! of filth! and misery! and smells! and winding
common stairs! and grated, unglazed windows on the land-
ings! and squalid figures looking down from two, three, four,
five, six, seven stories. . . . and every few paces a narrow court
running through between to more and more mysteries of stairs
and lofty crowded abominable dwellings. Some of the dark
closes and entries look most infernal.

It all stood in such stark contrast to their "orderly, clean, commonplace, well-behaved Manchester, it is hardly credible." The
graphic descriptions of the squalid life of large Scottish cities, such
as in *Sir Gibbie,* for instance, must have derived at least in part from
this evening's exposure to the realities of Edinburgh.

On July 5 he was reunited with his father's family and saw
again the countryside that he had not seen for seven years. To sit
beneath the trees in front of their ivy-covered granite home, drinking fresh country milk while sparrows twittered in the vines and
his little sisters brought various wildflowers for his admiration, or
to ride again over the lonely country lanes the mare that had given
him so much pleasure in his boyhood, was sheer delight for him.
And he had so much to share with his father: "Oh that fine old
man my father. He is the man to tell anything to. So open and
wise and humble and kind. He exceeds my expectation—God bless
him."[3]

Nor did MacDonald, now a comparatively successful man of
the world, feel as though he had to talk condescendingly to him.
"My father enters into Browning so—I have been reading several
[poems] among them 'The Spanish Monk.' He seems so to enter
into the dramatic." His father may have been making an unusually
earnest effort to be interested in poetry now that his son had
gained fame. Everything would have been delightful had it not
been for the sobering realities of Bella's condition: "Down in the
nursery lies my poor thin sister, very quiet—or rather sits, for she
sits in bed with her knees up and her head leaning upon them—
so thin is she. . . . she lies like a seed waiting for the summer to
which this summer is but a winter," he wrote Louisa.[4]

He had, however, to defend his beard. His father was more tolerant of it than he had expected, but his uncle James, who was already somewhat wary of his nephew because of his growing reputation for unorthodoxy, was pointedly distant, on one occasion offering him a guinea for it. MacDonald's ability to lapse into the native Scottish prompted some to overcome their distaste for his uncivilized appearance, but he was asked to speak from his home pulpit only twice, another speaker being secured while he was there. He blamed his full growth of black hair.

Another factor, however, may have been more the cause: the stern Scottish hesitation to accept MacDonald's insistence on the loving and childlike character of God. After his first sermon, one older woman of the congregation judged that he "went rather too far on the side of God's character"; but another remarked: "When I saw him in the pulpit . . . I thocht he lookit gey an roach like but or he had been speakin' long I just thocht it was like Christ himsel' speakin' to me."[5]

On July 24 he had the honor of performing the marriage ceremony of his cousin Margaret to Robert Troup, who was now the pastor in the Independent Chapel in Huntly. MacDonald presented them with an autographed copy of *Within and Without* as a wedding present. He was particularly moved when Bella, who had been trying to save some money for some time, gave him two sets of flannels for his winter wear. He knew the present took all the money she had saved and was sure she would be gone before he could wear them.

Meanwhile, Louisa was undergoing severe trials. She had undertaken a project of handpainting an ornamental table for her brother Alexander, for which he had promised her five pounds, but, again pregnant, she had not the energy or spirit to complete the task. She took the children to Liverpool to stay with the Sings and visit the Powells. Depressed and despondent, she blamed her own "unworthiness" as the cause of their inability to obtain much-needed money; the failure was a divine chastisement on herself.

Nor was this the only cause for disappointment. Her father came to the Sings' to visit with his two daughters, but the pleasure of his company was severely curtailed by the intimated comparisons between her sister's luxurious life and her own deprivation. She found her sister's actions patronizing, and her father's neglect to inquire into their financial condition with a view to extending some help most disappointing. Together with all this, their maid Charlotte had become impudent in manner and neglectful of her duty to help take care of the children. When the time came for Louisa to return to Camp Terrace, she was forced to endure yet a further humiliation. Having no money for the needed train ticket, she had to allow her sister to purchase it. Flora did it with a flourish; she secured first-class passage. Then, immediately upon returning, Louisa was met with a demand from their grocer that they pay their bill. Not knowing where else to turn, she wrote a friend of her father's in London asking for a loan of five pounds. He obliged with seeming kindness.

A great source of encouragement, however, was the reaction of the public to *Within and Without*. Reviews were appearing, for the most part containing hearty commendations, in such publications as *The Scotsman, The Globe, The Leader, The Brighton Herald,* and *The Morning Post*. The reviewer in *The Athenaeum*, although affirming that the poem had a "profound meaning which, on the first perusal, we cannot pretend to fathom," was filled with profuse praise: "Seldom have spiritual abysses been more thoroughly sounded,—seldom has despair had a more eloquent voice,—seldom has mystic sentiment been more beautifully interpreted."[6] Gratified and proud, Louisa faithfully sent the reviews north to her husband. MacDonald, who had been especially pleased when he arrived to discover that his father had already committed several key passages of his long poem to heart, was nevertheless dismayed when he, seized with fatherly pride, refused to allow his son to send a certain review back to Louisa.

Although apparently this saintly father could not see his own shortcomings, he was worried lest his son's newly acquired literary fame would turn his head. In his first letter to MacDonald after his return to Manchester, he warned him against becoming proud of his accomplishment. MacDonald responded:

> I hope I know enough of my own failings and ignorance, to keep me from becoming conceited and perhaps I don't think the success so great as you do. Certainly there is always danger, and perhaps a usually modest man may at moments be overfavourable in his judgments of himself. I think I have more consciousness of weakness than of strength. At least I have both. But our safety is in God's keeping not in our own. May He take care of me, and do what he will with me.[7]

Of all those who took interest in his poem, he was most pleased to learn through a mutual friend that Lady Byron, the poet's widow, was so moved by it she was writing her friends advising them to read it.

In early August MacDonald returned to his waiting family in Manchester, bringing with him a supply of clothing sewn by his mother and sisters to replenish his meager wardrobe: several shirts, a streetcoat, and "strong boots for winter." He also brought as housemaid Elsie Gordon, a young serving girl of his father's who wanted a larger experience of the world. She quickly proved to be a much-appreciated help to the beleaguered Louisa. Lily, Mary, and Grace would at last have a more dependable nurse.

Very shortly after MacDonald returned Bella died. But MacDonald's grief was soon countered by the unexpected appearance of John who, back from Moscow, was ready to accept a temporary teaching position at home. He intended to strengthen his fluency in German while he tutored here for a time, in order eventually to take a teaching position in Dresden. With George's help he was able to secure a post near Manchester. The two brothers were often together during the fall, greatly delighting in each other's company.

THIRTEEN

Yestereve, Death Came

So sure am I that many things which illness has led me to see are true, that I would endlessly rather never be well than lose sight of them.—Paul Faber, Surgeon

Returning refreshed from Huntly to No. 3 Camp Terrace, MacDonald plunged with renewed zeal into the tasks that lay before him. Then, exhilaration took its toll; his overexertion nearly cost him his life. He intended to go in one direction; circumstances would soon take him in another.

Except for a nagging cough, he felt well; and, although little actual money was as yet coming in from his efforts, he felt assured the prospects of earning a respectable living were now fairly clear. The group meeting on Renshaw Street seemed loyal, the anticipation of a good enrollment for a new lecture series for the fall was strong, and they intended to receive boarders from Owens College. Further, he was now considered a promising young poet by literary circles in London, so that he could expect to earn a larger portion of his income from his pen. His reputation was, in short, beginning to be established locally as a Christian teacher and preacher with a fresh and stimulating thrust and nationally as a writer to be watched.

Then, still another opportunity presented itself. A congregation at Bolton, an industrial city some eleven miles to the north, offered him their pulpit. Attracted to his teachings, they extended to him complete liberty to preach as he felt led. Being a "blue collar" congregation composed of workers in the woolen and cotton industries, they seemed to MacDonald to offer a balance to the more sophisticated and intellectual group to which he was already ministering. He agreed to try the situation for one year, the arrangement being that whatever offering was raised in the course of this time would be his. He estimated that he could expect to receive perhaps a hundred pounds annually. Spiritually invigorated, he gave himself to his many tasks with abandon.

Suddenly, however, in late November all these prospects collapsed. He began to bleed profusely from the lungs, and nothing availed to stop it. He was bid to lie in absolute stillness, with ice on his chest, and still the blood came, aggravated by a cough that he could not contain. The frantic Louisa summoned their friends for help, and help quickly came. Angela came from Liverpool, and the sisters-in-law of A. J. Scott frequently attended at MacDonald's bed. Very much weakened, his life seemed to be ebbing away before their very eyes. A telegram was sent to Huntly, and the parents still grieving from Bella's death faced the prospect of losing yet another son.

Finally, Dr. Harrison, a homeopath who was a faithful member of the Renshaw Street group, decided in desperation to bleed MacDonald from the arm in order to remove as much pressure as he possibly could from the lesion in the lung. Miraculously, the daring ploy succeeded. But the exhausted patient lay for weeks in utter weakness, his precarious constitution reluctant to right itself.

The passages in MacDonald's writings that speak of facing death in the full repose of faith have their origin in such firsthand encounters. One of his convictions was that a Christian teacher should present the nature of grace out of the fund of personal experience; MacDonald can never be accused of lacking in personal encounters with adversity. To him death was seldom far away, both in the loss of members of his family and in the tenure of his experience. The instance at hand is one of the occasions which he undoubtedly had in mind when he later wrote:[1]

Yestereve, Death came, and knocked at my thin door.
I from my window looked: the thing I saw,
The shape uncouth, I had not seen before.
I was disturbed—with fear, in sooth, not awe;
Whereof ashamed, I instantly did rouse
My will to seek thee—only to fear the more:
Alas! I could not find thee in the house.

I was like Peter when he began to sink.
To thee a new prayer therefore I have got—
That, when Death comes in earnest to my door,
Thou wouldst thyself go, when the latch doth clink,
And lead him to my room, up to my cot;
Then hold thy child's hand, hold and leave him not,
Till Death has done with him for evermore.

Such experiences are never free from existential fear, and the soul must work its way through each one, achieving afresh the equanimity of faith. MacDonald's prayer was not that he be steeled ahead of time for the next inevitable encounter, but rather that, when it came, he might not have to feel himself so alone.

MacDonald's previous episode of pulmonary hemorrhaging had come when he was beginning his first pastoral commitment at Arundel; this one came as he was beginning his second. In the first instance he was possessed with apprehension concerning his suitability for the demands of the pastoral ministry; he may have again been affected by a similar dread, both consciously and subconsciously. His keen conscientiousness, together with his capacity for excitement, goaded him into a too energetic response, and he put overly taxing demands on his weak constitution.

However this may be, he was reduced once again to utter dependence on others, forced by the sheer weight of circumstance to exercise all the humility that such dependence requires. Scott was a friend indeed during this period. He made the family's need known to friends of his, who responded and made some financial contribution. Then unexpectedly, on New Year's Day 1856, sufficient money came to meet all their mounting debts.

Three gentlemen appeared at the MacDonalds' door, none of whom he knew well, and presented him with a purse of thirty pounds, an offering which they had lifted from "a few friends." They offered it to him "in the most delicate and kind way," Mac-Donald told his father. "You will be interested to hear that one of the three is an Independent, another a Churchman, and the third a Unitarian." MacDonald's emphasis on transcending the sectarian spirit was evidently to good effect.

A sympathetic friend from Huntly sent him a bank order for five pounds. It was as unexpected as welcome. Then, some of his Bolton people called on him, bringing an entire quarter's salary in advance. They had paid him up to Christmas just before he was taken ill. The sum they brought, along with a private sovereign from one of the people, amounted to twenty-one pounds. "Since I wrote to you I have received 56 pounds" in all, the grateful invalid told his father with joy, adding, "This will leave something considerable over after paying all our present debts."[2] The congregation at Bolton were exercising genuine Christian charity. The fact that MacDonald could not have preached to them for more than two months during the fall renders the act the more impressive and suggests that his pulpit ministry was beginning to acquire some power.

Although MacDonald had many times prior to this crisis practiced a faith of complete reliance on God for daily sustenance, this experience brought him into a frame of mind characterized by a yet more quiet and consistent confidence in God to provide. He told Mrs. Ross in Huntly, the friend who out of meager resources had sent him five pounds:

> We are in the meantime free from any anxiety, and if we have not learned by this time to cast all on him who careth for us, I think we are getting to learn it. Indeed I have so much hope along with a little faith that I have not been troubled—scarcely at all. I can see more and more that nothing will do for anybody but an absolute enthusiastic confidence in God.[3]

No merely pious rhetoric this, but a tranquility of spirit hard-earned from experience.

On January 20, 1856, Louisa gave birth to their first boy, whom they named Greville Matheson, after MacDonald's good friend from Highbury days. But the proud father, although by this time up and about, was not regaining his strength as he should. The Scotts took him to their home at Cheetham Hill for quiet rest and encouraged him to take his family to live for a time in southern England, in the hope that cleaner air and a warmer climate would help restore him.

Louisa's sister Phoebe was to be married to Joseph King in London on February 20, so it was decided that the family would stay with the Powells for the wedding and then proceed to Devonshire in the southwest of England for rest and the longed-for recovery. The family took the journey well (Louisa too was far from strong), but the strain of the wedding affairs was considerable. In London, MacDonald thought he would consult his former physician, Dr. Williams, but he found the doctor too unwell to see him. He then went to see Dr. Wilkinson, a homeopath. He agreed with his Manchester physician, Dr. Harrison, that MacDonald's lungs were free from tuberculosis, but advised complete rest for a period of at least six months. So they tried to firm up their plans to go to Devonshire, in the southwest of England, for a couple months, and then, when summer was sufficiently settled in Huntly, they might be able to make another trip north.

That MacDonald consulted the physician Garth Wilkinson while he was in London is of special interest. Wilkinson was a Swedenborgian, and as such he would have had much in common with MacDonald. He was also an early student of the work of William Blake, being the first to print the *Songs of Innocence and of Experience* in 1839.[4] He may well have shared his enthusiasms for Blake's beautifully engraved works with his patient. The presence in MacDonald's writings of ideas very similar to Blake's is so noticeable that MacDonald must have had some early acquaintance with his work. Greville observed years later that MacDonald had in his library a facsimile of the original *Jerusalem,* a reproduction of *The Marriage of Heaven and Hell,* and a copy of Alexander Gilchrist's *Life of William Blake.* He could not have acquired the latter, of course, until after its publication in 1863, but the acquisition of some of Blake's works may have been earlier. MacDonald had a bookplate made that was a reproduction of one of Blake's engravings, showing an aged man entering the cave of death while from above springs the resurrected body in the full beauty of humanity.[5]

From London the family chose to go to Kingswear on the south coast of Devonshire, not far from Dartmouth. Taking lodgings that overlooked the mouth of the River Dart as it joins the Atlantic, both MacDonald and Louisa prepared for rest and recuperation. After spending the late spring in this bracing air they felt they were ready for their long-awaited trip together to Huntly. They returned to The Limes via Bristol, MacDonald wanting to see the publisher Bogue, who was seriously considering bringing out a volume of MacDonald's poems. From there at the end of June, MacDonald went by steamer to Aberdeen on his way to Huntly, Louisa and the children following by train through Manchester. After their twenty-two hour ride they arrived exhausted but jubiliant. Finally, Louisa and the children were able to meet MacDonald's father and his family, and the grandparents could become acquainted with three of their grandchildren. Lily had been left with the Scotts.

July and August were spent in Huntly, but the weather was perversely cold and damp. MacDonald remained weak and "lazy," as he told his sister-in-law Charlotte. "I scarcely do anything but read German stories and write a few verses now and then."[6] Among these stories was E. T. A. Hoffmann's *The Golden Pot,* an inspiring story that did much to shape his first adult fantasy, *Phantastes.*

It was apparent that MacDonald's health was not sufficiently restored for them to return to the rigorous schedule of duties in the adverse climate of Manchester, at least until after the upcoming winter, and perhaps not at all. Uncertain what to do, they even considered emigrating to Australia, but with little enthusiasm. "The idea was most unpleasant to me," he wrote Mrs. Scott. "I should not mind a voyage there and back after being scared with the idea of living there."[7] A trip to a milder climate was seriously considered; the future depended on his returning to health. But from where would the money for such a trip come?

FOURTEEN

The Obliged Person

*As you grow ready for it, somewhere or other you will find
what is needful for you—in a book, or a friend, or, best of all,
in your own thoughts—the eternal thought speaking in your
thought.*—The Marquis of Lossie

Lady Byron had read *Within and Without* shortly after its appearance, and, deeply impressed by its content, wrote the author.
To her great pleasure, she had found a poet whose talent was being
used to express a Christian view of life, uplifting and inspirational.
A warm correspondence followed. In spite of MacDonald's reluctance to accept the charity of others Lady Byron soon found a way
of helping him regain his health.

A woman of large moral purpose, she had married Lord Byron some forty years earlier on the strength of his promise that,
were she to marry him, he would reform. Envisioning how greatly
the world would be benefited if such a magnificent talent were
captured and transformed into a force for moral and spiritual en-
lightenment, she had consented. No sooner had she married him,
however, than she began to realize the impossibility of gaining her
ends; Byron had awakened on their wedding night, saw the light
filtering through the red curtains surrounding their bed, and
loudly declared himself to be in hell. In the days that followed he
had taken delight in constantly behaving in such manner that his
serious-minded bride became convinced he was mad. After a year
of such torment she separated from him. But Lady Byron's vision
of being instrumental in giving inspirational poetry to the world
had not diminished.

She learned of MacDonald's poverty and precarious health

through A. J. Scott. Desirous to be of help, but knowing how loath MacDonald was to receive money purely as a gift, she offered in March to employ him as a guide and tutor to escort her grandson to Paris, for which she intended to pay well. That ploy failing—MacDonald was too ill to consider such an assignment—she succeeded through a mutual friend, the Rev. Ross of Brighton (similarly to MacDonald, a clergyman who had been expelled from his church), in sending a gift of twenty-five pounds. She wished "to be considered the obliged person in my accepting it," MacDonald explained to his father.[1]

Then a very feasible way of aiding him to full health occurred to her. She suggested to Scott that a group of friends sponsor the MacDonalds on a trip to Algiers, she being the chief sponsor, in the hope that an extended period in the dry and intensely brilliant sunshine would turn his health around. The Scotts, anxious to contribute to the project, were able to raise considerable supporting money from various friends and donors. The entire effort seemed to the oppressed MacDonalds a direct expression of the grace of God.

The MacDonalds bid good-bye to Huntly in September of 1856 and proceeded to make the necessary arrangements for their departure. Mary, the weakest of the children, would go with them; the others would be distributed among various aunts. They went through Manchester down to London, checking on the state of MacDonald's publishing interests as they arrived. The publisher Bogue was delaying his edition of MacDonald's poems, but Longman's, pleased with the sales of *Within and Without,* intended to run another edition the following year. They were disappointed, however, that Lady Byron, herself in questionable health, had been forced to leave London for the more invigorating climate of the west. So MacDonald did not meet her before leaving.

They hoped to arrive at Algiers of November 2 and stay through the following April. On the eve of their departure, however, while with a large portion of the Powell family on an afternoon's outing—some in a carriage and some on horseback—the aged Powell was thrown from his horse. Insisting on remounting, he continued for some twelve miles. However, when passing the identical spot on their return, the horse threw him again, this time resulting in serious injury. So the MacDonalds stayed by his bedside for a week until they were assured he was recuperating satisfactorily.

They crossed the Channel from Newhaven to Dieppe, then traveled through Rouen to Paris. The weather was cold and wet, the hotels inconvenient. "Indeed if it were not for the hope that lies before, I should heartily wish myself back in England" he confided to his father-in-law.[2] They were fascinated, however, by the sights of the ancient city of Avignon. And when they were greeted in Marseilles by the sight of the blue Mediterranean under the warm sun, their mood quite changed, and they eagerly looked forward to the "promised land" of sunshine and rest.

MacDonald found Algiers deeply fascinating. As he stood amid the curiosities of this coastal city, set against the backdrop of the low Sahel range of mountains, the experience all but overwhelmed him. The streets were filled with noises: incessant military noises from kettledrums, the endless chatter of people jostling each other as they went to and from the market, and the shouts of artisans from their closet-like shops. Everywhere the buildings shone a dazzling white. To diminish the heat from the blinding sun, the natives whitewashed them inside and out twice a year. Narrow streets and passageways twisted in labyrinthine patterns. Over the cobblestones moved an incredible variety of people in multicolored costumes: French military uniforms, the splendid rainbow colors of Moorish and Jewish garb, the gracefully flowing Arab bernouse, and the traditional qamis shrouding the women.

Moving through the city dressed in his Rob-Roy plaid and Glengarry bonnet, MacDonald added yet another to the parade of costumes that made the streets so colorful. Absorbed with all the sights, he wandered among the shops as much as his health would permit, noting how the various artisans—tailors, shoemakers, tobacco-cutters—pursued their trades. Everything intrigued him: the way one Arab used his great toe in the operation of his turning lathe; the way a shoemaker used a stitch hitherto unknown to him.

However, colorful as it all was, his disciplined nature, accustomed to the order and pervading restraint of Britain, was disconcerted by the general disorder he saw: "The confusion here is enough to drive all rule out of a man's brain." But he also acknowledged, "There does not seem nearly the misery that we see in London or any of our large towns."[3]

The amount of time he could spend in the teeming city was limited. He had to find a situation in the country to accomplish the purpose for which he had been sent: to regain his health. Determined to situate themselves outside the city in order to get away from the noise and to take fuller advantage of the climate, they managed, after much searching, to locate such furnished quarters as their meager purse could afford. A large "Moorish house" belonging to a French officer, some two miles distant from the city, was available to them. There Mary would have ample room to play and chatter and still not disturb MacDonald when he felt strong enough to write. They quickly made the necessary arrangements to secure it. In one room, which had "a low groined roof with vaulted recesses on one side," they were able to have a French piano for Louisa's pleasure. In another they found a statuette of the Venus of Milo, which relieved somewhat the "picturesque dulness" of the place.

The floors throughout were paved with various colored tiles that extended some two feet up the side walls. But MacDonald's favorite color was red, and he was disappointed in "the utter absence of red in any combination." A huge French stove smoked incessantly whenever it was necessary to use it. But out the windows they could see in the distance the blue and purple waters of the Mediterranean, and when they sat on their terrace, they felt themselves "in the midst of the glowing world; the great hills in the distance, like an infinite hope, and the air filled with the odours of citron and orange blossoms."[4] Here amid the prevailing

silence they settled down to relax and receive the longed-for healing effects of the weather.

To their disappointment, the weather was not congenial for
long. An extended period of rain followed the advent of the new
year, intermingling violent storms of wind, lightning, and hail.
Days extended to weeks as one storm followed another. The natives rated it the most severe winter in thirty years. It did little for
MacDonald's health; attacks of bronchitis kept recurring. As the
days passed they could do scarcely more than sit inside and watch
the tempestuous sea in the distance.

The burden of such confinement, however, was somewhat
lightened by the presence of other British people nearby. An archdeacon and his wife occupied the top story of the house and not
far away lived a retired member of Parliament with his family of
daughters, the Leigh-Smiths. The MacDonalds at first found
them to be "rather fast, devil-may-care sort of girls" not to their
taste, but they came in time to enjoy their company and as spring
weather permitted, often took them on outings.

They also found the religious customs and ceremonies of the
natives interesting. They occasionally attended the Roman Catholic services, much to the surprise of the archdeacon living upstairs.
MacDonald had come to feel that every Christian church was but
another sect, and he was determined to look for the good in each.
They in fact planned to attend high mass on Christmas Eve, but
MacDonald became ill, and they were unable to go.

Especially curious to them were the local religious rituals and
rites, both of the black Africans, which they observed in the
streets, and of the Moslems. The rituals of the former, conducted
in the open air, were characterized by "intense bewildering noise"
from drums and castanets, and "a kind of frantic . . . dance." Mac-
Donald mused on them with a tolerant affirmation:

> May it not be . . . that even in this there are the first rudiments
> of the expression of an unknown need?—an inward prayer, that
> is yet so undefined as to take no embodiment in articulate

sound, but utters itself in howls and artificial noises? These too are the children of the one Father, and there may be even in these orgies something of prayer that reaches the ear that listens not for the form of the words, but the utterance of the need. And I could not help collating these barbarities with some forms of Christian worship, good enough in themselves, but which, when exalted into the place of essential duty, seemed to me equally senseless with these half-animal utterances, and far more provoking.[5]

The condescending attitudes of the Victorian Britisher to other cultures is painfully evident, but nevertheless the degree of affirmation in his judgments shows something of his comparatively eclectic mind. The human need for God was universal, and uninstructed people might well give seemingly lower forms of expression to that need. Professing Christians, possessing the greater revelation, had the lesser excuse when their worship practices included unrefined emotional expressions.

They found the services in the Moslem mosques more acceptable. On one bright moonlit night during the Fast of Ramadan they made their way into the city to see the principal mosque, brilliantly lighted for worship. Inside in an open court they observed the worshipers scattered in little groups as they now stood, now knelt, and now bowed low with their foreheads touching the ground, accompanied by the low intonations of the priest. A Moor who seemed to have some charge of the service occasionally waved them aside, but with a dignity that did not suggest to them that they were being bid to leave. The brilliant moonlight fell on a vine-shrouded tree in the outer court, as well as on the towers of the mosque, which rose high above and, intermingling with the flame of the various lamps, emitted a soft red glow.

That the MacDonalds embarked on such adventures separated them somewhat from their more insular British friends. They made an effort to become acquainted with what Arabs they could and came to admire them as a solid and dignified people. Mac-Donald saw in them something not only to affirm but also to emulate:

> One cannot help wondering, when he sees the little, jerky, self-asserting, tight-laced Frenchman beside the stately, digni-fied, reserved, loose-robed Arab, how the former could ever assume and retain authority over the latter. I have seen a power of contempt and repressed indignation in the half-sidelong look with which an Arab in a ragged bernouse regarded a Frenchman, who had tapped him on the shoulder with a stick to attract his attention. There is something in the bearing and manners of the Arab significant, whether truly or not, of a personal dignity far beyond that common to the German, or French, or English. Two of them came over to our residence to remove our piano before we left. A great proportion of the heavy carriage in Algiers is done by the Arabs slinging the weight on a pole which rests on their shoulders. Our breakfast being still on the table, I asked them to sit down and have some coffee; which they did without the least embarrassment, half-lounging on their chairs, and chatting away in bad French, aided by gesture, with a thoroughbred ease rarely to be seen in our own country. I was proud of them. Their religion teaches them that in the sight of God they are all equal, and they seem to believe it, more at least than Christians do; and this, combined with their fatalism, which naturally destroys all haste and perturbation, produces an indifferent stateliness of demeanor which many a man of Norman blood and fabulous origin might well envy.[6]

The months spent in Algiers not only effected a decided strength-ening of MacDonald's physical health, but they also strengthened his view of human nature in general.

Then disturbing news came from home. To his chagrin, Mac-Donald discovered that his brother Charles, having had significant business reversals, had gone so heavily in debt that his father now must assume responsibility for his bills. Charles's inclination to make somewhat risky business investments had caught up with him. Unable to right himself in England, he was preparing to embark for Sydney, Australia, leaving Jane behind. The family no doubt were haunted by memories of his uncle Charles's having absconded twenty years earlier and cringed from the irony.

Undertaking by letter to comfort his agitated father, who was at the moment, in spite of his own solid spiritual moorings, rather depressed about how meagerly all three of his sons were "getting on" in the world, MacDonald assured him that, as far as he himself was concerned, he meant to try to get something to do as soon as he returned. "For," he affirmed, "I must not be an invalid longer. Indeed I would rather die trying it, than live as we are doing now."[7] He determined in Algiers to return to an active life in England, though the effort might cost him his life.

As spring came on and the weather became more typically African, with the sun raising the daytime temperature quickly to one hundred degrees as the sirocco—the hot desert winds—blew, they knew it was time to leave. Although the months in Algiers had not worked a miraculous cure, MacDonald was feeling better. This respite from an English winter had not only saved his life but also invigorated him physically and emotionally. He had been able to do considerable writing, and although the publisher Bogue was no longer interested in his poems, he was now assured that Longman's was. They were committed to bring out this year both a volume of poems and also a second edition of *Within and Without*. At the beginning of May the MacDonalds packed, and on the ninth began the return journey. But where they would live in England was uncertain.

FIFTEEN

The Hues of Dreamland

*We have not yet enough speech to cousin the tenth part of our
feelings. . . . I can no more describe the emotion aroused in
my mind by a gray cloud parting over a gray stone, by the
smell of a sweetpea, by the sight of one of those long upright
pennons of striped grass with the homely name, than I can
tell what the glory of God is who made these things.—*
Robert Falconer

After a tedious and difficult summer spent mostly at The
Limes, the MacDonalds decided to move to Hastings. There he
was able gradually to further his career as a writer and a lecturer.
Financial independence was yet some distance off, but they tried
to take with grace the help willingly offered, believing God was
continuing to deal with their pride.

The ancient city of Hastings, with its rich historical heritage
and congenial climate, is situated on the Atlantic coast in Sussex,
some sixty miles south of London. A comfortable and flourishing
sea-bathing resort, it is for the most part nestled between two hills,
designated East Hill and West Hill, that rise rather steeply from
the sea. The old fishing town is at the bottom of East Hill, and
the beaches with their fashionable hotels stretch westward along
the coast. On the summit of each hill is a spacious parkland from
which there are panoramic views of city and sea. Gulls squawk
endlessly overhead.

Lady Byron hesitated about the wisdom of their move, feeling that the intellectual atmosphere there would not afford MacDonald the context he needed to carry on his lecturing; they should stay in London. But their primary consideration was MacDonald's health. Hastings promised to be more congenial, and it was, after all, not too far away. Brighton was also nearby, the home of their friends the Rosses, for whom MacDonald preached on at least two occasions that summer.

After much looking they found in the early fall a commodious thirteen-room home on the east side of Hastings, halfway up East Hill, with a sweeping view of the city to the west and of the sea to the south. Situated on the street known as the Tackleway, it was named Providence House, although the MacDonalds promptly renamed it Huntly Cottage. The thirty-five pound annual rent was within their means; Powell would help them with it if necessary.

Their presence at The Limes throughout that summer had been, they both felt, a rather severe burden, both on themselves and the Powells. Yet finding another place immediately, even if they could have afforded it, had hardly been possible. Louisa was far along in carrying their fifth child. Also, she had continued for a time to feel the effects of the hot desert winds that had struck during the last of their stay in Algiers and of the rough passage home.

Little Mary, who was "very thin and delicate—a most elvish creature," was also the worse for her Algerian experience. She had contracted an ophthalmia endemic to northern Africa. The disease would plague her eyes for several years; on some days she was unable to open them at all. Her buoyant and winsome nature, however, made her a favorite with all of the family. "We call her *elfie* when she is good and *kelpie* when she is naughty" MacDonald told his father with evident pleasure; these nicknames remained with her for the rest of her life.[1] Lily continually charmed all her aunts. Nevertheless, having to live with his family at The Limes had weighed on MacDonald's spirits.

Of all his trials MacDonald found the continual dependence on others the most difficult to bear. The seemingly never-ending precariousness of his health was hard enough to take, but his inability to support himself and his growing family without the constant dole of his father-in-law and various friends was yet more vexing. Not that he was reduced to begging; the help that had unfailingly come was extended freely and ungrudgingly from people who often contrived to make it appear as though it came from obligation. His and his family's needs had always been met; God was faithful.

In their dire straits Lady Byron again gave them help. Immediately after his return from Algiers, MacDonald had met her finally. On the first meeting they liked one another personally, and she invited him back to dine at her house on Dover Street. "If I can do anything for you, you must understand, Mr. MacDonald, it is rather for the public than yourself," she insisted.[2] Although she was not so wealthy that she could be lavish in support, she gave him twenty-five pounds, with the promise of double that amount by Christmas. MacDonald described her to his father as "a most extraordinary person, of remarkable intellect, and a great, pure unselfish soul. She has made a proposal to me to edit a number of letters which she has at different times received from distinguished persons. . . . If all goes well, and she commits the papers into my hands, I presume she will advance me a little money to work upon, which will deliver me from immediate difficulties."[3] Whatever became of this proposal is unclear, but her contriving to find an acceptable way of helping him is evident.

Assuming the prerogatives of friendship, she did not hesitate, however, to criticize when she felt it was in his best interests. Attending one of his lectures on poetry, she found the degree of emotion in his delivery "intolerable" and doubted if as a lecturer he would succeed. When she expressed her criticism to him, he responded that her candor was "a true sign of friendship" but added that some people liked his manner. To what degree he may subsequently have tried to alter his presentation is not clear, but their friendship allowed for frank exchanges. Once when she expected him as a visitor in London, she wrote:

You shall be treated most inhospitably—put into a room apart with a private entrance. . . . No note will be taken of your goings out and comings in. When socially disposed, you will *invite yourself.* My house has often been called Liberty Hall.[4]

He often took advantage of her hospitality, deeply grateful for her playful eagerness to be his friend.

He was also buoyed in spirits by the kindnesses of their many friends in Manchester and vicinity when he had been there to straighten their affairs, and especially by the opportunity he had to spend time with John. Charles, of course, was no longer there. But his favorite brother was settled as tutor at Barrow Hall, near Warrington, a position he found congenial enough. "John and I have been in the fields all the morning, and have found a pimpernel," he wrote Louisa.[5] Given the amount of poetry MacDonald had written since they were last together, and the prospect of a volume of his poetry appearing soon, the brothers had much to discuss.

Not only had he wanted to see John, but he longed to see his father again during that summer as well, imparting to him while they were yet fresh the many impressions he had of Algiers. The trip was a brief one, but he was afforded still another visit with his aging father and had time to "have a pipe together in one of the summer-seats by the Deveron" with his uncle. Louisa, unable to make the trip, was delivered of another girl; Irene was born on August 31.

Still another source of satisfaction amid the general difficulties of the summer of 1857 was the appearance of *Poems* by George MacDonald on July 3. The poems presented are typical of MacDonald's didactic efforts, but "The Hidden Life," containing many genuinely admirable lines, may well be considered his finest achievement in blank verse. MacDonald prefaced the volume with two sonnets dedicated to his father. Soon it was favorably reviewed in a remarkable number of leading literary magazines. *The Scotsman,* for instance, praised MacDonald for "the earnestness of thought" and the "deep simplicity and power of utterance" that, the reviewer affirmed, was consistently present in his work to date.[6]

Literary triumphs, however, did not take their attention long from domestic realities. Becoming situated in their new home was a large task. They made arrangements for their furniture and belongings to be moved from Manchester and also from the London warehouse where their things from Arundel still remained in storage. To their vexation, they discovered that these things had suffered general damage. Further, the cayenne pepper with which the carpets and curtains had been plentifully powdered to prevent infestation in storage now precipitated in MacDonald a violent bronchial reaction. He fled for a week to the Rosses' in Brighton, but when he returned, the residue still affected him.

Bravely, Louisa arranged the house and cared for the children with little help for a time but that of a fourteen-year-old girl. Unimpressed with either the girl's physical grace or mental ingenuity, MacDonald described her as having "joints like a Dutch doll, and a brain like a Dutch cheese."[7] An attempted jest, it nevertheless conveys something of his attitude toward serving help which he could indulge with apparently no qualms of conscience. Such help was necessary to them, not only because of their social standing, but also because MacDonald's health rendered him unable to help Louisa with normal household tasks. In short, he had to hire done what he felt he should be able to do for himself, and they had small funds for the hiring. The matter weighed heavily on his spirits.

Difficult as his situation was, he viewed it all as necessary to his spiritual need. "We must be saved from ourselves by very unpleasant things, and have no choice whether it shall by toothache or living on other people's means," he had instructed Louisa.[8] He was convinced that adversities in life kept him from pride or from thinking more highly of himself than he ought to think. A person must deny the self as the ruling center of his life, in order that he may live in an outgoing love. The ubiquity of this insistence in his many writings attests to the strength with which he continuously held the conviction. His many adversities through the 1850s help account for the pervading presence of this theme in *Phantastes*.

Given the difficulty people seemed to have in understanding his published poetry, MacDonald decided to try a different genre. He would write a fantastic tale in the tradition of the German fantasy writers. He thought he might attract a larger audience with such fiction, given its recent popularity. Carlyle's translations of German fantasies were popular, both Dickens and Thackeray had been successful in publishing Christmas fantasies, and Andersen's fairy tales were presently receiving considerable attention.[9] Loving literary fantasies himself, he undertook the task with zest, completing it in two months. "I am writing a kind of fairy-tale, in the hope it will pay me better than the more evidently serious works. This is in prose," he told his father. "I had hoped that I should have it ready by Christmas, but I was too ill to do it. I don't know myself what it will be worth yet—It is all I am able for just at present."[10] *Phantastes* readily manifests the influence of the German fantasy writers, especially Novalis and Hoffman. In terms of literary worth, it stands as one of his more enduring and provocative achievements.[11]

It occurred to him that the imaginative realm of Faerie offered an excellent metaphor for the world of spiritual realities. MacDonald felt his recent experiences had afforded him many insights into this higher world, a realm in which too few people had traveled very far. He was convinced that the world any person inhabits is that person's mind turned inside out; that is, a person sees the world according to his personality and background. Each person sees it differently; only the person who has achieved a certain level of sensibility sees its spiritual realities (that is, in terms of the metaphor, is able to see and enter fairyland). But discerning spiritual principles is not enough; a person must incarnate them. The archetypal image of a journey or a quest, therefore, which is a staple image in fairy literature, offered a ready metaphor for spiritual becoming. The questor matures as he journeys from experience to experience.

Phantastes offers a helpful reading of MacDonald's personality and the state of his thinking during this period. Anodos, the hero of the fantasy, is a thinly disguised projection of MacDonald's character, with its keen sensitivities, its intellectual curiosities, and its persistent childlike affirmation of the mysterious everywhere. His hero's name, *Anodos,* is a transliteration of a Greek term that can mean either "having no way" or "rising." In the tale Anodos has a series of adventures in the realm of Faerie which at first may seem to be random but which nevertheless issue in discoveries of deep truths that pertain to the spirit of man.[12] MacDonald had in mind his own seemingly random experiences of the last four years, which had issued in his deeper knowledge of the human spirit.

Anodos's spiritual growth derives from his imaginative perceptions achieved in Faerie, but this is not a realm alien to our world. Faerie is like a "marvelous mirror" held up to this life: In it otherwise ordinary things readily appear marvelous as they emit their spiritual reality. MacDonald's intention is to help the reader see the spiritual dimensions of this world. Much of the power of the tale derives from MacDonald's experiences; they reflect the aura of his deeply felt struggles and consequent spiritual insights.

The discoveries are not rational so much as intuitive. They are confirmed to Anodos by a wise mother figure who lives in a cottage in the middle of Faerie. He finds her cottage only after he has come utterly to the end of himself in a dreary wasteland beside a desolate sea, where he determines to die: " 'I will not be tortured to death,' I cried; 'I will meet it half-way. The life within me is yet enough to bear me up to the face of Death, and then I die unconquered.' " The basic spiritual imperative is that one must die into life.

Plunging in, he is to his amazement seized with overwhelming delight: "A blessing, like the kiss of a mother, seemed to alight on my soul; a calm, deeper than that which accompanies a hope deferred, bathed my spirit." Willingly dying to the self issues in life on a higher plain. Prior to this experience, Anodos had learned much in his various adventures concerning how nature and art minister to the spiritual development of persons, but it is only after he has abandoned the life of questing for self-satisfaction that he begins to experience life on a yet higher plain.

In the square cottage of the wise old mother, the Spirit of the Earth, Anodos moves through four doors respectively, one on each side, coming thereby into four different worlds. Each suggests some aspect of MacDonald's life: his childhood, his spiritual struggles and sense of failure, his dismay at his personal errors and gropings, and the folly of his rashness. After each experience the kindly earth mother sings him a song. These clinch the basic themes of the fantasy: behind the enigmas of life lies a benevolent Providence; wisdom is to forget the self, die into life, and live in an outgoing love for others.

The old earth mother assures Anodos that " 'In whatever sorrow you may be, however inconsolable and irremediable it may appear, believe me that the old woman in the cottage . . . knows something, though she must not always tell it, that would quite satisfy you about it, even in the worst moments of your distress." Then she sends him on his way with the commission: "Go, my son, and do something worth doing." A person's life is defined in terms of his deeds, not simply his perceptions. What the mind discerns must become incarnated in the life in order for it to acquire true moral worth.

Anodos goes forth to do good. The fantasy closes with his affirming the ultimate confidence he has acquired, the adventures of Faerie behind him:

> Yet I know that good is coming to me—that good is always coming; though few have at all times the simplicity and courage to believe it. What we call evil, is the only and best shape, which, for the person and his condition at the time, could be assumed by the best good.

Anodos possesses this truth intuitively not rationally; perhaps the chief danger he faced throughout his travels was succumbing to his Shadow, which symbolizes the cynicism that arises from a crassly rational approach to life.

The somber, self-denying aspect of MacDonald's convictions by no means canceled out his love of experience and his delight in all the simple aspects of life. To him self-denial was not life-denying but rather self-forgeting. Self-denial was the only means of coming into a realization, through the accompanying spiritual freedom, of the preciousness of life. In spite of his besetting poverty, ill health, general uncertainty concerning the future, and periods of deep depression, MacDonald saw life at its heart as thoroughly good and right.

It is in part because this optimism was not confirmed in experience by the surface appearance of things that his love of Faerie, or dreamland, was so strong. Faerie was a world in which he could contemplate what he felt was the true nature of the universe that in God's grace will yet be made manifest.

> The hues of dreamland, strange and sweet and tender,
> Are but hint-shadows of full many a splendour
> Which the high Parent-love will yet unroll
> Before his child's obedient, humble soul.
> Ah, me, my God! in thee lies every bliss
> Whose shadow men go hunting wearily amiss.[13]

This vibrant hope sprung from his faith, and he consciously tried not to impose it on life from outside. Rather he saw this hope as arising intrinsically out of the heart of things. In the passage quoted earlier, Anodos hears in the sound of rustling leaves of an ancient beech tree the assurance that a great good is constantly coming to him. One of the basic lessons Anodos had learned in his dying was that his passions were not thereby canceled but transformed to reveal the "glory and wonderment" in them. Both life and human nature at their core are wonderfully good and should be joyously affirmed.

Early in 1858, MacDonald delivered *Phantastes* to Smith and

Elder Publishers, and, to his delight, he received within two days a cheque for fifty pounds for the copyright. As he and Louisa assessed their situation things now looked more promising. They were in a commodious home, more securely situated than they had been since they had left Arundel. Although he could not be confident about his health, he was considerably better than before they had gone to Algiers. In spite of the fact that he was not well-known in this vicinity, his writing and lecturing soon consumed all his time, and he was able to maintain his family. As a promising young author his reputation was steadily growing.

Their growing family was a continuous source of delight. Their household was firmly disciplined, and their lives extremely well ordered. Although children in the nineteenth century led more regimented lives than children in general do today, they were nevertheless allowed to develop more fully in a child's world, freed from today's mechanisms and gadgetry. The MacDonalds' children, raised as they were with a firsthand relation to Faerie, felt the imaginative delight and sense of awe that such an orientation infused into their real world. Imaginative freedom served as a counterbalance to the strict discipline the parents maintained.

Without warning, however, early in February 1858, their family tranquility was shattered. News came that John was far from well. An inept doctor in Nottingham was doing him no good; his condition was rapidly deteriorating. In early spring he came to Hastings, weak, without appetite, coughing, and seized periodically with excruciating pain in the chest. Deeply alarmed, George and Louisa did all they could to get him to take nourishment: "He has been having rich gravy soup since he came, almost every day. . . . I hope he will eat a bit of pigeon," MacDonald wrote their anxious father.[14]

They consulted a doctor friend in Hastings, R. Hale, a homeopath, who discovered that John's left lung was diseased. He prescribed absolute rest for "eight or ten months." Hale insisted that he attend him as MacDonald's friend and charged nothing for his steady service.

The MacDonalds accepted their obligation to John with diligence, determined to do everything humanly possible to turn the course of the disease. Yet MacDonald quietly looked the dreaded end in the face. He wrote to Mrs. Scott in May, "I can hardly say whether John is better or not. I fear the disease spreads. He may be able to go to Scotland, but I doubt much if he will get through the winter."[15]

Meanwhile, Charles had returned from Australia and came immediately to Hastings to be with his brothers. George thought for a time he was a chastened and humbled man, but he soon saw that the old dreams of great affluence remained.

In each letter to his father MacDonald sought to ease his anguish: "I trust, my dearest Father, you will do about John as you did about me—just leave it to the Father of Fathers. If you are sure that one day you will say—I would not have it otherwise—let faith antedate the testimony, and say it now."[16] John's condition seemed to stabilize in May, and he determined to return to Huntly as soon as he could risk the journey. MacDonald philosophized to his father, discerning the will of God in their situation:

> How easy it would be for God to help us out of all these external difficulties—but it is not so easy to make us good. For that he suffers and we must bear some part of the suffering. His will be done. If he make your sons after (it may be) a long time, good men, you will be satisfied that none of them had the success which on many accounts would be desirable.[17]

Determined to return to Huntly, John went to London with MacDonald in June and sailed from there to Aberdeen, then traveled on to home. His condition deteriorated rapidly. He died July 7, aged twenty-eight, and his body was laid beside Alec's and Bella's in Drumblade churchyard.

John was no sooner buried than the grieving father, walking on his farm at dusk, had a vision of John hurrying by and bidding him to follow. He tried to do so, but with his wooden leg he was unable to keep up. The apparition of John disappeared around a bend as the road went toward the moor. Bewildered, he returned to his home. Although at the time he appeared to be in sound health, he was on August 24 seized with a heart attack, and within a few hours his spirit departed. The Celts have a strong tradition concerning second sight, in which an individual sees into the future and often his own death; this would appear to be an instance of it. The family, not given to expecting unusual supernatural manifestations, took it for such.

In the elder MacDonald's last letter to his son, written three days before his death, he commented on both George's brothers. Although he did attempt some humor to lighten George's spirits, his lingering grief over John's death rested heavily on him. He detailed the clothes left in John's wardrobe that the family was sending off to George, having taken great pains to clean each item so that no possibility of any tubercular disease remained. Of Charles, now back in Manchester and planning a return to Sidney, he wrote: "I have never had a cheque from him. . . . I have done him good once and again in my small way but he never showed the least disposition to return it." Then his mind fixed on his departed daughter: "This is the anniversary of dear Bella's death three years ago. O how much I have gone through in suffering in one way or another during the past three years and her death heavy very heavy as it was upon me was not the heaviest of my trials—Yet hitherto God has supported."[18] The final confidence provides a fitting summary judgment on his life. Three days later the MacDonalds received the telegram: "Your father after fourteen hours sickness died today at noon you will hear further by post." The two remaining sons rushed to Huntly. They buried their father beside his departed children in the churchyard of Drumblade on August 31.

SIXTEEN

Wish I Could

He was dead.—Yet his name will stand as the name of my story for pages to come; because, if he had not been in it, the story would never have been worth writing; because the influence of that ploughman is the salt of the whole; because a man's life in the earth is not to be measured by the time he is visible upon it; and because, when the story is wound up, it will be in the presence of his spirit.—David Elginbrod

Although MacDonald felt deeply the loss of his father—their relationship had been an unusually close and intimate one—he was not emotionally devastated. Theologically, MacDonald had become convinced of the essential spiritual importance of fatherhood, and he formed this conviction in part from the caliber of spiritual strength and fortitude he as an adult observed in his father's life.

As a child he had felt this bulwark of strength but had not understood it; as an adult he had taken its measure and found not a shallow piety sustained by sentimental cliches but something deep and awesome, to him unspeakably beautiful. He expressed his appreciation in the two poems to his father with which he dedicated his 1857 volume of poems.

> Thou hast been faithful to my highest need;
> And I, thy debtor, ever, evermore,
> Shall never feel the grateful burden sore.
> Yet most I thank thee, not for any deed,
> But for the sense thy living self did breed
> Of fatherhood still at the great world's core.

. . . I beheld my God, in childhood's morn,
A mist, a darkness, great, and far apart,
Moveless and dim—I scarce could say Thou art:
My manhood came, of joy and sadness born;—
Full soon the misty dark, asunder torn,
Revealed man's glory, God's great human heart.

MacDonald's perceptions anticipate what would be generally affirmed today: that a person transfers his experiences with his earthly father to the divine one. Because he saw his father as greatly admirable, he reasoned that the Divine Father could hardly be less so. Such thinking helped him to dismiss an image that he saw many of his fellow Scots entertaining: God as wrathful tyrant. It did not, however, lead him to minimize God's wrath (as do many who emphasize the Fatherhood of God), but rather to understand it as entirely corrective, never vindictive.

Returning to Hastings after his father's funeral, he tried to look the future solidly in the face. The climate on the southern coast had worked some improvement on his health, although he had to confront the reality that he would never be strong. Pastoral work was unthinkable, both because it put too large demands on his weak constitution, and because being in a position subservient to people who might oppose him capriciously was too irksome. He could lecture, and he could write. Lectures depended on his attracting sufficiently large audiences to make them pay; writing depended on his finding a genre that would sell. He was determined to support himself and his growing family or die trying. A sixth child, Winifred Louisa, was born November 6, 1858.

Lecturing began to bring in some much-needed money. During 1859 he was able to arrange, in part through the good offices of his providential patroness, Lady Byron, a series of lectures in London at the London Institution. His contacts in Manchester enabled him to arouse sufficient interest in a series there in the Royal Institution. His growing reputation also opened an opportunity to give several lectures in Scotland during that summer. He stayed in Edinburgh, with his uncle Alexander McColl, whom he admired greatly as a scholarly man, and went out from there to such places as Arbroath north along the coast.

As to his writing he searched for a medium through which he could express most effectively his convictions on the nature and importance of the Divine Fatherhood. *Phantastes* was, in the eyes of the critics, a colossal failure. The *Athenaeum* had run a highly deprecatory review, affirming that every author is permitted one mistake, and MacDonald had made his. "He seems to have lost all hold of reality," the confused critic judged and lectured on how a successful allegorist should "thrust the very handle of his meaning into your hand." He could see no meaning in *Phantastes*. "Mr. MacDonald has given us the shadow without the life which should cause it to him and account for it to us. Thus 'Phantastes' is a riddle that will not be read." It was, he concluded, a "confusedly furnished second-hand symbol shop."[1] MacDonald was crestfallen. If he were to continue to write, he must choose another genre. Given the continued success of *Within and Without*, he decided to undertake a second drama. This one would not be a closet drama in verse but rather one in prose, fitted for the stage.

Early in the summer of 1859, he set about his task. MacDonald's stepmother, whom he had been persuading for some time to pay them a visit, came to Hastings. After her brief stay he returned with her to Huntly, while Louisa and the children remained at Hastings. MacDonald took with him the beginnings of a manuscript of his new drama, intending to concentrate on it as much as was possible. In writing his daily letter to Louisa from Huntly, he commented: "I am very tired, dearest Louie, and must go to bed. I shall be at work at my play tomorrow I hope. Perhaps I have been sent here that I may write a good one, by having nothing at all to take me from it. But I feel it is difficult. I never felt this so much with anything else I have tried."[2]

He titled it *If I Had a Father*. Set in London, the plot concerns the quests of two fathers who are searching for their lost children and the experiences of the two children who have been separated from their respective parents by circumstance and who sorely need to be reunited with them. The play concludes with the expected reunions.

The plot is embarrassingly melodramatic, but the play is nevertheless sustained by firm and vivid character portrayal. This is due in part to MacDonald's realistic rendition of the dialects of the English lower classes. His ear for dialectical distinctions and his ability to capture their authentic flavor in print help make the dialogue live. In attempting realistic conversation he was making an interesting step in the direction of his later novels. Whether or not he seriously aspired at this time that his drama would actually be presented on stage, he entertained strong hopes that Smith, Elder, & Company would publish it as they had *Phantastes*.

Much to MacDonald's disappointment, however, they promptly turned it down as "useless." They wanted novels. "According to Smith, Elder, nothing is any use but a novel. Smith says if I would, I should have the publishers saving up their money to buy it! Of course that is nonsense, but it meant something. Isn't it a pity I can't. Wish I could," he wrote Louisa.[3]

Part of the reason the publishers were not willing to risk publishing his play was no doubt the cool response they were getting to *Phantastes*. Initial sales had been promising, but they soon fell off. Interest in published plays that had not been produced was minimal. Since George Murray Smith had no evidence that this play was producible, he declined it.

The words of Smith, however, remained in MacDonald's mind. He first thought that the writing of a novel was a task far beyond his abilities. But in April 1859, while staying in London at Lady Byron's during his lecture series, he decided to be bold and try. He turned the plot of *If I Had a Father* into a novel, which he titled *Seekers and Finders*. The transformation was a long and laborious task, and the finished product gave abundant testimony to all prospective publishers that the author had found it to be just that. After many rejections MacDonald finally set the manuscript aside, and it was never published. Many years later his sons Greville and Ronald came upon the manuscript among their father's things and considered whether they should try again. They decided the would-be publishers were right and destroyed it.[4]

Whatever talent MacDonald had as a novelist (and it may be argued it is in some respects considerable[5]), it was developed with much effort. His first attempt in the genre was too like an illustrated sermon for even his closest admirers. He had, however, a strong love of pure story, especially of story that presented the "marvelous," by which he meant some spiritual manifestation. He believed deeply, along with such religious teachers as Swedenborg and Blake, as well as with the German Romantics, that every aspect of the physical world and of human experience is an expression of spiritual reality and takes its form to express spiritual truth.

MacDonald was preoccupied with helping his readers to discern these spiritual realities. But because he felt these truths must be abstracted for the uninitiated—that is, they were not obvious and must be interpreted—commentary seemed unavoidable. The literary conventions of the day sanctioned authorial comment in the novel, and MacDonald did acquire the ability to express in an artistically acceptable manner his Christian meditations on his characters' actions. Indeed, such portions are, to anyone who is at all sympathetic with his views, the chief attraction and strength of the novels. But to a preacher, to comment is to preach, and preaching turns a story, no matter how well told, into an illustration for a sermon.

Sensing this dilemma and attempting to free himself, he undertook to tell a different type of story, simply for its own sake. He titled it *The Portent* and successfully placed it with the newly formed *Cornhill Magazine*. The novelist William Makepeace Thackeray, whom MacDonald met in May at a publisher's dinner given by George Smith, was the editor in 1859. *The Portent* appeared serially in the May, June, and July 1860 issues. Louisa was dismayed that the narrating voice did not attempt to tell the reader what to see in the story, but MacDonald insisted that the story had its integrity. While his effort did not especially please his wife, it did demonstrate to his contemporaries less interested in Christian ideas than he that he possessed an ability to tell a story unencumbered.

In a short dedication to his stepmother's uncle, Duncan McColl, he asserted with something of an air of apology: ". . . there ought to be a place for any story, which, although founded in the marvelous, is true to human nature and to itself." The "marvelous" in this story concerns the Celtic belief in second sight, and the plot is built around the occurrence of this spiritual phenomenon. It is the sort of thing that would naturally attract MacDonald's attention; the fact that it had seemingly so recently occurred in his father's experience enhanced its interest for him. After the story was well received as a serial in the *Cornhill Magazine*, Smith, Elder & Company brought it out as a novel in 1864.

MacDonald was then, by the end of the decade, decidedly more an author and lecturer on English literature than a Congregationalist minister. As his reputation as a writer grew he was more and more in demand as a lecturer to lay audiences. In July 1859, when an opening occurred at Bedford College, London, he applied and secured the Chair of English Literature.

Still living at Hastings, he again had to board with friends in London—this time with Alexander Munro, the sculptor—while he undertook his first series of lectures at Bedford College in the fall. He continued teaching there until 1867, earning from thirty to fifty guineas annually.[6] Now that he was no longer financially desperate, he refused for the remainder of his life to take remuneration for his preaching engagements. Before his father's death, he had asked him please to remove the "Rev." designation from his name. He no longer saw himself as a professional minister.

Encouraged by the warm reception his native Scots had given his lectures earlier in 1859, he returned to Edinburgh for another lecture series in mid-winter. Writing from Edinburgh to Louisa, he remarked: "The meeting was not large owing to the wet weather, but there were 600 perhaps."[7] That he was now drawing crowds of that size gives some indication of his growing popularity on the lecture circuit.

MacDonald was lecturing on English literature before it was being widely taught as a subject in the mainline colleges and universities. It was appearing as a subject of study in colleges such as Bedford, whose evening classes were designed to appeal to working men and women who wanted to improve their minds. People of the rising middle class were becoming increasingly interested in receiving instruction in the liberal arts, and the study of literature, not generally considered too demanding a pursuit, was felt to be nicely suited for the purpose. Early public lecturers on literature tended to emphasize the moral values the discipline offered.

Typically, these lectures attempted an overview of the poet's life and writings, drawing such connections as were apparent between the experiences of the poet's life and the themes of his works. MacDonald lectured on a wide range of poets. On April 23, 1860, he lectured on Hamlet at the Assembly Rooms, St. Leonard's. Very probably he was also lecturing during this time on Wordsworth and Coleridge, as well as on prominent poets of the English Renaissance. Later, when he was touring the United States, he regularly spoke on such figures as Robert Burns, Thomas Hood, and Shakespeare. In the summer of 1859, he submitted an article on the poet Shelley, which grew out of his lectures, for the 1860 edition of the *Encyclopedia Britannica*.

In his lectures MacDonald exercised a breadth of sympathy and depth of appreciation that sometimes took exception to generally held views. For instance, his lecture on Shelley closes with the following summary:

> Few men have been more misunderstood or misrepresented than Shelley. Doubtless this has in part been his own fault, as Coleridge implies, when he writes to this effect of him: that his horror of hypocrisy made him speak in such a wild way, that Southey (who was so much a man of forms and proprieties) was quite misled, not merely in his estimate of his worth, but in his judgment of his character. But setting aside this con-

sideration altogether, and regarding him merely as a poet, Shelley has written verse which will last as long as the English literature lasts; valuable not only from its excellence, but from the peculiarity of its excellence. To say nothing of his noble aims and hopes, Shelley will always be admired for his sweet melodies, lovely pictures, and wild prophetic imaginings. His indignant remonstrances, intermingled with grand imprecations, burst in thunder from a heart overcharged with the love of his kind, and roused to a keener sense of all oppression by the wrongs which sought to overwhelm himself.[8]

Robert Southey had castigated Shelley (together with Byron) as a member of the "Satanic" school of poetry. His assessment had been a widely accepted one; MacDonald was bold to attempt a public reassessment.

With MacDonald's growing reputation and his health now seemingly stabilized, the family decided to chance moving to London. The metropolis offered many more opportunities to attract lecture audiences. Lady Byron had long urged the wisdom of their living in London if MacDonald's health would permit it; now she was zealous in finding them a home. Convinced that she had one in hand, the MacDonalds relinquished Huntly Cottage and prepared to move, only to discover the arrangements in London aborted. Caught momentarily in an awkward situation, they were forced to take temporary quarters that Greville Matheson had found—somewhat beyond their means to afford—at 18 Queen Square, Bloomsbury. They moved from Hastings in late November 1859.

Despite Lady Byron's failing health she continued to do all she could for the MacDonalds. Her home was at 11 St. George's Terrace, in the fashionable area of Regent's Park. After they took up residence in London she would send her carriage for them to dine with her, confide some of her past with Lord Byron to them (she was normally quite reticent on the subject), and look to MacDonald for spiritual advice.

Frequent visits in her home opened to MacDonald an entrance into the literary and intellectual world of London. Henry Crabb Robinson, whose voluminous *Diary* gives an intriguing picture of the lives of nineteenth-century literati, met MacDonald at Lady Byron's on April 16; he depicts him as "an invalid, and a German scholar."[9] When Robinson died in 1867, he left MacDonald a generous legacy.

Lady Byron introduced MacDonald to several others, among them Mrs. La Touche (through whom he shortly came to know John Ruskin), Mrs. Margaret Oliphant, Charles Kingsley, Matthew Arnold, and Mrs. Reid (patroness of Bedford College). MacDonald, however, was not generally socially gregarious. He despised the masks people tended to assume in public gatherings, nor would he make any attempt to assume one himself. The presence of others in a crowded room sometimes pressed on him to nausea. Neither he nor Louisa had aspirations toward "high society." When occasions demanded, however, he could be a lively conversationalist. Mark Twain, in his *Autobiography*, classified him among "lively talkers" when he observed him at a social gathering.[10] MacDonald took a large-hearted interest in people whom he felt were spiritually sensitive and genuine, and some of his friendships were intensifying at this time. One was with Russell Gurney, the Recorder of London; another was with Frederick Denison Maurice, who was then rector of the Chapel of St. Peter's, on Vere Street. Maurice had introduced MacDonald to George Murray Smith, when he was searching for a publisher for *Phantastes* and was taking an active interest in MacDonald's emerging career.

But the closest friendship of this period was with Charles L. Dodgson, who, under the penname Lewis Carroll, would publish *Alice's Adventures in Wonderland* in 1865. He and MacDonald, perhaps the two most famous writers of children's literature of the century, had met in Hastings. Dodgson, who was lecturer in mathematics at Christ Church, Oxford, had a pronounced stuttering problem about which he had consulted James Hunt, a philologist and friend of R. Hale, the Hastings homeopath who was MacDonald's doctor. Hunt and Hale must have discussed their patients and felt they should know each other, because Hale promptly introduced the two at Hunt's house in Ore in 1859.[11] The relationship that followed soon became intimate; Dodgson began visiting so often that he was looked on as one of the family. He took pleasure in entertaining the MacDonald children with his acrostics, word games, puzzles, and fantastic stories, and was charmed with the intensity of their delight in his imagined world.

MacDonald's children figured in still another significant acquaintance with the artist Alexander Munro. He was commissioned to do a statue in Hyde Park and, deciding on a depiction of a boy on a dolphin, enlisted the four-year-old Greville as his model. Also, inspired by the appearance of MacDonald's long, black hair in the wind, he did a bronze medallion of him. One replica is today in the Scottish National Portrait Gallery in Edinburgh, and a second is in King's College, Aberdeen. Through Munro, MacDonald soon came to know several of the painters associated with the Pre-Raphaelite Brotherhood, such as the brothers Dante Gabriel and William Michael Rossetti, Ford Madox Brown, and Arthur Hughes. Hughes would do many vivid and compelling illustrations for MacDonald's works.

When Lady Byron, after an extended period of failing health, died in May 1860, MacDonald lost a close friend and benefactor. His tributes to her show how deeply he appreciated her largess. He dedicated his first published novel, *David Elginbrod*, to her "with a love stronger than death" and made her the model for the character of Lady Bernard in a later novel, *The Vicar's Daughter*.

Louisa was fond of relating later how, sometime following Lady Byron's death, she was out shopping one rainy afternoon and lost her purse on a bus. The family as a consequence found themselves completely without money and had almost no food in the house. They gathered in the drawing room and prayed for help. No sooner had they done so than they heard the postman's knock and, retrieving the letter, they found to their pleasure a check for three hundred pounds, an unexpected legacy from Lady Byron's estate.[12]

By this time they were living at Tudor Lodge, on Albert Street on the east side of Regent's Park. Regent's, with its innumerable flowerbeds of riotous color, expansive rose gardens, and wide, bench-lined walkways, is one of the most beautiful and spacious of London's many parks, a place the entire family often enjoyed. A smallish house of curiously different styling from the customary procession of more Georgian apartment facades that abut the street in typical London fashion, Tudor Lodge did possess a larger room adaptable for MacDonald's lecturing, had a garden for the children, and was more affordable than their quarters on Queen's Street.

Most assuredly it was Tudor Lodge MacDonald had in mind when he wrote in *The Vicar's Daughter:*

> I was surprised at the prettiness of the little house when I stepped out of the cab and looked about me. It was stuck on like a swallow's nest to the end of a great row of commonplace houses, nearly a quarter of a mile in length, but itself was not the work of one of those wretched builders who care no more for beauty in what they build than a scavenger in the heap of mud he scrapes from the street. It had been built by a painter for himself—in the Tudor style.

Although Tudor Lodge was somewhat small for their already large family, they found room for MacDonald's sister Louie to live with them. Her brother's position at Bedford College had opened to her the opportunity of attending there. The possibility was one of the first thoughts that had crossed MacDonald's mind when he first applied for the position; judging from his many references to it in the correspondence with his mother, everyone felt it was a significant opportunity. Securing the twenty-pound tuition fee seemed an insurmountable barrier to Louie's enrolling until Mac-Donald shared his plight with Mrs. Reid, "a widow lady with plenty of money and no children, who does more to support the Bedford Square College . . . than anyone else. . . . She offered at once to pay them [the college fees] and said she would love me for ever if I would let her do it."[13]

MacDonald's health was now sufficiently improved for him to sustain a demanding schedule. "I am better than I have been at this season for many years," he wrote his stepmother during their first winter back in London. "London, fogs and all, agrees with me better than any other place I know."[14] On another occasion he remarked: "I am much better and stronger. I really think I am growing stronger by degrees."[15] He went on to say that he attributed the improvement to his taking a bath each morning as cold as he could stand it. The invigorating effect of submersing in cold water helped his periods of depression and lethargy as well, for he was seized at times with a seeming mental paralysis in which, as he occasionally remarked to Louisa, he felt so "stupid" that he could not think. Not that he was now free from annoying physical difficulties—he never was—but they were not severe enough to be life threatening: asthma attacks, bronchial trouble, and "faceaches," by which he must have meant migraine attacks. But he was now able physically to support his family without doles from relatives and friends. His spirits were appreciably lighter.

And their family continued to grow. A second son, Ronald, was born October 27, 1860, at Tudor Lodge. For all his seriousness and earnestness MacDonald greatly enjoyed his family. He delighted to enter into their games and entertain them with stories, both realistic and fantastic. Participating in their lives was not a dutiful task but rather a natural delight. In his complex nature he loved the logic of children, their sense of wonder, their ability to see the mysterious in the commonplace, and their delight in the imaginative. The household rang with laughter when he entered into their games, sometimes on all fours donning a bearskin rug to play the part of a growling beast and sometimes wrestling with them on the floor.

Nor did his love of games stop with such romps. He was fond of whist, the Victorian forerunner of bridge. He and Louisa attended whist parties, and sponsored them in their home. Perhaps his favorite activity was riding horses; his novels readily attest to this love. He participated in at least one fox hunt while visiting an uncle of Louisa's in Wellingborough in the fall of 1863.

During the spring of 1862 Louisa was at Hastings for a time, nursing her youngest sister Caroline, ill with rheumatic fever. MacDonald's letters to her give some further depictions of family life: "Lily has been writing your exercise. But I think Elfie was hardly able. She carries her head on one side very funnily poor pet. Lily is just a little mother to them all—seeming to think of every one before herself."[16] Lily, then ten years old, seems to have carefully imbibed her father's teachings. She was becoming in a sense the center of the family, not simply because she was their firstborn but because the other children looked up to her, and the parents saw in her a compelling sensitivity to their concerns. Once when the family larder was especially low, she pretended she was not hungry that the other children might eat.

MacDonald delighted in overhearing their conversations. "The children are very good indeed. Gracie most amusing in conversation with the rest. She was proving the superiority of her spoon both in material and manufacture over those at the lodgings, but saying how she would part with it for you, as you were very poor. They brought it in that you wanted a bonnet very much. This was amongst themselves. I generally listen in silence."[17] He apparently found little difficulty in managing the household while Louisa was away. The Spartan character of their lives seems to have fostered a sense of fellow concern each for the other and even the chidren for their parents. Their poverty and frugality did not seem to make for covetousness and acquisitiveness, something we today might expect.

Some of MacDonald's finest fairy tales, such as "The Giant's Heart" and "The Light Princess," grew out of this period. He composed them for the delight of his children, who would gather around him on the floor to hear him recite. But he took the genre very seriously, believing that a good story should have an imaginative reach that arouses within the hearer a sense of wonder, so that he feels he has momentarily caught a glimpse of the eternal world. "I read Ulf and several other stories," he wrote to Louisa from one of his lecture tours, explaining how he was passing his time. "They are all translations and very bad ones. But as stories they just want the one central spot of red—the wonderful thing which whether in a fairy story or a world or a human being is the life—depth—whether of truth or humour or pathos—the eye to the face of it—the thing that shows the unshowable."[18] Having such an imaginative encounter gives as much pleasure to the adult mind as to the child's.

Inasmuch as many of MacDonald's fairy tales embody themes and contain symbolic patterns that engage the adult mind, rising to the level of myth, on occasion he would deliver one as a lecture to an adult audience in the front room of Tudor Lodge. The first publication of his fairy tales is in the novel *Adela Cathcart,* a work calculated for an adult audience, which appeared in 1864.

During the early 1860s Charles Dodgson, who found a similar delight in imaginatively participating in a child's world, became so much a part of the family they knew him as "Uncle Dodgson." He was, among his many pursuits, a photographer; he took some of the more frequently seen photographs of MacDonald and the family during this period. In 1863 he recorded in his diary that he had taken pictures of all the MacDonalds.[19] A retiring, nimble-minded man, he took great delight in exposing for the hilarity of children the conventions of the adult world as well as in simply contriving fantastic stories. He was adept at drawing caricatures, to the delight of MacDonald as well as his own children. One of several of his letters to Mary (apparently his favorite among the children, perhaps because of her delicate nature) communicates vividly the character of their fun. On November 14, 1864 he wrote:

My dear Mary,

Once upon a time there was a little girl, and she had a cross old Uncle—his neighbours called him a Curmudgeon (whatever that may mean)—and this little girl had promised to copy out for him a sonnet Mr. Rossetti had written about Shakespeare. Well, and she didn't do it, you know, and the poor old Uncle's nose kept getting longer and longer, and his temper getting shorter and shorter, and post after post went by, and no sonnet came—

I leave off here to explain how they sent letters in those days: there were no gates, so the gate-posts weren't obliged to stay in one place—consequence of which, they went wandering all over the country—consequence of which, if you wanted to send a letter anywhere, all you had to do was to fasten it on to a gate-post that was going in the proper direction—(only they sometimes changed their minds, which was awkward)—This was called "sending a letter by the post."

They did things very simply in those days: if you had a lot of money, you just dug a hole under the hedge, and popped it in. Then you said you had "put it in the bank," and you felt quite comfortable about it. And the way they travelled was— there were railings all along the side of the road, and they used to get up, and walk along the top, as steadily as they could, till they tumbled off—which they mostly did very soon. This was called "travelling by rail."

Now to return to the wicked little girl. The end of her was, that a great black WOLF came, and _____. I don't like to go on, but nothing was found of her afterwards, except 3 small bones. I make no remark. It is rather a horrid story.

> *Your loving friend,*
> *C. Dodgson*

One day Dodgson appeared at Tudor Lodge with a large manuscript under his arm, rendered by hand in impeccable calligraphy, complete with pages of meticulously wrought draw-ings. It was entitled *Alice's Adventures Under Ground*. He asked MacDonald to read it and render an opinion when he had the time. After reading it MacDonald suggested that Louisa read it to the children and gauge their reactions. The children were wildly enthusiastic. Greville, then six years of age, loudly proclaimed there should be sixty thousand copies of the work. Dodgson was emboldened to find a publisher. The result was *Alice's Adventures in Wonderland*, which appeared in 1865.

SEVENTEEN

Doing It Better

All a man has to do, is to better what he can.—Phantastes

Unable to interest any publisher in either his first attempt at a novel, *Seekers and Finders,* or his drama *If I Had a Father,* MacDonald was feeling unsure of himself as a writer. Yet the compulsion to write persisted. "I must try to write again—that is the only thing. But I don't feel very capable of it," he confided to Louisa in 1862.[1] His now heavy lecture schedule, tutoring, and also their frequent moving, had kept him busy, but he determined to make yet another attempt.

The possibilities for effective ministry that the novel offered remained on his mind. The success George Eliot was enjoying with her early novels that included clerical characters, such as *Adam Bede* (1859), encouraged him, and he thoroughly enjoyed her style. "I hope you enjoy *Silas Marner,*" he told Louisa soon after the appearance of this slight novel in 1861, judging it to be the best she had written so far.[2]

The frequent moralizing observations that Eliot makes on her characters' behavior must have suggested to him that, despite the failure of his first novel, it should be possible for him to present in an artistically acceptable manner a story focused on the behavior of people contemplated in terms of their being spiritual beings with eternal destinies. This was his compelling motivation.

He was further encouraged by a seemingly chance occurrence at one of the literary dinners sponsored by his publisher, George Murray Smith. Seated among the literati of the day, he overheard the journalist Manby Smith tell of reading a Scottish epitaph:

Here lie I, Martin Elginbrodde;
Hae mercy o' my soul, Lord God;
As I wad do, were I Lord God,
An' ye war Martin Elginbrodde![3]

MacDonald was struck immediately by the compelling logic and the pathos of this very human cry of the soul. Its theological implications answered to what he had long been feeling deeply. Prevalent current teachings on the nature of God tended to present him as arbitrary and begrudging in the exercise of his mercy, a being less compassionate than most people; such could not possibly be a true picture of God. People having been made in God's image, the deepest longings and highest hopes of the human heart must reflect the actions and attitudes of God.

The possibilities for a story were forming in his mind while the family made still another move. Tudor Lodge had become too small for their growing family. Louisa was again pregnant, and they speculated that dust from the clay in the yard might be aggravating MacDonald's asthma. In the late summer of 1862 they located somewhat larger quarters in the more fashionable district of Kensington, at 12 Earles Terrace, and prepared to move. A characteristic London dwelling with the facade directly abutting the street, it stood just off the bustle of Kensington High Street, affording MacDonald a better location in which to offer lectures to the general public.

Not being able himself to abide the dust occasioned by the moving and needing a change of atmosphere to help his asthma, he decided to take advantage of an invitation from one of Louisa's uncles, Mark Sharman, who lived on a farm in Nottingham, near Wellingborough, while Louisa supervised the move. Taking with him Gracie and "Goblin" (Irene), he went to enjoy a time on the farm while he furthered his writing. "Nobody could be kinder than uncle is," he wrote to Louisa[4] concerning Sharman, who met father and daughters at the train station with a dog cart and drove them to his stylish country home. "Since dinner I have been to see the horses and the pigs—both splendid—but each after his kind, as the bible says. Verily, there is one glory of horses and the other of pigs."

His stay on the farm offered him many diversions from the routine of his writing. Evenings were spent playing whist in the parlor (occasionally for trifling sums of money, the losing of which did not add to his pleasure). Out of doors was a stable of splendid riding horses, enabling him to indulge his love of riding. On at least one occasion he went fox hunting.

All the while the kernel idea implanted in his mind by the story of the Scottish epitaph was growing into *David Elginbrod,* which was to become his first successful novel. In writing it Mac-Donald drew on his true imaginative strengths. The title character, modeled on his father, analogizes the nature of the Divine Father in his relationship to humankind. He exemplifies MacDonald's preoccupation, apparent throughout the novels, to demonstrate that "the ideal is the real."

MacDonald's success in drawing Elginbrod is due in part to his ability to capture in print the distinctives of the Aberdeenshire dialect.[5] In this he is following the example of his famous Scottish novelist predecessor, Sir Walter Scott. But MacDonald tends to use his skill as a means of signaling a character's spiritual state: Those who speak pure Scots are more likely to be possessed of the virtues he recommends.[6] This skill, combined with his ability to describe natural scenes in a compellingly realistic manner—such as his description of the Scottish landscape in a snowstorm—mark MacDonald as a significant forerunner of the so-called kailyard—or cabbage patch—school of fiction, to which such later writers as J. M. Barrie belong.

To generate interest and suspense in the novel, MacDonald drew heavily on a range of Gothic elements: a ghost walk (upon which ghosts appear), secret passageways, seances, stolen rings of evil import, and the debilitating hypnotic power of Count von Funkelstein, a Bohemian mesmerist. The idea for Funkelstein arose out of MacDonald's experience. While living at Hastings, he and Greville Matheson had attended a lecture given by the popular mesmerist Zamoiski, propounder of a current theory on telepathy known as "Electrobiology." Responding to Zamoiski's challenge to any member of the audience to mount the platform and give his name, if he could, Greville went forward only to find he was suddenly unable to identify himself.[7] The incident had a deep effect on MacDonald, who was characteristically fascinated by any expression of seemingly supernatural energy. Transposing this character into his novel, MacDonald, viewing life from a Christian base, explained away what manifestations of the occult he presented, but nevertheless he used them heavily in the plot.[8]

The Christian ideal, beside being embodied in David Elginbrod, is also depicted in a fictional portrait of Frederick Denison Maurice. Shortly after the MacDonalds moved to London they began attending his services at the Chapel of St. Peter's. His appointment as vicar there was sponsored by the Office of Works, whose commissioner at that time was William Cowper, later to become Cowper-Temple, one of MacDonald's closest friends and benefactors. MacDonald was strongly attracted to Maurice's message because Maurice worked from a basic theological assumption very similar to MacDonald's, that is, a theology that does not correspond to the deepest thoughts and feelings of human beings cannot be a true one. Describing Maurice fictionally, MacDonald wrote:

> He trusts in God so absolutely, that he leaves his salvation to him—utterly, fearlessly; and forgetting it, as being no concern of his, sets himself to do the work that God has given him to do, even as his Lord did before him. . . . He believes entirely that God loves, yea, is love; and, therefore, that hell itself must be subservient to that love, and but an embodiment of it; that the grand work of Justice is to make way for a Love which will give to every man that which is right and ten times more, even if it should be by means of awful suffering.[9]

MacDonald's habit was to indulge in unrestrained hyperbole in depicting the ideal. But friends and opponents of Maurice alike attested to the quality of his Christian character. MacDonald was drawn to Maurice, as he was to A. J. Scott, because he saw each of them as standing at an infinite distance from the covert egoism existing behind the masks of humility so many Christian leaders wore. In commending Maurice's view of hell MacDonald was announcing his sympathy with Maurice in the current public controversy over its eternality. He defined his thinking on this subject in *Robert Falconer*.

David Elginbrod has an appreciable imaginative strength. It is, like the many novels to follow, a theological romance. Francis Hart observes that MacDonald's novels are at their best when they make "a movement back toward the visionary or fantastic," and in its merging of the real and the ideal this novel exemplifies the point.[10]

MacDonald submitted the novel to Smith, Elder, dedicating it to the now deceased Lady Byron "with a love stronger than death." But, to his dismay, they refused it, as did all the other publishers. Then a friend, Miss Jessie Ballantyne, visiting from Manchester, read it, was enthusiastic, and asked leave to show it to a novelist friend of hers. The novelist was Diana Maria Mulock (Mrs. Craik) of Hampstead Heath, whose religious novel *John Halifax, Gentleman* (1856) was immensely popular. Excited by what she read, Mrs. Craik took it to her publishers, the large firm of Hurst and Blackett, with the advice they were fools not to publish it. Impressed with her enthusiasm, they paid MacDonald ninety pounds and brought it out in the traditional three-volume format early in 1863.

It was immediately well received. The *Times* described it as "The work of a man of genius," and the *Athenaeum*[11] gave it a laudatory three-column review. *David Elginbrod* was destined to go through at least seven editions in MacDonald's lifetime and several more in this century.[12] In 1873 a German firm, Heydert and Zimmer of Frankfort, published a translation by Julie Sutter. The first of many American editions came out in 1879 as a volume of Munro's Seaside Library.

Henry Crabb Robinson was among the early readers who wrote MacDonald with congratulations: "I am heartily enjoying *David Elginbrod*. He is a glorious creature. Sometimes I regret that my want of familiarity with his dialect renders him not so perfectly clear to me as I wish all his words as well as doings to be."[13] John Ruskin was also among the novel's early admirers.

Ruskin was the most celebrated man of letters of the Victorian period to become a close friend of MacDonald. He had impressive stature as an art critic and philosopher with a strong bent for social reform. He first met MacDonald at Tudor Lodge. Mrs. Maria La Touche, a fashionable Irish woman who wintered in London and who admired both men, introduced them by bringing Ruskin to one of MacDonald's lectures. They had in common a background in Calvinist Christianity, a love of art, and a genuine concern for the poor.

Their most notable difference was that while MacDonald had moved toward an optimistic confidence in God as a benevolent heavenly Father, Ruskin had moved into skepticism. The relationship MacDonald had enjoyed with his father stood in contrast with Ruskin's tensions with his. Both men had the gift of being frank in their disagreements while allowing their friendship to transcend their differences. Although Ruskin demurred from a commitment to MacDonald's faith, he was nevertheless fascinated with it and looked to him for spiritual counsel.

Encouraged by the success of *David Elginbrod*, MacDonald decided to curtail his lecture tours and concentrate on story telling. Convinced of the value of story as myth, especially parable and fantasy, to minister to the needs of the human spirit, he conceived of the plot that became the novel *Adela Cathcart*. Turning from depictions of natural scenery and transcription of dialect, devices that had contributed so largely to the success of *David Elginbrod*, he chose an English setting and established a simple realistic framework for the presentation of numerous parables and fairy tales. By drawing on the popularity of the novel form, he hoped to achieve a better reception for his fantasies than he had with *Phantastes*.

The plot of *Adela Cathcart* is meager. A group of English friends are gathered at the home of Colonel Cathcart to spend the Christmas holidays. But the joy of the season is lessened by the curious illness of his adolescent daughter Adela, a malady for which the attending doctor can find no cure. As a guest the narrator suspects that her basic problem is one of the soul that must be addressed before the doctor can successfully treat the body. So he proposes that the various guests all tell a separate story each evening. The scheme works; Adela improves in soul and body.

Some of the stories that have such curative powers are among MacDonald's finest fairy tales, namely, "The Light Princess," "The Shadows," and "The Giant's Heart."[14] The others, of lesser quality, are nevertheless significant: "The Wow o'Rivven," "The Broken Swords," "The Cruel Painter," and "The Castle." A reviewer writing in the *Athenaeum,* however, was unimpressed. He suggested that MacDonald had "ransacked his desk for 'all old bits of writing he had in his possession'" and related them by a "story-telling club," an assessment that did not help sales.[15]

Among the noteworthy aspects of the novel are MacDonald's comments on the plight of women in contemporary society. Rather than simply making a plea for women's civil rights, he read their plight primarily in spiritual terms. The narrator observes concerning Adela:

> I watched everything about her; and interpreted it by what I know about women. I believe that many of them go into a consumption just from discontent. . . . The theological nourishment which is offered them is generally no better than husks. They cannot live upon it, and so die and go home to their Father. And without good spiritual food to keep the spiritual sense healthy and true, they cannot see the things about them as they really are. They cannot find interest in them, because they cannot find their *own* place amongst them.

MacDonald is inveighing against the dominant Victorian attitude that women were too delicate or frivolous in nature to adequately handle material of the same heft as men. He consistently sees them as quite as capable as men of achieving penetrating insights into the world of spiritual realities and needing such insights no less. While his handling of women characters does not in some ways vary radically from the norms of the time, he does show a dissatisfaction with the position his society allotted them, and his delineation of women and girls in the fantasies is considerably forward looking.[16]

The novel appeared on March 28, 1864, again published by Hurst and Blackett. Gratified, MacDonald sent a complimentary copy to his mentor A. J. Scott, who was in failing health. "The name of it is stupid," he observed, "but that is my publisher's fault, not mine. It is made up of almost all the short things I have written (some of which have been published before) embedded in another tale. Although slight, I don't think you will consider it careless, nor unworthy of filling a gap between the last and the next book which is on the way. I have dedicated it to Dr. Russell."[17] The "novel on the way" was *The Portent,* which had already been serialized in *The Cornhill Magazine.* It was brought out by his earlier publisher, Smith, Elder & Company, who, after seeing MacDonald's mushrooming success with *David Elginbrod,* was now willing to attempt another. John Rutherfurd Russell was a physician to the Homeopathic Hospital in London. MacDonald was convinced of the soundness of homeopathy, Russell having been a help to him.

He also remarked to Scott about his future plans: "Some day I hope to write a book good enough in my own eyes to let me ask you to allow me to dedicate it to you. I have long had one in my mind, for which I have some material ready—a life of the *Robert Falconer* who is introduced in *David Elginbrod.* For that I hope to be able to make the request." Encouraged by these successes, he was already shaping in his mind one of his finer works to come, *Robert Falconer.* "Till now I have been oppressed with work of one sort and another," he concluded. "Mrs. MacDonald is not at all strong yet. But we are going to Hastings for a little while, in the hope of her finding some strength in the breath of the sea."[18]

Louisa's weakness was occasioned by the birth on February 7, 1864, of Maurice, named after the MacDonalds' vicar. They had asked Ruskin to be godfather to their son, but he replied that he was still too much of a pagan to function in that role.[19] Maurice was asked, and he was delighted to do so. The letters he later wrote to his godson attest to the faithfulness with which he discharged the duty. The MacDonald family now consisted of four sons and five daughters. Louisa was feeling the strain of her many births and the demands of the growing family. She was, nevertheless, willing to bear still more should they come. "I'm sure it doesn't matter about having so many children—after all, you can't do what you ought for two so you may as well have eleven or twelve for that matter," she told MacDonald later, after the birth of their last.[20] The father was consistently proud of his children. He wrote his cousin Helen the morning of Maurice's arrival, "Another little boy arrived between five and six this morning. Louisa is doing very fairly, I think, and the bairn is *brawly*."[21]

EIGHTEEN

God's Steeples

Be willing to fail in what you have set before you, and let the Lord work His own success—His acceptable and perfect will.— Salted with Fire

"I have been amazingly well all winter," MacDonald wrote to Mrs. Scott early in 1865. "In fact I have turned a huge corner, and am past forty and invalidity. I can have a bad cold now without either bronchitis or asthma. I am amazed at myself."[1] He was seemingly healthier than he had ever been, and with his teaching and continued lecturing he was enjoying a steadier income. As a consequence, he felt perhaps at last he could do what he had long wanted—take a trip to the continent.

Ruskin regularly spent much time there, and he was filled with enthusiasm for the continent, its art and architecture and stupendous natural beauty. He kept insisting that MacDonald must see it all for himself, even offering to help him financially, if need be, in order that he might. In 1865, his urging prevailed. Ruskin was lavish in giving advice: MacDonald must go straight to Berne, avoiding Geneva, as the latter was "one wilderness of accursed gambling and jewellers' shops."[2] From there he should go to Thun, Interlaken, and Lauterbrunnen. MacDonald would receive in a brief period of time a variety of the most vivid impressions of the astounding natural beauty of the Alps.

MacDonald felt he could afford a two-week trek, so he with two friends decided to go directly down the Rhine and into the Alps. In the small party were William Matheson, his close friend from Highbury days, and William Sainsbury, a new acquaintance ("Very nice—always pretending to grumble. He is a gentleman.").

Alexander Munro had planned to go too, but at the last minute he sent a note to the group explaining that his wife objected to his going. So the three departed in mid-July, their wives evidently more resigned to staying in England.

As McDonald crossed the Channel to Belgium, he was haunted by the memory of Louisa's "sad face" as she saw him off. The tone of the letters he wrote all during the trip suggest his determination to atone, at least in part, for her being left behind by describing the sights in careful detail. Now well along in expecting their tenth child, Louisa could not possibly have gone. Bravely, she accepted her lot: a time alone with the nine.

She had one consolation: they decided to have Earles Terrace redecorated during MacDonald's absence. Consequently, she was reduced to taking the children to stay with relatives and friends. They spent the first week at Elm Lodge with her father and sister Carrie, the aged Powell being still spry but almost completely deaf. Carrie welcomed help in caring for him, but Louisa little needed the extra task. She proceeded to visit their friends the Rallis, at Cleveland House, Clapham.

Her letters to MacDonald describe her struggling to cope as best she could. Lily, Irene, and Winnie were soon sent to visit relatives; that left her with six. Grace, who seems to have been the most independently spirited of the family, cried so "crossly" one Sunday morning the entire family stayed home from church. In addition, Louisa was anxious about the colors of wallpaper and paint in Earles Terrace. And she was also worried about MacDonald's adventuresomeness: "I hope you won't try exploring by yourself. . . . I am not afraid of your doing it for the sake of saying you have done wonderful things but I am afraid of your doing it for the sake of getting 'divine air' from 'God's steeples.' "[3]

Louisa knew well her husband's tendency to extremes, and indeed his undertakings during the trip suggest her concern was well placed. He undertook extraordinary feats; the consequences were inevitable. In Antwerp the sight of the cathedral steeple piercing the sky so excited him he determined to climb to its very top. He was enthusiastic in the extreme: "God be praised for that spire. I would go up though my head ached and I seemed worn out. 616 steps, 410 feet—I made the others go. I was on the point of crying several times with delight."[4] Stairs and heights of any kind always fascinated him. When he first saw the lofty cathedral steeples of the continent (although there are steeples of magnificent height in England too) and then the Alps themselves, he was still further transported.

Climbing to the top of the Antwerp cathedral inspired the scene in his novel *Robert Falconer,* in which Robert goes to the same city and is arrested for climbing the cathedral spire and playing unbidden his Scottish folk tunes on the organ to the dumbfounded populace below. "But just think of a man being able to sit at a finger and pedal board—250 feet from the ground and play any time he liked on 40 bells yet higher—play to the whole city spread below. Oh how I should delight to build a cathedral tower and nothing else." The notion symbolically suggests the nature of his own aspirations in life. "God be praised was all I could say as the Arabs say when they see a beautiful woman. It has filled and glorified me, and I could go home again contented if I didn't see an Alp."[5]

But the experiences on the trip were not all positive. Both England and the continent were suffering under an especially oppressive heat wave that summer. Britishers, accustomed to a consistently cool climate, typically find any temperature above 80 degrees Farenheit stifling, and the soaring temperatures on this particular trip seriously marred their pleasure. "I have been sitting in the public room with bare chest," MacDonald complained from Antwerp, and in another letter confessed the party had long since quit wearing underwear.

Nor was the excessive heat their only source of discontent. The larger cities did not come up to their imaginative expectations: the streets were often drab, the smells were odious, and they felt "taken in" by some of the prices. Cologne was the most disappointing. "The smells are as bad as Coleridge says. . . . the rabble insulted us. We were infested with guides, and when we would not take any one or two were very impudent. The place swarms with them. . . . I believe they cheat us every now and then, and the money is horrid." Apparently the nineteenth century was not without its tourist traps. MacDonald was astounded to have to pay ninepence for a glass of lemonade. Wine was too "dear," and the Bavarian beer, which was cheap enough, was ruined with too much garlic for their taste. Sainsbury amused the party by counting the smells, insisting every building had one of its own, but MacDonald became completely exasperated. "Oh the damned smells!" he blurted to his wife.[6]

Further, a huge fire during their night in Cologne seemed to threaten their hotel. Lightning struck nearby during a violent thunderstorm, lighting a fire that flared right outside their windows. All night the silence was shattered with the watchmen's rattles and incessant bell ringing. With the morning light, when they were able to see comparatively little damage, they concluded that all the bells had been rung to scare away the devil.

As typical tourists they had difficulty with the language. MacDonald, adept at reading German, was nevertheless unable to manage his French. They commonly made comparisons between what they saw and the sights at home. "The roofs of Antwerp are all red with here and there a very black one. The look of the streets a little like Southampton. Here the roofs are all black and high, and the town is more like Aberdeen. Bells ever and not very beautiful. It sounds like a Scotch Sunday."[7] In Cologne the rather common European practice of "thousands of . . . respectable people drinking and talking in the open air at tables in the street," struck them as being quite vulgar; respectable Britishers would never conduct themselves so.

They had hoped the Rhine would be "nice" and went for a sail, but found it was little different from a sail on the River Lea at home. Sainsbury said the Drachenfels reminded him of Upper Clapton. MacDonald avowed, had he known what they were, he would not have gone out of Britain a step to see them. The cathedral at Cologne was scarcely more gratifying ("though very beautiful and very graceful [it] greatly lacks mystery to me"), and they left the city without regret. They all agreed a week in Wales would be worth two in Germany, but they remained certain a sight of the Alps would make it all worthwhile.

Indeed, their fortunes did take a turn for the better as they neared Switzerland. They stopped unexpectedly in a small town in France, due to an abrupt change in train scheduling. The apparent misfortune proved a happy one. MacDonald's spirit revived:

> Now you know I think that I don't believe in misfortune. Never was there a more delightful one than this. The town at which we stopped . . . is a French German one in Alsace. We have seen nothing interesting before. It lies off the railway. A policeman in a cocked hat and military clothes whom William persisted in calling a general officer took us to a tavern, and took his share of a couple of bottles of wine with us. But I must keep all these trifles for the children when I come home. But the lovely old town! with the water running through it and the fine old church and the pretty women and the quaintest houses with rows of windows one above another in every roof. I *must* take you there for a month some day. It is just the place to write a book in, and could be reached easily without going all the way we did. Will you come sweet wife?[8]

When they arrived at Strasbourg, they found it to be like Edinburgh but more "ancient and glorious." The cathedral was far more fascinating than that of Cologne. Built of red stone with glorious stained-glass windows throughout, it had "a huge organ hung against the pillars as if it had only been a kitchen clock." And the clock in the steeple was "full of moving figures and fantasies as big as a house telling everything that a clock could know about . . . the feasts of the church with women and cherubs and men that walk one leg after the other and goddesses and old Death and chariots and horses . . . more quaint than beautiful."[9]

The others in the party declared themselves unable to climb the tower and go up the spire, so MacDonald undertook it himself, going "as far as they would let me without an order from the mayor." The experience of the top so transported him that all his weariness and fatigue vanished. "How will it be when I get amongst God's steeples," he enraptured. "Are you tired? Don't lie down in the valley. Go up the hills—climb. Ah God it is easy to write. And it is easy for Him to breathe fresh life into us."[10]

The exertions to which his unrestrained enthusiasm prompted him inevitably took their toll. From Basel MacDonald wanted sorely to go to Schaffhausen. Ruskin had urged that at all costs he must see it. Going there necessitated a detour, however, to the northeast, and hence an added expense that his companions did not feel they could afford. MacDonald, less prudent, was determined to go, even if it meant he had to make the trip alone, while Matheson and Sainsbury went on to Interlaken. Then suddenly, he began to feel the effects of the climb of the steeple at Strasbourg. Severe lumbago and asthma came on him at once with such force that he could "scarcely crawl" or breathe, and the heat was stifling.

Seeing the strength of MacDonald's determination to go to Schaffhausen in spite of his ailments, Matheson decided to go with him after all, but the trip was a failure. His lumbago was further aggravated by his falling to sleep under only a sheet and awaking in the night chilled through. He was reduced to the humiliation, to say nothing of the pain, of walking doubled up: "Now I go about like an old man, and am ashamed of being stared at."

They proceeded to Interlaken and on to Murren, a village high up in the Bernese Alps. There the magnificent view of the Jungfrau as it towers 13,668 feet above sea level took his mind from all his ailments. He had to see the highest peak, all impediments notwithstanding.

And if I had seen nothing else, I could now go home content. Yet I am not sure whether amidst the lovely chaos of shifting clouds I have seen the highest peak of the Jungfrau. It is utterly useless to try to describe it. William and I agree about three things: 1. That it is beyond description. 2. That it is beyond memory. 3. That it is beyond photography. I hate the photographs. They convey no idea. The tints and the lines and the mass and the streams and the vapours, and the mingling, and the infinitude, and the loftiness, the glaciers and the slow crawling avalanches—they cannot be described.[11]

The magnificent scenes also silenced MacDonald's companions, who had been less than pleased with most of what they had seen on their trip thus far. They determined to go still higher and see still more, although this was possible only on horseback. Having secured mounts, they started from Lauterbrunnen. MacDonald was so impressed with the strength of his mare, named Mattie, that he vowed he would undertake "for a small wager" to ride her "down any staircase in London where she has room to turn the corners, and throw the reins on her neck too, though after all that is the only safe way. Such a climb first and then such a descent!"[12] When they neared the top of the peak they were climbing and the glory of the whole front of the Jungfrau with her uplifted Silberhorn burst upon him, "My mind could not take it in," he simply confessed.

Once he walked out on a glacier and came upon a cave. It, together with other such experiences, soon would find imaginative transmutation in *Wilfrid Cumbermede*. Emotionally and physically exhausted, however, he was ready to return to England, having been gone slightly over a fortnight.

Upon his return in August he received word of what at first seemed to him a capital opportunity. The Professor of Rhetoric and Belles Lettres at the University of Edinburgh, W. E. Aytoun, had suddenly died; a significant position for which MacDonald was suited in the academic world was now open. Having by this time an established reputation as a promising Scottish man of letters, MacDonald felt perhaps it was worth his while to apply for the chair.

He immediately wrote to his friend on the Greek faculty there, John Stuart Blackie, asking him frankly if he thought he had a chance for the position. An encouraging answer promptly came, so MacDonald immediately solicited letters of recommendation from all the literati he knew whose opinion might influence the Edinburgh authorities. He then decided to make a trip north and do what he could to further his candidacy. On the way he stayed with various friends, including Thomas Erskine at Linlathen, one of the more famous religious voices of the day.

Like Maurice and Scott, Erskine had a reputation for genuine godliness of spirit and attitude, together with a sense of justice and compassion that served to exclude him from the institutionalized church. He believed in the universality of the Atonement and the eventual restoration of all people to the unsullied divine image. The purpose of life was education rather than probation. He stood apart from both Presbyterianism and Anglicanism, quarreling alike with Arminianism, which he dubbed "a wolf in sheep's clothing," and with Calvinism, "a sheep in wolf's clothing." A barrister by training, he had retired in middle career when his brother's estate at Linlathen, near Dundee, came into his possession. Here he extended warm Christian hospitality to his many friends, most of whom were drawn to him by his persuasive insistence on the beneficent fatherhood of God. This, together with his broad interest in literature—he could discourse on the plays of Shakespeare as readily as on the Scriptures—rendered him a man of interest to MacDonald, who welcomed the opportunity to receive his famous hospitality.

Among the guests on this occasion at Linlathen was the bilious Thomas Carlyle, the eminent "Sage of Chelsea." He would be appointed rector of the University of Edinburgh the following November and give his inaugural address in April. MacDonald highly esteemed Carlyle.[13] The two had a considerable amount in common: both were Scottish in birth and loyalties, and both were staunch moralists. Both had moved an appreciable distance from their earlier Calvinist training. But whereas Carlyle now doubted the existence of a personal God and of a personal immortality, MacDonald's faith remained strong. Interestingly, both appreciated Erskine's firm assurances of the fatherhood of God, although for Carlyle these mainly aroused nostalgia for his past and the simple, strong faith of his now-deceased mother.

One of the strengths of MacDonald's character was his genuine interest in people who differed with him in matters of faith, so long as he felt they were sensitive, thinking people. As a result, he had by this time several friends among the intelligentsia on whom he could call for testimonials to help him in his candidacy. Among those who willingly responded were Arthur Penrhyn Stanley, Dean of Westminster, a well-known preacher who felt that Christian character was more central to Christianity than was doctrine; Norman MacLeod, a Scottish divine with a wide reputation for pulpit eloquence and practical philanthropy, who was the editor of the popular religious magazine *Good Words;* E. H. Plumptre, professor and dean at King's College, London; John Stuart Blackie, professor of Greek at the University of Edinburgh; John Ruskin; and Frederick Denison Maurice. The novelist Charles Kingsley, when asked, respectfully declined, explaining that he was backing another candidate, but he was nevertheless fulsome in his praise. Since A. J. Scott was now seriously ill, MacDonald used a prior statement from him that he had retained in his files.

David Masson wrote saying that he too was applying and expressed the hope that "we shall not, I am sure, be the less friends and well-workers to each other, in account of this temporary rivalry, however the event may turn out."[14] Ruskin wrote supporting MacDonald's candidacy in a tone of fresh and spontaneous earnestness that suggests much about the man as well as about MacDonald and evidences the state of their friendship at this time:

My dear Macdonald
I am heartily glad you are trying for this Belles Lettres

*Scottish Professorship—of all the literary men I know, I think
you most love literature itself; the others love themselves and the
expression of themselves; but you enjoy your own art, and the
art of others, when it is fine. I know you will do your duty
earnestly and wholly, in any position: and perhaps the desire to
make a Professorship real and useful is the first character which
should be looked for in a candidate; being one often wanting
even in the most able men. I am always glad to hear your
lectures myself—and if I had a son, I would rather he took his
lessons in literary taste under you than under any person I
know, for you would make him more than a scholar, a living
and thoughtful reader.*[15]

This was high praise. But, gratifying as it all was, MacDonald
found himself unable to generate any real enthusiasm for his candidacy. The task of candidating was a "rather weary and dreary
work," and he confided to Louisa that he did not feel right about
the events of the trip: "A cloud hangs over all my doings. It seems
as if something were going to happen." Again he wrote "I am sure
I shall feel relieved if I fail."[16]

And fail he did; the post went to Masson. The main reason
was probably the university authorities' view of MacDonald's
writings, such as *David Elginbrod;* he did not line up with the accepted orthodoxy and perfunctory pieties of the day. Although
his list of supporters contained many names that possessed conventional respectability, it did include a number whose thought
also was disturbing to the more conventional minds at Edinburgh.

Maurice, Ruskin, and Scott were the most offensive to the
conservative mentality. John Stuart Blackie, although he was on
the faculty at Edinburgh, was notoriously unconventional, not in
thought so much as in his appearance and manner. "People say
the less he [Blackie] has to do with the matter the better," Mac-
Donald confided to Louisa.[17] Nevertheless, he accepted the Black-
ies' invitation to entertain him immediately when he arrived in
Edinburgh with dinner followed by a musical event (the Christie

Minstrels). In writing to him afterward, MacDonald mused: "The right man has got the chair, and I am very glad, though I felt a wee bit disappointed for half an hour or so."[18] Failures, when they came, should be taken in stride.

Louisa, convinced that the Edinburgh climate would have consistently put her husband in ill health, was genuinely relieved when he did not receive the appointment. During this summer she had been having another difficult pregnancy, her problems not eased by MacDonald's absences. Especially annoying to both of them was her habit of waking at night, obsessed with various anxieties and concerns which in the light of day appeared of little consequence. Years later their physician son Greville would diagnose his mother as having an enlarged thyroid gland, which may have been a part of her problem at this time. "Do sleep at night and don't go fancying all kinds of things. You will trouble the brain of the little one," MacDonald tried to counsel tenderly in response to her writing to him some of her worst fantasies. "My love to all my chickens, and the one that is coming too. I hope it will be a little girl."[19] The last three children had been boys. But as it happened so was this one: Bernard Powell, born September 28, 1865.

NINETEEN

Broken Sabbaths

The chief difficulty in writing a book [is] to keep out what does not belong to it. —The Flight of the Shadow

By 1866 MacDonald had become a member of the Church of England. But he did not anticipate the degree to which he would be expected to sever his remaining ties with nonconformity. The result, however, was to the advantage of his career simply because he now preached less and devoted more time to writing. The works of this period give clearest definition to his most characteristic doctrines, especially his emphasis on the childlikeness of God and his denial of the eternality of the punishment of the wicked, and demonstrate how strongly he placed his emphasis on the spiritual aspects of people.

The decision to join the Church of England was not a momentous one as he had no difficulty in accepting the Thirty-nine Articles of the English Church. As a youth brought up in the dissenting church he had objected to the fact that some Anglican vicars appeared more worldly than Christian; he was interested in a purer fellowship. But through the years he had come to embrace a more eclectic attitude, recognizing that all sects had within them some members whose attitudes or practices were far from being Christian. He became an Anglican under the ministry of Frederick Denison Maurice at the Chapel of St. Peter's, Vere Street. In Maurice he saw a living example of how Anglicanism could produce godliness. Further, the Anglican Church offered him an experience of worship that Congregationalism did not, something that he had come increasingly to appreciate.

But it was not long until he discovered that being within the

Anglican Church exacted a price. In March of 1866 he began lecturing in the evening classes at King's College, London, to the working men and women who enrolled to advance their education. He lectured on Tuesday evenings from six to eight o'clock on literature from the time of Gower and Chaucer until 1625, and at the same time on Friday evenings he taught "Poetry and Poets of the last 100 years" together with "Prose Composition and Prosody." He enjoyed teaching and was pleased with the enthusiasm he was able to generate within his students. At the time of his appointment MacDonald told Principal Richard William Jelf: "All I can feel confidence in as to my ability for the post is the power of interesting my students. About that alone I cannot doubt."[1]

Aware that MacDonald preached as well as lectured, King's stipulated at the time of his employment that he not mention his connection with them in any advertising that he might do. MacDonald readily agreed; he never allowed any advertising whatsoever but simply announced his speaking engagements. A stern foe of all exaggeration and sensational statement, he knew the penchant of advertising to indulge in such, and he wanted no part of it. Inasmuch as he could control the matter, he chose to adhere as much as possible to a precise statement of truth in all things. He often said that if anyone thinks it easy to tell the truth, that person has not really tried.

He did, however, continue to preach in dissenting chapels when invited. Now, as a member of the Church of England, he suddenly found himself in the middle of controversy. In December 1866 he received a letter from E. H. Plumptre, dean and professor of New Testament and Greek at King's College. He complained: "The fact of your having preached at an Independent Chapel has become known here and people are talking of it. It is likely, I think, to be an occasion of offence both among the pupils and your colleagues." Preaching in a dissenting chapel was considered a hostile act against the official church of England, something no teacher in an Anglican college should do. Plumptre did not

wish to appear an opponent to Christian freedom, so he appealed
to MacDonald's desire to maintain peace, be charitable, and contribute to the working of "a greater good." He then posed what
MacDonald must have felt was a provocative question: "You have
a far wider sphere of influence as a religious teacher in your writings
than you can by any spoken words. Would it not be well to recognize in the circumstances of your life a definite *calling* to the one
work which it is not easy to recognize with equal clearness in the
other?"[2]

The letter touched MacDonald's sense of personal integrity.
He wrote Plumptre at once, insisting that Jelf be told, and explaining that he did not feel he could curtail his ministry, which
was important to him. He was first of all Christian, not Anglican;
his ministry was one of peace and reconciliation, not dissension.
Plumptre, wanting to put the matter to rest, begged MacDonald's
permission simply to show his letter to the principal. He did so
and reported to MacDonald: "The letter really moved him to a
glow of sympathy and made him find you better and *not* esteem
you less than before. Technically the view he took of the matter
was that what you had done had been in the character not of a
NonConformist preacher, but of a lay Churchman with a message
tending to reconciliation and brotherhood."[3] Evidently Jelf could
accede to political solutions when he chose. He had conducted a
strong crusade against Maurice several years earlier and secured his
dismissal from teaching at King's because they disagreed on the
issue of the eternality of punishment for the wicked. As regards
MacDonald, he requested that he, in public announcements of
his preaching, not use the name of King's College, a stipulation
MacDonald had no difficulty in satisfying. Apparently the matter
was laid to rest. MacDonald must have mused in retrospect that
indeed the sectarian spirit was not confined to dissenters.

Plumptre's remark that MacDonald's ministry through his
publications was decidedly larger than through his preaching was,
of course, very true. With the success of his early novels publishers
were open to his submissions, and he began writing indefatigably,

publishing steadily over the next thirty years an impressive body of work. He sometimes was working simultaneously on two and three novels at one time.

His writing together with his teaching at King's began to curtail his private lecturing at Earles Terrace, but he continued that too as long as they lived there. In a letter written to Louisa on his way to Edinburgh in 1865, he gave some instructions that reveal something of the terms between himself and his private pupils: "You had better tell Miss Metcalfe that a course will be at a guinea and a half a lecture." As far as subjects were concerned, he offered to take her "anywhere over the Literature—say a course on Spenser or on Shakespeare—or on various writers of a certain period—say the 16th century—or on Wordsworth or Sir W. Scott."[4] The range of possibility was quite large; evidently MacDonald felt comfortable working with the entirety of the English literary tradition.

He determined, however, to apply his energies to the writing of novels. He had found a way to express his Christian convictions that publishers would accept, and beyond his publishers a public was waiting to be reached. Further, writing novels fitted the nature of his convictions singularly well, inasmuch as a believable novel must present a plausible vision of life as people feel it and live it. So must a believable theology. A theology that did not answer to the deep longings of the human heart simply was not viable. He often alluded to Christ's question to the Pharisees when he condemned them for their distorted practices, "Why do you not judge for yourselves what is right?" (Luke 12:57 RSV). The presence of a true theology in a novel enhanced its sense of being a true vision.

His reputation now established as a promising young novelist, MacDonald turned to the *Bildungsroman* type, producing two of his finest works, *Alec Forbes of Howglen* and *Robert Falconer*. The *Bildungsroman*—or novels of apprenticeship—typically depict a child growing up and making various mistakes and false starts in life, until as a young adult he finds his true profession and a productive orientation to reality. Like the German folktales, also so influential in MacDonald's thinking, this genre originated with the Germans in the late eighteenth century.

This form became immensely popular in England throughout the nineteenth century. In the 1860s, Dickens's *David Copperfield* (1849–1850) and George Eliot's *The Mill on the Floss* (1860) were two of the most widely admired. MacDonald obviously had the latter in mind when he wrote *Alec Forbes of Howglen*. Set in northern Scotland, the story concerns the lives of little Annie Anderson (one of MacDonald's most appealing characters) and Alec Forbes, as the two grow up in the village of Glamerton. They are friends, not brother and sister, but they recall Tom and Maggie Tulliver in *The Mill on the Floss*. Annie's admiration of Alec is not unlike Maggie's attitude toward Tom.

Alec Forbes of Howglen is also similar to *The Mill on the Floss* because of the autobiographical elements present in both. Howglen, the Forbes's farm, is modeled on The Farm of MacDonald's youth. Murdoch Malison, the stern schoolmaster with "a quite savage sense of duty," is a depiction of the MacDonalds' first teacher, who bore some responsibility for the death of MacDonald's eight-year-old brother James. The "dominie's" maiming of his pupil Andrew Truffey recalls this pathetic incident. The blind Tibbie Dyster, whom Annie befriends and from whom she learns great spiritual wisdom, is a depiction of an aged and blind native of Huntly, Tibbie Christie. Like MacDonald going off to Aberdeen, Alec Forbes goes off to college and, in the competition gains "a small bursary." It is, of course, impossible to tell in any of these comparisons where fact leaves off and imaginative transmutation begins. To muse upon these parallels nevertheless enriches the experience of the novel.

The novel also demonstrates MacDonald's ability to re-create a child's way of looking at the world, certainly one of his strengths as a writer. His children are among his most memorable characters. They result in part from his love of children, but they also issue from his insistence that a childlike approach to life is essential to true spirituality, one of his most pervading themes.

MacDonald first titled his novel *The Little Grey Town* and submitted it to Hurst and Blackett early in 1865. They renamed it according to their notion of what would appeal most to popular taste, although it could as well have been named *Annie Anderson*. It appeared early that summer, the *Athenaeum* reviewing it on June 17.[5] The critic was filled with high praise: "It is something to rejoice the heart that even in these days a novel can be written full of strong human interest without any aid from melo-dramatic scene-painting, social mysteries, and the physical force of incidents." The source of interest, rather, lay in the "development of the inner life and spiritual history of all the characters." Interestingly, he concluded "it is not a religious novel, and yet the growth of the religious element in each personage is the pervading idea," and the doctrine of love is "worthily preached." MacDonald's strength as a novelist of the human spirit was gaining recognition.

The novel does not contain a strong father figure who functions as a spiritual mentor and MacDonald's spokesman, something few of the novels lack. His next novel, *Robert Falconer,* does. For some time he had been contemplating a novel that would depict the ideal Christian man. Chiefly he had in mind A. J. Scott as his model, together with a liberal portion of F. D. Maurice. In the letter to Scott quoted in the prior chapter, which accompanied his copy of *Adela Cathcart,* he expressed his intention "to do a better [novel] and one more worthy of being dedicated to you." He first created his ideal character, Robert Falconer, in his early unpublished work *Seekers and Finders,* made him to appear in an important role in *David Elginbrod,* and now concentrated on telling his story as a *Bildungsroman.*

Robert Falconer began to appear serially in the *Argosy* in December 1866, the final installment appearing in its November 1867 issue. Adding appreciably to the serialized version, MacDonald published with Hurst and Blackett the full novel in June 1868. The *Athenaeum*[6] devoted two columns to its review and, while the praise was perhaps not quite so fulsome as for *Alec Forbes of Howglen,* it was very strong. "It is a book to be returned to again and again for the deep and searching knowledge it evinces of human thoughts and feelings, not only in different phases of the same character, but in entirely different natures," the critic affirmed, lauding MacDonald's ability to set forth "the whole drama of life." *The Fortnightly Review,* however, was alarmed at the increasing didacticism of MacDonald's novels and, judging that his teachings were not only "wearisome" but also dissented "from the opinions which are held by any large body of believers," concluded his preaching was suicidal to his art.[7]

Again, the novel contains many autobiographical elements. Like *Alec Forbes of Howglen,* the action of the early portion of the story is set in a village in northern Scotland modeled on Huntly. Here young Robert, whose mother has died and whose father has mysteriously absconded, grows up in the home of his stern and crusty but tenderhearted grandmother. She is a direct fictional presentation of MacDonald's paternal grandmother, Mrs. Charles Edward MacDonald, whose son fled to America to flee the consequences of his irregular banking practices. It was zeal similar to hers that spread the "missionar' kirk" throughout the Lowlands and led to the establishment of the Scottish Free Church in 1843.

The fictional portrait has appreciable imaginative power. Convinced that her son, Robert's father, is lost and doomed to hell, she takes Robert's spiritual welfare as her preeminent concern, seeking to effect it by her most stringent understanding of Christian realities:

> To him she was wonderfully gentle for her nature, and sought to exercise the saving harshness which she still believed necessary, solely in keeping from him every enjoyment of life which the narrowest theories as to the rule and will of God could set down as worldly. Frivolity, of which there was little in this sober boy, was in her eyes a vice; loud laughter almost a crime.[8]

She is a prime illustration among MacDonald's characters of the type of person whose orientation to spiritual realities is in some respects sterling, and yet, failing to strike the proper harmony with the true tenor of human experience, is in other respects tragic. Such had become MacDonald's assessment of his background.

Many of MacDonald's earnest characters undergo not only severe afflictions from without but also deep agonizing from within. They often find themselves in a world they cannot understand, in which God is silent. One of the more notable is Eric Ericson, the distraught poet in *Robert Falconer*. MacDonald's model was his deceased brother John. Ericson's inner turmoil, as he scrutinizes life and wrestles in spirit with the enigma of the appearances of things, is a reflection of John's searchings and doubts.

MacDonald's long poem in ballad stanzas, "The Disciple," suggests the extent to which the spiritual struggle presented in Ericson's earnest questioning and Robert's looking toward what seems a deaf heaven was at times MacDonald's own. He may well have been composing this poem simultaneously with writing the novel, as *The Disciple and Other Poems* was also published in 1867. Its closing lines, "The man that feareth, Lord, to doubt, / In that fear doubteth thee," suggest that earnest spiritual questioning, directed Job-like to the throne of God himself, is an inevitable part of a whole Christian experience.

But MacDonald also had moments of certitude. In writing *Robert Falconer* he intended a novel that he felt worthy of dedication to A. J. Scott. Early in 1866, however, news came of Scott's death. Long in failing health, he had gone to the continent in the hope of regaining strength, but he died at Veytaux, Switzerland, on January 12. Receiving the news in early February, MacDonald penned the following to Scott's widow:

> *My very dear Friend,*
>   *May I come near you now just to let you know that my heart is with you? What else can I say? The best comfort is to what you know better than I do—the will of God—and the next best, that he who has left us was the best and greatest of*

our time. Those who know him best will say so most heartily.
But we have no more lost him than the disciples lost their Lord
when he went away that he might come closer to them than
ever. Life is not very long in this place, dear Mrs. Scott. All we
have to mind is to do our work, while the chariot of God's
hours is bearing us to the higher life beyond.[9]

He felt the loss of Scott very deeply. When *Robert Falconer*
was published in mid-1868, the flyleaf bore the tribute: "To the
memory of the man who stands highest in the oratory of my
memory, Alexander John Scott, I daring, presume to dedicate this
book."

The theme of estranged relationships between parents and
children, with eventual reconciliation, also figures in *Annals of a*
Quiet Neighbourhood, although less prominently. It began to be serialized in the *Sunday Magazine* in October 1865, being completed
in the September 1866 issue, and then was published in book
form at the very outset of 1867, over a year earlier than *Robert*
Falconer. In it MacDonald departed from the *Bildungsroman* type
and a Scottish setting to compose a purely English story. Drawing
on his pastoral experiences, he wrote the story of the young Rev.
Harry Walton as he tries to bring Christian truth to bear upon
a variety of human dilemmas in a small English village very like
Arundel.

Immediately well reviewed, the book proved immensely popular, going through eleven editions in MacDonald's lifetime. It
was the first of his novels published in America, Harper of New
York bringing out an edition in 1867.

In comparing the presentation of the cleric in *Annals of a*
Quiet Neighbourhood with Anthony Trollope's very popular novel
of clerical life written some ten years earlier, *Barchester Towers,* Mac-
Donald's characteristic emphasis becomes apparent. Both novelists
concentrate on character portrayal and detail the commonplace
and the usual. But whereas Trollope presents his clerics as beings
little different from barristers or university dons in their humanity

and ambitions, MacDonald draws Walton as a man of spiritual dimensions with concern for the spiritual welfare of others and with an interest in life as a process of events and circumstances that answers to those concerns. MacDonald's work is less entertaining than Trollope's, but it possesses a dimension Trollope almost entirely overlooks.

Less popular in its own time, but containing some of Mac-Donald's most memorable work, *Dealings with the Fairies* also appeared in 1867. He dedicated it to his children and appended the epigram, "Where more is meant than meets the eye." It contains five fairy tales: "The Light Princess," "The Giant's Heart," "The Shadows," "Cross Purposes," and "The Golden Key." All of them present some aspect of the soul's orientation to spiritual reality. The first three had already appeared in *Adela Cathcart*. "The Golden Key" is a vision of the sweep of life from the time a person's spirit is awakened, through successive steps of purgation, until progressing beyond what the human imagination can reach. It succeeds in arousing the sympathetic reader's imaginative longings after the eternal as do few pieces of literature and is arguably the finest fantasy MacDonald wrote.

MacDonald also achieves in "The Golden Key" his most vivid imaginative expression of his vision of the childlikeness of God, a concept that he does not see as contradicting, but rather as complementing, his insistence on the divine fatherhood. To look closely at the image of God here presented is to understand more precisely what he meant when he kept insisting that the God he worshiped was not the same as the God his fellow men worshiped. The image of the Old Man of the Fire—a surrogate in the story for a high revelation of God—as a little naked child, arranging little colored balls in patterns of infinite meaning, gives memorable expression to the paradox he saw in God's nature.

He presented a very similar vision in expository prose and enlarged on it in yet another publication of 1867. Together with the imaginative literature, *Unspoken Sermons* appeared in April, the first volume of a series of three. (The next two would appear in 1886 and 1889.) The incredible number of MacDonald's publications that appeared in 1867 attests to the state of his health and energy during the mid-1860s.

In the initial sermon, titled "The Child in the Midst," Mac-Donald develops the analogy that God is most like a child, rather than like "a great King on a grand throne, thinking how grand he is." It is clear, however, from the sermons that follow that Mac-Donald's God retains a goodly portion of Calvinist sovereignty. His main point is that God is inexorable in love, a "consuming fire," determined to create an ultimate purity in humankind.

He contends therefore that God's love coalesces with his wrath; they are in the final analysis indistinguishable. Jesus came to take away the sins of the world, not simply their divinely instituted consequences, as he saw too many evangelicals teaching. He affirms that all those for whom the eternal fires of God's wrath, burning in the outer darkness, are necessary, will find that God in love will spare no effort to effect their turning toward their purifying, painful and prolonged as the process may be.

In the publications of the latter part of the decade, therefore, MacDonald energetically maintained doctrines that were deeply offensive to some people committed to Reformed theology. He came out strongly on the side of F. D. Maurice (as well as the Unitarians) in the contemporary controversy concerning the duration of punishment of the wicked in the next life. He hoped for the eventual salvation of all people. (But in a manner quite different from the easy salvation the term *universalism* generally implies.) On the flyleaf he drew an analogy to Christ's opposing the religious authorities of his day: "These ears of corn, gathered and rubbed in my hands upon broken Sabbaths, I offer first to my wife, and then to my friends."

TWENTY

A Goodly Heritage

But it was better perhaps that she should be left free to follow her own instincts. The true teacher is the one who is able to guide those instincts, strengthen them with authority, and illuminate them with revelation of their own fundamental truth. —Alec Forbes of Howglen

MacDonald is not among those who would define spirituality as a quality that is the antithesis of physical reality. He remarks in *David Elginbrod*, "Life intelligently met and honestly passed, is the best education of all." The idea reflects his approach to life: he tried to face difficult issues head-on, learn from his experiences, and modify earlier positions if necessary. This distinguishes him from Christians who approach life deductively, working from their doctrinal positions.

He came increasingly to believe that the conscientious and sincere person learns God unconsciously from life intelligently met. His later works reflect this conviction.

Two areas of his life during this decade illustrate the working of this concept. One is his view of education. Early in his career he strongly advocated that children should imaginatively scrutinize life. As they became curious about a thing they should receive instruction. His working with his children, however, led him to curtail his early enthusiastic insistence on the role of imagination in the learning process. The second area is that of the problem of pain in life. During the last part of the decade his own pain and adversities issued in his wrestling in his writings with the importance and effects of suffering.

On January 23, 1867, the last of the children, George

MacKay, was born. His name honored his great-uncle, whose daughter, Helen Powell, was his godmother. The MacDonald family, now completed, numbered eleven children. At the time Lilia was fifteen years of age, Mary thirteen, Caroline twelve, Greville just turned eleven, Irene nine, Winifred eight, Ronald six, Robert four, Maurice almost three, and Bernard one. Things were never dull. The parents bestowed on their children liberal quantities of both love and discipline. They delighted in the individual personalities and manners of each yet tried to instill in all a sense of love and responsibility to each other and to the family unit.

Louisa, writing from Brighton in 1866, where she together with the children were vacationing with her father and sister, gave a vignette of family life. They all went out riding in a little goat chaise after dinner. Maurice, who was "very very cross and continually contradicting every body himself included" in his shrillest treble voice, did not "at present conduce to the family bliss." Greville was "very good and only uncomfortable because he [had] no one to teaze," and Lily was "as sweet as Lily can be and brighter than she usually is."[1] Greville was often teasing his sisters, especially Winnie, a practice that may have been an attempted compensation for the fact that he had more difficulty learning his lessons than did the girls.

Both parents seem in their letters to refer to Lily, Mary, Greville, and Maurice more frequently than to the others, but this is not necessarily out of a sense of partiality. Maurice had a "bewitching" personality; Greville was the firstborn son and had a learning problem; Mary was especially frail, quiet, and thoughtful; and Lily was magnanimous in the self-effacing and loving attention she bestowed on the other children and her parents.

Lily's age and disposition, together with her witty scrutiny of people, rendered her in many ways the center of family attention. When the family played charades, as they often did, her ability to mimic other people, reproducing their manner and idiosyncracies, was extremely entertaining. She had as well acquired an unusual degree of maturity for her age, and she was so willing to accept responsibility that MacDonald and Louisa soon began leaving the children in her charge on selected occasions. Not unlike her Aunt Charlotte in the Powell household of a few years back, she came to occupy the position of intermediary between the other children and the parents.

Mary, as the second child, also readily accepted a large share of responsibility for the younger ones. On another occasion Louisa confided to her husband: "My baby [Bernard] was just an angel to me last night. His smile though not an archangel's was very delicious and love implanting. He has never cried once at night and Mary manages him so nicely in the morning. She is very sweet and helpful. I think already both Lily and Mary's price, if not above rubies yet, exceeds garnets, don't you?"[2] "Far above rubies" measures the value of a virtuous woman as described in Proverbs 31:10. The passage gives a listing of qualities that defines the standard of womanhood in the Victorian mind. Certainly both parents took the shaping of their children's virtue as their most basic responsibility.

Next in importance to their children's developing virtue was their acquiring an education, to which the parents both gave careful attention. They were determined to help them all to develop their minds to their fullest capabilities. While MacDonald was in Switzerland, Lily went with Greville and Winnie to visit their Aunt Helen and Uncle Alex Powell. Louisa, desiring that Lily advance her education while she was there, told her to read history. When Lily asked *what* history, her mother responded she had no particular historical period in mind.

> I only thought you know least about Ancient History and we wanted you to be *studying* something. I dare say if you ask Miss Miller she can give you some book, if it is ever so elementary you won't mind, and then after you have read a few pages of it, make some questions for yourself about it, and answer them on paper next day.[3]

Louisa seemed to view the mental exercise of reading and acquiring comprehension as more important than the specific subject matter. Biographies were another matter.

> I think Papa and I would rather you would not read Charlotte
> Bronte's life just now. It will do you more good and less harm
> in a year or two. It is very exciting and not just the kind of
> excitement you want just now. I am glad you have such a lot
> of nice books. Do you get Winnie and Greville both to read
> to you?[4]

Such strictures indeed give us pause today. The book in question probably was Mrs. Gaskell's *Life of Charlotte Bronte* (1857), which became controversial because it contained some allegedly libelous statements. Generally considered a masterpiece of biography, it is difficult to understand why it should be kept from a thirteen-year-old girl.

MacDonald had strong opinions concerning the process of education, and he practiced them on his children. He found considerable wisdom in the writings of Sir Francis Bacon, and among Bacon's remarks he was fond of quoting was, "Wonder is the seed of knowledge." The successful teacher should awaken within his pupils a curiosity and desire to know and must not try to impose materials on them until that desire is present. When the desire to learn a thing is so strong that students ask to be taught, the teacher should then lead them to discover it for themselves.

The fact that MacDonald detailed this approach in *David Elginbrod* shows that it was much on his mind during the early 1860s as he was coming to terms with how to educate his children. Evidently, his trying to teach them caused him to modify his earlier theories; in the *Bildungsroman* novels of the middle of the decade he showed his characters profiting from more traditional educational practices.

Greville's experience helped to alter MacDonald's thinking. Writing years later as an aged man, Greville mused on his education with mixed feelings.[5] In the main he affirmed the highest respect for his father and gave him great praise. He recalled that MacDonald's remembrances of his own father's practices had governed his relations with all his children. MacDonald said of his father that he never denied him as a child anything he asked, and he wanted his own children to be able to say the same about him. Greville did. He praised his father's patience and unqualified tenderness whenever a child was sick or repentant.

Nevertheless, he felt his father did not fully understand him. His older sisters took more quickly to MacDonald's approach to the educational process than he did. Musically inclined, Greville did well on his violin, loved painting, and avidly enjoyed his father's fairy stories. But MacDonald's attempts to teach him geometry and Latin by imagination and desire rather than by memory and proof were unproductive (although they apparently succeeded with his sisters).

Greville's problem was due in part to a hearing handicap, which was not recognized early enough. He was generally a slow learner. Lily wrote to her mother concerning his obtuseness:

> I was up at 6 o'clock this morning and practiced till 7 and then helped Greville with his poetry. The poor boy is so slow over learning it. He doesn't know more than half of it and today Mr. MacClare [their tutor at the time] examines them in poetry. But it seems impossible to cram Greville, however much one grinds it into him.[6]

As a result of Greville's lack of success MacDonald simply quit trying to teach him what he evidently had no desire to learn. He was careful not to leave the impression that the boy's inability in any way diminished his love and esteem for him. For instance, on hearing that Greville was not feeling well, he wrote: "Your news of Greville makes me a little uneasy; but I know you will do what is right with him. What a dear boy he is! I suppose it is the effects of cold he is suffering from."[7] The subjects Greville could not master were left for him to acquire in his formal schooling, which came later.

MacDonald made clear to his children that whether they succeeded or failed in life (that is, as people at large judge success or failure) was no great matter. What did matter was their conduct, their obedience to God, and their personal integrity. Greville recounts the story of how, when he was nine, he received a gift of a box of tools, which gave him great delight. He succeeded in building many childish specimens of which he was proud. But he recalls how, having on an occasion made a box that was somewhat less than a product of his best effort, his father counseled: "If ever you do anything badly and content yourself with saying, 'Oh, that'll *have* to do!' then you may be sure it *won't do at all!*"[8]

Greville's formal education as a child, which began in 1867, was only moderately more successful. Having a high-pitched voice, together with a passion for music, he won a place in the children's choir at King's College, where his father was teaching in the evening school. The distinction carried with it the prize of a paid education in its boarding school. As an adult he retained vivid memories of the system of fagging[9] practiced there, of his receiving ridicule for his long hair (thanks to his mother's love of it), and of the difficulties of being at the bottom of the class. When he did do acceptably in an examination, the family was as jubilant as he. His perseverance prevailed in the end. Later, when he entered college, he managed to set a good record. He grew up to be a physician, surgeon, and author.

An important milestone in Greville's education occurred during the summer of 1867, when MacDonald took a parish for the summer in the far west of England, in Kilkhampton. They had cottages in Bude, a village built on the cliffs of Devonshire overlooking the Atlantic. Also with the entire family were MacDonald's stepmother and sister Jeannie, together with Octavia Hill, then a young and attractive social worker. Hill, a protege of Ruskin's, took a warm interest in Greville's learning difficulties and undertook to teach him the rudiments of Latin grammar. Early each morning she took him across the breakwater to where it ended on a huge rock. There, surrounded by the sea, they conjugated Latin verbs. He may well have been prompted in part by the determination to impress this pretty young woman, but Hill's more traditional approach to understanding Latin syntax succeeded where MacDonald's approach had not.

In both going to and returning from Bude, MacDonald and his wife found it necessary to split the family and travel separately. During the third week in June 1867, Louisa left for Bideford, taking with her Lily, Greville, Ronald, and MacKay, while MacDonald stayed behind with the balance of the family. He had to complete some writing before he left, and his asthma was bothering him. But he found caring for half of the family no burden: "The children are wonderful. No more trouble than if they were— I don't say men and women—but angels in heaven, who had outgrown human experiences."[10]

Louisa's first experience of Bude, on the contrary, was quite traumatic. Her colorful recounting of the incident reveals something of her own imaginative verve. She excitedly expressed to her husband both her terror and her ensuing delight.

> *Dearest Husband,*
> *This place is more delightful than I can give you any idea of. [But] . . . all day—no half the day, yesterday, I thought the hills and the sands hideous. Dearest, you had better divorce me at once. I thought all day yesterday that I would send you in my resignation. I meditated throwing myself down from the rocks but then I thought the sea might wash me up again and then the expense of the funeral deterred me! Well, I can't come to confession yet. It is too dreadful. But suffice it to say I have already become the most notorious visitor in Bude. . . . We walked our legs off, cried our eyes out, wrote our fingers off, dispensed shillings, offered rewards, suspected the innocent . . . and finally sent to Stratton, not for the doctor but for the crier, and, 5 minutes after he had proclaimed Mrs. MacDonald's shameful character all through this populous town, a girl*

*brought me in my little brown purse with 14 (pounds)—12—6
and a button. The screams and shouts of joy in the house were
deafening. The place turned suddenly beautiful again. . . . I
still wished to be allowed to remain the unworthy wife of George
MacDonald the Prophet.*

For them in their straightened circumstances to have lost that
much money would have meant great distress indeed.

They fell in love with the sleepy little town. Louisa, raving
over the fresh, clear, pure air, urged her husband to hurry to join
them. When he and the balance of the family did, they found the
area delightfully scenic and the air wholly invigorating. MacDonald, regimenting himself to as demanding a schedule as his health
permitted, wrote tirelessly on his next novel and preached in the
church at Kilkhampton. He was writing *The Seaboard Parish* plus
readying *Guild Court* (which was being serialized in *Good Words*
throughout 1867) to appear as a novel. But he found time as well
to enjoy the seaside with his family.

Greville recalled the summer as an especially joyous one for
the children, highlighted by those occasions when his father
would play with them by the sea, racing along the breakwater with
Maurice and Bernard held one under each arm or wading with
the family in the shallower waters.[11] MacDonald's love of the sea
took them there at times when more cautious souls stayed away.
"It was high tide last night and I took them all to the breakwater.
Lily and I went over two or three times and did not get wet. We
were the only people that went."[12] The summer at Bude appreciably invigorated him.

MacDonald fictionalized many of his experiences in his novel
The Seaboard Parish. A sequel to *Annals of a Quiet Neighbourhood*,
the story chronicles the life of the Rev. Harry Walton as he dis-
charges the duties of a vicar in a temporary parish by the sea. His
daughter, injured from a fall from a horse, remains an invalid
throughout the novel, which allows MacDonald to explore more

deeply than heretofore the problems of the suffering of the innocent. How the sufferings and adversities of life could be justified in terms of a loving God is one of the basic concerns of *Guild Court* and the pervasive concern of *At the Back of the North Wind,* which began to be serialized in *Good Words for the Young* in 1868 and was published by Strahan in 1871.

Among his imaginative writings, MacDonald's most artistically successful handling of the problem of pain occurs in his book for children, *At the Back of the North Wind,* in which he intermingles fantastic or dream episodes with more realistic ones. He succeeds in creating symbols, metaphors, and poetic statements to present a compelling vision of a paradoxical relation of chaos and order at the heart of reality and of a fusion of the supernatural with the natural.[13] The story concerns a London cabman's sickly son who, in dreams occurring during periods of delirium, is visited by the North Wind, a beautiful woman of supernatural powers. She personifies those adversities in life out of which good may come. Carrying him with her wrapped in her long and lovely hair, she takes him along on her providential errands. To be at her back is to be in tune with the nature of things so that one is not defeated by adversities but is able to help good emerge from them. MacDonald has in mind biblical assurances that the righteous person is not to be afraid when things seem to go wrong but is to trust (e.g., Psalm 112:7). The narrative in its realistic portions shows Diamond, the little boy, working to effect good in the lives of people oppressed by dire circumstances and reversals.

A portion of the appeal of this story lies in its tone, which is affirmative but not dogmatic. The North Wind herself is not all knowing. She exercises faith that the errands she executes—for instance, she sinks a ship, resulting in the loss of lives and fortunes—will ultimately issue in a great good that all can affirm. She hears the sound of a "song" that, although it is far-off and long in coming and she cannot now understand its meaning, nevertheless assures her that "all is right." When it finally arrives, it will satisfy all objectors.

Since she appears to Diamond in dreams, MacDonald raises the issue of the validity of good dreams, or imaginative longings (an issue that concerned him all his life, and has its final treatment in *Lilith*.) North Wind assures Diamond: "The people who think lies, and do lies, are very likely to dream lies. But the people who love what is true will surely now and then dream true things."[14] North Wind appears to different people in different forms: to people of low development, she is hideous. Only to people spiritually alive and attuned to her true nature, such as Diamond, does she appear beautiful. MacDonald will develop this concept later in his Curdie stories.

At the Back of the North Wind stands in interesting contrast to *Gutta Percha Willie*, a children's story that appeared serially in *Good Words for the Young* during 1872 and was published by Henry King in 1873. In it MacDonald tells another story of a boy of ideal nature. Gutta-percha is a coagulated, rubber-like material sometimes used for making molds, since it fits itself to the irregularities of almost any shape; Willie is a boy of an unbelievable adaptability whose great curiosity and ingenuity enable him to learn many crafts and excel in contriving inventions of his own. He is told early in his life that God is always working in his universe, and Willie's industry comes from his determination to follow the pattern God has set. The book was not successful, inasmuch as Mac-Donald made little attempt to give the story dramatic interest. Nor did he introduce fantasy elements, the area in which his talent was strongest. Given the rate at which he was producing material, artistic unevenness should not be surprising.

When the summer at Bude drew to its close, MacDonald had a considerable amount of writing yet to do to meet his schedule. Louisa left in early September, taking part of the family with her, while he stayed into early November. Hers again was the task of engineering a move to the new home they had located before going west. The completed family required yet larger quarters than those at Earles Terrace. No longer dependent on MacDonald's lecturing and private tutoring for a living (although they were still in

George MacDonald, at the height of his long career.

George MacDonald, circa 1860.

Louisa Powell MacDonald, circa 1860.

The MacDonalds' graves in the Stranger's Cemetery, Bordighera. Lilia, Grace, Louisa, and George MacDonald's ashes are buried here.

London: J.M. Dent & Sons, 1905, repr. 1913.

George MacDonald as he appeared on the frontispiece to his long poem, *A Book of Strife in the form of The Diary of an Old Soul*.

George MacDonald with his sons at Porto Fino (from top left, clockwise) Bernard, Edward Troup, Robert Falconer, Maurice, MacKay, George, Greville, and Ronald.

Louisa with daughters at Porto Fino (from top, clockwise) Irene, Lilia, Winifred, and Grace.

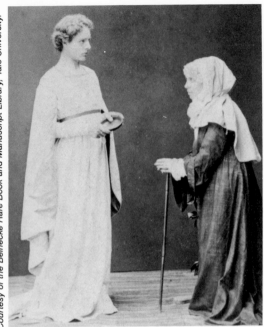

Scene from the family's
dramatic presentation of
Pilgrim's Progress: Mistress
Muchafraid (Louisa)
meeting the Messenger
(E. R. Hughes).

George MacDonald
dressed for the role of
Mr. Greatheart in the
family's dramatic production
of The Second Part of
The Pilgrim's Progress.

GMDW.

Casa Corraggio, Bordighera, as it appeared near the turn of the century.

The complete MacDonald family, 1876, together with prospective son-in-law
E. R. Hughes. Top row: Grace, Greville, Mother, Lilia, Ted Hughes, middle
row: Ronald, Robert Falconer, Irene, Father, MacKay, Mary, bottom row:
Maurice, Winifred, Bernard

The Farm, now called Greenkirtle, on the edge of Huntly, where George MacDonald was raised.

The Huntly Castle, which captured MacDonald's imagination as a child.

The chapel, King's College, Aberdeen, where MacDonald enrolled in 1840 and graduated in 1845.

Arundel street, with plaque by the door of the newly married MacDonald's quarters.

The Trinity Congregational Church, Arundel, where MacDonald was
minister, 1850–53.

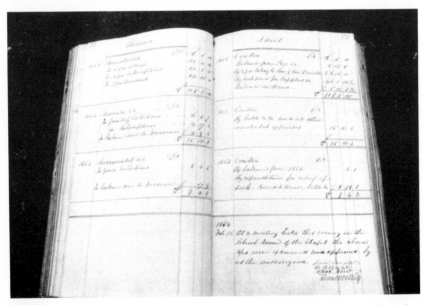

Entries for the year 1853 in the ledger of the Trinity Congregational Church,
Arundel, recording MacDonald's drastically reduced salary. Right-hand page,
second entry: "By ½ yrs. salary to Rev. G. MacDonald £6.16.0."

148 Charles Street.
Oc. 8, 1872.

My dear Mr. Longfellow,

It is most kind of you to ask us to sup with you, and more than I could have looked for. We will do so with very great pleasure.

Will you allow me to inclose two tickets for the lecture. I hope I shall not give a very bad one, else I shall feel that I do not deserve your company afterwards.

Yours most truly
George MacDonald.

A letter to Henry Wadsworth Longfellow, written during MacDonald's lecture tour of America in 1872–73.

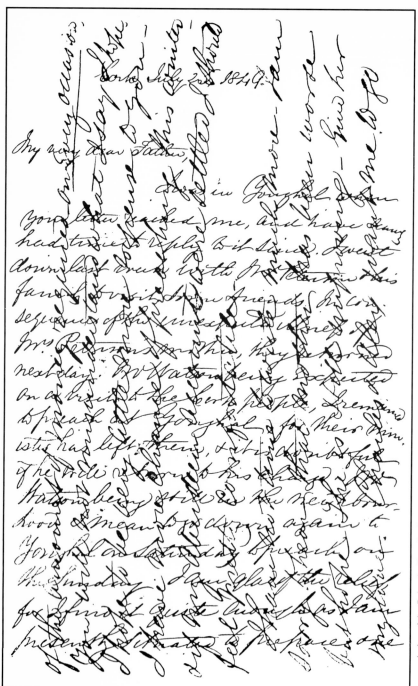

First page of a letter written by George to his father, cross-written to save postage.

My dearest Bob — I send you this paper
to shew you in what neighbourhood we arrived
on Sat'y & slept & dined & breakfasted &
supped — but oh! the walks we have had!
and the water we have seen & the thunders
of water

DINNER.

we have heard

Dear Bob Monday, March 31, 1873. I hope you

are all well —

are we are

SOUP.
Chicken

FISH.
Boiled Haddock, Egg Sauce.

BOILED.

Corned Beef,   Chicken, Egg Sauce,   Ham
Tongue,   Mutton, Caper Sauce.

ROAST.
Lamb,   Mutton.   Ribs of Beef,
Turkey.   Chicken.

ENTREES.
Minced Fowl with Ham on Toast.
Stewed Giblets, Dublin Style.
Wings of Turkey, Butter Sauce
Salad a l'Allemande

SAUCES.
Worcestershire,   John Bull,   Harvey,   Anchovy,   Jocky Club.

VEGETABLES.
Turnips.   Rice   Squash.   Tomatoes   Cabbage.
Onions,   Hominy,   Potatoes—Boiled and Mashed.

PASTRY.
Indian Pudding, Wine Sauce   Cherry Pie.
Apple Pie,   Vanilla Ice Cream   Fruit Cake
Sponge Cake,   Wine Jelly.

DESSERT.
Raisins,   Nuts,   Apples,   Coffee.

Seats at Dinner Will be Served thirty minutes only.
All Meals, Lunches or Fruits, sent or carried to Rooms will be charged extra

Give my love to

going straight

when

shall be in over

Queen's drive

we have been over

Niagara where we

Letter written on an American hotel dinner menu from Louisa to her son
Robert.

George MacDonald's bookplate, from an engraving by William Blake (enlarged).

rather meager circumstances), they looked for a more open and airy location, apart from the bustle of London, and were able to secure The Retreat, a commodious house of Georgian design, located in Upper Mall, Hammersmith (in western London). Certain family and friends were pledged to help Louisa with the move, among them Edward Sharman and Annie Munro. MacDonald, not wanting to precipitate another asthma attack and having to meet his publisher's deadlines, stayed at Bude.

The Retreat offered many advantages. The Upper Mall bordered the Thames, which flowed by quietly and serenely, so they were always conscious of the river's presence. Enough traffic passed on the river to keep it a constant point of interest, and on boat race days the spectacle offered great excitement. Out back was a garden covering a full acre, with a huge sprawling tulip tree and a stable, where for a time they kept a cow and a horse. Entering from the street into a hallway, visitors mounted the stairs to a commodious living room (the servants lived "below stairs"), with bedrooms yet above.

The family was excited about the prospect of being situated in their new home, which they were having painted and freshly decorated during the summer. But for Louisa, the move was hectic. When it was over, she wrote MacDonald that a moving day would make "a grand *Hell* for misery—misery enough to make one so wicked one would never be able to want to repent."

Her exasperation reached its peak when, waiting in the empty rooms of their new home late at night, they finally heard the four moving vans approach. The driver came to the door to announce he must have his money, twenty-two pounds, before they would begin to unload. Horrified, Louisa protested that the agreed price had been five pounds ten. The foreman laughed: "That was 5 pounds 10 *per load*," he said. Then the realization struck her: "When we came to think of it," she later told MacDonald, "we saw 4 van loads, 8 men, 4 horses all day could not be [gotten] for 5 pounds 10. But 22 pounds is preposterous. They must get more than 10 pounds profit."

When she had not the money to pay, the foreman commenced to depart with the goods for a warehouse, assuring them they would be charged with the extra trips. "I was in despair," Louisa wrote. "Then Ewing remembered that he had a blank cheque in his pocket. He wrote it for me—22 pounds. It was very good of him, wasn't it?" It was midnight before the workers began unloading, and Louisa was obliged to direct them where to put everything. "There wasn't a bed or wardrobe in its place and I was so hideously tired I could hardly direct anyone and there were 8 men all about the house carrying things and no candles except in bottles."[15] Finally, when sufficient beds were assembled for the family's sleeping, the men agreed to leave and return the following day to finish arranging the furniture. "I had some whisky which did me good," Louisa confessed concerning her day's end.

TWENTY-ONE

Anxiety to Entertain

He was confident that only the personal communion of
friendship could make it possible for them to believe in God.—
Robert Falconer

Now that the MacDonalds had more commodious quarters, more secure finances (they were never free of financial concerns), and MacDonald's health seemed stabilized, he applied himself to a very ambitious writing and lecturing schedule. The family also enlarged their social life. They began giving family entertainments for their friends, but their socializing did not stop there. They were concerned for the poor and deprived, and they expended a considerable effort to entertain them as well. The family's avid interest in drama helped them to entertain both groups, and they often tried to integrate the two.

At The Retreat the MacDonalds' interest in acting began to flourish and became an important part of their family life for many years. "The coachhouse is finished and has a lovely border devised by Mr. Cottier one day he was here. And there is a lovely stage being put up with *GAS LIGHTS* and we are going to act there,"[1] Lily excitedly told Mary, dramatizing the depth of her feelings by writing *gas lights* in large, fancy script across the middle of the letter.

Cottier was an artist friend whom they employed to help decorate The Retreat. His tastes, in line with contemporary styles, were bold and pronounced. He decorated MacDonald's study with a wallpaper of crimson flock background and a black fleur-de-lis design. MacDonald, who as a child was especially fascinated with the night sky and who all his life vividly remembered a childhood dream in which the ceiling of his bedroom was filled with the moon and stars, had the ceiling of his study painted a dark blue containing a smattering of silver and gold stars and a silver crescent moon.[2]

Their interest in drama had its inception with Louisa's observation of how strongly the fairy tales gripped the children's imaginations. At play they pretended to be the various characters from the stories, especially those from their favorite fairy tales, the Grimm Brothers'. Fascinated, she began to assist them by turning portions of the stories into little scenes for them to act out.

This beginning soon grew into a consuming interest. Lily was especially adept at acting, but most of the children took an avid interest. By the time they were situated at The Retreat, with more room in which to express themselves, the boys constructed a moveable stage for the yard. E. R. Hughes, nephew to the artist Arthur Hughes, MacDonald's illustrator, painted designs on curtains that Louisa and the girls sewed together. A rendition of "Beauty and the Beast" was an early favorite production in this contrived theater, as was Dickens's story "Haunted Man, the Tetterbys," rewritten as a drama by Louisa, to which she added three scenes of her own. The family referred to it simply as "Tetterbys."

MacDonald himself maintained a steady interest in the theater, both the activities of his family and the London professional stage. He had attended the theater since coming to London as a tutor in Fulham. Now sometimes he would go with one of his friends, such as Arthur Hughes. But his interest in 1868 was not primarily entertainment. On one occasion, when he and Hughes had seen a play MacDonald felt was "absolute dreariness," he explained to Louisa that he meant nevertheless to increase his theater attendance that summer to become more familiar with the mechanics of play writing. "It seems to me a great chance of doing something for them, that so many people should be gathered together night after night in London—and fed with husks like swine and not sheep—forsaken in fact by their shepherds and handed over to false teachers or at least poor rickety shepherds and tooth-less dogs." His recent success at writing novels notwithstanding, he did not see being a novelist as his ultimate calling and was wist-fully considering writing dramas. "I don't know yet what espe-cially God made me for," he confessed, adding, "I have done very little if anything that is first-rate and I feel as if I could do a good many things I have not tried yet. I must have a try at the stage."[3] Perhaps his continued inability to arouse the slightest interest in "If I Had a Father" finally deterred him from carrying through with this intention, for there is no evidence that he actually began writing another drama.

When his family showed such delight in acting, he did what he could to encourage the interest and had the coach house in the yard remodeled into a small theater, complete with the gas lighting that so pleased Lily. He also allowed the family to use one end of his large upstairs study for another stage, and many dramas were put on there as well. Thus the family interest flourished, with MacDonald himself taking active roles when his schedule would allow it. They began to undertake Shakespeare, with MacDonald playing Macbeth opposite Lilia as Lady Macbeth.

However widespread this interest was in the family, it is clear that it centered in Lily. Greville remarked of her that by the time she was eleven, she knew intimately all of Shakespeare.[4] Her talent in acting elicited praise in all who saw her. She was fascinated with every aspect of the London stage, the actors, and even the dress and manners of the theater-going public. She wrote her sister: "But Mary, the dresses, the ways, of all these pre-raphaelite Dames and damsels. They stood under the trees and bit apples just like Mr. Rosetti's pictures. Mrs B[urne] J[one]'s dress was the lest [sic] peculiar and she wore bright blue muslin with ropes of bright green beads round her neck and green in her hair."[5] MacDonald's acquaintance with several in the Pre-Raphaelite brotherhood would have intensified his daughter's interest in their posturing. The MacDonalds' closest acquaintances in the group were Sir Ed-ward Coley Burne-Jones and his wife.

Their growing circle of friends enjoyed the entertainment not only of the family dramatic presentations but also of their appreciable musical talents. The family began holding open house regularly on Sunday evenings. These occasions sometimes began with tea, followed by a dramatic presentation, and concluding with an evening meal. At other times they would begin with "a supper of cold joints, hot potatoes, milk puddings, bread and cheese," after which friends would gather for an evening of music and readings.[6] Sometimes they would give little concerts, with Greville playing the violin and Grace excelling at the piano with her interpretations of Beethoven, Chopin, and Schumann. The family also sang (except MacDonald), and at the Christmas season delighted in giving concerts of Christmas carols. These evening occasions often concluded with MacDonald reading from Scripture and literature—Shakespeare and Renaissance or Romantic poets—and with prayer.

The quality instruments that the family enjoyed came in good part from friends. One piano had come from Ruskin. During a period of financial hardship in 1866, MacDonald had borrowed a sum of money from his friend. When he sought to repay the loan, Ruskin refused to receive it, saying simply that he did not need the money, whereas MacDonald did. But MacDonald insisted that Ruskin keep the check he had sent. A few days later a handsome grand piano was delivered to the MacDonald home. No other gift could possibly have delighted them so much.

Interestingly, in late 1868 a somewhat similar incident occurred. On another occasion of financial need, MacDonald had borrowed fifty pounds from Russell Gurney, and he too was loath to receive MacDonald's cheque in repayment. Gurney promptly sent a cheque for the same amount to Lily, saying she would "value it the more as being part of the fruits" of her father's "talent and industry."[7] Louisa suggested the money be applied to a piano for her. The use of two pianos appreciably enhanced the family's concert performances.

Nor were these family performances presented to their circle of intimate friends alone. One practical expression of MacDonald's attitude toward the poor and underprivileged occurred at least once each summer when the family would invite a large assembly of underprivileged people to The Retreat to serve them with a meal and then entertain them with music and drama. Such occasions would conclude with a period of games and folk dancing.

MacDonald's contact with a specific group of poor people came through Octavia Hill, the bold and untiring social worker who was a close friend of the family. Beginning when a teenager as a drawing pupil of Ruskin's, she had become interested in his social philosophizing on how the poor should be helped. Due to the Industrial Revolution, masses of people were crowded into slum areas in the great cities of Britain, locked into living in deplorable quarters and laboring long hours for little pay in the great factories of the time. The nation was incredibly slow in enacting meaningful laws for social and labor reform. Thinkers such as Ruskin did much to raise the consciousness of the privileged ruling class to the plight of these people, but it took the practical ingenuity and unflagging energy of someone like Hill actually to change the way some of the poor lived.

When Ruskin learned of Octavia Hill's plans and intentions for slum renovation, he used some of the large fortune he inherited from his father, who had died in 1864, to purchase specific slum areas and to sponsor their renovation, all under her direction. She was also successful in persuading other philanthropists to make similar investments. Working largely without salary, she made a gallant effort to afford the underprivileged an opportunity to live cleanly and decently, so that her name has become permanently synonymous with successful social reform.

Hill was an admirer of MacDonald as well as of Ruskin. "MacDonald's lectures are indeed a success," she wrote to a friend. "He often nearly brings tears to my eyes by the beauty and truth and suddenness of what he says."[8] She had been with the MacDonalds during their summer at Bude and was frequently at The Retreat. MacDonald was in turn very interested in her work and would go into her renovated slums to speak to the tenants.

While Victorian England was nominally Christian, many among the working class were unchurched. Sensing his uncondescending sincerity, many responded to him as he talked to them simply and directly, using moral anecdote and fairy story to arouse an interest in the teachings of Christ. The large numbers of underprivileged people who came to the "entertainments" at The Retreat were mostly from among Octavia Hill's tenants.

MacDonald's thinking concerning the poor was influenced by Maurice as well as Ruskin and Hill. One of the reasons MacDonald was attracted to F. D. Maurice was his advocacy of what was known as Christian Socialism. The program these Christian (not Marxist) Socialists advocated emphasized individual responsibility as well as social reform by the application of Christian principles to all social relationships. With typical Scottish sternness MacDonald insisted on the need of the poor to better themselves. They must be given adequate opportunities, something many sadly lacked. When anyone whose life was at low ebb needed to be taken in and helped to make a new start, The Retreat was open to them, while the MacDonalds did what they could to help them turn their lives around. It was not unusual for a penniless person or a drunkard trying to reform to live with the MacDonalds temporarily. Not all such attempts issued in successful rehabilitation, but many did.

MacDonald expressed his thinking concerning the poor in several instances, but perhaps as succinctly and forcibly as any in *Robert Falconer*. Falconer spends his life working among the poor in London. Some of his thinking directly echoes the scheme of Ruskin and Hill:

> To provide suitable dwellings for the poor he considered the most pressing of all necessary reforms. His own fortune was not sufficient for doing much in this way, but he set about doing what he could by purchasing houses in which the poor lived, and putting them into the hands of persons whom he could trust, and who were immediately responsible to him for their proceedings: they had to make them fit for human

abodes, and let them to those who desired better accommodation, giving the preference to those already tenants, so long as they paid their reasonable rent, which he considered far more necessary for them to do than for him to have done.[9]

This is precisely what MacDonald's friends were doing. Octavia Hill was famous for not giving anything as a dole, but rather for working unstintingly to enable the poor to help themselves. She was, at the same time, careful to ensure that Ruskin made a five-percent return on his investment.

Ruskin was present at The Retreat when the first of these "entertainments" was held in June 1868. Writing him immediately after the occasion, MacDonald thanked him for his gift of some engravings of Turner. "I do not deserve such exquisite things. But I am indeed delighted to possess them," MacDonald commented. Then he apologized to Ruskin for not having paid him sufficient attention, and in so doing conveyed an interesting feeling about the event:

> My wife and I are troubled in our minds that in our anxiety to entertain the poor people, we neglected to make proper provision for our other guests. I believe you went home half dead with unfed fatigue. It was our first attempt, and we shall do better next time, I hope. We ought to have had one room in the house provided with refreshments, but everything was sacrificed to the one end, which I hope was at least partially gained. I also have to regret that I talked conceitedly to you. But you will forgive me, and I shall be cured of it in time.[10]

Ruskin expressed his esteem of MacDonald at this time not only through tasteful gifts, but also by being present to encourage the efforts of the family. Greville records that, although Ruskin was shocked at the number of guests who, in his opinion, came improperly dressed, he nevertheless entered heartily into the dancing at the conclusion of the day.[11] When the MacDonalds held more of these events, they enlisted several of their friends to help serve.

It was MacDonald's nature to establish intimate personal relationships with a certain few people to whom he felt strongly attracted. Whether he liked a person deeply seems to have depended on his assessment of that person's spiritual sensitivity and overtly kind and loving ways. He made it a point, however, to be meticulously congenial and sympathetic with everyone, fixing them with his penetrating blue eyes and expressive face. The result was a coterie of people who paid him warm homage.

One such was William Carey Davies. The son of a dissenting minister and on the verge of disillusionment with Christianity, he enrolled in one of MacDonald's classes at King's College. MacDonald's teaching had a crucial effect on his life, giving him an orientation to Christianity that his background had not. MacDonald resigned his post at King's on March 27, 1868, citing his literary engagements that were "now more remunerative and more numerous."[12] But Davies went with him, becoming his secretary, accountant, and proofreader. He served in these capacities over a great deal of the remainder of MacDonald's career.

The admiration and homage that several people extended to MacDonald did not always involve a complete agreement with his views, nor was MacDonald piqued by a friend's disagreeing with him. Earnestly applying to himself his teaching on the necessity of self-abnegation, he remained free of that large view of self that characterizes some religious leaders, so that they attract a cultic following. In 1868, when MacDonald sent him a copy of his *Unspoken Sermons,* Ruskin replied: "They are the best sermons—beyond all compare—I have ever read. . . . But I feel so strongly that it is only the image of your own mind that you see in the sky!"[13] Such comment would not have altered MacDonald's attitude toward his friend.

Another instance of a friendship that surmounted differences of opinion was with J. MacLeod Campbell, the popular Scottish divine. Like Scott and Maurice, Campbell had clashed with the Presbyterian authorities over the issue of the universality of the Atonement. They had found him guilty of heresy and deprived him of his living. He proceeded to establish his own church in Glasgow and conducted a large independent ministry there until his death in 1872. The precise nature of his disagreement with MacDonald is unclear, but he was a forthright man who spoke his mind. MacDonald was evidently aware that Campbell held a low opinion of some of his work, but he was determined that their friendship surmount their differences. In 1868, as MacDonald was looking forward to a lecture tour that would take him to Glasgow, he wrote Campbell, intending to stay in his home while there, and remarked:

> I have been working very hard since I came home, and so I daresay have you. And I suppose you think some of my work had better be left undone. Never mind. We won't quarrel about it. Time will bring out the event of things. Meantime whether we agree or not, you are a downright good fellow, and I hope to know more of you. I hope too you will say of me, as the man replied to the appeal of his dying wife—"Oh middlin', jist middlin?"[14]

MacDonald had a persistent love of Scottish garb and maintained his own supply. Because Campbell was having a Glasgow tailor make a kilt for him, he sent along the desired measurements: waist, thirty-two; seat, forty-three; length, twenty-six. Putting these together with the fact that MacDonald's height was five feet ten and a half inches gives a fair idea of his profile. An interviewer later described him as:

> a tall impressive-looking man, a little high-shouldered, and not without a tendency to Scotch gauntness, the head well shaped, the features fine, the whole expression noble. Hair long and flowing to the shoulders, full beard and moustache, which, like the hair of the head, was grizzled. I was much struck by the broadness of his Scotch accent.[15]

He was quickly impatient when he felt someone was ready to take advantage of him. He had begun an association with the energetic publisher Strahan, who brought out *Dealings with the*

Fairies in 1867. When Strahan, apparently in response to some reader dissatisfaction, had suggested that something MacDonald had written was either not orthodox or not pious enough, Mac-Donald exploded to Louisa: "What does Strahan mean by sending me such rubbish? If he thinks to turn me into a slave of *Good Words* and *Good Words* into a slave of such foolish people, I shall soon cut my moorings."[16]

Guild Court had been serialized in *Good Words,* the magazine Strahan was behind, in 1867. *The Seaboard Parish* was appearing throughout 1868 in the popular *Sunday Magazine.* "I will give him a finishing story of the vicar's for the Sunday if he likes, but if he is going to turn goody with *Good Words,* it has seen the last of me." He was adamantly against having his work altered in any way. After these novels had been serialized they were published as novels. The process was a tedious one and involved MacDonald in an immense amount of work, for which he felt he was inadequately compensated. "I would rather have 800 pounds for a novel not first in a magazine than 1000 pounds for one in a magazine. It is such a bore."[17]

Although his novels were now commanding such prices, the family seems always to have been financially stressed. "No more money to send my little woman at home. She must hang on as well as she can for a day or two and let me know when she can't any longer, and I will contrive something," he lamented on one occasion.[18] At another time he assured Louisa that he would write Strahan for an advance of ten pounds to enable her to meet their obligations.

Sheer financial need forced him to maintain a vigorous schedule of lecturing. He would take publisher's proofs with him and work assiduously on them, while continuing his writing when he could. Immediately after Christmas of 1867, he left—this time accompanied by Louisa—for a lecture tour of Scotland, visiting Huntly during a busy itinerary that had them crisscrossing Scotland during the snow and cold of a virile winter. Marischall College of Aberdeen had engaged the painter George Reid to do MacDonald's portrait. They stayed at the Geddes's, making a trip out of Aberdeen to lecture in places like Glasgow or Banff and then returning for another sitting.

Everywhere they went they were very well received. MacDonald was beginning to be heralded in Scotland as a novelist in the tradition of Sir Walter Scott. A young girl, learning of Reid's commission, pressed Reid to introduce her to the author of *Alec Forbes of Howglen,* but he firmly refused. During one of the sittings, as the fire in the grate languished, the painter rang for more firewood. He was startled to see this same girl, appropriately dressed for the task, respond to his call, rebuild the fire, and tidy the hearth. After she left, when MacDonald happened to remark on her beauty and grace, the embarrassed Reid explained her ruse. When MacDonald realized to what effort she had gone simply to see him closely, he called for her and gave the interview she had exercised such ingenuity to secure.

In each city he commanded huge crowds. Louisa told Lily: "There was such a crowd in the afternoon at the chapel yesterday—1200 they say, and such a number of young men. It was really a fine sight."[19] And again: "There was a famous attendance at the lecture last night. Quite an ovation at the last. He has been received every where with enthusiasm. Papa read more beautifully than ever."[20] Perhaps prompted in part by MacDonald's popularity among the Scottish people, the University of Aberdeen bestowed on him the honorary degree of Doctor of Laws in 1868. Evidently their scruples over *David Elginbrod* were not so great as those of the University of Edinburgh, where three years earlier he had failed to secure a Chair.

Having established a strong reputation both in Scotland and in the Manchester area, MacDonald returned to these places most often. He was in Manchester in the spring of 1868 and again in the fall, the latter itinerary including Nottingham and Lancaster. Early in January of 1869, he left for yet another lecture tour of Scotland, committing himself to a demanding schedule.[21] He was not feeling well when he left, and in Glasgow red stains began to appear on his handkerchief. He took to his bed, but left it to do his lecture, to the amazement of his hosts. He told Louisa:

> Pulsford [his host at Glasgow] is full of astonishment at what I can do. He says if any six doctors had seen me yesterday they would all say I must not speak. I am not at all sure, all but impossible as speaking has appeared even to myself before beginning, that it does not do me good. Don't be uncomfortable about me, love: I will send for you or come home to you at once, if I break down.[22]

At home Louisa was incapacitated with headache and toothache; nevertheless, she implored him to allow her to come to him to do what she could. He refused, and kept going. "I had a full house—full to the doors last night—1200" he wrote from Edinburgh.

Still refusing to rest properly, he undertook another series of lectures in Yorkshire in April. There he found himself unable to function acceptably, forgetting the commonest words, blundering, and floundering in his speech when he got excited. He had to write Strahan saying he could not meet a deadline for the next installment of his story *At the Back of the North Wind*, which had begun in November 1868, to run serially in *Good Words for the Young*. In addition to all his other work MacDonald had also agreed to be the magazine's editor. He would soon pay a grievous price for his persistent overexertion.

TWENTY-TWO

As If an Awful Destruction Were Most Likely

A good man I do not doubt he was; but he did the hard parts of his duty to the neglect of the genial parts, and therefore was not a man to help others to be good.—Wilfrid Cumbermede

Although the lessons from life that school the spirit can be hard earned, to say the least, MacDonald never seemed to waver in his conviction that life should be heeded and its lessons honored, as though it were a kindly mentor. In 1869 he was to learn that he must quit overtaxing his delicate constitution, but the lesson he felt life most consistently taught was that each one should affirm life while denying the self. Seeing in many evangelicals precisely opposite perspectives—they tended to deny life and inflate the self—he sought in his writings to expose such attitudes for what they were. The quantity of the evangelical spirit in Louisa's family kept him well abreast of the type.

"Tomorrow the first end of my prayer will come at last. I shall be with you—Oh I have gone through some of the folds of the shadow of death since I saw you, but the light has never ceased to shine."[1] Desperately ill, he was writing from the train that was bringing him home from an ill-fated excursion to the north.

Finally recognizing his need for a period of rest and relaxation, he and Louisa had given some thought to going to Switzerland.

He had, after all, promised Louisa to take her there when he could. However, he remembered with distaste the stifling heat of that summer and was reluctant to chance anything similar now. Then, quite unexpectedly, an invitation came for him to make a yachting trip, with a group consisting mostly of Scottish clergy, up the west coast of Norway, "a good deal farther north" than Trondhjem. They were hoping to sail around the Lofoten Islands. It promised to be ideally cool and relaxing. Louisa, typically self-effacing, readily sacrificed her pleasure to his. Switzerland was forgotten, and he accepted.

The opportunity came through Alex Stevenson, a wealthy mine-owner in Newcastle, whose merchant cousin John owned the yacht. Christened *The Blue Bell* and rigged as a schooner, its one hundred twenty tons offered all the amenities and luxuries of the day. Planned to intermingle business with pleasure, the trip was scheduled to leave on June 10 from Largs.

Lily and Gracie accompanied their father to Alexandria in Dumbartonshire, where the girls stayed at Tullichewen Castle with their friends the James Campbells. MacDonald was relieved that John Stevenson would accompany him from there to Glasgow: "It is a comfort, when one is tired especially."

MacDonald's letter written as the yacht was embarking exhibits an intermingling of excitement together with some seemingly minor annoyances concerning his health. He was delighted with the sparkling whiteness and cleanliness of everything and by the way "we just crept along as swiftly as in a dream" as they departed. Especially amusing were the dining tables, so constructed that they remained level while the ship tossed. During their first dinner they were in a "near Squall," causing the ship to make "off like a wild thing," and "the consequence [of the tables remaining level] is that taking yourself for level, they look as if they were tumbling, and you can't imagine how the things can stick on them at such an angle. It was with great difficulty that some of our party could keep their places at the table because of their chairs sliding away with them to the other side."

Some threatening problems did annoy him: a developing sty, a knee that was "very troublesome sometimes," and a "shivering-fit after I got into bed," which made him fear he may be getting ill. But the trip promised him plenty of time to rest. "I fear I shall write very little. I enjoy being on the deck and doing nothing."[2]

As it happened he did write "very little" but not because he was enjoying himself. On Saturday his knee became so swollen and inflamed that all were alarmed. On Sunday night they docked "on the coast of Ross shire" to summon a doctor, who confined him entirely to bed with poultices and leeches to be applied periodically. For ten days he lay in the best cabin in the yacht but one without "window or porthole," so that the startlingly beautiful northern coastline was lost to him. On hearing of his condition Louisa urged his return: "I trust you will come home straight from Trondhjem. Ah! do dear—only perhaps you may get better by that time, and then the North Wind might after all comfort you in that long hair."[3] Louisa's imagination was gripped by an image from his recently completed tale, *At the Back of the North Wind*. The idea suggested by the imagery in the story—that solace is available to one who receives adversity in the proper spirit—was about to be put to severe test.

"Sleepless nights, weary days—pain, pain, wouldn't eat—could scarcely read, no woman near to attend him—not one face he had ever seen before about him—the most horrible noises incessantly going on about and around him," Louisa later bewailed as she described the situation to MacDonald's aunt.[4] He would have welcomed some reading, but the only novel aboard was "that awful *Vanity Fair*." Something of Carlyle he found "instructive but not quite so instructive as dreary." And so passed a weary time while he hoped for improvement.

But his condition worsened. He lost his appetite so that all he could consume was weak beef tea. When they arrived at Trondhjem, they summoned another doctor, who lanced what was by this time a huge abscess that began about four inches up the side of the leg and spread all over the knee.[5] Now physically weak and in great pain, he was left on board while the others went on excursions into the countryside. When they learned that the steamer *Norway* was bound for Newcastle-on-Tyne, they made arrangements to place him on board—he had to be lifted through the skylight on a stretcher—to convey him back to England.

At Newcastle, Alex Stevenson met him and accompanied him to London, where the anxious family received him. Louisa related: "I was to meet him at King's Cross, and oh . . . I shall never forget what I saw on arriving at the Platform. There was an invalid carriage and in it a man propped up with pillows looking as if he were in the last stage of consumption, with a horrid cough. I could scarcely believe for a minute that it was George. He could hardly raise himself. His eyes were sunken his checks hollow and he was so weak that his voice as hollow as his cheeks could not speak."[6] Greville remembers thinking, when he first saw his father, that he was dead.

At last back in his own bed he "looked all round the room and cried with thankfulness." A vase of sweet peas, his favorite flower, was by his side. When he was ill, Louisa's "nursing" was indispensable to him. Louisa told his aunt: "Oh it was wonderful to see him sleeping, sleeping on and on like the stillest sleep of an infant. He says tho' it was nearly worth it all—the wonderful effect of the blue sky just above him as they laid him on the floor of his cabin when they took the skylight up—when they lifted him up with cords. It was as if he looked out from his grave the tall mast of the vessel rising from his cabin—that and the blue sky was all he saw then he felt his Resurrection was come but I should like you to hear him tell this. It was his one spot of Joy."

The "one spot of joy" notwithstanding, he had been nearer to death then he had yet been with his earlier bouts of hemorrhaging from the lungs. Typically, he put the entire experience in positive perspective: "He says . . . he had never had anything but the luxury of illness before and it was well that he should know its real misery." And Louisa saw a further positive reason for the experience: "He said wherever they carried him people looked at him so, he looked like a hero coming from the wars, and 'alas!' he said, 'I had done nothing for anybody'. But he had suffered intensely and who shall say those sufferings were not for other people in what he may hereafter write."[7] Whatever he felt he was learning he determined to pass along to his readers.

It was, however, some time before he had energy to return to his writing with vigor. He seemed to Louisa to be dreadfully altered, having lost all "animal flow of spirits which makes him so pleasant to strangers generally."[8] He and Louisa took a leisurely boat trip up the west coast to Oban in Scotland in the early fall, hoping to be reinvigorated. They briefly visited Huntly; the children remained at home under Lily's care.

The first writing he did after his ordeal was probably *Ranald Bannerman's Boyhood,* which began to appear serially in *Good Words for the Young* in November 1869 and ran through the following October. The difficulty he had in warming again to the task of writing accounts for the slight character of that strongly autobiographical work, a thinly disguised account, with sundry additions, of his boyhood in Huntly.

Louisa remarks in the letter quoted above that he had a "very good engagement" to write a new novel. It is quite probably *Wilfrid Cumbermede,* which began to appear serially in *St. Paul's,* of London, in November 1870. After running for a year it was published as a novel. MacDonald received twelve hundred pounds from Strahan for the copyright.[9]

Wilfrid Cumbermede is an interesting work for several reasons. One is the strength with which MacDonald works out his themes. Returning to the *Bildungsroman* form, he tells the story of Wilfrid's growing up, with an uncle for his guardian, in relatively modest circumstances but in proximity to the huge country estate of Moldwarp Hall. His uncle, a meek and kindly man, willfully keeps Wilfrid in ignorance of the fact that the boy is the rightful heir to Moldwarp Hall simply because he wants Wilfrid to acquire virtue before he comes into such a position of wealth and prestige.

The uncle, however, suddenly dies, and Wilfrid learns of his heirship gradually through a series of incidents. By the time he is sure of his right and is in a position to claim his legacy, he discovers he can do so only by bringing great deprivation to Mary Osborne, the woman he loves. She is married to Wilfrid's enemy, and the couple is living at Moldwarp Hall. To claim his right would be to evict his beloved. He resolves his dilemma by an act of utter self-abnegation—he forgoes his claim to Moldwarp Hall. He allows his enemy and his beloved to continue living there and leaves them in ignorance of his sacrificial largess.

His action is depicted as godlike. As the novel concludes, Wilfrid muses on what he has learned:

> If all love be not creation—as I think it is—it is at least the only thing in harmony with creation and the love of oneself is its absolute opposite. I sickened at the sight of myself: how should I ever get rid of the demon? The same instant I saw the only escape: I must offer it back to its source—commit it to him who had made it. . . . I saw too that thus God also lives—in this higher way. I saw, shadowed out in the absolute devotion of Jesus to men, that the very life of God by which we live is an everlasting eternal giving of himself away.[10]

Self-abnegation is the essence of the divine nature; those who would be children of God should emulate the pattern.

In the story MacDonald sets this act of self-sacrifice over against the general manipulation and possessiveness that he saw in many professing Christians of the evangelical mindset. In Mr. Osborne, Mary's father, he creates perhaps his most compelling evangelical. Osborne's religious dogmas and attitudes are the chief source of frustration for the main characters. They are so life-denying that he drives his earnest but questioning son Charles, Wilfrid's bosom friend, to suicide and keeps his daughter from returning Wilfrid's love. "An Evangelical of the most pure, honest, and narrow type . . . he looked as if the care of the whole world lay on his shoulders, as if an awful destruction were the most likely thing to everyone, and to him were committed the toilsome chance of saving some.''[11] He is filled with distrust and suspicion, preoccupied with finding evil in things and condemning them, rather than with discerning the good and affirming it. These attitudes are in reality a subtle but terrifying display of selfism. However well-meaning the father is, the result of his actions is negative and destructive. In sharp contrast, Wilfrid's self-sacrificing action marks the pattern of true religious conduct. The theme of the destructive nature of selfism, which was a dominant idea in *Phantastes*, receives here another strong delineation.

This novel is also interesting in the way MacDonald draws on his trip to Switzerland in 1865; he describes Wilfrid's outing in the Alps and elaborately describes their beauty. A larger point of interest, however, are the oblique references to Ruskin's infatuation with the young Rose La Touche, one of the more intriguing love affairs of the century.[12] Ruskin's wife had their marriage dissolved in 1854, alleging Ruskin's "incurable impotence." Annulments or divorces were quite rare at that time, and the affair, occurring as it did in the life of a public figure, created no little notoriety. But Ruskin later confided to MacDonald that his unwillingness to consummate his marriage was because of a basic incompatibility between him and his wife and not from any physical inability.

Among Ruskin's friends of long standing was the Irish would-be intellectual and woman of letters, Mrs. Maria La Touche, the woman responsible for first introducing MacDonald to Ruskin. She was married to an Irish banker and industrialist of strong Calvinist commitment. He was a domineering and authoritarian man, a Baptist, and a follower of the popular evangelical preacher Charles Spurgeon. She spent her time between Ireland and London, often bringing her attractive daughter Rose with her. As Rose was growing up Ruskin exercised what appeared to be simply a paternal interest in his friend's daughter, who responded by treating him with great fondness. But in 1866, as she was blossoming into young womanhood, he, at forty-seven, confessed his love to her and proposed marriage.

Understandably confused by his ardor, Rose told him he must wait until 1869, when she would be twenty-one, for her answer. Her parents, learning of the situation, whisked her back to Ireland and forbade correspondence between her and her would-be lover. Their main objection was not the age difference so much as the fear that if the marriage produced children, the grounds for the annulment of Ruskin's first marriage would become invalid. Rose could find herself with offspring who, in the view of the courts, would be illegitimate. Ruskin was left to languish in unrequited love.

When the designated year arrived, Rose was still unable to make a clear decision, and Ruskin was obliged to continue to wait. MacDonald, finding himself in an unenviable position as a friend of both Ruskin and the La Touches, tried to find some resolution to the situation. This whole tumultuous affair was going on at approximately the same time that he began writing *Wilfrid Cumbermede*.

Later, in 1872, MacDonald received from Rose some anguishing letters and became alarmed. Her mind was obviously in turmoil, and her health was deteriorating. She had been psychologically disturbed for some time. He therefore contacted Ruskin, who was on one of his many trips abroad, and arranged for him and Rose to meet at The Retreat. The two met there that summer, as well as at the home of the Cowper-Temples. It was apparently a helpful time for both, but Rose, still disturbed by their differences, especially regarding Ruskin's faith, continued to demur about their marriage. She was drawn to her father's faith; Ruskin was openly skeptical of Christianity, although he continued to admire MacDonald and even had several conversations with the Rev. Charles Spurgeon. Rose returned to Ireland, her health continued to deteriorate, and she died in 1875.

MacDonald, of course, would not have known what the outcome of this affair would be when he was writing *Wilfrid Cumbermede*, but it would appear that his knowledge of John La Touche offered him a model for his character Mr. Osborne and

Rose for Mary. Ruskin's father had also been of this mold. Mac-Donald may well have had Ruskin's spiritual state in mind—his objections to Christianity, together with his differences with his father—as he drew Charles Osborne's anguishing ambivalence between an attraction to Christianity and an inability to accept it. Wilfrid's unrequited passion for Mary Osborne, which ends in Wilfrid's making a godlike renunciation for her good, could represent MacDonald's view of Ruskin's affair, together with the course of action he was advising as best for Ruskin and Rose.

MacDonald's father-in-law was also uncomfortably close to the Osborne mold. Many of his negative and domineering attitudes may be mirrored in this fictional character. An incident occurring near the end of his life illustrates the point. Nearing ninety, Powell remained a formidable man, of independent mind, strong evangelical opinions, and stoic attitudes. Among his convictions was the belief that Christians in the next life would be so "spiritual and different" that they would recall nothing of the past, and thus have no memory of other people. Kept by his persuasion from anticipating reunion with his beloved wife, he grew sadder as he grew older, giving his family genuine distress.

Godwin and Charlotte tried to cheer him into looking forward but to no avail. He took their efforts in stoic silence while they were present, but after they were gone he never failed to denounce them angrily as "soft pious twaddlings." There was no marriage or giving in marriage in heaven.

One night, when Caroline was listening to her father read some chapters out of The Wisdom of Solomon from the Apocrypha, she ventured to ask if he would be willing to read some words from "another old Jew." She then fetched him Browning's "Rabbi Ben Ezra." "Browning—Who's Browning?" he asked. She knew that had it been Tennyson he would not have read one word. He began as if to make fun of it, but he soon became more thoughtful and then began to weep. He especially liked the stanza:

And I shall thereupon
Take rest, ere I be gone
Once more on my adventure brave and new
Tearless and unperplexed
When I wage battle next
What weapons to select, what armour to indue.

One night shortly afterward, unable to sleep, he lay awake praying that he might have fresh powers and fresh strength to begin the battle once more in another world, and he thought that God promised it to him. Apparently to him the most satisfying metaphor for life beyond as well as for life here was one of pitched battle. Life was replete with things to oppose. MacDonald respected his father-in-law for Louisa's sake, but he found much to oppose in the type of Christianity he embraced. Powell died June 20, 1870, a somewhat happier man for having encountered Browning's poem.

The elder Powell's death was followed in three months by that of his son Alexander, husband of MacDonald's cousin Helen, who kept a dairy near Liverpool. He had been ailing for some time.

Immediately on hearing of Helen's loss, MacDonald penned her a letter of condolence. Burdened with work and in ill health himself, MacDonald wondered if he could avoid making the trip north. He wrote his brother-in-law Joshua Sing inquiring whether Helen would be offended if he did not come to the funeral. "It could be a somewhat serious loss to me at a time when I need every penny I can get, to make up lee-way and even to keep going. But I should not let this prevent me, nor other things either, if she would be in the least hurt or disappointed by our not going."[13] Evidently Sing judged MacDonald's presence was needed, for they went to Liverpool for three days.

The incident sheds interesting light on MacDonald's relationship to Helen Powell. He had felt some attraction to her when he was in college, having written her a number of poems. Their occasional correspondence through the years was characterized by a sprightly tone of banter and a certain assumed intimacy. It is also evident that MacDonald respected his brother-in-law. But when the latter died, the fact that he did not feel it necessarily incumbent on him to go to the funeral, and that he wrote his other brother-in-law inquiring whether Helen would miss him if he did not come, suggests that he did not view their relationship as being unusually close.

Later, Helen sent MacDonald several of her husband's things. Grateful, MacDonald put them to good use. MacDonald's mother was asked to stay with Helen while she disposed of the dairy and then to come down to spend the remainder of the winter with the MacDonalds at Hastings.

TWENTY-THREE

Ask Me Anything You Like

Oh dear! What a mere inn of a place the world is! And thank God! We must widen and widen our thoughts and hearts. A great good is coming to us all—too big for this world to hold.—MacDonald to Louisa, October 26, 1891

His reputation now well established, MacDonald's books were being reissued as newer ones kept coming out. Strahan published in 1872 new editions of *Annals of a Quiet Neighbourhood* and *The Seaboard Parish,* along with the newly written *The Vicar's Daughter* (the three are sequels), thereby putting on the market his own editions of the set. By this time two new editions of *David Elginbrod* had also appeared, by separate publishers. MacDonald was being widely read. His unrelenting attacks, however, on attitudes and doctrines widely held in Victorian Christendom, such as his portrait of Osborne in *Wilfrid Cumbermede* and his rejection of the eternality of damnation in *Robert Falconer,* raised many objections to his work. Laity questioned his doctrinal soundness; critics suggested that his seeming fixation with such themes marred the art of his work.

Several reviewers, such as one writing in the *Fortnightly Review* in 1868, complained that he had become "increasingly didactic" since *David Elginbrod,* his novels showing "a lamentable falling-off in artistic method and purpose."[1] His books were admirable if he would put his preaching aside. MacDonald probably had such criticisms in mind when he wrote in *Guild Court,* "nothing in which the art is uppermost is worth the art expended upon it."[2] Art, like all things rightly viewed, should serve the spiritual ends of life. American reviewers tended to be more enthusiastic concerning MacDonald's preoccupatin with concerns of the human spirit but would have liked more action and adventure. One especially praised *Alec Forbes of Howglen* but expressed unhappiness with the author's inability to depict "excitement and great passion."[3]

While his work by and large continued to receive the praise it had drawn at first, the public was now aware not only that his preeminent concerns were religious but that many of his religious positions were singular. Rumors that he was writing heresy began to circulate. Once when Louisa stepped into a Hastings bookstore to get some pens the owner called her into the corner of his room and asked if it was true that her husband absolutely denied eternal punishment and the incarnation of Christ in *Robert Falconer*. He said he had all MacDonald's other books in his library, but a lady had come to him in great distress begging him not to sell that one because of those two things. He was worried about the effect of the many copies of *Unspoken Sermons* he had sold. Louisa, with a bit of asperity, told him she did not think he would find anything worse in *Robert Falconer* than in those sermons.[4] The type of person who wants to know all about a book without reading it is not confined to the twentieth century.

Some of the many who did read MacDonald's works and were unhappy with what they found wrote to tell him so. Patiently, he tried to answer all his mail, even though to do so impinged seriously on his time. The task was often a weariness to him, especially when the writer seemed to be deliberately misunderstanding what seemed to him obviously plain or when a writer would attempt to conceal identity. The following response to a woman who attempted to remain anonymous is a good illustration of the skill he developed in responding to his objectors. He managed to tell her without being offensive that her manner of approach was less than honest and her question less

than perceptive. At the same time he expressed a spiritual message
that was singularly calculated to her need:

> *Dear Madam,*
> *. . . I cannot understand how after reading many of my*
> *books—as you say—you should suppose I believed such things as*
> *you seem to take for granted I do believe concerning the future*
> *state of the greater number of those whom God has*
> *created. . . . I can only say that if you find it taught in the*
> *bible that God created beings merely to suffer and die, then the*
> *God of the Bible must be a false God. But I do not find that in*
> *the Bible. It would be useless for me to spend my time in saying*
> *over again what I have said so often in print, and I can afford*
> *neither that time nor the labour involved. But if you read*
> *either* Robert Falconer *or the* Unspoken Sermons, *you will*
> *find a great deal of what I have to say concerning those*
> *matters.*
> 　　*Be sure if you go on enquiring you will find the truth—*
> *enough of it to keep you alive and wishing for more, and that is*
> *enough for us at a time. And be sure that if you raise the*
> *highest structure of imagined loveliness, truth, grandeur and*
> *graciousness, of tenderness and self-denial, of love that will*
> *punish fearfully rather than leave the beloved in sin—I say,*
> *construct as you will, God will tower above it all, greater and*
> *grander and lovelier, even as the heavens are higher than the*
> *earth. In him is no darkness, and you are bound to understand*
> *him to your measure.*[5]

The facility with which he found people misunderstood him
may well be one reason he obviously labored and so often repeated
himself in some of his writings to make his points crystal clear.
His willingness to be the patient mentor is apparent in his extant
letters to his children as well. When MacDonald was recuperating
from his close encounter with death during the summer of 1869,
Mary, or Elfie as he was fond of calling her, wrote to her father

when he was resting at Dovedale, a scenic glen southeast of Manchester. Evidently, she found herself unable to love God as she felt she should and, perplexed about her spiritual state, wrote her father and frankly told him so. Both the tone and substance of his response suggest much concerning his nature and his relationship to his second daughter:

> *My darling Elfie,*
>
> *. . . . I will with all my heart try to answer your question. And in order to make it as plain as I can, I will put the answer in separate parts. You must think over each of them separately and all of them together.*
>
> *In order to any one loving another, three things are necessary:*
>
> *1st. That the one should be capable of loving the other, or loving in nature*
>
> *2nd. That the other should be fit to be loved, or loveable*
>
> *3rd. That the one should know the other.*
>
> *Upon each of these three points respectively I remark:*
>
> *1st. Now we are capable of loving, but we are not capable enough, and the very best, the only thing indeed that we can do to make ourselves more capable is to do our duty. When a person will not do his duty, he gradually becomes incapable of loving, for it is only good people that can love. All who can love are so far good. If a man were to grow quite wicked he could only hate. Therefore to do our duty is the main thing to lead us to the love of God.*
>
> *2nd. God is so beautiful, and so patient, and so loving, and so generous that he is the heart and soul and root of every love and every kindness and every gladness in the world. All the beauty in the world and in the hearts of men, all the painting all the poetry all the music, all the architecture comes out of his heart first. He is so loveable that no heart can know how loveable he is—can only know in part. When the best man loves*

God best, he does not love him nearly as he deserves, or as he will love him in time.

3rd. In order that we should know God, and so see how loveable he is, we must first of all know and understand Jesus Christ. When we understand what he meant when he spoke, and why he did the things he did, when we see into his heart, then we shall understand God, for Jesus is just what God is. To do this we must read and think. We must also ask God to let us know what he is. For he can do more for those who ask than for those who do not ask.

But if it all depended on us, we might well lose heart about it. For we can never do our duty right until we love God. We can only go on trying. Love is the best thing; the love of God is the highest thing; we cannot be right until we love God. Therefore we cannot do right—I mean thoroughly right—until we love God. But God knows this better than we do, and he is always teaching us to love him. He wants us to love him, not because he loves himself, but because it is the only wise, good, and joyous thing for us to love him who made us and is most lovely.

So you need not be troubled about it darling Elfie. All you have to do and that is plenty is to go on doing whatever you know to be right, to keep your heart turned to God for him to teach you, and to read and try to understand the story of Jesus. A thousand other things will come in from God to help you if you do thus.

I am very very glad you asked me, my child. Ask me anything you like, and I will try to answer you if I know the answer. For this is one of the most important things I have to do in the world.

Mamma sends her dear love to you.

Your father[7]

The lines of communication were evidently quite open between father and daughter. MacDonald's tone of commendation, fatherly concern, and careful attention to the issue at hand did much to ensure they would remain so. Busy as he was, he did not neglect giving careful attention to the task of raising his children, feeling that it was one of his primary obligations in life.

Not all the children's concerns were quite so ideal as Mary's. Greville asked his mother once, as a young boy might, "Mamma, shouldn't you like to be a highwayman?" "No dear, I don't think I should particularly," was the reply, to which he responded: "Oh, wouldn't you? I should awfully." "So you see his morals have not grown since he left home," Louisa wryly commented to her husband.[8] Louisa gave no indication that she was overly concerned about her son's ill-placed enthusiasms.

One of the family's stronger concerns was for Greville to do well in King's, where he had secured a scholarship because of his singing abilities. He mastered his studies only with great difficulty, so that when he passed an examination, he had cause to feel a special sense of achievement. The family was quick to support and congratulate him, and such encouragement helped him greatly.

In 1871, Greville was invited by a doctor friend of MacDonald's to spend the summer with him at Jedburgh. A bachelor, the doctor rode on horseback to visit his patients, and for the summer took his young guest along. Greville took such delight in accompanying him, that, when he returned to his home, he announced that he was determined to study medicine.

The parents were extremely apprehensive. They entertained a keen sense of Greville's limitations and did not want him to become involved in a program of study that would only overwhelm him and result in serious discouragement. MacDonald himself, as a young man at King's College in Aberdeen, had given serious thought to becoming a doctor, and he was quite aware of the demanding course that lay ahead. After careful consideration and prayer the parents decided to help him try to take a realistic view of his prospects but not to stand in his way.

Greville's resolve was adamant; he undertook the task, applied himself with vigor and concentration, and did well in his studies. The family was exceedingly gratified. In part, his success was due to his doctor friend's having detected one cause of Greville's former scholastic difficulties: he had a hearing impairment that was more serious than anyone had known. The doctor discussed the matter with the parents. After the problem was detected steps were taken to remedy it, and Greville's education thereafter progressed with less difficulty.

During the time when Greville was attending boarding school, the family was spending more and more time down at Hastings. By the spring of 1870, MacDonald still had not fully recovered his health from his yachting trip and seemed plagued with more frequent attacks of asthma and bronchitis. Further, Louisa was exhausted to the point of breakdown. Thinking the sea air might restore them both, they engaged temporary lodgings at Caroline House, then took more permanent ones in 3 Reculvers Cottage. Later, in 1871, they secured the more commodious Halloway House. For the remainder of their tenure at The Retreat, they maintained some quarters in Hastings, and part of the family was often there.

They enjoyed Hastings so much that they began to give serious thought to renting The Retreat as a furnished home and staying permanently by the sea. This proving impractical, they continued to maintain two places, tending to spend the winter down at Hastings and the balance of the year at The Retreat. Two and a half hours by train took them from one place to the other.

MacDonald's recommendation to Mary that she give special attention in her Christian life to a careful study of the life of Christ suggests the consistency of his views. He believed it was essential to maintain an active sense of Christ as a person and friend, an elder brother, rather than to abstract him into a theological entity. The only way to come to love God is to "know and understand Jesus Christ." This conviction no doubt prompted his publishing

during the summer of 1870 *The Miracles of Our Lord*. He undertook to present the miracles not in abstract theological terms but
as human events occurring in the lives of ordinary people, so that
the reader feels the humanity of Christ responding compassion-
ately to human need. MacDonald tended to interpret the miracles
not as events violating or suspending the laws of nature but rather
as accelerating their working. God is constantly working in his
world, turning water into wine, stilling storms, making people
well, and so forth; Christ's miracles present his doing these acts in
a moment of time, rather than in hours or years, as the case may
normally be.

He dedicated the work to F. D. Maurice, "honoured of
God." Maurice's ministry was considerable to the MacDonalds
during their London years, as, in addition to his sermons, he often
called at The Retreat when MacDonald or one of the children was
ill. In 1866 Maurice was made Knightsbridge Professor of Moral
Philosophy at Cambridge, and he tried for a time to hold that
post simultaneously with conducting his Vere Street ministry. The
demands of the two commitments were too strenuous, however,
so he was forced to resign his church. "Mr. Maurice is to make
up his mind this week whether he gives up Vere Street. If he does,
'Oh! the difference to me,'" Louisa lamented to Lily.[9]

Later that year several of his friends raised a collection for him,
as a gesture of love and honor. MacDonald was active in spear-
heading the effort. A portion of a letter in which he invited a
woman friend to contribute to the fund conveys something of
MacDonald's esteem for Maurice, together with revealing Mac-
Donald's attitudes about money:

> I have such a sense of the sacredness of money, and such a
> conviction that it is only the vulgar mind which regards it as
> an unclean thing—because in secret it worships it—that I
> would gladly prevail on Mr. Maurice, should the amount be
> large enough, to accept our love in the form of the gold of
> God's making, that he might do with it as he would. But if
> he should, for his own sacred reasons, decline to accept it in

this form, I should turn it into that of such books as should make him feel rich in their possession.[10]

When Maurice died in 1872, the family felt a keen loss.

The Princess and the Goblin, one of MacDonald's finest fantasies, was written during this period. It began to appear in serial form in *Good Words for the Young* in November 1870. He felt it was a product of his best effort. In a letter to R. W. Gilder he remarked that "in the sense of miserable demerit every one may sometimes hope that he may be doing something beyond the reach of the fire"; he probably would have placed this fantasy in that category.[11] He was the more dismayed, therefore, when sales of *Good Words for the Young* began to drop off, and his story was blamed. Strahan remarked to him that he felt the magazine had "too much of the fairy element" in it. "I know it is as good work of the kind as I can do and I think will be the most complete thing I have done. However," he concluded to Louisa, "I shall drop that sort if people do not care about it. Perhaps I could find a market for that kind of talent in America—I shouldn't wonder."[12] Inasmuch as the writing of fantasy was MacDonald's forte, the reluctance of the Victorian public to respond to his work is the more lamentable.

He was further chagrined when he felt rebuffed by an author who took offense when MacDonald, as editor, rejected his work and ran his own. "Mr. Gilbert would have cut me yesterday in an omnibus—if I had let him. They say he thinks me just the devil—Poor man! he is always threatening his solicitor upon some one or other." MacDonald found pettiness especially annoying, but he knew well the disappointment of having one's work rejected. "I am more and more glad I am to be rid of the editing," he confided to his wife.[13]

The Princess and the Goblin develops with subtle imaginative power the principle that a person must believe in the existence of spiritual realities before one can either discern them or live in harmony with them. The story is about the eight-year-old Princess Irene, who lives in a castle halfway up a mountainside, and Curdie, a somewhat older miner's son. Deep within the mountain, near where Curdie and his father work, is a colony of kobolds or goblins—distorted and devilish beings oriented to the darkness—who oppose the miners and intend them harm. In the far reaches of the upper story of the castle, Irene discovers a mysterious and kindly old lady, her great-great-grandmother Irene, who exercises benevolent power over people's lives.

Perhaps the most powerful scene occurs when Irene, after she succeeds in rescuing Curdie trapped in the mines, excitedly takes him to meet her great-great-grandmother and discovers, to her dismay, that Curdie cannot see her. Instead he sees only "a tub, and a heap of musty straw, and a withered apple, and a ray of sunlight." "People must believe what they can, and those who believe more must not be hard upon those who believe less," the grandmother consoles Irene. Curdie's skepticism prevents the grandmother from revealing herself to him. But, because Curdie is a boy of the right potential, he is later able to see the grandmother, and he acts heroically in faithful obedience to her.

The story is not allegorical, but it does contain symbolic suggestions and mythic power. The structure of the novel's setting, with the grandmother living in the heights of the castle and the goblins living deep below ground, while Irene dwells in the middle, suggests something of a Christian view of the structure of the soul. The spiritual nature, which only certain people acknowledge, seems to dwell in the uppermost reaches of the psyche. MacDonald sees the human merging with the divine in one's spirit (both are named Irene). The baser instincts seem to dwell below. The ego can know spiritual freedom in communion with the former, or it can be enthralled and imprisoned by the latter. Richard Reis observes that this model of the human mind anticipates Freud's.[14] It is also basically Pauline.

Strahan published *The Princess and the Goblin* separately in 1872, with thirty woodcut illustrations by Arthur Hughes. MacDonald was pleased both with the substance of Hughes's drawings and with the fact that Hughes's name appeared with his on the cover. Strahan had also brought out the previous year a beautifully bound and boxed ten-volume set titled *Works of Fancy and Imagination*. The set included MacDonald's fairy stories, poetry, *Phantastes*, and *The Portent*.

However, the jolly and bumptious Strahan, by this time an intimate friend of the family, was partial to the novel *The Vicar's Daughter:* "I like *The Vicar's Daughter* much, very much," he wrote Louisa with flamboyant hand. "I had the proper sensations on reading it this morning. The spine is the true literary barometer, and just as the currents are cold (as they were today) so (in my experience) is the work likely to move and impress."[15] He had paid MacDonald one thousand pounds for it. The story contains in the character Lady Bernard a flattering fictional portrait of Lady Byron.

Finally admitting the necessity to take a respite from his work, MacDonald and Louisa, together with Lily, went with George Reid on a short vacation to Holland in the early fall of 1871. Another trip, however, was decidedly more refreshing. To get inspiration for a new novel that would depict life in the fishing villages to the north of Huntly, among which he had spent time as a youth, MacDonald made two trips there, one in April 1872 with Louisa and the second in May with Maurice. He and Louisa thought they would unobtrusively spend a quiet time, uninterrupted by people. The keeper of the hotel told them on arriving, however, that they need not think to pass anywhere unrecognized. Finding themselves beset with local fans, they managed hastily to secure the nearby estate of the Countess of Seafield, who was visiting in London at the time, for the weeks they spent in Cullen.

The Scottish surroundings did what Europe had failed to do: "Papa seems so quietly happy. He enjoys going out so much and loves talking to all the fisher people and country folk and they really are so nice though not nearly so pleasing or polite as the Highlanders," wrote Louisa to Lily.[16] Material was taking shape in his mind that would issue in a different type of novel, *Malcolm*, concerning the lives of fishing people.

In the middle of their relaxation, with Louisa relieved to have "no bother with housekeeping," a telegram came from Lily that Emma, a young servant, had come down with the measles. Louisa hurried back to take charge, while MacDonald stayed to finish his research and then to lecture at Dundee, Liverpool, and Leicester on his return.

Louisa had a reputation for being an especially tender nurse, an activity that took an appreciable amount of her time. The family experienced much annoyance from the diseases of childhood, many of which hardly concern us today. For instance, in the summer of 1869 mumps went through the household, afflicting all the children within a few weeks. They also frequently had boils and sties, rare ailments today due in large part to altered hygienic practices. MacDonald often complained of having painful sties, as well as debilitating headaches. One of Louisa's abilities was the capacity to be both sympathetic and tireless in such strenuous situations.

TWENTY-FOUR

Becoming Fond of America

*To set out free, to walk on and on, without a notion of what
at any turn of the road is to appear—it is like reading a story
that comes to life as you read it! And then in the last chapter
to arrive at the loveliest lady in the world, her whose form
and face mingles with every day-dream—it is a chain of gold
with a sapphire at the end of it—a flowery path to heaven!—*
Warlock O' Glenwarlock

James T. Fields, visiting in England in 1869, had suggested
to MacDonald that he seriously consider coming to America for
a lecture tour. The widespread popularity at this time of lecturing
in America had grown out of the Lyceum of the early part of the
century. The Lyceum was a well-organized attempt to raise the
level of education and awareness of the people by providing free
lectures across the nation on various topics. By the 1860s entrepre-
neurs such as James Redpath of Boston had constructed commercial lecture bureaus on the foundation of the Lyceum. They
engaged both native American and popular European speakers,
arranged their tours, and sold tickets to their appearances. The
more popularly interesting or entertaining of these speakers could
command large sums of money, perhaps five hundred dollars a
lecture or on occasion even as high as one thousand dollars.[1]

Naturally, MacDonald was attracted to the prospect of being
amply paid for his work. But his primary motivation was to teach
his interpretation of life to as many as he could interest. Americans
were showing an increased interest in his writings, especially in *The*

Vicar's Daughter, which had been published in Boston in 1871, and in *Robert Falconer,* but in the absence of effective international copyright laws, MacDonald was receiving no royalties. Harper of New York had brought out *Annals of a Quiet Neighbourhood* in 1867 and *Guild Court* in 1868, and Routledge of New York had published editions of *The Princess and the Goblin, Ranald Bannerman's Boyhood,* and *At the Back of the North Wind* in 1871. Gratifying as his growing popularity may have been, MacDonald was nettled to receive no royalties from pirated editions and hoped that by cultivating contacts with the publishing world in America he might be able to secure some badly needed income. And, of course, he would have opportunity to meet the young nation's literary greats. "Mr. Field's invitation goes for something. It ensures familiar intercourse with Emerson, Longfellow, Lowell, and all the rest of them," the enterprising Strahan observed.[2]

MacDonald had been aware for some time of his growing reputation in America. Some American visitors had found their way to The Retreat, and he had received glowing statements of the excitement his writings were generating. In 1869, while he was on his trip to Norway, Louisa related how, when making a social call in Brighton, she had encountered an American lady devotee who gave some shrewd advice: MacDonald should not publish another book in England without making an arrangement with an American publisher that it should come out there simultaneously. She said that Browning did this, along with others of less note, and that it was the only way MacDonald could hope to receive fair income. She told Louisa people in America were "greedy" for MacDonald's books. "They are talked of as a new gospel," Louisa affirmed to MacDonald.[3]

Assured of an enthusiastic reception, in early December of 1871 MacDonald wrote to the firm of Messrs. Redpath and Fall of Boston, putting himself "in their hands." But, in keeping with his principles of personal integrity and humility, he would make no claims concerning his abilities nor allow any boasts in advertising. Further, he was reluctant to commit himself to a firm date for departure because of the serious illness of one of his closest friends since Highbury days, Greville Matheson. He had already this year lost F. D. Maurice in the spring and Norman McLeod, editor of *Good Words,* in July. Then Matheson died in early September.

In spite of his grief MacDonald was excited when arrangements were set to sail from Liverpool on the nineteenth on *The Malta* direct for Boston. He hoped Mr. Fields would be able to meet them when they arrived, "for we shall be so lost in your huge country if left to ourselves." Their only sorrow was the necessity of leaving ten children behind. "Perhaps however it would be harder to leave only one," he mused.[4]

Greville was elected to accompany his parents; the others remained at The Retreat. Throughout their eight-month tour that took them west as far as the Mississippi River and north into Canada, their letters convey their excitement at seeing America, enjoying its hospitality, experiencing its sheer vastness in comparison to the relatively comfortable distances in Britain, and being the objects of so much appreciation, evidently quite deeply felt. They also offer a vivid picture of American culture in the 1870s. The unexpectedly more primitive conditions for travel and lodgings, however, together with the appreciably more rigorous climate than that to which they were accustomed, worked serious hardship on them. The fatiguing schedule Redpath had arranged for them was often jeopardized and on occasion altered.

The Fields met them when they arrived in Boston Harbor on September 30. The crossing had been swift and peaceful; nevertheless, Louisa had been confined to her cabin almost all the time with seasickness. The congenial hospitality of the Fields delighted them, as did the "newness, strangeness, clearness and brightness" of seemingly everything in America. Their hosts lived at a fashionable address—148 Charles Street—where majestic American elms (a tree unfamiliar to them) made Gothic arches over the avenues lined with stately red brick homes.

Louisa found Mrs. Fields to be "true through and through—much educated but no false polish," and they soon became genuine friends. Fields was "very, very amusing—full of anecdotes—and exceedingly kind, a great mimic evidently," who told his stories with dramatic flair.[5] Greville told Lily: "Mr. Fields is forever telling us funny stories and he does it so remarkably cleverly that we roar with laughter."[6]

They were pleasantly surprised at how seemingly English the people were and at how much Boston reminded them of a continental city, such as the Hague. The speech spoken by some—"a fashionable English drawl . . . mixed with the American nasal"—they found somewhat amusing. Boston became the base to which they returned after going by train to various single lectures or brief tours. Greville soon wrote:

> I am getting very fond of Boston; it is so much nicer than any other of the large cities I have seen. It seems quite English and so I feel quite at home in it. New Yorkers and Philadelphians complain of its crookedness and say they can never find their way about. This is because both these cities are so very regular—all the streets are parallel or at right angles to one another. It is quite painful to me![7]

He found it difficult to appreciate the efficient angularity of the layout of the typical American city; the meandering streets and "roundabouts" of Boston were much more like home.

But most difficult was the task of adjusting to the schedule of meals: "They keep a most hospitable table and if you could but eat enough at once—or rather at twice—we should do excellently but it is difficult for us to manage at first," Louisa wrote Elfie. "They have a sumptuous breakfast at 8—dinner at three—and coffee and tea with thin biscuits and iced water at seven." Nevertheless, they decided that, "modified," they "should like to do something like it at home," where several smaller meals during the day was the rule.[8] They also came to prefer the predominance of sunshine in America to the frequency of overcast skies of England ("when the sun shines, How it shines!"), and they were delighted with the glory of the red and yellow leaves of October. The heat, however, was quite another matter; they found it almost impossible to bear.

They were soon introduced to the literary greats of Boston. Their introduction to Harriet Beecher Stowe taxed their social tact and grace, inasmuch as she had recently published an interpretation of Lady Byron's life uncongenial to MacDonald's view.[9] Emerson, together with his wife and daughter, came to lunch on October 5; the same afternoon the MacDonalds called on Longfellow, who proudly showed them through his hundred-year-old home, once General Washington's headquarters. Oliver Wendel Holmes came to a tea the Fieldses gave in the MacDonalds' honor. They would also have met James Russell Lowell had he not been visiting in England at the time, but his sister had them to tea.

Longfellow was present at MacDonald's first lecture in America, given at the Union Hall at Cambridgeport, "beneath the classic shade of Harvard," as the reporter for the Boston *Journal* phrased it, on October 10. Interestingly, the Russell Gurneys were also present, Gurney being in America because he had been appointed as British representative on the commission to settle British and American claims arising out of the Civil War. They made a special trip from Washington to Boston to hear MacDonald's first American lecture, one on Robert Burns.

The lengthy accounts the American press tended to give MacDonald's lectures from city to city preserve a fairly detailed picture of these occasions. The reporter for the Boston *Journal* described him as a man of medium height with an earnest face, wearing "a full, shaggy beard. A few silver threads tell of the maturity of middle age, and he wears glasses. His manner is easy and graceful, and his speech is difficult to describe, combining a distinct tinge of the broad Scotch with the English accent." After beginning his account with several blatant inaccuracies—he presented MacDonald as a graduate of St. Andrews who at first settled in Aberdeen until "outspoken liberal ideas" drove him into a writing ministry—he described the occasion at length.

After preliminary remarks on Burns, MacDonald quoted liberally from the poems, his voice vividly conveying the inimitable charm of the Scotch. He read the entirety of "Tam O' Shanter" with such verve the audience was thoroughly entertained, especially with his animated rendition of the storm:

> The wind blew as 'twad blawn its last;
> The rattling showrs rose on the blast;
> The speedy gleams the darkness swallow'd
> Loud, deep and lang the thunder bellowed;
> That night, a child might understand,
> The Devil had business on his hand.

He treated Burns's drinking songs, making clear that he did not condone the drinking; Burns's worse habits—his "weakness for sensual pleasures"—soiled "the white robes of his innocence."

MacDonald closed by affirming that Burns's remorse was bitter and that he died at the age of thirty-seven because God saw "he was fighting on and making no headway." He closed with an appeal to men to make the best of themselves with God's help, for "the best in a man was the man." The audience thundered their applause. The reporter judged that the people enjoyed "especially the passages in which the high-toned morality of the man burst out with fervent earnestness."[10]

MacDonald had used Burns's life and a selection of his poems to present his own views of the importance of the spiritual and to inculcate moral principles. His lecture had popular appeal because of the earnest, conversational manner—he always spoke without notes—in which he emphasized and reinforced attitudes held in esteem by his audience and because of the charm and power of his readings. The novelty of his Scotch-English accent added appreciably to the effect. With the variations that are inevitable in extemporaneous speaking, MacDonald gave this lecture more frequently during his seven months in America and Canada than any other.

The enterprising Redpath, seeing, not altogether to his pleasure, that he had engaged an appreciably greater lecturer than he had at first thought, remonstrated: "See here, Mr. MacDonald, why didn't you *say* you could do this sort of thing? We'd have got 300 dollars a lecture for you! Guess the Lyceums all over the United States'll think they've *done* Redpath and Fall, sure! You make me sick! Yes, Sir."[11] Then he proceeded to arrange a grueling schedule, with lectures throughout New York, Massachusetts, and New Jersey, as far south as Washington, D.C., and east to Buffalo, before Christmas. Typically, he assigned four lectures a week, but the destinations, being far apart, involved much traveling, with several social occasions and receptions interspersed. "The bear's keeper has not lengthened his chain to our vision beyond the 23 of December," Louisa wryly observed, playfully using her nickname for her husband but apprehensive concerning his health.

On October 21 they were in Philadelphia, where MacDonald lectured in the Academy of Music to a crowd of over three thousand. "Papa says he never saw *such* an audience. It made him rather nervous at first but he rushed into his subject and he held their attention wonderfully." MacDonald was made confident by his hearers' obvious appreciation. Then, at the end of the lecture, the rapport became yet stronger:

> There was a bit of fun at the close. He could not get off the stage. The curtain down behind was so heavy he couldn't get out. He went from one side to another, to get an exit but not finding one and the people beginning to clap him at last he bounded onto the stage box where we sat. It was funny to see him stepping or jumping over the red velvet cushions. They clapped him again, and the laughter was hearty and cheery.[12]

The reporter covering the event remarked that there was a suggestion "of the Frenchman" about MacDonald "in vivacity and nervous enthusiasm" and observed that he talked "much as he writes in his novels, in crisp, impulsive sentences, by no means always rounded into finished rhetoric." He concluded that the rest of the tour would be successful, "for what the critics may fail wholly to admire, the people will choose to love."[13]

The evening following the Philadelphia lecture, the MacDonalds were introduced to New York literary society at a reception at the Park Avenue home of J. G. Holland. He was the editor of *Scribner's Monthly,* a magazine fast gaining a large reputation for its combination of high literary quality with its emphasis on the art of magazine illustrations. The event commemorated the second anniversary of the magazine's founding. Some of MacDonald's poetry had already appeared in its pages; much more would follow in the months immediately ahead. Holland, who obviously admired MacDonald, was a man not unlike him—a layman of serious moral and spiritual concerns, who had written some novels but who wanted above all to be known as a poet.

Louisa found the New Yorkers "outrageously kind and flattering," more so than the Bostonians. Among the many people they met at Holland's was his managing editor, Richard Watson Gilder, who was also a distant relative of MacDonald. A simple-hearted and sensitive man of large affections and an aspiring poet, he had been corresponding with MacDonald since 1871. He would be an intimate correspondent for years to come. Bret Harte, the short story writer, was also present.

On Monday, October 28, they were in Amesbury, Massachusetts, where they were overnight guests of "one of the greatest of the American poets," John Greenleaf Whittier. "It was such a sweet little house he lives in and it was so simple and quiet—it was like a little holy rest when we got into it. A number of Scotch people were there. Many of them came to speak to Papa both before and after the lecture," Louisa wrote the children.[14] Greville was quite impressed with the "dear old gentleman, a Quaker," whose "thees" and "thous" and "thy" sounded "so pretty," and with the general deportment of the Amesbury audience.

He told Lily that the audience at Amesbury was really the

best that his father had ever had, because "they clapped and laughed quite in the right places. . . . In all the other halls," he explained, there had been a burst of laughter "at two words which invariably come in the Burns lecture, viz: 'Devil' and 'drunk.' These two words generally act like magic on the dullest audiences but last night no more notice was taken of them then any other words except one or two silly girls who giggled."[15] After the lecture two Scotsmen made MacDonald a present of Whittier's works in two volumes, and the next morning Whittier said to him, "It is not fair that thee should get it all," so he made Louisa a present of "The Pennsylvania Pilgrim." Whittier considered that long poem, then freshly off the press, his best effort.

Scarcely having been in America a month, MacDonald had been celebrated in Boston, New York, and Philadelphia. He had met most of the well-known in the American literary world of the time and had established a reputation as a significant lecturer. The seven months ahead seemed to hold high promise.

TWENTY-FIVE

A Different Class of People

*I learned that he that will be a hero, will barely be a man:
that he that will be nothing but a doer of his work, is sure
of his manhood.*—Phantastes

Back in England, a reporter observed with a dilettantish air:

> An American paper thus alludes to Mr. George MacDonald,
> who is sharing the honours with Froude, Tyndall, and Ed-
> mund Yates on the other side of the Atlantic just now—
> "George MacDonald . . . is having a quiet, good time in Bos-
> ton, walking or driving every day, and wearing, like a true
> Highlander, the Scotch bonnet, with the insignia of his clan.
> Very fond of horses is George MacDonald, and driveth four-
> in-hand." Very few of his own countrymen, I should imagine,
> were aware before that to his many other gifts and accomplish-
> ments the author of *David Elginbrod* added the ability to drive
> four-in-hand.[1]

The ability to control correctly a four-horse team was more highly
esteemed in America, it would seem, than in England. MacDonald evidently took opportunity to indulge his love of horses and
display his skill in handling them. But, although it was true he
was in general enjoying himself, once the lecture itinerary began
in earnest he had not nearly so much leisure as the English reporter
intimated. Nor was it long before reversals began to occur.

The hectic pace, with new people and experiences met at
every turn, first began to oppress Louisa. At the Fieldses' home
she was often confined to her room with violent migraine attacks.

Then, early in November, she caught her foot in her dress going up the stairs in a guest's home, stumbled, and fell, receiving a bruise that confined her to her room. MacDonald was obliged to continue his lecturing unaccompanied. Further, she found train travel difficult: "The instant I get into the cars I feel sick," she explained to the children. "They all have a hot stove in them. Windows are never opened till *I* get in—then up goes my window directly—only sometimes it is too cold for Papa and so close to us to be able to bear it open long and the motion is much more than on our railroads."[2]

Their schedule demanded constant travel, frequent socializing, and invariable dependence on the hospitality of others: "The most of our days are spent either 'in the cars' (that is on the railroad)—or in company—or in bed which we hail as 'oh! bed oh bed, delicious bed,'" Louisa explained to Winnie. Nor could they adjust to the early risings: "*Everyone* wherever we go has breakfast at 8 o'clock or 7:30—but then we are so glad of it when we do get it. Imagine our feelings when they tell us after a reception— after a lecture—after a six hours journey and a lot of talk, at twelve o'clock at night that they breakfast at 8 and have prayers before that!"[3]

The Fieldses gave a reception for the MacDonalds on November 9; however, MacDonald was forced to excuse himself, having a gumboil so severe he could scarcely open his mouth to utter a word. But their minds were momentarily taken off their ill health by the great Boston fire, which, breaking out that same night, raged on to destroy property estimated at over fifty million dollars. During the reception news came of the uncontrolled flames that were threatening even the stately mansions of Charles Street. The Fieldses frantically began packing their valuables while their commercial properties were going up in flames.

Excitedly, Greville attempted later to describe to Winnie the dimensions of the disaster:

He [Fields] and I went out about eleven o'clock to see how it was looking. This will give you some idea of the intensity of it. When we were nearly half a mile off the fire on the common and the moon was nearly full and shining as bright as ever it did, the glare of the flames obliterated one shadow which the moon would have made and cast one right in the opposite direction!

On Sunday he did nothing but go about the ruins and burning buildings the whole day.

There is something most touching and sad about it all. Nearly a hundred acres which the day before were worth millions of money are now lying in burning masses and smoke and not worth a cent. Over all this vast extent of ground you can't distinguish one street from another and here and there are poor Irish women guarding their few old chairs and a rickety table with an old dutch clock and a few other little ornaments.[4]

While the Fieldses assessed their losses, the MacDonalds were taken to the Cunninghams' home in nearby Milton. Together with having boil, MacDonald had become asthmatic and had bronchial difficulties.[5] Over a week of lectures were canceled while the exhausted lecturer was nursed back to health. Apparently he spent part of the time while recuperating perfecting his lectures on Thomas Hood and Tennyson, for he turned more frequently to these poets' works when he resumed his lecture schedule on November 18 in New York.

Then he began spitting blood and was forced to admit that he had taken on too ambitious an itinerary. They decided to resign themselves to earning less money from their tour by cutting down on the number of lectures. Louisa efficiently proceeded to delete some from their schedule for each week; she also began to make plans to spend the weekend of November 23 resting at the Gurneys' home in Washington.

On Monday following a weekend of rest, the Gurneys saw

them on their way for the eight-hour trip to Jersey City, purchasing the finest of traveling accommodations for them. But after a lecture at Plainfield on Tuesday the twenty-sixth, MacDonald began chilling and continued spitting blood. Dr. Cole, a physician whose hospitality they were enjoying, forbid his continuing his schedule. On December 1, when it was thought safe for him and Louisa to travel, they returned to Washington to the Gurneys'. All lectures were canceled until Christmas, including, much to MacDonald's disappointment, a trip to Chicago.

Fall, of Redpath and Fall, hurrying from Boston to discuss with MacDonald his future itinerary, found he was too ill to be seen, and was obliged to talk with Louisa alone. He was most anxious for the lectures to resume. Louisa explained to the children: "They say that Mr. MacDonald has brought out a class of people quite different from the ordinary lecture goers and they think he will *draw* anywhere, so don't get too angry with the newspaper writers who tirade against him. They are not the fair representatives of the public."[6] Louisa was referring to a sheaf of newspaper clippings covering the lectures that she was enclosing with her letter, some of which were less than complimentary.

But the managers of the lecture bureau shrewdly observed that the readers of MacDonald's works, who were now coming out in large numbers, were not among those who normally attended their public lectures. They were the more religiously oriented who appreciated MacDonald's novels for their moral and spiritual concerns and were attending the lectures for the same fare. They came not only with a knowledge of the novels but with a deep sense of gratitude. *Robert Falconer* seems to have been the favorite.

Louisa observed, in comparing MacDonald's audiences to those of other lecturers:

> Papa's reception is of a very different kind. It is so deep in the
> hearts of the people—not the showy ones but the true ones.
> A Chicago lady I saw last night could not tell me about her

reading his books without tears coming so fast down her face, she had to stop talking of it, and of her mother's reception of the books, but to Papa she said little very little—but how she looked at him. Such people one thanks God for.[7]

Such people tended to appreciate MacDonald's simple and unaffected manner. Reviewers, on the other hand, that tended to write hostilely of his unadorned and seemingly unpracticed manner of delivery, were measuring MacDonald against the studied polish of the typical lecturer–entertainers of the time.

This bifurcation of attitude can readily be observed in the reviews. Newspaper evaluations of his presentations varied sharply. The account of MacDonald's lecture on Tennyson given in Jersey City and reviewed in the *American Standard* is an example of the more severe:

> There was nothing like an attempt at oratorical display in the lecture, and his rendering of Tennyson hardly met with sympathy from most of his hearers. His reading . . . was marred by the sharp falsetto voice, by just the faintest cockney taint and the rising in inflection at the end of each sentence peculiar to Englishmen and annoying to Americans. . . . Fortunately perhaps, the speaker's favorite passages were not those best known to the audience, and they were thus spared the mangling of some of the purest passages in the English language by a reading which was simply execrable.[8]

The very accent that charmed some this critic found annoying. He would have preferred a more stylized and rhetorical elocution.

By way of contrast, a reporter for the Wilmington *Every Evening* quoted with approval a laudatory account of MacDonald's lecture on Thomas Hood given in The New York *Evening Mail*:

> It was very noteworthy how he took complete possession of his audience. His sympathy for Hood and with the people before him, were alike surpassingly full. It is the chief characteristic of the man, this fellow feeling for all humanity, for all

God's creation; we feel indeed with this great-souled man as though

> "Within the shadow of that great heart,
> He sheltered all the universe."

This was what told. The speaker was by this all embracing sympathy wholly *en rapport* with his hearers. The effect was heightened by the manner of his delivery, which was without notes and in a hesitating, searching fashion that produced the sensation of a direct soulful talk with each one before him.[9]

The Wilmington reporter observed that the *Mail* was not given to indiscriminate praise, and such a compliment meant all the more. Such reviewers saw dimensions in MacDonald the first simply did not. The difference, at least in part, lay in the degree of sympathy with his religious values.

MacDonald especially needed to draw on his spiritual resources as he lay incapacitated and homesick at the Gurneys', while they did all in their power to help him. Dr. Cole of Scotch Plains came on his own behest, volunteering to be of what help he could. Louisa was as usual his constant nurse, while Mrs. Gurney took turns with her in reading aloud to him. Once, Louisa recounted to the children, "Papa moaned (in his sleep). . . . I said 'what's the matter dear' to wake him from an unpleasant dream as I thought it must be—'I'm not asleep but I do so want to see Bobbie and Maurice' and he said it in such a tone."[10] MacDonald was longing to be home, and he seemed to have little hope that he would be able to go on lecturing.

The letters bear abundant testimony to the difficulty both he and Louisa felt in being so long parted from their children. But for them to return home prematurely would mean their losing the opportunity to make a considerable amount of money (although they never received so much as they could have, had Redpath and Fall been willing to renegotiate his contract and pay MacDonald proportionately to the crowds he was drawing). Further, at home he would simply have had to return to his writing, an effort he found as strenuous as lecturing.

His depression notwithstanding, MacDonald experienced a steady recovery at the Gurneys', so that he felt able to resume his schedule sooner than anyone thought. He therefore kept a commitment to appear at the First Congregational Church in Washington on December 11 and at the Maryland Institute in Baltimore on the thirteenth. He also managed to attend a limited number of social affairs. At one reception given by the Gurneys for MacDonald and Professor John Tyndall—British physicist, natural philosopher, and atheist, who was also lecturing in America at the time—an ambitious young socialite was determined to impress MacDonald by appearing to be very familiar with his writings, although she really knew nothing about him. When she pressed a friend to lend her all of the works of the "celebrated writer," her friend thought she was referring to Tyndall and obliged her by sending all of the celebrated scientist's works. She read them avidly, cramming as much information as she could. An amused social columnist gave the following gossipy account of what happened when at last she met MacDonald:

> She had the honor of having Mr. McDonald presented to her, and on the first favorable opportunity she opened on him:
>
> "Oh! Mr. McDonald, I am so delighted to meet you. I have read your beautiful books."
>
> George McDonald bowed gracefully.
>
> "I do think your 'Fragments' so lovely."
>
> George McDonald stared like a featherless owl.
>
> "But the most thrilling of all is the 'Glaciers of the Alps.'"
>
> The poor pen driver could not utter a word. Indeed he seemed to be catching his breath as if he had received a blow below the belt.
>
> "And how brilliant you are on Light and on Sound! Do, Mr. McDonald, tell me how you produce such beautiful things."

The Englishman came to the conclusion that the little
girl was chaffing him, especially as some audience smiles in the
immediate neighborhood told him certain people were being
amused, so he colored up to the hair, and fled the encounter
in such confusion that the company feared he was suffering
from a relapse of his late sickness. But we are happy in saying
that it was only a slight attack of *cram infantum Americanus,*
and that he is now convalescent.

Greville, in his biography, gives an altered account of the conclusion to the incident, having his father rescued by Mrs. Gurney,
who, he recalls, led the frustrated girl to Tyndall.[11]

Feeling "wonderfully well" after these experiences, in spite of
the extraordinarily cold weather, they left by night train on Sunday, December 15, for New York, for lectures in Buffalo and Auburn. They found appreciative audiences, but the rigors of
traveling all but undid what progress toward health MacDonald
had made at the Gurneys. Louisa expressed her frustrations in hurried prose to R. W. Gilder, with whom they were planning to
spend Christmas:

> Another hideous journey here changing waiting in choking
> dirty rooms and then poked into a steaming car with the door
> flinging open just in his face every 10 minutes—arrive at last at
> Auburn, 10 P.M.—an open sleigh to meet us—has brought on
> his cough again. A warm room waiting us, but no supper to
> be had, our last meal having been at twelve. "Never give travel-
> lers or any one supper after ten o'clock." We did however coax
> out of the landlord a jug of milk and some bits of bread. The
> warm room shortly converted into an oven hot enough to
> bake ten poets and ten wives—couldn't cool it—effectually
> kept one poet and one wife awake and restless till past one
> o'clock. So this morning it is no wonder that his cough is
> rather troublesome.[12]

MacDonald also described the night at Auburn to Lily as a
low point in their experience but added that it all suddenly
changed:

I thought as I lay in bed last Thursday night after a lecture that I should have to give up. My chest was so bad and I could not rest. The stove which had been burning like a demon, and making us miserable with red-hot heat, for we could not control it much, went out, and the room grew cold. A great storm of wind, mixed with small snow was roaring outside, and I felt it blowing on my face as I lay, and everything seemed against me. But what do you think? I grew easy and calm and restful, and fell fast asleep, and woke indescribably better, and have been better ever since. For there had come a change, it was a great south wind that blew into the room and all about me. Like so many of God's messengers, it had *looked* fearful to my ignorance, when it was full of healing. Mamma too . . . was much better.[13]

They resumed their journey invigorated, stopping en route to New York City to spend three days with Mrs. Langdon, Mark Twain's mother-in-law, in Elmira. During this and subsequent stops at Elmira a friendship developed between MacDonald and Twain.

MacDonald wrote to Lily on her twenty-first birthday, expressing his heartfelt wishes for her:

May you have as many happy birthdays in this world as will make you ready for a happier series of them afterwards, the first of which birthdays will be the one we call the day of death down here. But there is a better, grander birthday than that, which we may have every day—every hour that we turn away from ourselves to the living love that makes our love, and so are born again. And I think all these last birthdays will be summed up in one transcendent birthday, far off it may be, but surely to come—the moment when we know in ourselves that we are one with God, and living by his life, and have neither thought nor wish but his—that is, desire nothing but what is perfectly lovely, and love everything in which there is anything to love.[14]

Letters from their father were relatively rare, Louisa being the chief correspondent. This one illustrates how, when he did write, his thoughts often dwelt on hope for a future in a higher world, where human nature would be different from what it is here.

Keenly disappointed that their schedule did not allow their seeing Niagara Falls, they nevertheless allowed Greville to go by himself and then meet them in Elmira. "I shall not try to describe it—it is too impossible," the excited Greville wrote Lily. "If you imagine it grander . . . than you can believe or fancy it to be you will have a better idea of it than I could possibly give you."[15]

The children in turn wrote their parents long accounts of how they spent their Christmas, each opening a modest gift from their parents, together with packages from relatives and friends who were especially careful to see that their holiday was a happy one. The MacDonalds went from Elmira to Jersey City on the twenty-fourth, intending to spend Christmas with the Gilders. A conjunction of untoward circumstances followed. A severe winter's storm rendered the night bitterly cold and snowy, MacDonald was severely asthmatic, and Gilder's confused understanding of their destination resulted in their not being met at the depot. Greville and his mother were barely able to get MacDonald to a hotel without his completely collapsing, the subzero air cutting his lungs like a knife. Gilder finally found them and took them to his home, where they had a belated Christmas.

The threat to his health notwithstanding, MacDonald, finding that he was unable to extricate himself from a lecture appointment in Newark on the twenty-sixth, summoned sufficient strength to meet it. Prior announcement had been made in the newspapers that the event would not be canceled; hence, MacDonald kept his word, despite the continued severity of the weather. "There has been no such storm as this for many a year; the horse cars were struggling with the elements, almost in vain; and walking was well nigh impossible."[16] He knew that *some* would come expecting him to be there. Instead of the baker's dozen expected, over one hundred fifty were present. The following

Sunday he preached to an audience of twenty-five hundred in the Association Hall.

By this time the proceeds from his lecturing were putting MacDonald on his feet financially. From Elmira he transferred over twenty-two hundred dollars (which converted to four hundred pounds) to his bank in England and then sent Lily instructions to discharge some apparently long-standing debts. They also packed and sent a variety of items—some things they were not using, others they had collected—to Halloway House, telling the children they would be amused to unpack it. Louisa asked them, however, not to read Mark Twain's books until they came, as she wanted the pleasure of reading them aloud to the family. She apologized for there not being more gifts for the children in the box: "Everything is just like what we have only about 4 times the price."[17]

MacDonald maintained a curtailed lecture schedule during January. He was well received at Princeton Seminary on the sixteenth ("All the divines and the young men, 500 students, listened to him last night. Imagine *Macbeth* in a Presbyterian Church! This is quite the hot bed of the old Theology too."[18]). The Burns Society of New York, having issued an invitation to MacDonald to be their guest at the poet's annual birthday dinner, was delighted when MacDonald appeared adorned with not only his kilt, but also sword, dirk, and skian dubh.

Somewhat refreshed, they left on January 26 for Mark Twain's home in Elmira, from which, after a day's respite, they embarked on a three-week tour of western Pennsylvania and Ohio. Whatever hardships they had experienced thus far in traveling were quite surpassed by those of this trip. Greville foresaw the difficulties ahead as he wrote to Maurice: "There is a terrible journey in store for us tomorrow—two days! But we may be much longer for the snow is so deep that the engines find it hard work to get along and are sometimes delayed very much."[19] He was right. What should have been a three-hour trip to Williamsport took nineteen. Stalled trains necessitated their spending "the whole of the cold, dark night with these wretched seats and wretcheder surroundings," extending their two-day trip to over three.

When they were able to travel in compartments or have access to lounge cars, their trips were more bearable, but such luxuries became rarer the further west they went. By the time Louisa reached Dayton, Ohio, she was filled with utter disgust. She vented her feelings to her children from her hotel room there:

> I am on the sofa after having scoured myself and garments from the thick black of Pittsburgh and cars—Pittsburgh a place that for blackness and darkness beats Manchester and Birmingham hollow—at least any experience that I ever had of either. We left it yesterday morning at nine o'clock and were traveling all day—except when we were stopping. . . . it was 12:30 before a ramshackly omnibus ejected us into this hotel whence we were glad enough to escape from the coarseness and oaths and indecencies of the men inside, not to mention over again that daily trial to our commonest feelings of cleanliness and sense of the fitness of things—their beastly habit of spitting streams of tobacco juice all round you. The longer the journey the harder they spit and the demonlike noises that precede the operations are quite as trying to one's nausea—making nerves as the sight of the brown puddles all across the floor when you have to walk through them and take your seat down amongst them. It turns us so sick when we have to sit for hours in the common cars. I can't describe to you the suffering it inflicts on my backbone and the back of my throat resists the sounds so severely as to give earache, sorethroat and strangulation all in one.[20]

The newspapers contained fulsome accounts of each lecture, accompanied with elaborate descriptions of MacDonald. In Cincinnati, MacDonald gave his most popular talk, on Burns, the first night and talked on *Macbeth* the second. Both were fully covered by the *Enquirer,* which proceeded to described him as

> a medium sized man, of about forty years of age, and rather *distingue* appearance. . . . He wears a dress-suit of black, a white

cravat, and a vest showing an amplitude of snowy shirt front. His manners on the rostrum are easy, his voice clear and melodious, with a very decided Scotch dialect. He would be recognized by any one who met him, and heard him talk as a thoroughly cultivated Scot—a clergyman, perhaps, if it were not for the handsome seal ring he wears upon his left hand.[21]

MacDonald was no doubt surprised, if he read this, that his ring marked him as being no cleric. He loved color and finery and dressed handsomely when he was able to do so. One reporter remarked he wore a black-and-white double neck-tie, a sparkling diamond breast-pin and jeweled studs, and a massive watch chain "conspicuous with pendant charms," and then quickly observed: "MacDonald evidently dresses to please himself, not his audience. For if there be anything unmistakable about his manner it is a triumphant unconsciousness, a *naiveté* and naturalness which have not a suspicion of acting or affectation in them. He is thoroughly self-possessed and in earnest, and of course self-forgetful."[22]

From his study of *Macbeth*, together with his seeing a mediocre performance in an American theater, MacDonald became excited about the possibility of acting it, with him and Lily taking the lead roles. He suggested the idea in a letter to his daughter, saying he would have Macbeth's part memorized by the time they returned home. "I am inclined to try how it feels to be a murderer," he mused.[23]

By February 19 they had made their way back through Altoona to New York. Greville concluded, writing from Altoona: "We shall be back in New York on Wednesday and are going to Dr. Holland's. . . . I do not think we shall be in that city for a long time; . . . Father does not know in the least what he will have to do after that."[24]

TWENTY-SIX

The West at Last

Did I tell you that I have not seen Mrs. Croall? But she must be very nice. Her copy of Coleridge's Poems is much worn with use.—MacDonald to Louisa, August 1884

"We are on the top of a hill here and the scene is simply magnificent. On one side of the house is to be seen the Atlantic which is a most perfect blue and then this contrasted with the white hills; and the numbers of snow-covered islands dotted about, and the ships with their white sails all spread; all these together make it most lovely."[1] Greville was describing to Grace the scene from the Cunninghams' home near Milton, Massachusetts, where they had gone for a short rest.

As soon as the MacDonalds returned to New York, Redpath and Fall proposed a full schedule of meetings. They had in mind, first, that MacDonald give a further series of lectures near New York City and Boston, together with a trip into Vermont; then, that he try again to make a trip to the west, going as far as Chicago, with a sally into Canada. Although the earlier trip to these destinations had been canceled, the people there were still waiting to hear the celebrated novelist.

MacDonald agreed. During the final week of February, he gave several lectures in the New York area, while staying with the Hollands. Then they set out for Boston. But at Northampton, on the February 26, Louisa became so fearful because of MacDonald's extreme fatigue that she wrote Mrs. Cunningham at Milton asking if they could retreat there for a short rest ("You see we both turn to you as to an American Mother. My husband said when I proposed writing to you, 'Ah, Yes, I could rest there!' ").

Receiving a warm reply, she proceeded to contact Fall, insisting that a tour of Vermont be canceled.

After a reception in their honor at the Fieldses' on March 1, they took a week of rest at the Cunninghams'. Then MacDonald made more appearances in the Boston area, in such places as Peabody, Georgetown, and Lawrence. On March 20, they set out for Chicago, a trip filled with adventure.[2] Already they were deeply yearning to return to England.

Several aspects of the trip were becoming tedious. The constant dinners and receptions, however well intended, were wearying. MacDonald wrote Mary, who was visiting in Liverpool, "Give my love to Aunt Flora, and tell her for pity's sake not to have roast turkey for dinner the first day we come home. Turkey, turkey, turkey for ever and ever here, and the very smell of it makes me feel sick. Dear good kind people! It is a shame to complain; but I am getting off my feed again!"[3] Also, he was asked everywhere to repeat his Burns lecture ("they like to hear a Scotchman read Burns"), so that, even though he tried to vary each presentation, the mere repetition wore on him.

En route to Homer, New York, on a tight schedule—they had but thirty minutes to go from train station to lecture hall for the address—the train became stuck in the snow; consequently, by the time they arrived the audience had dispersed. MacDonald agreed to stay over and lecture the following night, after which, to his chagrin, he was presented with only a third of his expected fee, "in consequence of his not keeping his engagement."

The spectacle of Niagara Falls, however, seemed "to wash out" all their troubles, and the brief visit to Canada invigorated them ("when Greville took off his cap and said 'God save the Queen' and I sang 'God save the Queen', Papa said 'God save the Queen' "[4]). Greville's thoroughly English loyalties found exuberant expression when he discovered how much more like the English the Canadians were than the Americans. He explained to Mary from Toronto how immediately different the manners of the people appeared: "As soon as we crossed the Niagara river it was immediately perceptible: everyone was so obliging and polite and the railway officials ready to do or tell you anything—so different from the American officials."

Their British sense of class distinctions was also more at ease:

> Mother says that she has been addressed as Maam by a servent [sic] for the first time since we have been on this continent as in the States it is only your equals that call you Sir and Maam, but, I suppose, that servants, considering themselves as your equals, deem it degrading to address you in anyway that smacks of respect.[5]

The more egalitarian spirit of American society seemed to escape their sympathies.

As they journeyed back to the United States, however, their respect for it returned. They marvelled at its vastness: "Fancy their lakes are so big that you might drop the whole of England Scotland and Wales into the middle of them quite easily . . . and their rivers are so tremendous that the Thames seems quite a small river by the side of any of them almost." When at last they arrived in Chicago, the spectacle of the city reborn from its great fire (in 1871), together with its sheer immensity, overwhelmed them: "This is the most wonderful city in America—in some respects the most wonderful in the world," MacDonald wrote to Fields. "Its resurrection is like something out of the Arabian Nights. It is surely destined to be one of the first in the world." He added that the long trip, with its somewhat relaxed lecturing schedule, actually had invigorated him: "With various vicissitudes, I am, I think, really better now than when I left home, and confidently hope to return in better health than when I left."[6]

They were guests at the home of Rev. Laird Collier, 847 Indiana Avenue, a Unitarian clergyman, recently widowed. ("He is immensely enthusiastic, but the most curious man altogether that we have met; . . . and yet the good and earnest and spiritually minded are all alike here—as they are all the world over."[7]) Their schedule being less congested, they took some time to enjoy their host and surroundings.

After their recent experience of the Boston fire they were the more amazed with how quickly the devastated areas of Chicago had been rebuilt. The three and one-third square miles of the heart of the city was all restored "in most magnificent style! I think I never saw such gorgeous buildings in all my life; it beats New York to 'Smithereens' in the architecture of both business and private houses. Of course there is not the regularity about it like that city," Greville explained to Grace. He liked the people's gusto of spirit:

> You know that Chicagoans are noted for boasting and bragging and they laugh at poor Boston for trying to have a fire there and indeed they crow over it for its complete failure as they consider the fire which we witnessed there. . . . if ever I turn out bad and come to this country (for that is the only reason I should have for coming) I should set up in this city. There seems such an openness and freedom about it.[8]

Behind his statement are the shadows of his great-uncle Charles, who in the early part of the century had fled to America to escape the arm of Scottish justice. Chicago seemed the ideal place, should he ever have to "start over" in life; barring such necessity, however, he was clearly making no plans to come.

Returning eastward, they had occasion to visit with more of their relatives in Ann Arbor, Michigan.[9] After lectures in East Saginaw, Flint, and Detroit, they made a sally into Montreal, where MacDonald lectured on Burns on April 28 and Hood on the twenty-ninth. On May 3 they were back in Boston for a matinee. In spite of the date it was "horribly cold and wet . . . snow thick on the ground when we came out of the hall."[10] Then on the fifth they returned to New York and the hospitality of the Hollands before making still another trip to the Boston area.

Good-byes were difficult in both places, but the simple earnestness of their New York friends made bidding farewell to them more difficult still. While they enjoyed the more ostentatious and lavish hospitality of Boston, they did not feel as warmly about it: "But [as] we left Charles St. both Papa and I felt very much the same as we do when we leave Aunt Helen and yet how I shame myself for the ingratitude of it!" The opulence of their relatives the Powells and Sings in Liverpool had always made them feel somewhat uncomfortable, and they could not help feeling similarly now. Louisa explained, clinching the moral point:

> They were so kind to us always and were the first to take us in and to make us feel that their house was a home. But the relief, the ease, the homefeeling when we came in here [the Hollands'] again to these dear simplehearted kind people made me feel for the 100,000th time how simplicity of heart and truthfulness of nature triumph over money, refinement, artistic taste, education, and every thing else.[11]

On Sunday, May 18, MacDonald preached his last sermon in America from Dr. Bacon's pulpit at the Orange Valley Congregational Church near Bloomfield, New Jersey. Occasions to preach had increased during his stay in America as people discovered the power of his manner. One reporter captured something of the effect he felt, an effect MacDonald consistently achieved. After describing him as "a man with shaggy beard and tall . . . of earnest demeanor, clear and forcible in speech, with an expression of face which is a sermon it itself," he reproduced the scene:

> One could imagine, as Mr. Macdonald read the fortieth chapter of Isaiah, that they were listening to the prophet of old. It was not reading. It was not recitation. The words which found expression through eye and lip came from the heart. "Comfort ye, comfort ye, my people, saith your God. . . ." And when, after a prayer which must have reached God's throne, he dismissed us . . . we fain would have lingered and listened longer; would have caught that spirit of God which seemeth to swell, in George Macdonald, richly. For one cannot listen to Mr. Macdonald without being stimulated to something nobler and purer.[12]

Although some reviewers found fault with MacDonald's manner as a lecturer, all who described his preaching attest to his extraordinary power. Before leaving New York a church on Fifth Avenue offered him their pulpit, at a salary of twenty thousand dollars annually, but MacDonald did not seriously consider the offer.[13] He disdained preaching for money where it was not absolutely necessary, and such a salary seemed extravagant.

A group of New York literati, headed by William Cullen Bryant, editor of *The Evening Post,* arranged a final lecture and formal farewell at the Association Hall, New York, on Thursday evening, May 22. MacDonald spoke on *Hamlet,* after which he bade his American friends farewell:

> For the kindness I have received in America I am very grateful. We came to you loving and knowing that we should love yet more, and, instead of being disappointed, with our hearts larger for the thoughts of so many more friends than we had before; and if word of mine could be of any value, the love between the countries will surely be at least a little strengthened by the report of your goodness which in honesty we are compelled to carry back with us. Never let us misunderstand each other, whatever we do. Let there be no lies between us, and let us know that whatever reports and vague rumors of dislike and annoyance and ill-natured criticism arise, they arise only among the triflers on both sides, and the thinking and honest men of both sides are just like each other, and they care for each other and believe in each other. There is nothing between them. I trust and hope that we in England and you in America, who have the same blood, and the same language, and the same literature, the same Shakespeare, not to speak of the same Bible—whatever our little bickerings be—will only be the better friends for any word that compels us to explain what we mean to each other.[14]

On May 24 they set sail aboard the Cunard Royal Mail Steam Ship *Calabria.* In Louisa's final letter from America the words ecstatically tumbled from her pen: "Oh my boys, my little and big boys, my heart swells so big so big to think of seeing you so soon—it will be very soon after you get this and my dear dear gentle girls. I shall really shall I really have you again. God be praised for the hope even."

A reporter summarized the effect of MacDonald's American trip:

> A few days ago Dr. George Macdonald, the most *spiritual* and poetic novelist of the day, left these shores to return to his native country. . . . his homely, stirring, beautifully simple words . . . have left an echo in the hearts of every one who heard them, which will never quite die out. More than any living man we know of, Dr. Macdonald has the rare power of inspiring his readers and hearers with a personal affection and love for himself. They feel that in him they have a true man, with the brain of a poet and heart of a child; a man who could never be other than simple, and honest, and loveable; with a peculiarly refined and healthy nature, full of sweetness and warmth and light.[15]

We may cringe at such reporting today, but much evidence suggests that for its time this is an accurate statement of the impression MacDonald had made. Judging from the number of American editions of his works, his popularity continued to flourish in America throughout the remainder of the century and well into our own.

TWENTY-SEVEN

Sweeping the Floors in the Temple of Life

Life is a thing so deep, so high, so pure, so far above the reach of common thought, that, although shadowed out in all the harmonic glories of colour, and speech, and song, and scent, and motion, and shine, yea even of eyes and loving hands, to common minds—and the more merely intellectual, the commoner they are—it seems but a phantasm.—Paul Faber, Surgeon

Back at The Retreat, MacDonald's study was echoing with young voices singing "Lift thine eyes" and "Hearts feel that love thee." Lily had taken Mary, Grace, and Ronald with her from Halloway House back to The Retreat, where they were cleaning and painting to have all in order for their parents' return. They studied the night sky in order to get the moon and stars painted on the blue ceiling of their father's study positioned as realistically as they could.

Paper had to be hung straightly over walls so uneven with "extraordinary angles and lumps" that they struck Lily "as if a corpse was bricked up and had burst through."[1] The more tired they became and the more their bones ached, the lustier they sang and laughed, lapsing into what Mary called "the imbecility of fatigue." Perhaps no incident in the lives of all the MacDonalds, parents and children alike, gave them more joy than that of their return to their children. Nine months' separation for a family so closely knit in spirit had been a severe trial. When the entire family was at last reunited, excited conversations conveyed what the many letters had not.

MacDonald returned invigorated in spirit but weary, the grueling pace having drained him physically. Lecturing had been highly rewarding; he had been yet more highly celebrated in America than at home. He strongly entertained the prospect of returning next year for another tour, but the family would be disappointed if he did. For now, he must return to his writing, which he was finding increasingly onerous.

The excitement he felt from reunion with his children soon gave way to utter exhaustion. For weeks he was unable to pick up his pen. They went on some outings in an attempt to recoup his energies and restore his ability to concentrate. "How you would, both of you, have enjoyed yesterday with us in a boat all day on the Wey, a sleepy, lock-restrained, willow-garlanded, green, meadow-banked tributary of the Thames!" he wrote to Fields. "You have far grander rivers, but they don't go to sleep like some of ours, as if they never wanted to leave the grass and the flowers and the overhanging trees."[2] Gradually he recovered strength to return to his writing.

He first tried to revise the drama *If I Had a Father* that had been lying in his drawer for some fifteen years. During his tour of America their hosts had on a number of occasions entertained them at the theater. The dramas they had seen on the American stage, which seemed to him so lacking in moral and spiritual quality, strengthened his conviction that he should try again to get his work produced. So he set about reworking it. After an "actor-friend" who read the play advised MacDonald to reduce it in length and make it less "poetic," he proceeded conscientiously to apply the advice ("Scissors are cheap, and heart-strings may be severed, so I have cut and will come again if needful.").[3] He sent a copy to Gilder and also one to Fields to see if either could arouse interest in it through their respective contacts in the theatrical world. Gilder induced an American producer to take time to read it, but that was all that came of the matter.

That MacDonald put revising his drama ahead of completing his novel *Malcolm* attests to the strength of his desire to be a dramatist. But he also had great enthusiasm for his story of Scottish fishing life. He had done considerable research on the project during the two trips he had made to Cullen in the spring of 1872. The degree to which the plot drew on the traditions and habits of the "fisherfolk," distinct from those of both Highlanders and Lowlanders, demanded that he return to the area, for he determined to be sure of his information. Louisa, Grace, and Lily went with him on a trip there in the fall of 1873, the group spending some time in Huntly as well.

By Christmas of 1873, he was still only two-thirds done with the story, and the *Glasgow Weekly Herald* was anxious to begin running it serially. When the installments finally began to appear, a great demand for the successive issues arose among the Scottish people, who asked, not for the *Herald,* but for "Makim."[4] The novel was published in 1875 in book form simultaneously by Henry King & Company, London, and Lippincott, of Philadelphia, in whose luxurious home the MacDonalds had stayed during their American tour. He would at last begin to receive some financial return for his being one of the most widely read novelists in America.

In *Malcolm,* MacDonald seems determined to write a more artistically sophisticated story than heretofore but one in full accordance with his understanding of the nature of true art. Compared to the other novels there is a relative absence of the preachments of the narrator. The story progresses well as a story, with MacDonald's typical spiritual concerns being more deeply positioned in its form and texture. Nevertheless, on one occasion in the heart of the narrative, after MacDonald indulges a comment on the action, he pauses self-consciously to affirm his attitude toward art in its relation to life:

> But, alas, it was not Lady Florimel who thought these things! Looking over her shoulder, and seeing both what she can and cannot see, I am having a think to myself.

"Which it is an offence to utter in the temple of Art!"
cry the critics.

Not against Art, I think: but if it be an offence to the
worshipper of Art, let him keep silence before his goddess; for
me, I am a sweeper of the floors in the temple of Life, and his
goddess is my mare, and shall go in the dust-cart; if I find a
jewel as I sweep, I will fasten it on the curtains of the doors,
nor heed if it should break the fall of a fold of the drapery.[5]

This complex Victorian analogy suggests that MacDonald
chose to serve life over art and was determined that his art do likewise. He was at the same time quite aware of the increasing cry in
his day—one that was soon to pervade the Modern literary period—that art should accomplish its ends entirely by indirection,
the artist making his art reveal life by means of form and image
alone and not by offering any direct statements of intention. He
does seem to be giving more deference to that ideal in this novel
than he did in his earlier works. But in MacDonald's universe the
ultimate work of art was a human life of moral and spiritual
beauty; he considered valid only those artistic qualities in his novels that would help his readers achieve such lives. He wanted his
literary art, therefore, to be a means to this end.

A prominent theme of the novel—the need of the human
soul to be rightly related to its true parents and hence by analogy
to God—is embedded in the form of the story. MacDonald develops this idea through the foundling theme. Malcolm, an ideal
youth, is brought up by Duncan MacPhail, a blind Gaelic piper
not his true father. Malcolm's father is the local Marquis of Lossie;
hence, Malcolm discovers he in reality belongs to the aristocracy
and comes into possession of a large fortune on the death of the
present marquis. His emotional odyssey suggests by analogy that
of the soul that is uncertain of its origins, fearing they are evil, and
at last learning its true divine derivation.

After having put considerable time and energy into *Malcolm*,
MacDonald was pleased with the finished novel, feeling that he
had achieved a more well plotted story than heretofore.

Lippincott of Philadelphia and Henry King of London published the book in 1875.[6] *Malcolm* was enthusiastically reviewed in *The Canadian Monthly.* "The story has more of a plot than some of the author's works," the reviewer observed, "but its interest depends much less upon that than upon the pourtrayal [sic] and development of character, the exquisite and poetical descriptions, and the beautiful thoughts with which it is profusely enriched." The writer enlarged upon each of these with appreciable praise but was especially impressed with MacDonald's ability to see the supernatural within the natural, observing that "in our matter-of-fact and material age, such qualities are by no means superfluous, as a counteractive to the self-sufficient hardness of positivism."[7]

Besides his work during this period on his drama and on *Malcolm,* MacDonald was also busy with his poetry. For the Christmas of 1873, the MacDonalds had printed a collection of his translations of selected German poets for distribution to their friends. Some of these were poems of Novalis, early versions of which were similarly privately printed in 1851. Never being quite satisfied with his work, MacDonald kept fine-tuning these poems, so his translations exist in many versions, "so anxious have I been" he said, "to do them justice both as to meaning and form."[8] They were collected and published under the title *Exotics* by Strahan in 1876. Included with the poems of Novalis are some of Schiller, hymns of Luther, and some Italian poems. Twelve of them had already appeared in *Scribner's,* as Gilder was fond of MacDonald's poetry and readily published it.

While MacDonald was thus occupied with his career, the children were growing into adulthood. When he, together with part of his family, was at Huntly in the fall of 1873 finishing research for *Malcolm,* a letter from Octavia Hill came to Lily, who had seemed somewhat depressed, proposing an outlet for her outside the home. Hill regularly offered entertainments to the poor in her housing projects as an important part of her therapeutic program. Needing someone to plan and manage these, she wrote asking Lily to accept the position of being her "Master of the Revels."

An army of assistants could be enlisted to do much of the actual physical work involved, Hill assured her. But performers had to be scheduled; rooms cleaned, arranged, and decorated; invitations issued; food ordered; and the events made to occur with spirit and verve. Lily was the ideal person for the post; she eagerly accepted. The opportunity to have more of an interest outside the home was a welcome relief from her many responsibilities within the family.

This also compensated for the fact that Mary, not she, was the first of the daughters to become engaged. William Matheson, some twenty years her senior, was much attached to Lily, needing only the slightest encouragement to become her suitor, but she was unable to see him in any other light than that of an affectionate elder. It had been apparent for some time, however, that Mary was finding an ardent suitor in Ted Hughes. A nephew of Arthur Hughes, MacDonald's illustrator, he was a strikingly handsome and talented young artist in his early twenties, whose features resembled, many said, that of a Greek god. For the last half-dozen years he had been one of the children's closest friends.

One sultry Friday afternoon in late September, when the Arthur Hughes family was visiting at Halloway House, the MacDonald children restlessly awaited Ted's joining them from his school in London for an extended weekend. There followed several days packed with exciting activities that all enjoyed, but none so much as Mary. On Monday they set out in a wagonette, with seventeen in the party, for the two "Ancient Towns" of Winchlesea and Rye to view the church and monastery ruins, which date to the time of Chaucer. At Rye they had a picnic, drinking ginger beer while Greville cooked mushrooms over a fire. Then they played running games, nearly laming themselves among the ruins as they made flying leaps to escape being caught.[9] Before their return Ted, Mary, and Winnie climbed by themselves around the tops of the ruined walls. The following day Mary sat as Arthur Hughes drew her, while Ted read to them from Thackeray's *The Virginians*. This was the weekend that Ted proposed; he had loved her, he said, since he was fourteen.

Shortly thereafter Louisa announced the glad news by tele-gram and letter to all their relatives that their "twelfth" had been born: Ted had been received into the family as Mary's betrothed. MacDonald heartily embraced him; Louisa was ecstatic. Ted promised to be the perfect son-in-law: gentle-spirited, of noble purpose and bearing, highly talented, and, above all, entirely de-voted to Mary. And Mary, in her mother's fond eyes, was "loveli-ness itself." When the newly engaged Ted came one cloudy Sunday morning and joined the family walking to church, the sun briefly broke through, shining only on Ted and Mary. It seemed a divine benediction.

Life at The Retreat was now more demanding than ever. To supplement their income, the MacDonalds took in children to tutor. Some came to them by the term, others by the year; Lily, in addition to her duties with Octavia Hall, had large responsibility for this project as well. Some, such as a girl named Wentworth, became an intimate part of the family.

In addition the MacDonalds found a larger portion of their time now devoted to entertaining, as many of their American ac-quaintances appeared at The Retreat on return visits. Among them were Mark Twain, whose hospitality at Elmira they had greatly enjoyed, and Mary Mapes Dodge from Newark, whose ex-tremely popular children's book *Hans Brinker, or, the Silver Skates* had established her among the foremost authors of children's books of the period.[10]

The position of The Retreat on the Thames made it an attrac-tive spot from which to view the annual boat races between Ox-ford and Cambridge—a competition that still arouses great national enthusiasm in England. The willingness of the MacDon-alds to hold open house to their wide circle of friends resulted in their having many visitors during such occasions. In 1875 Tennyson paid them a surprise visit. MacDonald was delighted with his two- or three-hour stay, especially with the interest he showed in MacDonald's library. Seeing a fancy copy of *Ossian* in Gaelic—one that MacDonald had secured from his Uncle

MacKay—he begged the privilege of borrowing it.[11] Numerous lesser luminaries also came to call, so that MacDonald found he had to curtail the amount of time he could give to them in order to keep up his rigorous writing schedule.

Intending to secure another respite from his routine and also, of course, to earn additional money, MacDonald entertained strong hopes of returning to America for a lecture tour. When the 1874–1875 season proved unfeasible, he made plans for the following year. Writing to Fields, he proposed that Fields and his wife visit Britain early in the summer of 1875, returning with the MacDonalds to America in the autumn. To put his health at less risk, MacDonald intended this time to arrange for a series of lectures in larger cities, with fewer stops at smaller towns. A second tour would mean another break from composing novels; "I get very tired of writing," he confided to Fields.[12]

But as 1875 came it became increasingly doubtful that the trip could be undertaken that autumn. Mary was not well. As early as September 1874 Louisa had noted to Lily that she looked "worried and white and distracted" and had arranged for her to spend time by the sea. Though frail, she had been the most energetic of the girls (years earlier Charles Dodgson had taught her to box); now she seemed listless. MacDonald too found that his old and persistent ailments were increasing. The atmosphere of The Retreat, they began to think, might be responsible for their weakened health, with the frequent fogs hovering over the Thames, emitting a fetid atmosphere when the river was low.

Perhaps a home in a more secluded, rural setting would afford them the needed change in atmosphere and at the same time offer MacDonald some of the isolation that he needed from their many callers. No sooner did they begin their search than they found that Great Tangley Manor, a long, low and many-gabled old farmhome with a great thatched roof located in Surrey, south of Guildford near Wonersh, was available, furnished, for six months. They engaged it in early April 1875, while they continued their search for more permanent quarters. MacDonald was delighted to have a house "built when Shakespeare was a boy—in 1582—of great oak beams within and without."[13]

Taking a contingent of the children, Louisa went to scout out their new, if temporary, home, and expressed her delight with their newly found seclusion among "charming lanes and sloping hills and woods" abounding all around them.[14] They were soon settled there.

The family now could take long hikes in the rural setting. Between their excursions they read aloud to each other such things as MacDonald's sermons in the morning and Hawthorne's *The Blithedale Romance* in the afternoon and evening. Life at Tangley for the short time they were there was a welcome change from the city, in spite of minor annoyances, such as having to get someone to exterminate a nest of rats from under the lobby floor. "All we want here is for me a pony or donkey chaise and for you a horse," Louisa resolved. [15]

So she purchased for MacDonald a little horse named Kitty, and he began to work regular rides into his busy day. Within a few months Louisa had two ponies. Not far from the Manor was Blackheath, an open area in which MacDonald delighted to ride. "I walked the mare up to Blackheath, and have had the first real enjoyment of country that I have had for many a day. . . . I found it nearly perfect—the day warm without being too hot up there— the finest heather perhaps that I ever saw, and a thousand dainty interminglings of wildness and culture."[16] Some of their relatives thought their keeping a horse was too obvious a luxury for the family, but the animals afforded MacDonald needed recreation as well as providing a pastime for the children. MacDonald's brother-in-law Joshua Sing was among those who objected, but nevertheless, when finances were low he contributed to the mare's keep.

"I almost think it is the very place for a story I am thinking of," MacDonald remarked concerning Blackheath.[17] Just having finished his fantasy *A Double Story*[18] (which was being serialized in *Good Things,* and which was about to be legitimately published in

America by Dodd, Mead, and Company), he was beginning to form in his mind the narrative for his next novel, *St. George and St. Michael*. The role horses play in the plot of that story was shaped no doubt in part by his daily riding that summer. Also, the rich historical associations of Great Tangley may well have induced him to undertake a historical novel.

For this the second of his researched novels, MacDonald attempted a historical one set in the 1640s, during the English Civil War. The period held considerable interest for him; he had already published in 1868 *England's Antiphon*, a series of essays on early poets, and had lectured extensively on Renaissance and seventeenth-century literature. He stated in a note at the conclusion of the novel that his main sources of material for this narrative were "Mr. Dircks's *Life of the Marquis of Worcester,* and the *Certamen Religiosum,* and *Golden Apophthegms* of Dr. Bayly."

MacDonald undertook in the novel to show the folly of sectarianism, one of his most deeply held convictions. He presented an impartial view of both sides of the conflict, the Puritan and the Royalist, creating characters of admirable moral fiber and courage existing in each camp. He showed people from each side acting honorably in support of their loyalties. But he emphasized that the quality of a person's humanity depends on the motives for and the moral quality of his deeds, not the "rightness" of his opinions: "A man may be right although the creed for which he is and ought to be ready to die, may contain much that is wrong. Alas! that so few, even of such men, ever reflect, that it is the element common to all the creeds which gives its central value to each."[19]

MacDonald received five hundred pounds from the *Graphic* for *St. George and St. Michael,* which began appearing serially on April 24, 1875, and ran through October.[20] Henry King then published it as a three-volume novel in 1876, with twenty-five woodcut illustrations by Sydney P. Hall.[21] The novel was immediately pirated in the United States.

TWENTY-EIGHT

A Most Enchanting Situation

If I had not the hope of one day being good like God himself,
if I thought there was no escape out of the wrong and badness
I feel within me and know I am not able to rid myself of
without supreme help, not all the wealth and honours of the
world could reconcile me to life.—The Marquis of Lossie

In December 1875, the Cowper-Temples asked MacDonald to visit Broadlands, their elegant estate near Romsey, Hampshire. The stately Palladian mansion was situated amid six thousand acres in the Test Valley, with the Test River quietly meandering by the house and huge copper beach trees studding the riverside lawns. Designed by Lancelot "Capability" Brown, the famous eighteenth-century residential designer, the refined interior was complemented by original paintings, porcelain, and pieces of sculpture. It was the epitome of the English country home.[1]

MacDonald had known William Cowper for some time as he was a fellow communicant at St. Peter's, Vere Street.[2] He was a distant relation of the poet William Cowper, after whom he was named, and stepson of Lord Palmerston, the distinguished prime minister under Queen Victoria. Having inherited Broadlands from Lord Palmerston in 1867, Cowper and his wife went there to live two years later. In 1870, after also inheriting the Temple properties, he and his wife changed their name to Cowper-Temple, and then, in 1880, to Lord and Lady Mount-Temple. An energetic man of deep religious convictions, he heeded Maurice's call to espouse Christian Socialism and used his various offices in

Parliament to advance a number of humanitarian reforms intended to raise the quality of life of ordinary people.[3] Maintaining the most eclectic of Broad Church mentalities, he was as well an outspoken advocate of temperance and vegetarianism and he strongly opposed vivisection. Together with his wife, he had a strong interest in spiritualism.[4]

His wife, Georgina Cowper-Temple, a pious woman of sweet and gentle spirit, was of a deeply religious nature with a compelling curiosity concerning all things supernatural. Although deeply interested in Christianity and a woman prolific in philanthropic acts, she was reluctant to claim to be a Christian.[5] Deeply distressed by the death of her mother in 1861, she had turned to spiritualism in the hopes of finding some assurance of immortality. Later, in penning the family memoirs, she referred to the practice of attempting communion with the dead as "so alluring, so bewildering, and so utterly disappointing; but still furnishing to the material mind a new basis of belief."[6] Possessing great grace and beauty, she had been an ideal embodiment of femininity for Ruskin ever since he had first seen her, and they were close friends.

She had taken an active interest in Ruskin's affair with Rose La Touche, even to the extent of arranging some of their clandestine meetings at Cowper-Temple residences. In the spring of 1875 Rose had died, and Ruskin was beside himself with grief.[7] In an effort to console him the Cowper-Temples invited him to occupy a suite of rooms at Broadlands and sought to help him religiously. Ruskin had long been curious about spiritualism, maintaining an open mind toward it and vacillating between belief and skepticism.

Ordinarily, MacDonald would have been delighted with the invitation to visit Broadlands; this time he went reluctantly. He told Louisa as soon as he arrived: "I don't see much good of my coming. I wish I were back with you." Not that he was not glad to see Ruskin, for he was. His discomfort was prompted by the presence of Mrs. Edward Acworth, wife of a physician in Brighton, who had a reputation as a successful spirit medium. "I don't take to her much, but Ruskin is very interested in her. . . . She has seen and described, without having ever seen her, Rose, whispering to Mr. Ruskin. He is convinced. I am not—but I shall not refuse to hear her talk, if as Annie offered, she gets her on the subject."[8] Annie Munro, sister of the sculptor and an old friend of the Mac-Donalds, was a governess for the Cowper-Temples.[9] She had met MacDonald at the station and anxiously told him about Mrs. Acworth.

MacDonald's attitude toward spiritualism, and all aspects of the occult, is plain enough from such novels as *David Elginbrod:* he suspected it was evil. He was quite aware of the biblical injunction to abstain from participating in such activity, and he sought to honor scriptural precepts. Nevertheless, the frequency of reference in the novels to evil characters possessing supernatural powers shows his fascination with all manifestations of the supernatural. In *Paul Faber, Surgeon,* he admits the possibility of such occurrences, but indicates he is quite content with the memory of the departed, letting the sense of absence achieve its spiritual value.[10] On this occasion his lively curiosity kept him from refusing to listen to Mrs. Acworth, should the subject be broached, as no doubt it was.

In spite of their differences of opinion on the validity of spiritualism the Cowper-Temples' esteem of MacDonald was steadily growing. In the fall of 1875, the MacDonalds' lease of Great Tangley Manor having expired, they sought to locate in the southwest in the hopes that the climate there would be more healthful for both Mary and her father. Beginning their search in the area of Broadlands, they temporarily took Kensington Villa in Bournemouth and continued looking for something more suitable.

Then, happily, they located a freshly built house at Boscombe, "in a most enchanting situation . . . on the edge of the cliff, facing the sea with a garden looking down the chine." Louisa had some doubts about it accommodating all of them comfortably for long, "but at Christmas and in a summer holiday we might all be comfortable together and those are the only times we could be all there together."[11] They named it Corage, the first word of an anagram MacDonald formed from the letters of his name, "Corage! God mend al!"[12]

The distant sound of the sea, together with the murmur of the wind through the surrounding pine woods, was a constant source of pleasure to them whenever they were there, somehow suggesting to them that all was ultimately well with the universe. They found two girls who were willing to stay in the house the year around, with their rent paying the lease. Therefore, adding this property to the other two they were maintaining did not represent a large additional drain on their straightened finances.

Here they took Mary in hopes of inducing her recovery. In early July she had come down with quinsy—a severe inflammation of the throat—and possibly scarlet fever; the doctors could not agree on the diagnosis. Her fever rose nightly to frightening levels, with her bones aching. Louisa faithfully gave her rubdowns morning and evening, and MacDonald waited on her as he could, helping her with such menial tasks as putting on her stockings when her bones ached too severely for her to do it herself. Typically self-effacing, Mary showed deep appreciation for the help everyone extended to her and daily tried to see signs of her own improvement for the family's sake as well as her own. "How dreadfully dreadfully thin she has got though her face is beginning to look more red . . . I think," the distraught Louisa wrote Lily.[13] As the days passed Mary showed signs of improvement. By early December she was more consistently cheerful than she had been for some time, and the family was heartened.

MacDonald too found the new situation congenial to his health and hence to his ability to concentrate. "Not for a long time have I been able to work so steadily, and I hope my work will turn out better for it," he remarked. Louisa was pleased that once again he was "in great spirits. . . . You should have heard him gossiping with everybody in the little shops."[14] Having arranged for his horse Kitty to be sent down by train, he was delighted that she neighed as soon as he went into the train car to receive her. She was so gentle they let her loose on the platform.

The family found a "beautiful new stable" for her, through the fir wood.

Now Louisa too could ride. MacDonald's good friend Henry Cecil, who had been a fellow teacher with MacDonald's brother John at the Sheffield Academy in the 1850s, lived nearby. At the time the MacDonalds moved to Boscombe, Cecil's wife was dying of tuberculosis. After her death Cecil made a present to Louisa of his wife's two shaggy Shetland ponies, together with their chaise and harness. Named Zephyr and Zoe and often referred to simply as the "Z's," they delighted Louisa, who would have enjoyed them at Tangley. Now, she often joined her husband in outings through the pines and along the beach.[15]

One day Cecil showed to MacDonald one of his prized possessions, a kind note from Thomas Carlyle, with the august Carlyle's autograph. MacDonald asked the loan of it to show it to another friend. Later, when Cecil asked for the return of his treasure, MacDonald, to his very deep chagrin, could not find it, although he made an exhaustive search. Deeply distraught, he sought relief by a direct appeal to the dyspeptic Carlyle. After gingerly explaining the situation MacDonald made his plea:

> My heart is sore for my fault and his loss. I am not a careless man, but here is carelessness. I have lost my evening's work, which to a man who works steadily, is no little punishment. But the loss of tomorrow's is threatened also by my mental disquiet, and the only thing that has brought me relief is the thought of troubling you—happily not with the heartache I beg you to take from me. Now to put my request plainly—a cry to my big brother to come to my help. Will you, out of your humanity, dictate again a few words to my friend, founded on the contents of this letter, and send it with your own autograph signature to me, that I may give it to him instead of the other. Then I shall have courage to confess my failing. Do not write a word to me: I do not deserve it. I am ashamed of thus troubling you. But someday, I trust, on the other side, I shall thank you for a kindness which lightened a

real burden, when our life here has become the dream which,
real as it is, Novalis says perhaps it ought to become.[16]

MacDonald's former acquaintance with Carlyle made him bold to
proffer his request, casting it in his most engaging style. No records
of the outcome remain, but Carlyle could hardly have refused.

At Corage MacDonald completed his novel *Thomas Wingfold,
Curate*. "My book which Routledge is about to publish in
America I count one of my most important," MacDonald told
R. W. Gilder. "Whether it will be largely read I can hardly form
a conjecture even. Some of it is necessarily a little difficult. It is just
being finished off—six months work."[17] MacDonald's misgivings
about its reception were correct as far as the reviewers were concerned. The *Athenaeum* gave it only a paragraph, remarking it was
largely given over to religious discourse and hence "more directly
controversial" than his previous novels. *The Fortnightly Review* gave
it a lengthy summary, but only to illustrate the reviewer's "pain
and diffidence" in reading it. He conjectured it would please only
those "who like a sandwich of sermons and sensation." The British critical establishment had become increasingly disdainful of
MacDonald's using fiction to convey his message.[18]

So also had the religious right. George McCrie had published
The Religion of Our Literature in 1875. Measuring contemporary
literature according to his understanding of orthodoxy, he felt
Longfellow to be the truest poet of the time and heartily attacked
such authors as Carlyle, Tennyson, and Browning for their heterodoxy. He included MacDonald among those who derived an unorthodox theology from "mere moral sentimentalism," and who
taught it "with all the earnestness" of missionaries.[19]

MacDonald may have had McCrie in mind when he wrote
his most doctrinally comprehensive Christian novel to date. He
tells the story of Rev. Thomas Wingfold, a young curate who, having been challenged by George Bascombe—an honest, self-assured
atheist—whether he really believes anything he professes, is forced
in honesty to admit that he really does not. Contemplating

whether he should not therefore resign his position, he discovers that he really wants the gospel story to be true. Consequently, he seeks to represent honestly to his parishioners the steps he takes to discover its authenticity. The plot traces these successive steps in his spiritual odyssey.

MacDonald believed this novel important for at least two reasons. First, he had found a way to successfully convey the heart and substance of his Christian convictions in story form. He had, of course, been attempting this in each novel he had written, but always a certain tension existed between story and Christian thought. In this novel he kept the tension at a minimum by deriving the dramatic energies for the plot from the struggle in the main characters to believe and repent.

Second, the novel represented his response to many of the issues confronting the contemporary church, beginning with the validity of belief itself. He addresses the range of critical attacks against Christianity that were being leveled during the nineteenth century by the secular world: the historicity of the miracles attributed to Christ, the nature and authority of the biblical text, and Darwinian evolutionary theory. Since to him evolutionary growth seemed to be a basic principle in the world of the spirit, and the reverting to lower forms of life through immorality a constant possibility,[20] he finds little difficulty in affirming a version of evolution. He also explores what it means to be Christian in the marketplace and the issue of personal immortality.

His strongest appeal is to the Christian's personal experience, consistently insisting on the centrality of Christ and the importance of personally obeying his commands, as opposed to simply making rational assent to a creed. Wingfold never arrives at any dogmatic creedal affirmation. His convictions spring from his encounter with the Spirit of Christ through the Bible. Seeing such beauty and loveliness in the story of Christ, he becomes willing to lay down his life, if need be, on the chance that what the Bible presents is true. For, "even if there be no hereafter," Wingfold affirms, "I would live my time believing in a grand thing that ought to be true if it is not. No facts can take the place of truths; and if these be not truths, then is the loftiest part of our nature a waste."[21]

A basic component, therefore, of Wingfold's religious experience is the strength of his human desire. If MacDonald had McCrie's criticism in mind, he boldly commits himself to the validity of judging a Christian theology on the basis of something akin to "moral sentimentalism." But the novel is at the same time the most Christocentric of MacDonald's works, offering an imaginative apologetic for Christianity that stands in sharp distinction from a rationalist defense. Wingfold becomes increasingly convinced of the truth of the gospel by the grandeur of the biblical story of the life of Christ. "No woman, no man surely ever saw him as he was and did not worship," he concludes.[22]

Thomas Wingfold, Curate closes with an affirmation of personal immortality. MacDonald's mind never being far from the subject, he may have been prompted to concentrate on it at this time because of Mary's worsening situation. In his prior novel, *St. George and St. Michael,* he included a scene of the death of a saintly child named Molly, which was one of Mary's nicknames. Now he thought often on it, for the possibility of Mary's dying was quite real. The bond between Mary and her father was especially strong. In one of her letters Mary showed deep concern for her father when, having left The Retreat one morning for London, he returned within a few minutes ill and in great pain, to the alarm of the entire house. "I am so sorry papa is still so poorly" she wrote Lily. "I wish I could do something for him. (Doesn't that last sound like a gushing young lady? but I am his daughter)."[23]

The family increasingly concentrated their attention on Mary's health. When for a time she seemed to improve at Corage, Ted's visits would occasionally arouse her to the exertion of playing the piano to accompany him on the violoncello. But Ted's father— long seriously ill—was dying, and he could not come often. When, in September 1875, it became apparent that there was no real improvement, MacDonald, Louisa, and Mary went to Nairn, in northeast Scotland, again in the hope that some change in climate would work the longed-for change in health. Now both Mary and MacDonald were seriously ill: each was coughing, running high fevers, spitting blood. Further, MacDonald was swinging in moods between exhilaration and depression. The excitement of the trip and the change of scenery seemed at first to effect a change in Mary, but as the days went on, they saw it was another false hope.

Then, to everyone's consternation, Mary began to withdraw, seemingly having no interest in anything. Having formerly been so full of energy and exhibiting a lively interest in life, she now became a puzzle and source of perplexity to all the family. "She is very cold, goes out in a seal skin in the sun and yet is not warm," Grace observed, at a loss to say more. The doctor ordered her to eat raw beef and never to go more than an hour and a half without eating something. In a sisterly attempt to arouse her Lily wrote her a long letter from Tangley, evidencing her desperate concern: "Come down! Come down! come down and see the sun, come and see the moon . . . come and see the cows and calves. . . . come and see the sun set and get strength enough to see it rise. Come and look at the holly hocks and sun flowers. One group of hollyhocks we saw tonight is like nothing but the pink of your dress and the colour your cheeks should be."[24] But now nothing seemed to stem her steady deterioration. Bewildered, Grace queried her mother: "I am so glad Papa is a little better but oh why does Mary get worse instead of better?"[25]

TWENTY-NINE

Taking His Yoke

And if we try to put his yoke on, and do not know the way,
will he stand by and give us no help? Would that be like
Him?—MacDonald to Louisa

After returning from America the future had for a time appeared quite promising, but now trial seemed to follow trial. Mary's ill health was a constant heartache, MacDonald's a severe distraction. His work was increasingly disdained by the established critics, who thought he should confine himself to writing art that would entertain. Publishers were paying less for his work, and financial needs steadily mounted. Circumstances that would overwhelm most people with discouragement, however, seemed to intensify his faith. When things were lowest, something always turned up. He derived strength from his steady conviction that his calling was to serve his generation. The truths he was bringing were having a large distribution, in spite of critical antagonism. And he had many friends.

"I hoped in God, and will hope in him even if that worst of earthly evils, debt, should overwhelm me," MacDonald remarked to the Cowper-Temples at a time in 1877 when he was feeling the heavy weight of unpaid bills.[1] In spite of his most conscientious efforts to remain solvent, creditors were always waiting to be paid. In drawing the portrait of Rev. Walter Drake, in the novel *Paul Faber, Surgeon* that he was writing at the time, MacDonald portrayed something of his feelings during his worst moments. Drake, a retired Congregational minister, was on the verge of suicide because of the burden of bills, which, on his small income, he was unable to pay. "It was the shame—the shame he could not bear!"

MacDonald wrote. "Ought he to have been subjected to it?" MacDonald was able to enter into the feelings of his fictional character because of his own experiences, but he was convinced that God was allowing his trials to keep him humble.

It was true that he was working constantly, turning out novels at a rate few writers could match, and their sales were brisk. But the pirating of his books by unscrupulous publishers in America not only kept him from receiving what was his rightful due for his work, but it also kept the market price of his novels down, such publishers being able to sell for less. His authorized publishers, therefore, were not able to charge what they otherwise would have, and MacDonald's royalties lagged. Further, his friend Strahan had broken with his partners. Trying to publish on his own on a smaller scale, Strahan was unable to match his former offerings for new work.

In addition to his grueling pace of writing MacDonald was lecturing steadily, offering during the winter of 1875–1876 one course of afternoon lectures at the home of Lord and Lady Lawrence and another at the home of the Russell Gurneys. "Can you think of any other place we could *scheme* for lectures in?" he asked Louisa.[2] The family was ready to give up The Retreat to lighten their expenses, but no one showed an interest in taking it.

The costs of raising so large a family, many of whom were now in expensive teenage years, seemed ever rising, and the expense of maintaining three dwellings, necessitated by reasons of health, was no small factor. As the children grew they had to be started in life. Greville was doing well in his medical studies, and in the spring of 1876 earned one of three available scholarships whereby he was able to complete his work. But he still needed money to live at school. The children took music lessons, and Irene, who showed artistic talent, was enrolled in the Slade School of Art on Gower Street. Doctor bills too kept coming not only for Mary and MacDonald but also for Maurice, who had contracted a severe infection—a large cyst on his leg—and needed medical attention for an extended period of time.

All this weighed especially on Louisa, whose equanimity under stress was not so steady as that of her husband's. Then while at Hastings she conceived a plan—they would offer public dramatic productions, charging a modest admittance.

Putting on family plays had been a family hobby for some time, and their interest and enjoyment in it had grown, not diminished. Strahan had published Louisa's little collection entitled *Chamber Dramas for Children* in 1870. The MacDonalds had furnished dramatic entertainments for Octavia Hill's tenants for years, and they had given a number of presentations for friends at The Retreat. When a friend of Lily's had sent her the script for a farce titled *Obstinacy,* she responded, "It has amused us extremely and must go very well when quickly played." Gathering courage, the family presented it to the assembled students at the Working Women's College in London in May 1876. They were delighted to find it a rousing success.

Now, with Louisa's inspiration and the children's enthusiasm, they secured suitable public facilities and set to work in earnest to prepare productions worthy of the public's paying money to see. The prospect excited them. Not only did they feel satisfaction from the chance of acquiring some much-needed earnings, but they had found another enjoyable outlet for the girls' flair for sewing and artistic design in the assembling of costumes and painting of backdrops. After having successfully presented *The Tetterbys* at Miss Kingsbury's Convalescent Home in Hastings they believed they were well on their way.

The local newspaper responded with favorable reviews and encouragement; Lilia's appreciable acting talent carried the day. They soon had in their repertoire a number of their own versions of dramas, among them *Beauty and the Beast, The Tetterbys,* and a fairy tale, *Snowdrop*. During the winter of 1876, as Lilia remarked, "We screwed our courage to the sticking point and bid our pride farewell" by taking the Bournemouth Town Hall and presenting public performances of their "little plays." Buoyed by considerable audience enthusiasm (one friend came eleven times to see repeat performances of the same play), the following summer they presented several private performances in London. They would have done many more, but MacKay came down with scarlet fever, forcing a momentary rest.

Their most successful play was their version of Part Two of *Pilgrim's Progress*. They first performed it at Christchurch, Hampshire, on March 8, 1877, which, whether by plan or happenstance, was the MacDonalds' twenty-sixth wedding anniversary.[3] Louisa's inspiration to produce their plays proved fortuitous. The family's endeavors as an acting troupe continued for a number of years, adding no mean share to family finances and providing another means of religious expression that many found inspiring and helpful.

Family members assumed parts that each played regularly, so that in the normal course of life they frequently called each other by their role names. In *Pilgrim's Progress* the part of Greatheart was first played by Ronald, but MacDonald, who had not been a part of the original public venture, allowed himself to be persuaded to assume the role at a performance at Grossenor House, London, on June 8, 1877. His handling of the part proved so successful that it became his regular role. They sewed for him a majestic black robe covered with gold sequins, which, when combined with his flowing beard, the fixing power of his blue eyes, and his voice at once gentle and authoritative, created an impression of great spiritual significance. For the final stirring scene they painted idyllic designs on large curtains as a backdrop, which they referred to with just pride as the "Beulah curtains."[4]

The Princess Louise was present at their premier performance of Bunyan's classic. Some twenty-five years later, when Winifred was introduced to the princess as the daughter of George MacDonald, she remarked, "Oh, I saw him act once! I am right, am I not? He was the author of *Robert Falconer*?" When Winifred registered her surprise at the princess's memory, Princess Louise

remarked, "I think you would like to know that my mother—
Queen Victoria, you know—gave that book to *every one* of her
grandsons."[5]

Not everyone, however, was immediately enthused. Mac-
Donald himself, when he first heard of the plans, had some hesitation. But when he felt the strength of Louisa's conviction that
this was a project the Lord had assigned her, he acquiesced. Characteristically, he concluded that this reminder of his inability to
provide entirely for his family's needs was a needed check on his
incipient pride. Greville also felt some embarrassment about the
venture and did not participate in the undertaking. Some of Louisa's more society-conscious sisters looked askance at this new venture, feeling that it was degrading for the family to make such a
spectacle of themselves.

In a letter to their cousin Mrs. Frank Sharman, MacDonald
labored to make very clear that any hesitation he may have originally felt was not motivated by what "society" might judge concerning them: "What society so-called . . . may say or do about
it, I simply will not heed one straw." He went on to explain, "We
are only taking up an art that has been unjustly undervalued and
left too much to unfit representations," a sentiment he had long
entertained as he had tried to penetrate the theatrical world with
his attempts at writing drama. If the world of professional drama
would not present plays focusing on moral and spiritual themes
as he desired, his family would in their humble way undertake to
do it. "The time is short, and there is none for humbug, whether
social or ecclesiastical—there is time only for truth and justice and
graciousness and lovingkindness, and we hope to learn and teach
some of all these," he explained. "What God has put in us, we
will let come out, and not be ashamed."[6]

The spiritual needs of his society were increasingly apparent
to him, and he felt his calling, as well as that of his family, to
be the servants of his age, regardless of public opinion. That this
conviction had been brought into focus by the dramatic endeavors
of the family may in part account for the emphasis on servanthood

in his next novel. MacDonald turned to complete the story of Malcolm, which, as he had assured his readers at the conclusion of that former novel, required another book. He had probably been working on it to some extent while he was writing *St. George and St. Michael* and *Thomas Wingfold, Curate;* now he resumed the story in earnest. Titled *The Marquis of Lossie,* the novel offers a detailed exploration and development of the theme of servanthood. The conflict between the popular conception of servanthood and a Christian understanding of it is a chief source of dramatic tension throughout the plot.

As in *Malcolm* MacDonald pays the ultimate compliment to the ideal teacher in the character of Mr. Graham, a *stickit* minister. "It may seem incredible that one so young as Malcolm should have been able to talk thus," MacDonald remarks concerning his hero's spiritual wisdom, but "it must be remembered . . . that the advantage to such a pupil of such a teacher as Mr. Graham is illimitable."[7] There is, of course, a generous amount of MacDonald's self-image here; in the eyes of the world he too was a failed minister who must find means to teach other than the pulpit. Like Graham, he was in his view the ultimate spiritual teacher, bringing truth to bear upon his hearers; like Malcolm, he would serve people by persuasively presenting a vision of the attractiveness of virtue and goodness.

MacDonald saw himself as a servant who must inevitably experience rejection. The people at Arundel had looked on him as their servant, desiring that he serve them on their terms. He intended to serve on truer ones, modeled on the life and attitudes of Christ. The general reading public wanted entertaining art, not serious contemplation of the spiritual realities permeating life. But since the kingdom of heaven was, at least thus far on earth, a matter of the rule of God in willing hearts, he must patiently continue to persuade. He was not unmindful of the scriptural promise that the saints will one day rule with Chirst as kings and priests to God and had as well a vision of the more regimented form that rule might take.

The Marquis of Lossie was published in 1877 simultaneously in England and America, Hurst & Blackett bringing out the English version and Lippincott's the authorized American version. Serially, it ran in *Lippincott's Magazine* from November 1876 through September 1877 and in Scotland in the *Glasgow Weekly Mail*.[8]

Another outlet for MacDonald's determination to serve his age presented itself through his growing friendship with the Cowper-Temples. They conceived the scheme of opening the spacious grounds of Broadlands each summer to religious conferences that would concentrate on the deeper Christian life.[9] They were careful to define their purpose in terms of their seeking a fuller experience of the presence of God on the basis of their common life in Christ. They agreed to avoid any working for doctrinal agreement or any attempt to establish a new sect. Christians of all sects were invited, discussions of doctrinal distinctives were forbidden, and quiet fellowship in the seeking of God consumed their time.[10]

On the spacious lawns at Broadlands, not far from the River Test, stood a grove of copper beeches, one of England's most beautiful trees. Named for the deep purple appearance of their leaves, these trees stand rotund and stately, in shape not unlike the American maple. Under such a spreading canopy large groups assembled from morning to twilight, composed of some Americans, such as Persall and Hannah Smith (at whose suggestion and under whose guidance the conferences were organized), and some Europeans, as well as a generous variety of representatives from the range of English denominations, Anglicans to Friends. Many church leaders, such as Canon Wilberforce, attended.

The purpose and character of these meetings was in harmony with MacDonald's sense of the underlying unity of all who were Christian in heart and will and with his conviction that the purpose for Christian assembly was actively to seek wisdom and help from God in obeying his precepts. He delighted in the Broadlands conferences, insofar as they offered a forum in which Christians could attempt to realize what he referred to in *Paul Faber, Surgeon* as "the ecstasy of the shared vision of truth, in which contact souls come nearer to each other than any closest familiarity can effect." He was one of their most inspiring teachers.[11]

MacDonald's relationship with Georgina Cowper-Temple, one of his more intimate, existed within the context of this ideal. He was prone to sentimentality in his relationships to people whose sensibilities matched his own; his expressed attitudes toward her present a good example. The MacDonalds had been friends of the Cowper-Temples since the early 1860s; their mutual interest in Ruskin's ill-fated love affair, the MacDonalds' moving to Corage, and the conferences at Broadlands, all served to deepen the relationship. He now looked on her as his close sister in the faith, found her to be more eager to learn than anyone else he had known, and treated her with great spiritual interest. He referred to her as his "sister," his "angel," and his "great, great princess grandmother" (cf., *The Princess and the Goblin*).

In March 1877, Georgina, much aware of the MacDonalds' financial straights, raised a sizeable purse and presented it to them. Many of MacDonald's friends contributed, but the lion's share likely came from the Cowper-Temples.[12] Like the Rev. Walter Drake in *Paul Faber, Surgeon,* whose debt-ridden condition was suddenly relieved by his inheriting a fortune, MacDonald also unexpectedly came into, not a fortune, but nevertheless a good amount of money.

MacDonald's reply to her kindness suggests the religious sentiment that permeated their relationship. "Sometimes I do not know how to thank God for a special gift," he wrote, "because from him it is all and equally gift. But I can thank him for making me the surer that he is and that he does care for the sparrows. This kindness of yours also is only just like you and your goodness to me and mine has been just a part of the Father's and in thanking you I thank him." MacDonald had in the past refused gifts which he considered doles or had treated them as loans which he meticulously repaid when he had been able, but of this gift he wrote: "I do not think it will do me the harm now it once might have done, for I feel my stay here so short that I shall not begin to love the world now—if for no other reason, yet because it is no use." Further, he felt this gift differed from others in the purity of the motives behind it. "I would gladly owe no man anything but love. And for this which you and my other friends have given me I do not feel that I owe anything but love. What is given me is mine, and love to boot. If I did not believe in the love, however unmerited, I could not take the money." Apparently the purse came with the qualification that only a part be used for daily expenses. He wrote, "The portion you allow me to use takes a load off me." It must, therefore, have been a sizeable sum for the other portion gave him grounds to hope he would in the future, could he add some to it, be able to build a home. "It may be good for me however to have a few years in a house we can call our own, and therefore I think that, as God has sent me this towards one, he may be meaning that I shall be able to add to it in the years to come so that I may be able to build or buy someday."[13] The hope would be realized within a few years when they would build in Bordighera, Italy.

The necessity to take Mary to southern Europe or Africa for the winter, however, took precedence over any plans to build a home. That she had an advanced case of consumption was now painfully apparent. The family remembered what a winter in Algiers had meant to MacDonald thirty years earlier and determined to do something similar now for Mary. When MacDonald shared their decision with his fellow Christians gathered at the Broadlands conference in August 1877, Lady Ducie, a much-traveled guest, urged them to go to Cairo, Egypt. Assembled under the beeches, they offered special prayer for her as she lay at Corage, spitting blood. "Poor pet Mary!" MacDonald sighed. "But Love is Lord of all and all shall be well. I *will* trust."[14]

THIRTY

The Hill of Difficulty

Our Lord never mentions poverty as one of the obstructions to His kingdom, neither has it ever proved such; riches, cares and desires He does mention.—Weighed and Wanting

For a time Mary appeared too ill to travel, and the family feared they would have to abandon their plan to winter by the Mediterranean. But then she rallied, the doctor gave permission for her to go, and they hurriedly made their plans. Although they had had to lease The Retreat for another year, they still were hoping someone would take an interest in subleasing it. Lily and Irene worked hard to pack their things with a view to their not returning. They thought it would not be difficult to rent Corage for the winter, ponies and all. But what if the ponies were not wanted? They could hardly bear the thought of selling them.

They hurried to set out before cold weather came, having decided that Louisa would go with a part of the family while MacDonald remained behind with the rest. Besides Mary, Louisa took with her Lily, Irene, and Ronald, together with a maid for Mary and an Italian-speaking friend, Hatty Russell, whose mother lived in Nervi, a suburb of Genoa. Ronald's main function was to carry Mary. A large group of friends appeared to see them off the morning of September 25. Mary felt awkward and embarrassed.

Hatty Russell's accompanying them seems to have been the determining factor in their deciding to go to Italy. A more worldly, prudent family might well have gone elsewhere. Italy was in a state of political turmoil, both from within and from without. Since Victor Emmanuel II had come to the throne in 1861, numerous internal revolutions had occurred. He had but recently added

Rome to his domain. The famous Triple Alliance with Germany and Austria-Hungary, which Italy sorely needed to diminish the threat of French expansion, was not formed until 1882. It was an uncertain time. But MacDonald seems to have been unconcerned with contemporary politics, except insofar as he saw moral implications. "I know more of the politics of the kingdom of heaven than I do of those of this world," he mused to Georgina Mount-Temple. "At least, if I do not, I am in evil case."[1]

The travelers crossed the Channel at Folkestone and engaged a coupe—the half-compartment at the end of a European train—for Mary's comfort, although the cost seemed prohibitive to Louisa. "You must not mind that," MacDonald told her. "I see more and more how to be able to trust, and I think we shall always find that we can get through." He was, however, uncertain whether he would be able to put together sufficient money for him and the remainder of the children to join them; they might have to winter apart. In the back of his mind was the intention of making another lecture tour of America the following year, which would "clear up a good deal" of their financial troubles, but that was a year away.[2]

The travelers hurried through Paris to Menton, a small town on the French Riviera just adjacent to Italy, and took temporary lodging at the Pension Americana. The beauty of the orange trees, palms, and maritime pines, together with flowers, blooming cacti, and the brilliantly deep purples and reds of the bougainvillea vines, filled them all with amazement, but especially Mary, who had longed to go abroad if she were able. Only the mosquitoes, which they had constantly to "grab at," gave them annoyance.

They were dismayed with the appearance of Nervi—one long, narrow, drafty street. It was, however, in many ways an Italian Hastings, with the hills dotted with homes and steeply declining to the sea. Nearby were tourist and fishing industries. Their spirits soared when they learned that a large villa at an easy distance from the shops, named the Palazzo Cattaneo, was available for lease at a little over twenty-two pounds per month. With spacious gardens of orange and lemon trees, it was beautifully situated on a terraced hillside; precipitately below, the sea sparkled in the sunlight. Surrounding it was a high stone wall on which sat, to their delight, huge pots containing still more orange and lemon trees. They decided to take it temporarily, even though Louisa feared she would have to be taken up and down the steep hill in a sedan chair. It promised them ample room and beautiful surroundings while they looked for more permanent quarters.

Meanwhile MacDonald, amid the welter of boxes stacked everywhere at The Retreat, sat in a makeshift study and looked out on the thick fog of a London fall as he tried to complete *Paul Faber, Surgeon*. The money he could receive from it would enable him to settle their bills and take the remainder of his family to Italy. Winnie and MacKay were with him, while Grace and the balance of the children were at Corage.

That summer Greville had been one of three (from among seven candidates) who passed their medical examinations, and he went on to receive honors. Now excited at already having seventeen new patients with which to begin his practice, he came to see his father in the evenings when he was able. "You would like to hear the way the boy talks," MacDonald proudly remarked to Louisa. "He is a boy no longer, however. One thing he sees plainly—the elevating power of suffering."[3] One evening MacDonald was suffering from an aching tooth, and Greville brought a leech to apply to his gum. When it escaped its vial, Winnie was beside herself with fear until it was retrieved. The thought of an unsupervised leech crawling somewhere on the premises was more than she could take.

MacDonald was unable to fend off bewilderment with their situation. "Is it not a strange time for us, my dearest?" he asked his wife. "I have once or twice been tempted to feel abandoned—in this messy and struggling existence—I mean the houses, etc., and not being very well. But I know very much better—and my inside house is pretty well supplied with the necessaries of life. But it is a touch of the valley of humiliation or the hill Difficulty rather." His imagery is that of *Pilgrim's Progress*. Mary's plight weighed constantly on him. "My love to my little sick dove," he wrote. "Tell her to keep a big heart for God to fill for her. When I was a boy my desire was to be loved; but now my prayer is to be made able to love. . . . We have hardly a glimmer yet of what we have to learn in that way, and therein lies the secret of bliss."[4]

Having two volumes of his novel, *Paul Faber, Surgeon,* completed by October 1, MacDonald took them to Strahan in the hopes of his running them serially in his new publication, *Day of Rest.* Strahan demurred, however, thinking the work too philosophical for his purposes. It would, he said, put things in readers' heads they had never thought of, and on reflection MacDonald agreed. Strahan, nevertheless, liked it well enough to promise to publish it as a novel when it was finished, but he could offer MacDonald only four hundred pounds, payable in three months, for the rights of publication. Disappointed since he was accustomed to receiving twice that amount and more for his work and he considered this novel his finest thusfar, MacDonald nevertheless accepted. "It does seem notable," he mused to Louisa, "that just when we seem to need it so much, I am likely to get less than I have had for the last ten years—surely the intention is to keep me from trusting anywhere but in the *giving* God."[5] When Cowper-Temple learned of the situation, he offered to endorse Strahan's bill, so it was "as good as gold" in the eyes of the bank.

Exhausted to the point of collapse, MacDonald took to his bed. "Never had I so many worldly mosquitoes about me," he wrote Louisa, "but they don't get within my curtains much. I grow surer and surer. Winnie nurses me so sweetly and Grev too— and I don't think I shall be long ill. I have seldom been quieter in mind—than just this day—but I am sometimes hard put to it with the Apollyon of unbelief."[6] His spirit typically vacillated between the abyss of doubt and the repose of faith, as the frequency in his novels of clashes between characters concerning the truth of Christianity suggests. He had a personal need, it would seem, to wrestle constantly with the basic issues of Christian belief.

It is also true that these tensions within his spirit helped generate the appreciable energy needed to maintain his rigorous writing schedule and to achieve continuously, as he did, further religious insight. In *Paul Faber, Surgeon* he had been imaginatively posing a case against Christianity and countering with a case for it. This emotional drain, combined with their domestic difficulties, now drove him to bed with a variety of pains, especially in his side, and "a rather quick pulse." The doctor diagnosed pleurisy and prescribed cotton wool, together with linseed poultices, for him to apply to his side.

He lay day after day, reading the Bible or Shakespeare when he could, but his strength did not return. He wrote a note to Georgina at Broadlands: Would she return to their #15 Great Stanhope Street residence and receive him for a few days? "It would be like a fairy story to have you to take care of me," he wrote. "I would pay you with things out of the New Testament. It is much much to ask, but what are you my sister for if I am going to be doubtful before you?"[7] The Cowper-Temples telegramed their eagerness to serve him in any way they could, and MacDonald was soon surrounded by the Christian love and temporal elegance of their London residence, while Winnie finished cleaning and packing at The Retreat.

Sensing that the ponies might be the reason why Corage was not yet leased, the Cowper-Temples offered to keep them at Broadlands. Georgina would delight to drive them, she assured MacDonald. It was a great weight off his mind as he simply could not bear to sell them. They offered to take Kitty as well, but then a Mr. Plumer offered to purchase her. MacDonald set the price at fifty pounds, saying he thought she was "very cheap at that." Then he added: "But if you give me that for her and after trial come to think her not worth it, I hereby promise to return you the difference between your estimate and mine. . . . I should have a horror of getting more than she was worth from anybody."[8] One of his most rigid principles was that each person should try earnestly to establish equitable worth in all his financial dealings.

As MacDonald slowly regained some strength at Great Stanhope Street, his daughters were busy getting The Retreat ready for a new tenant. All their boxes were moved to River Villa, the house immediately alongside The Retreat, which they decided to retain, Greville and one of his school chums agreeing to live in it with a Mrs. Morris to cook for them. But MacDonald was still far from sure that, when all the bills were paid, enough would remain for him and the remainder of the children to make the trip to Italy. "I have been writing cheques a good part of the morning. I cannot yet see how the thing is to come, yet I think it will come. . . . certainly we could live on much less out there. I should be quite content with macaroni."[9] He thought, if he were absolutely forced, he could ask his brother-in-law Joshua Sing for the loan of one hundred pounds.

Then good news came from Italy. Louisa and the children were settling at Palazzo Cattaneo, and the gentle Italian fall seemed to be working wonders for Mary, who was reviving in body and spirit. Louisa wrote of the improvement cautiously, not wanting to raise false hopes, but Mary continued to rally. "How gladdening your news about Mary is!" MacDonald exclaimed. "What if our blessed Father should leave her to us yet! I did think he was going to take her. And we don't know yet."[10] Further, Louisa had boldly explored the possibility of doing public dramatic performances for the benefit of the large English-speaking community in the resort area of Genoa, and she had solid indications they would be well received. The proceeds could make a large difference in their family finances.

She asked Grace to pack and send all their costuming and backdrops. "The acting is a great relief to me," MacDonald admitted. "It makes a strong point for justification in going." He calculated that, with all expenses paid, he would have only fifty pounds left, which would have to be applied to the rent for the Palazzo Cattaneo. Then Cowper-Temple prevailed on him to take a gift of two hundred pounds. "I tried to refuse it," MacDonald explained to Louisa, "but it wouldn't do. . . . He came and said he wanted me to do him a favour. I was so pleased, thinking he really wanted me to do something for him."[11] All things now seemingly arranged, they went off to Broadlands to set things in order at Corage. Since it was not yet taken, it would be placed in an agent's hands.

Then MacDonald received a pleasant surprise, just in time to tell Louisa in his birthday letter to her. The Queen granted him a Civil List Pension which would yield him one hundred pounds annually. He could only conjecture why it should come at this time; Cowper-Temple assured him he had had nothing to do with it. Perhaps Princess Alice had instigated it, Georgina suggested. Or perhaps Lord Beaconsfield, whose office assigned such boons, had been prompted by reading some favorable reviews.[12] In any case, elated not so much with the money as with the honor, MacDonald summoned his best formal style and expressed his gratitude to the Earl of Beaconsfield, through whom the grant had come.

> *Nov. 3, 1877*
>
> *My lord,*
>
> *Permit me to return by your lordship, with all loyalty and service, my grateful thanks to her Majesty for the honour and benefit her Majesty has been pleased to confer upon me through your lordship. The honour of her Majesty's notice is more to me than the benefit of her Majesty's gift, welcome as the latter must be to one dependent on the uncertain returns of literature.*
>
> *Were it allowed me to hope that this favour had in any measure resulted from your lordship's estimate of my standing in the profession, it would add to the pleasure of being thus the recipient of her Majesty's goodness.*
>
> > *With sincere thanks*
> > *I am*
> > *Your lordship's obliged and obedient servant,*
> > *George MacDonald*

"The Queen is not quite so stingy as I had prognosticated," Greville confided to Winnie.[13]

The final obstacles to MacDonald and several of his children's leaving were overcome; they made plans for a quick departure. Louisa was urging them to hurry because Mary had again taken a turn for the worse. MacDonald was prepared for such word.

> If we have to be sorrowful, we shall sorrow together. Only I will not bow my head before death. I will not acknowledge concerning death what our Lord denies of it. If we only get near to him, we shall more and more feel it a delight that he should do with us as he pleases, for it is all in such love as we only sometimes get a glimmer of now. He shall have his own of me, I would say, but for fear of boasting.[14]

Ted at first intended to accompany them, but circumstances kept him in England until early the following January. Louisa, in motherly solicitude, wrote wondering if they ought not to encourage Ted and Mary to marry. Would MacDonald not have married her if he had known she were dying? Of course he would have, MacDonald assured her, but perhaps Ted was simply shy. In any case the matter was for them to decide. As he pondered the matter he showed Louisa's letter to Georgina, and they discussed it. When later, after he arrived in Nervi, he told his wife what he had done, she was sincerely offended, feeling that he had betrayed her confidence and trust. Shamefacedly, MacDonald wrote to Georgina of Louisa's dismay and hoped she did not think ill of his wife because of the proposal.

After warm good-byes had all been taken, and the "Z's" comfortably stabled at Broadlands, MacDonald and his children left Southampton on Tuesday, November 6. After a rough passage they stayed overnight at Havre, then hurried on without stop until they reached Genoa, to be greeted, not as they had expected with sunshine and gentle breezes, but with cold wind and rain. It struck MacDonald as an ill omen. Louisa and Ronald met him at the station in Genoa, and after an overnight there they went on to Nervi. After laboring up the hill amid the olive and orange trees MacDonald got his first glimpse of the palatial residence Louisa had engaged. Hurrying to Mary, he found her bright-spirited but thinner than when he had last seen her. "I feel just like a badly cut nine-pin," she quipped. "When I try to stand up, I tumble over before the ball touches me."

Then, making him shut his eyes, they led him through a large white oval hall, containing a huge chandelier, to show him their surprise. Beyond a latticed opening, he saw a little private chapel, the walls lined with crucifixes and toward the front a little marble altar, with a madonna quietly presiding over the whole. Behind the curtain one of the daughters was playing "Abide with Me." MacDonald was deeply moved to have "a little core of rest in the heart of the house—a chamber opening out into the infinite,"[15] although he was quick to observe it fulfilled its purpose only if the worshiper had a similar chamber within his heart where the Son of Man reigned. The owners were immensely pleased when they learned their new tenants did not intend to close off the chapel or remove the images, although the MacDonalds did cover some of the crucifixes with little curtains.

He found Palazzo Cattaneo larger than he had expected, more stately than comfortable, and the decorations, to his taste, all bad. Yet, on the whole it pleased him. From the room Louisa had designated as his study, a shutter allowed him to overlook the large dining hall from near its ceiling, like, he said, "a benignant gnome, or evil djinn." To his delight, when Louisa played the piano, the music drifted upward to where he was working. Out the window lay a large, beautifully terraced garden filled with orange trees. And down the slope to the west shimmered the waters of the Ligurian Sea, placid and clear, dotted with little sailing vessels. The Russell Gurneys came to join them for Christmas. A special bottle of wine was opened, and they offered many thanksgivings.

THIRTY-ONE

Let Us Go On

One of the best of men said to me once that he did not feel any longing after immortality, but, when he thought of certain persons, he could not for a moment believe they had ceased. He had beheld the lovely, believed therefore in the endless. —Warlock O' Glenwarlock

MacDonald's delight in his new surroundings rapidly grew. He now had greater solitude, cleaner air, and more beautiful sunsets than in England, all of which seemed somehow to come from the Ligurian Sea. "Railways and factories and dirt and smoke don't go very far after all," he mused to the Cowper-Temples. "It is delightful to think that even in this world the precious sea keeps a wide solitary space for us."[1]

In the evenings he looked westward from Palazzo Cattaneo across the bay below him to catch the unique quality of each day's sunset. "They are different from the sunsets of either England, America, or Algiers—the prevailing characteristic being the soft blending of dull tender colours as if every hue were wrapt in a twilight of its own—a twilight made of thoughts of other colours—like the hues, rather, of a Roman scarf." One particularly breathtaking one, with the sea appearing "a still lake of gold under a red canopy," prompted the thought that he should attempt to keep some record of these aesthetic delights, but he quickly rejected the idea in favor of another spiritual surmise: "This profusion of passing, untreasured, never-repeated, unrecorded splendour, makes me wonder whether all our recordings are not a heaping up of treasure after a worldly sort. When we are well up the hill, we shall no more—perhaps—think of treasuring a poem, or a drama, or writing a book. . . . We shall share our poems and our music, like eloquence, fresh from the heart, and let them go, no more to be recalled than last night's sunset."[2]

But what delight he felt was sorely frustrated by Mary's continued decline, her body now little more than skin and bones. When Ted came to be with her early in January, she seemed to rally momentarily. Her suffering, meekly borne, was a great weight on the entire family. "I can hardly trust myself to write about our Mary," MacDonald confided to the Cowper-Temples. "But God is with her, and she clings to him. Surely he will take her as easily as may be consistent with her good entrance into the more abundant life."[3] Ronald later told Burne-Jones in London that the sweetness of her spirit did not fail until her bodily strength was all but gone, and even then there were flashes of her characteristic brightness. Her suffering ended on April 27, 1878. Her sisters made her pall from silk intended for her wedding dress.

Their faith notwithstanding, the family, having put so much effort into ministering to her, felt a great emptiness for a considerable time. All the assurances of Mary's happily living somewhere seemed to Louisa of little relevance to her present need to talk with and minister to her child, a need that obsessed her throughout the year. Six months later, on her birthday, MacDonald made a quiet plea to her in verse to take courage:

> To tell thee that our blessed child
> Is watching thee from somewhere nigh,
> Mourns with thee when thy agony grows wild,
> Sits sometimes by thy bed while slow the hours go by,
>
> Were but to mock thy weary pain
> With pleasant fancies of a half-held creed,
> To gather up and offer thee again
> What thou hadst cast away as nothing to thy need.
>
> But when the Shepherd great was dead
> Death did but let the Shepherd's glory out:

> She heard his voice and followed where he led—
> He were no Shepherd now, not leading her about.
>
> Take courage fresh, my Wife, this day
> Step out with me to find her new abode;
> We go together, cannot lose the way,
> The wearier our feet, the shorter still the road.
>
> Let us go on. We do not care
> For aught but life that is all one with love:
> We seek not death, but still we climb the stair
> Where death is one wide landing to the rooms above.[4]

Distraught in spirit and utterly exhausted from her care of Mary, for months Louisa was unable to leave the house except in a wheelchair. Greville came to spend the summer with them.

Octavia Hill was also a visitor during this difficult period, but her presence—because of her need—served only to add to their trauma. Her health, having steadily weakened for some time under the strain of managing her housing projects, was now on the verge of breakdown due to an unpleasant relationship with Ruskin. She had given her life and great energies to social programs shaped and financed by him, and now, having become a notable social reformer in the eyes of the general public, she found he had drawn her into an ugly public quarrel.

It seems a third party had misrepresented some of her statements to Ruskin, he had written her asking for an explanation, and a correspondence had followed in which the basic misunderstanding grew beyond proper proportions. Ruskin proceeded to publish their correspondence in his *Fors Clavigeral*, a sort of one-man magazine he published periodically from 1871 to 1884. Beginning in 1878 to experience a series of delirious illnesses that steadily increased toward the end of his life, he was already giving evidence that his emotions were becoming unstable.[5] The MacDonalds, with Octavia as their guest, found themselves drawn into the strong emotional energies of the quarrel at a time when they little needed another emotional trauma. "Our dear

Ruskin has been behaving very naughtily to Octavia, and has troubled her much," MacDonald diplomatically remarked to Georgina.[6]

Still another sorrow came in early June with the news of the sudden death of Russell Gurney. A close friend and benefactor of the MacDonalds since their early days in London, his long and distinguished career in public service had been to MacDonald, like that of William Cowper-Temple, an impressive embodiment of the ideal of Christian statesmanship. His final boon to MacDonald was a five-hundred-pound legacy, coming now at a time when it was much needed.[7]

Throughout this difficult winter and spring, MacDonald was working on the third volume of *Paul Faber, Surgeon*, which he considered the best of his novels. Like his character Robert Falconer, who was introduced in *David Elginbrod* before he received an entire novel devoted to him, Paul Faber had appeared in an earlier novel, as a dedicated atheist doctor in *Thomas Wingfold, Curate;* now MacDonald devoted a novel to "his story." Many of the other characters of the former novel appear in this one also.

Wingfold and his wife Helen present a model marriage relationship in this novel, enhancing one of its main themes: the spiritual significance of sexual love. MacDonald had been insisting since *Within and Without* that the relationship between the sexes was greatly enhanced by a full orientation of the partners' awakened spirits toward God and that married love was one of God's chief channels of grace. He gave the theme its most thorough development in this novel, contrasting the marriage of Thomas and Helen with that of Paul Faber and his bride Juliet, a relationship spiritually askew and traumatic.

MacDonald undertook to manifest through the story that all true love is sacramental; to abandon oneself to love is to participate, whether or not consciously, in the reality that is God and may well be the means of the soul consciously discovering him. He also took occasion to repudiate with vehemence the double standard of sexual morality that pertained widely in his day: virginity the ideal for single women but covert promiscuity accepted as normal for men.

He combined the sexual theme with the nature of scientific positivism and its insufficiency as compared to Christianity. As in *Thomas Wingfold, Curate,* where MacDonald addressed current issues in biblical scholarship and offered his response, so in this novel he confronted the challenge of a strictly positivist, rationalist, and materialist approach to life. In considering this as the largest issue besetting the church of his time, MacDonald stands in interesting contrast to contemporary evangelicals who were expending considerable energies grappling with the issue of Darwinian evolution, which hardly concerned MacDonald.

Paul and Juliet are brought through their experience of life into contact with a reality that is quite beyond the reach of science and that is thoroughly paradoxical in nature: mutual dependence makes for individuality; sacrificing the self issues in freedom; ever to lose oneself is to be godlike.

The book closes with their having found an orientation to life, which, if maintained, will allow them consciously to grow into fuller spiritual health. "Why should I pursue the story further?" he asks:

> The true story has no end—no end. But endlessly dreary would the story be, were there no Life living by its own will, no perfect Will, one with an almighty heart, no Love in whom we live and move and have our being. Offer me an eternity in all things else after my own imagination, but without a perfect Father, and I say, no; let me die, even as the unbelieving would have it. Not believing in the Father of Jesus, they are *right* in not desiring to live.[8]

The vision with which his writing career began twenty years earlier—that the essential need of people is to find and obey God as their heavenly Father—is unchanged; the literary vehicle he uses to express it has steadily improved.

In December 1878, just prior to its publication, MacDonald dedicated the novel to William Cowper-Temple. He wrote a sixteen-line poem, beginning "Clear-windowed temple of the God of grace / From the loud wind to me a hiding-place," in which he graciously acknowledged his large debt to the Cowper-Temples for their help during a difficult time. When Cowper-Temple wrote expressing his honor at the dedication, he complimented MacDonald on his intention in his novels to draw believable characters ideal in virtue. Pleased, MacDonald responded: "Your letter says of my books just what I try to go upon—to make them true to the real and not the spoilt humanity. Why should I spend my labour on what one can have too much of without any labour? I will try to show what we might be, may be, must be, shall be—and something of the struggle to gain it."[9] A clearer statement of his motivating purpose would be difficult to find.

Although the purpose for their coming to Italy seemed to have failed with Mary's death, a benefit soon appeared. In the Italian sun and air MacDonald began feeling better than he had ever felt before. Although it took no little effort, he climbed daily up the hill to breath the clear air and enjoy the view at the top. Beyond the spiritual analogy, which was never lost on him, he literally felt himself improving physically as he did so. Both asthma and bronchitis seemed to have disappeared.

Then word came that William Morris, whose publication of the long poem *The Earthly Paradise* in 1868–1870 had established him as one of the most popular of contemporary poets, was interested in taking The Retreat, so the burden of that lease would now be lifted.[10] When they added the crucial consideration that living in Italy was so much cheaper for them, staying seemed the logical course. Even though Corage still was standing empty back at Boscombe, they nevertheless would be financially ahead if they remained. And they never enjoyed outdoor life together so much as they did now.

When their lease expired at Nervi, they were pleased to locate a similar place in nearby Porto Fino, the Villa Barratta. Like the Palazzo Cattaneo, it was situated on a steep hillside overlooking the sea—this time, a bay filled with yachts and sailing vessels.[11] To the west and south they could look out to sea, with its perfection of blues and greens, over the top of a little isthmus where the picturesque village of Porto Fino rested, with its quaint shops, outdoor "restaurantes," and local fishing industry.

To the east they could see down the coast almost to Spezzia, which lay around a corner. Miles of terraces on the sloping hillsides, with their lush growth of palm and maritime pine trees made the area, MacDonald avowed, the most beautiful he had ever seen. Three miles away at Santa Margherita they could catch the train into nearby Genoa. Since there was no carriage road between them and the station, they secured their own boat for rowing across the bay. MacDonald reveled in the solitude; they might go months here without seeing a visitor.

Now that they were seriously considering adopting Italy as their second country, they had to come to terms with the language. They engaged a young lady from Florence named Verita, who spoke no English, to come live with them for several months in order to make them talk, if she could, Italian.[12] With increased health and solitude MacDonald was spending more time in his study, both writing and studying scripture. Through the 1870s his interest had steadily grown in the Greek manuscripts of the New Testament. "Still . . . the great sweet book, so wise, so simple, so daring, yea—infinite—grows upon me," he confided to the Cowper-Temples.[13] He was especially interested in the rich semantics of the Greek words and began to spend considerable time comparing variations in the earliest texts.[14] "Papa and Greville are Greek Testamenting together" Louisa had remarked to Lily on an earlier occasion.[15] He did not trust the lexicons put together by the theologians because they concentrated only on biblical Greek; he preferred the more complete ones that included the meanings of the words as used by the classical authors.

In league with the Cowper-Temples he devised for his study purposes an interleaved New Testament that combined various Greek texts with the King James translation. They had it bound, with an appropriate plate on the front, and sent it off to him shortly after he took up residence in Italy. He exclaimed in gratitude:

> What do I not owe you for my New Covenant! I use it every day, and had no idea before how useful the Greek would be to me. Oh how much more precious already even than before is the word of it to me! Some difficulties are quite cleared away by the Greek—or it suggests possible explanations where I must ask a scholar before I am certain.

At the same time he kept from reverencing the text as such; he was interested in the Living Word, and, as he made clear in *Thomas Wingfold, Curate*[16] he felt the Spirit of God purposefully kept the church from having a pure text simply in order to avoid the worshiping of the text itself. The Word of God lives in the hearts of obedient followers, not in the volume of a book nor in words as such: "The English is vanishing from me as inadequate—and so will the Greek by and by, and nothing be left but The Word," he affirmed.[17]

The nature and character of the obedience that people should practice to Christ as the Word is the basic theme of his next novel, *Sir Gibbie*. He commenced *Sir Gibbie,* most of which was written at the Villa Barratta, within a few days of finishing *Paul Faber, Surgeon*. Although the family was living on considerably less (and more enjoyably) than in England, MacDonald found he could not slack his writing pace; he was being offered less and less for his novels. For instance, in 1872 he had received one thousand pounds for *The Vicar's Daughter,* not one of his better efforts. He began writing *Sir Gibbie* on the strength of an offer of one hundred ten pounds. Yet many critics would hail this novel as his best. The pirating publishers, now working in considerable volume, had lowered their prices as low as twenty cents per volume, and legitimate publishers were forced to lower their prices accordingly. The author was ultimately the one that suffered the most. As MacDonald totaled his income for 1878, he found he had made approximately half what he did the year before.

But with improved health he was able to write more steadily than ever. He finished *Sir Gibbie* before the end of 1878, and it began appearing serially on January 4, 1879, in the *Glasgow Weekly Mail*. Hurst and Blackett's edition appeared that May, and Lippincott of Philadelphia brought out their edition soon thereafter. "I hope you will like my *Sir Gibbie*," MacDonald told Helen Powell. "I was a good deal hampered from never having been in the parts I tried to imagine. I should not wonder if you liked it as well as any thing I have done."[18]

Greville regarded *Sir Gibbie* as "at once the most direct and most beautiful" of all his father's works, as well as being "the most picturesque of his Scottish stories."[19] Similarly to *Alec Forbes of Howglen* and *Robert Falconer*, this novel fits loosely into the *Bildungsroman* tradition, as Gibbie, a mute street waif, is shown growing into manhood and inheriting a baronetcy. But contrary to the normal pattern of the *Bildungsroman*, Gibbie makes no false starts in life. He is "one of those natures to whom obedience is a delight—a creature so different from the vulgar that they have but one tentacle they can reach him with: contempt."[20] He lives "in the holy carelessness of the eternal *now*."[21] To see a truth and to do it is one and the same thing with him. Gibbie is a prime instance of the degree of success MacDonald enjoyed in making his good characters real and attractive. Gibbie is a Christ figure in whom MacDonald worked out an important theological concept, but he is not wooden. He exists as a believable, sympathetic, and attractive character.

The reviewer in The *Athenaeum* dismissed *Paul Faber, Surgeon* as another "lay sermon" of MacDonald's; therefore he found "little to criticize from a literary point of view."[22] The one who reviewed *Sir Gibbie* expressed much the same attitude but acknowledged that the story, whatever "antagonisms" it may raise in its depictions of religious instructors, had "power, pathos, and humour." Its fault, he said, was "the noble one of too exalted an ideal for most people."[23] The *British Quarterly Review,* on the other hand, ran highly laudatory reviews of both novels,[24] praising them for the very aspects to which the reviewer in The *Athenaeum* objected. "In no other author do we get the same wealth of moral and spiritual thought," the reviewer wrote in his comments on *Paul Faber, Surgeon.* "He seems to have a special faculty for getting at the heart of man and of nature." These assessments epitomize the two types of contemporary views of MacDonald's work. Those who approved of his Christian interpretation of life tended to be lavish in their praise; those who objected to his views tended to dismiss his work as nonliterary.

THIRTY-TWO

Learning Slowly and Stubbornly

Memory is a dreadful thing—a heart sickening thing—until Hope helps us—and then it is the sweetest, best help to Hope.—Lily to Nelly

The MacDonalds were finally adjusting to Mary's death when another sorrow occurred. Fifteen-year-old Maurice, so loved by the entire family, took a severe cough and fever; his lungs became congested; and in just over two weeks he died. The family was emotionally crushed; MacDonald and Louisa were all but overwhelmed. Yet out of the emotional devastation MacDonald's vision of the nature of spiritual realities became yet deeper and fuller, motivating him to produce two compelling novels and his best volume of poetry.

Like Mary, Maurice was meek and gentle spirited, a boy of unusual promise, perhaps MacDonald's model for Gibbie in the novel he had just completed. Thin and agile in build, he had been athletic, with a reputation of being the best among the boys in swimming and diving. If he had a fault, his mother avowed, it was overexertion: walking too far, swimming too long, or wandering about regardless of wet or rain. He had been often ill, a large sore on his leg two years prior being the most serious of his maladies.[1]

Possessing as he did a quiet, ready smile, Louisa had often referred to him as "angelic"; MacDonald had hopes of his entering some form of the Christian ministry. All the family enjoyed his keen wit and clever impersonations in charades. Louisa jestingly warned that he should take care lest he become the "funny man" of the family.

In their dramatic productions his talent was second only to Lilia's. During the eighteen days of his illness, Louisa nursed him indefatigably, with Lily, Grace, Bob, and Ronald anxiously helping. During the final ten days, Louisa hardly slept, being forced by the children to leave the bedside only when she became irrational with fatigue.

Once MacDonald took his boy's hand and quoted: "Let patience have her perfect work, that ye may be perfect and entire, wanting nothing" (James 1:4). Attentive, a minute later Maurice asked his father to repeat the verse. The incident made a deep impression on MacDonald and, transformed by his imagination, would be reflected in his forthcoming novel, *Warlock O' Glenwarlock*. The family was awakened by Maurice's scream early on the morning of March 5, 1879, an excessive hemorrhaging followed, and he died at two o'clock that afternoon.

MacDonald's grief and indignation almost overwhelmed him when he learned that the local church would not receive the body of his boy for burial in their graveyard. Nor could they lay him with Mary at Nervi, authorities not allowing a grave to be reopened within twelve months of burial, so that his coffin could have been placed, European fashion, on top of hers. Their only choice was to take a spot beyond the wall of the graveyard, on the rocky hillside, where a section was allotted for strangers and heretics.

The church is situated on a curving finger of land jutting out into the sea, which forms by its embrace the little bay where the village of Porto Fino sits below. All is visible in the near distance from the Villa Barratta, perched on the hillside across the bay. Not far from the church stands Brown Castle, an ancient fortress looking out to sea. Between the two on the rocky heights stand a variety of trees, mostly maritime pine and cypress, keeping solemn watch. An iron gate through the crypt-filled stone wall surrounding the little church graveyard opens on this rugged area of large boulders. Beneath one, which acted as a shield from the sea spray when the winds were high, they secured a grave.

Mrs. Russell Gurney, with her son and daughter who had been visiting the MacDonalds, returned from Mentone to be with the family in their grief. Some of the silk used as Mary's coffin cover—which had originally been purchased for her wedding dress—also became Maurice's coffin cover. On it his sisters sowed the emblem of a crimson cross, taken from their costume for Greatheart in *Pilgrim's Progress,* a part he had sometimes played when MacDonald was not available. His body was buried by moonlight the night of March 6, Ronald and Bob carrying the coffin bareheaded up the steep, stony path, the family following. Robert held the lantern as an aged clergyman, Rev. Woodruff from Nervi, read the simple graveside service.

"What shall I do for Patience and Submission?" Louisa imploringly asked her sister Charlotte. The thought that Maurice and Mary were now together yielded them some measure of solace. MacDonald's grief was deep, profound, and prolonged. Nevertheless, out of this period of extremely painful trials came a yet greater deepening of his convictions concerning spiritual realities and his commitment to them. The more that was taken from him in life, the fuller his true life in God seemed to him. While his longings for immortality increased, so did his vision of the spiritual wealth of complete personhood.

He first gradually came to terms with his grief by applying himself to writing a calender poem with a separate verse for each day of the year, which he would later title *A Book of Strife in the form of the diary of an old soul.* For December 30, he wrote:

> Twilight of the transfiguration-joy,
> Gleam-faced, pure-eyed, strong-willed, high-hearted boy!
> Hardly thy life clear forth of heaven was sent
> Ere it broke out into a smile, and went.
> So swift thy growth, so true thy goalward bent,
> Thou, child and sage inextricably blent,

Must surely one day come to teach thy father in some
heavenly tent!

The image of Maurice's becoming a being of great spiritual stature
in glory yielded him consolation.

Other visitors at Villa Baratta that spring were Richard Gilder
with his wife Helena and child Rodman. On learning that Gilder
was ill and needed a change of climate, both MacDonald and Louisa wrote assuring them that Villa Barratta was their home in Italy,
and they should come at once. When the Gilders arrived, the
MacDonalds, considering whether to return to England that summer, were busily preparing for some local productions of *Pilgrim's
Progress,* thinking to raise money for their trip. At first they had
hesitated to resume their dramas so soon after the death of one of
their best actors, but they found they were now able to see a spiritual light and truthfulness in Bunyan they had not felt with such
force before. Playing the drama gave them solace.

This was not the first presentation of their plays in Italy. Almost immediately upon arriving, on December 8, 1877, they had
rented the Villa Novello at Genoa for presentations of *The Tetterbys*
and *Obstinancy* for the English-speaking community. The good reception their audience gave them on that occasion, and the
much-needed money they received, encouraged them to mount
the effort again. They had a stronger sense than ever that their
work was bringing important spiritual benefit to their audiences.

They gave several performances in the Genoa area later that
spring and also many in England that summer. "We are now, as
you may have heard, turned into a sort of company of acting stroll-
ers—I mean strolling actors," MacDonald quipped to Fields, "and
have a good reception and tolerable results. . . . People seem a
good deal interested in our attempt."[2]

Their determination to return to Britain was clinched one day
when a large package of "Scotch luxuries" arrived, courtesy of
Helen Powell, much to MacDonald's delight. The haggis, oat-
cakes, shortbread, and rock candy were all it took. "Nothing

agrees with my construction so well as the meal of my youth—in any and every shape, and when I can't eat nothing else I can eat that," MacDonald wrote in gratitude.[3]

Before they left, however, they had to secure a place to live when they returned, their lease now up at the Villa Barratta. They cast their eyes westward along the coast dotted with resort towns, each with its sandy beaches, luxurious verdure, and clean, well-ordered demeanor. From among them they choose Bordighera, a picturesque town of yellow stucco buildings and tiled streets, home to twice as many English as Italians. They were attracted to its level terrain, so distinctly different from the steep hillsides where they had been living, and also to the fresh and invigorating sea breezes. Behind the village to the north the maritime mountains sloped sharply upward, and to the west they seemed to descend into the Ligurian Sea. Generally serene and still, the waters to the south spangled in the sun, with the frequently present haze in the distance making it impossible to discern where the sea merged with the sky. Between the sea and the village was an extensive beach and a mile-long promenade. Using the large purse that had been raised for them two years earlier by the Cowper-Temples, they were now prepared to buy and settle permanently in Italy.

The Villa Patrick was for sale in Bordighera, and they took an option on it. It appeared to them a good place to live for "a few winters till we are called, I hope, to the high countries," MacDonald explained to Fields.[4] With Maurice's death following so closely on Mary's, the world seemed a more bewildering place than it ever had before. They intended to have inscribed in the front hall, "And they confessed that they were pilgrims and strangers on the earth," for that captured their mood (Hebrews 11:13). "There is no time for anything but getting ready to go," MacDonald told the Cowper-Temples, as he set his face toward "the high countries."

By the middle of May they had returned to England and settled again at Corage, which had never been let. It was the same as they had left it, minus the aged ponies, which were now the possession of Mrs. Russell Gurney. From this base they traveled throughout the south of England, giving their plays in places where friends had worked hard to make suitable arrangements. Often a friend would buy a block of tickets to a performance, distributing them to others as gifts.

Among the plays they were performing regularly now were Corneille's *Polyeuctus* and Shakespeare's *Macbeth*. The success of the venture pleased them; they were received with consistent acclaim. MacDonald performed such parts as Mr. Greatheart and Macbeth with relish. His deeply felt reverence in the presence of any issue bearing on the eternal verities, together with his flowing beard and sincere demeanor, added appreciably to the overall effect. Consistent with his frugal use of time, he corrected galley proofs between his cues.

After one performance in 1881, a woman approached him, commended him on his performance, and proceded to tell him of the extreme disappointment of a little girl who was prevented by illness from being present. MacDonald took a piece of paper, wrote on it, and gave it to the woman, saying, "Give her that with my love." On the paper was written:

> Pain and sorrow,
> Plough and harrow,
> For the seed its place to find;
> For the growing
> Still the blowing
> Of the Spirit's thinking wind;
> For the corn that it will bear,
> Love eternal everywhere.[5]

He was unwavering in his conviction that all disappointments of good people will one day yield some further evidence of God's love.

Returning to Corage in the autumn of 1879, they began to give serious thought to giving up their option on the Villa Patrick and staying in England. Formerly they had planned to return that October to take up residence in Bordighera, but, having made no binding commitment there and now delighting in their English home, they tried to settle in at Corage. The family kept Christmas there, and MacDonald sat down to return to *Mary Marston,* his current novel. But his old complaints began to plague him, and he was forced to bed for a great many days in January. "I find I am not to live here, for I cannot work for illness," he concluded.[6] Clearly, they should return to Italy for the sake of his health.

The prospect of returning to Italy was a difficult one for Lily. In England she had strong intentions of allying herself again with Octavia Hill in her work with the poor. When the decision was made for the family to return to Bordighera, she said, "Ah, then I shall never be able to work for Miss Octavia. How can I give up that hope?"[7] She nevertheless decided to go with her parents rather than stay in London without them.

While they were at Corage, MacDonald printed at his expense a group of poems that he had been working on for some time, which he titled *A Book of Strife in the form of the diary of an old soul,* which appeared in January 1880. The printing, though done by Unwin Brothers in London, was small and distribution was private. Arthur Hughes undertook to handle the copies, sending them to anyone who would write him, price three shillings. After Ruskin received a copy, he praised it in his Oxford Lectures as being "one of the three great sacred poems of the nineteenth century."[8]

It consists of three hundred sixty-six seven-line stanzas, one for each day of the year, including leap-year. An intimate revelation of MacDonald's mind, it records his moments of doubt and anguish, his gropings after insight, his affirmations of hope, and his moments of inner triumph. Addressed directly to God, it is more the record of a monologue with God that the reader is privileged to overhear than a devotional guide.

MacDonald told Georgina Cowper-Temple that he looked over it "with more interest than I have yet felt for a book of my own," apparently because he had some trepidation concerning how the very private quality of these devotional musings would appear in print. "I think it is not a failure," he judged, "but a great deal will depend, not only on the degree and kind of spiritual training but on the mood of the reader."⁹

A perceptive judgment. MacDonald was well aware, but without the slightest trace of arrogance, that very few people are capable of entering into the intense spiritual longing after God and tender devotion to him that characterized his life and even those only on specific occasions. A person of extreme moods, he appreciated the role of mood in spiritual states of the soul and the difficulty on any given occasion of generating a desirable one. Many readers, gripped by a congenial state of mind due to experiencing deep grief or passing through deep trial, find this the most helpful and deeply penetrating of any of MacDonald's devotional writings.

It is an indispensible source of material for anyone desiring a better acquaintance with the state of MacDonald's spiritual life and the quality of his odyssey as it came to greater intensity during the time of the deaths of his two children. The themes of the novels he would now write derive directly from his experiences. He became preoccupied with the desire to experience what lies beyond death, believing it was a more complete union with God and a greater freedom from the negative energies of the self. As he contemplated his experience he concluded God was asking of him a yet more complete willingness to relinquish all enjoyments that in any sense might detract from the realization of this divine union:

> Take from me leisure, all familiar places;
> Take all the lovely things of earth and air;
> Take from me books; take all my precious faces;
> Take words melodious, and their songful linking;
> Take scents, and sounds, take all thy outsides fair:
> Draw nearer, taking, and, to my sober thinking,
> Thou bring'st them nearer all, and ready to my prayer.¹⁰

A compelling paradox presented itself to him, one that greatly stimulated his story-telling imagination: as a person relinquishes things in order to achieve fuller communion with God, those things are in that fellowship with God restored. Since for the Christian possessions acquire their full significance and import only in God, the Christian alone possesses the earth. Therefore, things seen in this light are "nearer." The result to the soul in this spiritual transaction is yet fuller being.

The novels MacDonald now wrote show how he imagined these themes expressed in human experience. *Mary Marston,* on which he was working at the time of Maurice's death, contains these themes in good measure; his next, *Warlock O' Glenwarlock* is replete with them. In *Mary Marston,* Mary, a draper's daughter, experiences great deprivation but because her first consideration in life is service to God by serving others she is more than compensated by the spiritual riches she acquires in the end.

The idea of a person complete in virtue is a concept that is "beyond most people," we are told, in that they have neither the capacity to receive it nor much interest in being such a person themselves. While most people tend to see complete maturity in virtue as madness, in terms of eternal reality it is the norm for sanity. "For my own part," MacDonald affirms, "until I shall have seen a man absolutely one with the source of his being, I do not believe I shall ever have seen a man absolutely sane."[11]

These themes constitute another version of the need-for-a-father theme. The only way to become complete in virtue is to be at one with God the Father; without him the ideal is impossible. MacDonald insisted, however, that the pattern for the complete person lies deep within people; it is not something God imposes on them from without, as though it were foreign to their natures. The pattern is the image of God in which people are created and which is perfected only as the individual cooperates with the continuing efforts of God the Father to finish his creation.

In telling Mary's story MacDonald concentrated on the role interpersonal relationships, and especially love relationships, play in the development of the individual toward what he called "the pure human." He undertook to show in this novel, as he did in

Paul Faber, Surgeon, that love and marriage are intended in the divine ecomony to be among the most powerful of God's channels of grace, whereby he works to refine people's natures and to help them grow in virtue. But love is not the sole channel; poetry and music also play an important part.

Although a devoted Christian girl, Mary develops as a person through the poetry of such authors as George Herbert and John Milton. These arouse her imagination and awaken her to the world of spiritual reality: "Mary came to know of a land never promised, yet open—a land of whose nature even she had never dreamed—a land of the spirit, flowing with milk and honey—a land of which the fashionable world knows little more than the dwellers in the back slums."[12] While literature plays a role in Mary's maturation, music ministers to the spiritual well-being of Joseph Jasper, the blacksmith violinist whom Mary marries in the end. People in the novel who have an intellectual grasp of Christian truth but lack an aesthetic orientation tend to be narrow and mean-spirited.

MacDonald affirms that true artistic expressions are gifts of God to humankind—expressions of the Spirit that is in the world and that is ever trying to arouse the spirit lying deep within a person. When, through sacramental grace, the Spirit without reaches and enlivens the spirit within, then salvation occurs, and the person is set on the road of spiritual becoming. Perhaps the finest expression of this idea is found in *Thomas Wingfold, Curate*:

> All about us, in earth and air, wherever eye or ear can reach, there is a power ever breathing itself forth in signs, now in a daisy, now in a wind-waft, a cloud, a sunset; a power that holds constant and sweetest relation with the dark and silent world within us; . . . the same God who is in us, and upon whose tree we are the buds, if not yet the flowers, also is all about us—inside , the Spirit; outside, the Word. And the two are ever trying to meet in us; and when they meet, then the sign without, and the longing within, become one in light,

and the man no more walketh in darkness, but knoweth whither he goeth.[13]

As is generally true in the novels the theme of spiritual becoming is inversely related to the hierarchy of the British class system, a hierarchy against which MacDonald often railed. His indignation was prompted not by a desire to do away with it—he was not especially democratic in his thinking—but by his perception that it seemed persistently to conflict with the hierarchy of true being. In a more ideal society people would be arranged on a social scale according to their moral and spiritual qualities, so that power and influence would be in the hands of truly worthy people. So it will be in the kingdom of God. But in this social world, class status is too often based on material riches; the system rewards attitudes of snobbery and greed. The biblical statement appears in the novel as a refrain: "there are first that shall be last, and last that shall be first" (cf., Matthew 19:30).

In *Warlock O' Glenwarlock* MacDonald does not repeat the sexual themes, but he does continue to work with the concept that deprivation in the pursuit of virtue will yield rich reward.[14] He now emphasizes the necessity for patience in loss. The patience that he counseled Maurice to exercise on his deathbed is illustrated in the story by the hero, Cosmo. His nature and disposition suggest that in creating him MacDonald was idealizing his late son.

While Cosmo enjoys life and nature, he yearns after a lovelier nature than what exists before his eyes. He senses in the nature around him an air of mystery—"the form the infinite first takes to the simplest and liveliest hearts"—and this creates within him a "mighty hope." Such yearning after the infinite marks him as a being with large potential for spiritual growth, and the novel traces his spiritual progress through a series of onerous trials.

A part of his reverence for his origins is a deep love and respect for his father; MacDonald develops the father-son theme as thoroughly and carefully in this as in any of his novels. Although a Scottish laird and member of an ancient family, Cosmo's father is quite poor. It is only by pawning a family heirloom that he is able to send Cosmo to college. Like the author, Cosmo attends a "university of the north," takes a tutorship during an interim in his college years, is financially unable to go to Germany to complete an education in chemistry, and thus decides to be take a permanent position as tutor.

What happens next teaches him the utter need for patience in the face of extreme deprivaton. After falling deeply in love but supposing he has lost his beloved to another man, Cosmo returns to Castle Warlock, to find his father in ill health and the family fortunes at still lower ebb than he had realized. He works as a common laborer, then falls desperately ill. Grizzie, the family's faithful servant (and one of MacDonald's more memorable peasant characters) is reduced to begging for their daily food. Then they discover hidden in their castle a cache of family jewels that, when sold, brings Cosmo great wealth. His father dies in peace, an aged man, and Cosmo, as the story closes, marries the girl whom he thought he had lost to another man.

The plot is strained, but MacDonald offers his readers a paradigm for spiritual maturity. Cosmo is the ultimate Christian hero, who though he is brought through suffering to utter depths still trusts. The depiction reveals MacDonald's reading of his own experience:

> To trust in spite of the look of being forgotten; to keep crying out into the vast whence comes no voice, and where seems no hearing; to struggle after light, where is no glimmer to guide; at every turn to find a doorless wall, yet ever seek a door; to see the machinery of the world pauseless grinding on as if self-moved, caring for no life, nor shifting a hair's-breadth for all entreaty, and yet believe that God is awake and utterly loving; to desire nothing but what comes meant for us from his hand; to wait patiently, willing to die of hunger, fearing only lest faith should fail—such is the victory that overcometh the world, such is faith indeed.[15]

A casual reader opening to such a passage might view it as the ultimate in rhetorical flourish, but this is MacDonald's own reality as he went through the dark night of his soul. The imaginative strength of this novel (it is one of his better ones in spite of its melodrama) derives from the stimulus his suffering worked upon his imagination.

Also, with Mary and Maurice no doubt on his mind (and perhaps for Georgina Cowper-Temple's benefit as well) MacDonald gives early in the novel a complete repudiation of spiritualism. In a conversation between Cosmo and his father on the subject of ghost stories, MacDonald takes occasion to remark:

> It seems to me that the most killing poison to the imagination must be a strong course of "spiritualism." . . . I care not to encounter its mud-larkes, and lovers of garbage, its thieves, impostors, liars, and canaille, in general. That they are on the other side, that they are what men call dead, does not seem to me sufficient reason for taking them into my confidence, courting their company, asking their advice.[16]

The repudiation is vehement. MacDonald does not here deny a spirit medium's ability to communicate with the dead. He rather asserts that the dead who are thus contacted are but the scum of life. That a person's departed loved ones maintain an interest in earthly affairs must, like assurance of the divine care, remain an item of faith.

Warlock O' Glenwarlock appeared in the early summer of 1882, with a dedication to Mrs. Russell Gurney, which concludes:

> Then down thy stream, with hope-filled sail,
> Float faithful, fearless on, loved friend;
> 'Tis God that has begun the tale,
> And does not mean to end.

MacDonald wrote his cousin Helen, who was one of his avid readers, that he was sure she would enjoy the novel. When she sent him as a gift a book containing several castle etchings—presumably in return for his having sent her a copy of the novel—he confessed that the sole model and inspiration for his creation of the castle in *Warlock O' Glenwarlock* came from a little drawing of "Tilwhilly" castle,[17] which he had never even heard of until he saw the picture in I. I. Stevenson's *House of Architecture*.[18] He went on to tell Helen, most revealingly:

> I wish I could see all these places [pictured in the book]. I am often terribly hampered in my stories by sheer ignorance. I have seen so little of Scotland or any other place. Aberdeen, Banff, Cullen, and Huntly are the *only* places I knew when I left at the age of twenty, and I have never been but once for as long as months in Scotland since.[19]

This statement should go far in dismissing the widespread assertion that MacDonald spent time during the 1842–1843 interim in his college studies cataloguing a library somewhere in the north of Scotland. MacDonald's experience of his native Scotland had great depth but not geographic breadth. His ability to depict it and its manners so compellingly sprang much more from his vivid imagination than from his memory.

Having been published immediately in both England and America, *Warlock O' Glenwarlock* appeared in a second edition the following year in England and in 1885 in America, enjoying wide popularity. MacDonald must have felt he had encountered the ultimate in gullibility when he received a letter from an American family in the West named Warlock, who thought they were related to the family in the narrative. They asked, please, would he send them the exact address of the castle, information on any relatives still living, and whether he knew whatever became of the horse that played a part in the story.[20]

THIRTY-THREE

Because God Does Not Forget

The one secret of life and development, is not to devise and plan, but to fall in with the forces at work—to do every moment's duty aright—that being the part in the process allotted to us; and let come—not what will, for there is no such thing—but what the eternal Thought wills for each of us, has intended in each of us from the first.—Sir Gibbie

Confident that the Villa Patrick would be waiting for them when they returned to Bordighera, the MacDonalds left England in February. Grace and Lily accompanied them, while the boys stayed at Corage with Winnie and Irene under the supervision of Jessie Sharman, one of Louisa's cousins. However, they discovered when they arrived that the owner had changed his mind and was no longer willing to sell. MacDonald lamented to Georgina that they had come to buy and now felt sold instead. They were, however, allowed to live in the Villa Patrick temporarily while they found another place.

They began to wonder whether it might be possible for them to build their own home. Bordighera, famous for its palms (the palm fronds for Palm Sunday observances in Rome regularly come from there) and gentle climate, seemed the ideal location. The climate was consistently pleasant with the temperature never falling below freezing. Flowers of every kind flourished: the sky-blue agapanthus, bougainvillea vines blanketed with rich pink and purple blooms, the lantanas with yellow and rose, and cacti like miniature trees with soft pastels. Orange and olive trees abounded. Regular breezes blowing from the sea kept the air fresh and invigorating, an ideal antidote for a bronchitis and asthma sufferer like MacDonald.

They soon became excited about the prospect. Checking on the price of land and possible construction costs, they discovered they could afford it, using the money that the Cowper-Temples and other friends had presented to them. An English friend in Bordighera introduced MacDonald to an Italian architect who impressed MacDonald with his honesty and willingness to design a home to their liking. MacDonald gave three days to doing nothing but drawing preliminary plans for the architect. Louisa remarked that the task seemed to give him as much renewed life and energy as the original trip to Italy two years earlier. He now could fashion his study to his heart's desire and also a large room that would function not only as a place for living and entertaining but also as a small auditorium for Sunday evening gatherings.

He decided immediately that he would not preach publicly in any of the churches in Bordighera as he feared a sect forming around him. Realizing that he was beginning to have a considerable effect on Christendom, he was the more cautious that he not defeat his purposes by in effect forming another denomination. Zealous for the truth alone and unwilling to proclaim that his thinking offered the last word on Christian doctrine, he was most careful that his influence be as much for good and as little for evil as he could help. He avoided any systematized presentation of his ideas. In *Weighed and Wanting*, which he was working on at the time, he revealed some of his thinking:

> The ruin of a man's teaching comes of his followers, such as having never touched the foundation he has laid, build upon it wood, hay and stubble, fit only to be burnt. Therefore, if only to avoid his worst foes, his admirers, a man should avoid system. The more correct a system the worse will it be misunderstood; its professed admirers will take both its errors and their misconceptions of its truths, and hold them forth as its essence.[1]

Well-meaning admirers could do great damage. Nevertheless, a teacher must fulfill his calling to teach. They decided that any who chose could join them for Sunday evening family worship, and he would confine himself to readings and devotional homilies.

Lectures on literature to the English community in Bordighera were also a possibility. A large, suitably arranged room could accommodate their dramatic presentations, concerts, and dances. So with many expectations they planned a room measuring fifty-two by twenty-six by thirteen feet within a structure four stories high, oblong, of light gray stone.[2] They quickly settled on a name for their new home: Casa Coraggio. The corner lot they chose was diagonally across the street southeastward from a Scottish Presbyterian Church, but MacDonald, now long removed from that aspect of his heritage, chose to worship at All Saint's, the local Anglican Church standing an easy walk farther to the east. They soon were active members of the congregation, with Louisa playing the organ for services and training the choir.

Although the residence they planned was of appreciable size, they were aware that their family was diminishing and few would be at home any longer for extended periods. Greville had decided to establish himself in London. He had tried the life of a ship doctor, having taken a voyage aboard the *Kashgar*, a steamer bound for Bombay and ports in China. But he found that type of life too idle and monotonous. Ronald would soon be going off to college, and Robert was planning for a career as an architect.[3]

It appeared that Lily too might soon be leaving home. She had met Charlie Granet de la Rue, a handsome and refined young man who stood to inherit a sizable fortune. Their relationship quickly developed into an intimate one, so that it appeared they would soon marry. MacDonald saw in marriage a means for Lily's maturing in understanding the meaning of love and wrote in *A Book of Strife*:

> Thy ways are wonderful, Maker of men!
> Thou gavest me a child, and I have fed

And clothed and loved her, many a growing
   year;
Lo, now a friend of months draws gently near,
And claims her future—all beyond his ken. . . .
Then first, I think, our eldest-born, although
Loving, devoted, tender, watchful, dear,
The innermost of home-bred love shall know![4]

But what her father had imagined was not to be; Lily refused
de la Rue's proposal in August 1879, to MacDonald's dismay. "I
am sorry, very, for poor Charlie," MacDonald told Louisa. "But
anyway it will do him good." He evidently considered him somewhat deficient as a future son-in-law but added, "There are not
many who would, I think, break up the family less than he
would."[5] MacDonald was content to leave the matter with God
and Lily.

After Charlie persisted, however, Lily reconsidered, and they
did become engaged. But then his wealthy aunt, on whose largess
his entire financial future depended, objected so strongly to Lily's
acting in public that she vowed to disinherit him if he married
Lily without her agreeing to act no more. For Lily's part she would
rather forgo the fortune than her acting. When he refused this
prospect, she refused him, not wanting to marry someone who
would so confine her. "You are quite right that things must have
been for the best with me," she wrote Janie Cobden Unwin afterward. "God gives me a light heart. I thank him."[6]

Grace's future seemed more promising. She was engaged to
Kingsbury Jameson, a "really good, true, earnest, and very loveable fellow," a cousin of Ellen Gurney's, who was studying at
Cambridge for the Anglican priesthood. He held his prospective
father-in-law in highest esteem, having been influenced toward the
ministry by his writings. The MacDonalds were as pleased with
the expectation of this union as they had been with that of Mary
to Ted Hughes. Ted, who had spent much time with them after
Mary's death, returned to Italy with them in 1880, where he

found solace sketching among the olives and cypresses. Louisa said that his life was to them a continual example of trusting, patient resignation.

Weighed and Wanting, the novel MacDonald was working on during this period, shows even more than *Mary Marston* his preoccupation at this time with the problems of courtship and marriage. Much of the plot focuses on the threat of an unsuitable marriage, no doubt in part inspired by the possible union between de la Rue and Lily. Like a number of MacDonald's novels, this one offers the temptation of a too autobiographical reading. The reader may be inclined to see Raymount, the author father, as MacDonald; Mark, a son who dies in the narrative, as Maurice; Hester, the heroine, as Lily; and her lover Lord Gartley and his aunt as de la Rue and his aunt. Some similarities do exist. But the novels are not literal transcripts of actual life.

MacDonald would find inspiration for his stories from events and people in his experience, but his very active imagination transmuted the material into something quite distinctly fictional. The novels reveal MacDonald's state of mind and thought during any period of his life but do not directly depict his life or that of his family and friends.

The text of *Weighed and Wanting* also shows MacDonald taking another controversial theological stance. Pondering more pointedly than in the prior novels the question "What is man?" he boldly insists on a theological view of human origins distinct from the prevailing theologies of his day. He exclaims:

> I repent me of the ignorance wherein I ever said that God made man out of nothing: there is no nothing out of which to make anything; God is all in all, and he made us out of himself. He who is parted from God has no original nothingness with which to take refuge. He is a live discord, an antitruth. He is a death fighting against life, and doomed to endless vanity; an opposition to the very power by whose strength yet in him he opposes.[7]

In affirming that God created man "out of himself"—or, as he would say later in *Lilith*,[8] "out of his own endless glory"—he was making an important exception to the Augustinian doctrine, widely accepted in Christendom, that man was created out of nothing. He now saw that position as a logical impossibility: there never was a place where God is not; God is all in all.

A result of this idea is, of course, a denial of the Calvinist doctrine of total depravity that sees the human heart in its depths as thoroughly corrupt. The corruption that a person sees in human nature, MacDonald suggests, comes from a source less deep, that of the self that has "usurped the consciousness" and polluted it. Beneath this usurping self is a soul that has come from God and that, however dimly, still retains some vestige of the divine. People, having been created out of God, will find no possible satisfaction in anything less than a full return to him. These assertions form an important doctrinal underpinning for his view of eternal punishment, which he had made clear in such earlier novels as *Robert Falconer* and which he would thoroughly reaffirm at the conclusion of his career in *Lilith*.

MacDonald probably felt compelled toward this conclusion in the interests of consistency. He taught that not only can people not find any refuge apart from God, but for them eventually to learn virtue is an eternal necessity. The idea is not that God is a tyrant who will use whatever pain and horror is necessary to have his way, no matter what.[9] It is rather that the very nature of God and of the entirety of his creation demands and his endless mercy will work relentlessly to effect a final reconciliation of all things.

In *Orts,* the collection of essays he published in 1882, MacDonald continued to develop his view of human nature, especially regarding the role of the imagination. Most of these essays had been written earlier and had appeared in various publications over the span of his career. The first two essays, "The Imagination, Its Function and Its Culture" and "A Sketch of Individual Development," however, were recently composed.[10] They suggest that he was concentrating on this subject at the time; his fiction would bear this out.

He sees the standard for imaginative thinking in God (shades of Coleridge), who, he stresses, is immanent. All of nature, which is constantly being created by God, is a result of God's imaginative thinking. Not unlike Blake, he insists that the person who is thinking with proper imaginative insight perceives the spiritual within the physical, God in things. The poet's task is thus both priestly and prophetic—to give fresh and compelling expression to the invisible truths of God as they are resident in the things of this world, allowing them their moral and spiritual impact. Mac-Donald's vision focuses on what people must experience to be brought to a proper orientation with the world of the spirit.

The Princess and Curdie, published in 1882, illustrates this preoccupation and provocatively insists that valid perceptions of the spirit world are dependent on personal moral quality.[11] A sequel to *The Princess and the Goblin,* its large theological implications are well integrated into the story, which concerns Curdie's adventure after he had lapsed for a time into the spiritually commonplace. He again encounters the great-great-grandmother Irene, who commissions him for a task and prepares him spiritually to fulfill it. His task is to go to the city of Gwyntystorm and rescue it from the control of evil people. The king and his princess, Irene, are helpless, being held by the people of the court, who are seeking to seize power and execute their designs. Curdie engineers their rescue and the restoration of the king to his righteous rule. Eventually, Curdie and the Princess Irene marry and rule well. But after their demise a wicked king arises; Gwyntystorm again relapses into wicked ways and is destroyed.

The ending emphasizes the seriousness of evil. If there is no effort to effect and maintain the good, things degenerate to evil: the earthly kingdom of Gwyntystorm collapses and disappears from the face of the earth and is replaced with a wilderness of wild deer and running streams. Evil is ultimately self-destructive. The reader is left to ponder that those who perpetrated the evil will suffer the just consequences of their actions in eternity, until the evil within them is in turn destroyed, and they begin the long process of learning obedience and the necessity of righteousness.[12]

Two themes in the story are of particular interest. One is Mac-Donald's view of human nature, which quickly divides people into the two categories of righteous and wicked. The categories are defined in terms of either progressing in life toward a greater goodness or regressing toward a deeper wickedness. The Uglies are formerly wicked people who have sunk to become animals and who have since begun to learn righteousness. MacDonald's fertile imagination devises for each a shape that is appropriate to the particular type of evil to which it had succumbed in life. They have now begun the long road of becoming fully human in righteousness. The story implies that such long experience, in which one learns righteousness by the doing it and comes thereby to appreciate what true freedom is–and love it and seek it–is necessary to their final spiritual health.

The second theme is the perception that people serve God as they imagine him and that they are not able to serve a God higher than they are capable of imaging. In one of MacDonald's most memorable scenes, when Curdie and his father Peter meet the great-great-grandmother Irene, she appears as a shining figure in resplendent glory, so that "all the beauty of . . . the whole creation, seemed gathered in one centre of harmony and loveliness in the person of the ancient lady." The coarse-minded miners, on the other hand, see her as Old Mother Wotherwop and assign her a number of other names according to their natures, superstitiously attributing to her a range of unworthy activities. The grandmother explains:

> It is one thing what you or your father may think about me, and quite another what a foolish or bad man may see in me. For instance, if a thief were to come in here just now, he would think he saw the demon of the mine, all in green flames, come to protect her treasure, and would run like a hunted wild goat.

I should be all the same, but his evil eyes would see me as I was not.[13]

In the larger sweep of his thought MacDonald would insist that, these things being true, it is important for people to become carefully acquainted with the biblical Christ that their image and concept of God be accurate. In his novels he illustrates abundantly the idea that so many who call themselves Christians entertain inadequate and distorted images of God and are therefore really serving in self-centeredness aspects of their own natures.

THIRTY-FOUR

Easy to Please; Hard to Satisfy

There is so much in us that is beyond our reach!—Paul Faber, Surgeon

The MacDonalds built Casa Coraggio large enough that they could continue to offer a home to needy people and orphan children.[1] For instance, they had not been in Italy long when they met Madame Desaint, a young, poverty-stricken, consumptive woman who had been divorced and disowned by her husband and who had two small girls, ages one and two. Realizing that she was dying, she was beside herself with concern for her children's future, being totally without means of support. The MacDonalds took them in and made them a part of their family not long after they settled in Italy.

When it appeared in 1879 that they might again take up residence in England, they brought the Desaints there in January of 1880. They placed Madame Desaint in a hospital for consumptives at Bournemouth and cared for the children. After she was partially restored to health she lived with the family for seven years before her death; the girls were tutored by the MacDonald children.[2]

The family returned to England in the summer of 1880 as a family acting troupe. They had rented Steinway Hall in London for two days each week from the middle of May to the middle of July for the performance on alternate days of *Pilgrim's Progress* and *The Patient Grisiel*. On the free days they took private engagements. They badly needed whatever money they could raise to ship the remainder of their furniture to Italy and to buy additional furnishings for Casa Corragio.

When they went back to Italy in the autumn, they were anxious to begin decorating their new home as soon as it was finished. They brought many things from London to help furnish it. Construction had gone quickly, so that by Christmas of 1880 they were able to begin to move in. Making the transition from the Villa Patrick was difficult. Their furnishings, stored in England and now en route by ship to Italy, had not yet arrived as promised, so they were forced to improvise. The ship carrying their belongings was expected late in January, but bad weather kept it from arriving and increased the family's apprehension concerning the safety of the cargo. MacDonald, who did not believe in insuring one's goods or life, would never purchase any insurance. The shipment did not arrive until well into the spring, but all was safe.

Meanwhile, the family tried to make as much furniture as they could. Lily, having learned the art of upholstering, covered chairs and ottomans that the boys assembled until her fingers were raw. Others stained woodwork and painted walls. Louisa wanted her sitting room painted a soft red, and Grace exercised her artistic skills by painting a eucalyptus leaf design over the walls. Since they did all the interior decorating themselves, and their home was quite large, it took them well over a year to complete.

Although the house was barely furnished that first Christmas, they conceived the idea of doing Christmas *tableaux vivants,* with separate silent and motionless scenes of the Annunciation, the Visit to Elizabeth, the Shepherds' Visit, and Mary with the Infant Jesus and St. John.[3] The Desaint children performed the parts of the Christ Child and John the Baptist splendidly, adding greatly to the success of the whole. Invitations were issued to the English residents of Bordighera for one day and to the Italians the next. They were especially pleased to have over one hundred Italians attend.

As soon as they were able they also began their weekly practice of opening their large drawing room on Wednesday afternoons and Sunday evenings to whoever would care to come to a reading or a service. These occasions soon became very well attended. Visitors were met at the door by Bernard and MacKay, who would silently wave them up the handsome staircase. On the landing two smaller boys—orphans who had been made part of the family—would show them to the drawing room. There Louisa and her daughters, tastefully attired, would greet them and help them to coffee or tea. For a time people would chat in groups around the lofty room. One guest described the scene:

> The window-curtains, of dark-blue velvet, form a curious contrast to the olive-green walls; the floor is carpeted chiefly by rugs of various sizes and shapes; here and there bright bits of color are skillfully introduced in the form of a Genoese veil carelessly thrown over the pianoforte, a yellow shawl hanging over the back of a chair, a few deep red and blue vases, half a dozen oranges scattered among the arrangement of crimson and violet anemones adorning the deep shelves of the high oak chimneypiece. . . . Every effect of color is evidently the result of careful study. Mr MacDonald's special chair is a shade of the darkest green, but its sombreness is lightened by a judicious touch of brighter drapery carelessly hanging on the arm.[4]

At an appropriate time MacDonald would enter, dressed in a black velvet coat and crimson necktie, his beard now quite silvery and flowing, and assume his chair. After a few preliminary remarks he would begin reading on the Wednesday afternoon sessions passages he had chosen from such poets as Wordsworth, Burns, Cowper, and also figures less familiar today, such as Samuel Rogers. His Scotch accent lent a charm to his expressive intonations, and his commentary on difficult passages was seasoned with pronouncements into human nature and experience, so that many who came once returned frequently. On Sunday evenings he would deliver a seemingly extemporaneous talk on some scriptural passage, interspersed with Louisa's piano playing and often with her and the daughters singing. MacDonald's closing prayer, delivered with simple and fervent earnestness, sent people on their way hushed and thoughtful.

The spring of 1881 brought both alarm and joy. Grace had been poorly all winter. Her lungs had become diseased, and her breathing was so difficult she had to be on a portable respirator. But in April, being improved, she was married to Kingsbury Jameson. For legal reasons the service had to take place in Rome, so the MacDonalds took advantage of the opportunity to see some of the sights and ruins in the "Eternal City."

After Jameson stood his exams at Cambridge at the end of the term (where he passed fifth in the first class), he and Grace enjoyed an extended honeymoon in Switzerland. He was ordained in the fall and received an appointment as curate at All Saint's in Bordighera. There he read the service many times a week and occasionally preached, pleasing everyone by keeping his homilies to ten minutes. He and Grace occupied two rooms on the upper floor of Casa Coraggio, and the MacDonalds secured his services as tutor for Bernard and MacKay.

With the advent of hot weather in the summer of 1881, the family was quite happy to return to the cooler climate of England. Although MacDonald thoroughly enjoyed the heat, Louisa found it oppressive. That summer they added to their repertory Part One of *Pilgrim's Progress*. To MacDonald's mind, the two parts together made an especially beautiful and spiritually satisfying whole.

By 1882 the MacDonald children were giving frequent dances in the drawing room for the youth of the neighborhood, with Louisa playing familiar waltzes on the piano. "Our boys, and in fact the whole of young Bordighera, have gone mad on the subject of dancing, and have been giving dances all over the place," Lily explained to her friend Jane Unwin. "No one minds amusing themselves in a humble way."[5]

They also erected a stage at one end of the room and played *Domestic Economy* for their friends, with the audience laughing so hard at times the actors themselves broke down and laughed too.

Next, they mastered Shakespeare's *Twelfth Night*. Their friends' immense enthusiasm for their performance encouraged them to give public presentations. They engaged the Theatre of Cannes, a fashionable city on the French Riviera just beyond Nice, and announced a performance for January 11, 1882, offering the best seats at thirty francs each. Mrs. Crowe, one of their friends among the socially prominent, "was very kind in puffing the thing for us," Lily explained to Jane. Lily played Viola; MacKay, Valentine; Bernard, Sir Toby Belch; Ronald, Malvolio; Robert, Fabian; Winifred, Olivia; Louisa, Maria; and MacDonald, the priest. Other parts were played by various friends, with a huge bulk of a man, Clarence Bicknell, playing Orsino. He was, Lily remarked, "a regular whopper of a stage duke in blue satin garnished with yellow." His was the only costume they felt unequal to making.[6]

The presentation was quite successful. The manager of the Cannes theatre made a great point of how, when he had formerly engaged the best of French artists, the audience was meager, but when the MacDonald troupe played, the size of the audience was quite beyond everyone's expectations. Encouraged, the troupe went on to engage facilities and give performances at the nearby resort towns of Menton and San Remo. The money they earned made an important and much-needed contribution to family finances and helped them to complete the furnishing of their spacious home.

Meanwhile, MacDonald was working on another novel. He chose to write a sequel to *Sir Gibbie*, developing the story of the peasant poet, Donal Grant, and naming it after its hero. MacDonald's mind was evidently occupied with the spaciousness of a large dwelling; he developed the plot around the multitude of rooms in a huge castle and invested the rooms themselves with metaphorical significance in a manner reminiscent of *The Princess and the Goblin*.

The labyrinthine character of the castle (through whose mazes Donal deftly finds his way) is likened to the heroine's confused psychological state. The metaphor works not only to suggest the complex nature of the inner being, but also to suggest how a change is possible. People inherit their natures from their ancestors as they do their houses. They may "remodel" themselves to resemble more nearly "godness" by setting their will to eradicate with God's enabling grace whatever tendencies are offensive. In placing great emphasis on the freedom of the will MacDonald draws on an Augustinian model of the nature of humanity.

As the plot unfolds Donal and Arctura discover deep within the bowels of the old castle a hidden chapel that had been walled up and forgotten for generations, and the elaborate metaphor is complete. The chapel at the heart of the castle is like the divine self forming the essence of each person; it must be brought back to life by discovery and conversion.

> "I will clean out the temple!" said Arctura, speaking as if to herself. . . . "I will pull down that wall," she went on, "and the light shall come in again through those windows, and astonish the place with its presence. And all the house will be glad, because there will no more be a dead chapel at the heart of it, but a living temple with God himself in it—there always and forever."[7]

The focus at the end of the novel is on the repentance of the thoroughly evil Lord Morven, a satanic figure who had been wielding power in the castle, though it belonged rightfully to Arctura and not to him. When Lord Morven is finally broken, MacDonald explains: "He who will not let us out until we have paid the uttermost farthing, rejoices over the offer of the first golden grain in payment. Easy to please is he—hard indeed to satisfy."[8] The final sentence is in microcosm MacDonald's view of God in his relation to people's spiritual growth.

The subject of conversion, of course, often recurs in MacDonald's novels—for example, the marquis in *Malcolm* and Redmain in *Mary Marston*. But Lord Morven is the most villainous of those who repent. As MacDonald's thinking focused more on the spiritual categories of the righteous and the wicked, his novels became yet more concerned with repentance, conversion, and spiritual becoming.

The frequency of various conversions in his collection of short tales, *The Gifts of the Child Christ and Other Tales,* that he published in 1882 (during the time he was writing *Donal Grant*), underscores how much the subject was on MacDonald's mind in the early 1880s. His disillusionment with human nature was steadily growing. In the earlier novels conversion mainly involves reorienting the thinking; in the later ones it tends to become more of a violent emotional experience. More emphasis is placed on the chastening of God, who may use extreme circumstances to produce repentance.

The title story of the collection contains a daring artistic ploy. In it MacDonald undertakes to illustrate how God's punishment, or chastening, is really an act of love that serves to awaken the spirit and initiate "fruits of righteousness," which are appropriate attendant attitudes. Sophy Greatorex, a child neglected by her father and stepmother, longs to love and be loved. When she hears her pastor say that God's chastening is a sure sign of his love, she prays that the Lord will "chasten" her. On Christmas Eve, while she is asleep, her stepbrother is stillborn.

Early on Christmas morning she creeps down the stairs, intensely expecting a visit from the baby Jesus on this his day. When she sees the dead infant dressed and laid out upon the bed, she delicately takes it into her arms and comes momentarily to see him as the Christ. As she patiently waits for her treasured Christ Child to awaken, the reality that she is holding a dead infant gradually dawns on her. When her father, a proud man who has long neglected her, comes upon her and the baby, his eyes are suddenly opened, and he is converted. A "new covenant" begins to exist between father and daughter as a loving relationship is established.

Other estrangements are also reconciled as a consequence of little Sophy's identifying her stillborn brother with the Christ Child and weeping for him. Therefore, the child that came on Christmas Eve was indeed a surrogate for Christ to Sophie as that is how her childlike faith saw him. The incident echoes the concept MacDonald shaped in *The Princess and Curdie*—that God presents himself in various forms appropriate to a given individual's need and is accurately recognized by the spiritually sensitive person, although crass sensibilities fail to understand.

The story symbolizes how God expresses his chastening or his wrath. A few years earlier, MacDonald had told Louisa that he longed to draw or paint the angels with the seven last plagues, every one a wrath of God. He said he would use Octavia Hill's face for one of them, F. D. Maurice's for another, and their "own Bogie's" (Robert) for yet another.[9] These faces represented to him corrective love actively expressed, with its object the inducing of righteousness.

MacDonald's using the image of a dead child in this manner is, to say the least, startling, but he handles it delicately and within the aura of the story convincingly. The *Athenaeum*, in its review of the collection, remarked: "There is something repugnant to one's notions of reverence in the conception of the incident on which the first story turns, but there is nothing coarse in the method of its treatment."[10]

The theme that true conversion is a change of heart that issues in reconciled or renewed personal relationships occurs in many of the other stories in this collection. They are all well-told tales, demonstrating MacDonald's ability to sustain tone and achieve a pleasing unity in shorter fiction.

Artistically, perhaps the most notable in the collection is a fairy story, "The History of Photogen and Nycteris." Symbolically, the tale suggests the tragedy of lives that have narrow and circumscribed views of reality and the evil of those who may be responsible for people entertaining such inadequate views. The tale describes the machinations of Watho, a wicked witch with "a wolf in her mind," so that she cares "for nothing in itself—only for knowing it." She contrives to control the lives of two children born in her castle, Photogen and Nycteris, so that Photogen is raised to know only daylight and Nycteris only darkness. As

Photogen and Nycteris grow to adulthood they each love the world as they know it, hating and fearing its opposite. As young people they separately escape the witch's power and meet. Nycteris helps Photogen overcome his fear of the night by showing him its beauty and how to avoid harm in it, and in turn Photogen helps Nycteris to become accustomed to the glory of the day.

They kill a wolf (Watho incarnated), marry, and live happily, each coming to love the characteristic element of the other better than their own. Together, their view of reality is now whole and complete. MacDonald observed in *Donal Grant* that "to make things real to us, is the end and the battle-cause of life."[11] To be complete human beings requires being oriented in spirit to all aspects of life—its glad, active, daylight facets, as well as its pensive, sorrowful, nighttime elements. The Wathos of life—those who take a cold, rationalist approach to knowledge and presume to act as guardians and dictators over the lives of others—reduce their victims to people who see only part of reality.

MacDonald probably had in mind self-appointed guardians of people's religious convictions, the like of which are present in all sects. (He worked out a similar theme in the earlier story "The Giant's Heart.") Once such wolves are recognized and slain, their victims are freed to come into a larger understanding of and appreciation for reality.

MacDonald completed this collection of tales by including as the final entry his drama, *If I Had a Father.* Having tried intermittently since its conception in 1859 to arouse some publisher's interest in it, he finally resorted to bringing it out in this way. He must have been chagrined at the reviewer's remark in The *Athenaeum:* "Of the last and longest piece, 'a drama,' it is hard to say anything good, the incidents and plot being tame and trite to a degree, while it is heavily handicapped by the hideous Lancashire dialect." The critic concluded: "On the whole, Mr. MacDonald is more successful in more serious efforts."[12] It is difficult to conceive of anything being more serious to MacDonald than the theme of this drama, the quest for a spiritual father.

THIRTY-FIVE

And Yet Again

Be sure God will not take you away, if it be better for you to live here a little longer. But you will have to go sometimes: and if you contrived to live after God wanted you to go, you would find yourself much less ready when the time came that you must. . . . no one can be living a true life, to whom dying is a terror.—What's Mine's Mine

The insistence that an open-eyed orientation to things as they are is a requisite for spiritual maturity continued to be the guiding theme in both MacDonald's fiction and nonfiction as the decade progressed. The individual must alertly receive what life offers, rather than, as he saw most people doing, pursue chimeras and elusive joys of one's own definition. Although personal experiences lead to severe struggles with doubt, nobility of soul consists in doing one's duty when one sees it.

By 1883, the many rooms at Casa Coraggio were filled with guests. Some were students sent by monied English parents to be tutored and taught music by Louisa and the children; some were orphans; and others were simply needy people whom the Mac-Donalds were helping get on their feet. They also took in as they could people who were ill and needed nursing. "King" Jameson and MacKay, walking one day through the streets of Bordighera, were accosted by an elderly lady who asked: "Can you please tell me where George MacDonald's sanitorium is? I hear it is a very good one." When King responded he did not know there was such a place, she insisted: "Oh! but there is, and I shall go and ask at the hotels till I find out." MacKay stepped behind a paling to conceal his laughter.

There was also a steady stream of friends and relatives coming to visit from Britain. Georgina Mount-Temple was convalescing from a fall, and she and her husband took nearby Casa Margherita for the winter of 1883. Exchanging London for Bordighera was, Mount-Temple remarked, "like passing from earth to the happy home our eager hearts expect."[1] MacDonald's stepmother paid them an extended visit in the winter and spring. Writing to his cousin Helen in his native Scotch, MacDonald humorously remarked: "My mother's the healthiest ane in a' the hoose. She's gran'—an' aye helpin' a'body."[2] When her visit was over, Robert accompanied her as far as London; the remainder of the family made their summer's journey to England in June.

On March 17, 1882, Grace, to the great delight of her parents, gave birth to her first child, Octavia Grace. The MacDonalds' pleasure was the greater because the Jamesons were living in the same house with them. But it was becoming increasingly apparent that Grace was not well, and her health became a constant cause for apprehension. "Grace is a little better," MacDonald told Helen Powell. "But we are very doubtful about her sometimes. Her child is a darling."[3]

In an attempt to stem the deterioration of Grace's condition, King Jameson built a home just a few doors away from Casa Coraggio, which they named Casa Grazia. Of gray, granite-like stone, it was designed throughout with Grace's health in mind. As many windows were installed as possible, with large folding doors between rooms and high ceilings to allow for the free passage of air. To allow Grace to spend as much time as possible lying in the sun and air, a hammock was slung by the large bay window in the morning room. The house incorporated many modes of ventilation, with special ventilators over doors, windows, and fireplaces.[4]

In spite of all their efforts, however, the dreaded end came on May 5, 1884. Yet again thrown into grief over parting from a beloved child, Louisa unburdened herself to Charlotte:

Her departure was far more terrible and difficult than Mary's. Oh—so terrible—but her cry of Father take me at the last was so fervent and strong. We knew it was a struggle after that. Surely sometimes Death comes to the saints in a Demon shape—especially those who have had no great knowledge of the struggles with him before.[5]

The body lay in state two days at Casa Coraggio before being buried in the corner of the newly established Stranger's Cemetery in Bordighera, the first to occupy a grave there. Flowers from friends in Bordighera poured in to Casa Coraggio in such quantities that Louisa found it all but overwhelming. As when Mary and Maurice died, she was again seized with great grief. The sight of the flowers, she said, almost made her hate them. Some solace came when she saw how the flowers not only helped fill the grave and cover it but also the entire area around.

MacDonald took his daughter's passing with somewhat more composure: it was God's will. He was, through this experience, acquiring a yet fuller sense of oneness with God. Later that same summer he remarked parenthetically to Louisa: "I feel as if I could not call myself by my name but in the name of God. Is it a feeling to be understood?" (August 1, 1884).[6] Now that yet another child had departed for "the high countries," his expectation to join them soon strengthened. The Christian hope provided a deep mine of consolation. Having so recently worked through the entire process of loss, grief, and strengthening of faith, he with Louisa bore Grace's passing with less prolonged agony than had been the case with Mary's and Maurice's. It was the family's custom to make regular trips to the graves at Nervi and Porto Fino, tending them and providing fresh flowers (something Europeans in general do with remarkable faithfulness). Lily roots were planted on Grace's.

Kingsbury Jameson remained very much a part of the MacDonald family, and Louisa took upon herself the task of being a mother to little Octavia. That summer part of the family went again to England, but they did not attempt to perform their dramas without Grace. MacDonald committed himself to an extended lecture tour of England and Scotland, while Louisa, Winifred, King, and Octavia spent the time at Bude, where the Joshua Sings joined them for a visit. Lily stayed with Irene and MacKay to run Casa Coraggio, while Bernard, of somewhat more independent spirit, unexpectedly decided to spend the summer at a chalet in the Swiss Alps, tutoring some English boys there. Greville, having decided to try to set up a practice in Florence, had moved from London and was often at Casa Coraggio. This summer he was planning on taking lessons in Italian with Lily. Lily and Irene were also taking voice lessons from a professional teacher ("a nice little ex-prima-donna . . . who knows what she is about").

In Bude, Louisa and her party secured for their lodgings West Cottage, the same place they had occupied seventeen years earlier, during the summer of 1867. She no sooner arrived than a flood of vivid memories came to her of family life as it was then: of MacKay as an infant and of Maurice, who even at three and a half years of age began to produce his wise, philosophic sayings that seemed so beyond his years. Suddenly at times she heard Mary's pixyish laugh and saw Grace poring over her drawings. Then little Octavia would burst into the room, recalling her to reality. "She is such a duck of ducks," Louisa wrote to Lily, "coining words and being so funny and sweet and naughty in a mild way all in 4 minutes or less." Bounding upon her grandmother's bed one morning to arouse her from sleep, "Ou's are lazy 'ittle pigs so get up," she announced and tried to imitate some pigs she had recently seen. Her grandmother found in her quite enough to keep from dwelling morbidly on the past.[7]

Meanwhile, MacDonald, accompanied for a time by Ronald, left London for Leicester and Edinburgh, where he gave a number of lectures, especially on Dante and Macbeth. He had been told it was absurd to expect an audience of any size in Edinburgh in August, but the crowds exceeded all expectations. "I find myself more popular than I knew," he explained to Louisa. A professor at Edinburgh told him the only fault of his presentation on Dante was that it gave him too much to think about afterward, a compliment that could hardly have been more pleasing to MacDonald. Another avowed he was ready to stand an examination in Mac-Donald's novels. His friends begged him to bring the family and do *Pilgrim's Progress* there, confident they could fill an auditorium holding one thousand people. He began talking to Louisa about coming for a week of performances the following June.[8]

Going northward through Aberdeen toward Eirboll and Inverness, he stopped for a few days at The Farm. There he visited with his cousin James, who now occupied the family place, and intended to preach in the home church. But just as he mounted the gig to go to the morning service, he came down with such a severe hemorrhaging of the nose they had to summon a doctor, who promptly packed his nostrils and told him to stay in bed. There he lay until Thursday, forced to cancel his engagements to the north and west. He felt thwarted and disappointed. He had been contemplating another novel of Scottish life, this time set in the Highlands, and had intended to find some inspiration by visiting some of the highland countryside while he was in the far north. Now he found he must hurry back south as soon as he was able to travel. He commented to Louisa:

> It is a great disappointment not to have seen something of the country—the more I learn of it the more I wish to see it. I presume I have been stinted in such things that I might turn the more to others. Only to be sure my loving desire for them now is strong, as it was not before, though I am not likely to have it gratified much in this world—I mean in this body. But that is a trifle; it matters nothing, or is all the better.[9]

He concluded the entire incident was a signal that he must seek still more teaching directly from God before he wrote.

By Friday he was able to resume work on his critical essay on *Hamlet,* which he had been working on whenever he could during this trip. On Monday he felt well enough to leave for the south to meet Louisa at Leicester. At the beginning of his lecture tour, when he had learned Louisa too was ill, he wrote that he did not intend ever again to leave her. They knew how, he said, to take care of each other better than anybody else could.

Meanwhile, back at Casa Coraggio, Lily was managing affairs. She paid the bills of butcher and baker and in general tried to make the meager family funds match their needs. "Everything is so jolly," she remarked to her mother, "Except the hardness of your money getting, and our money spending."[10] She also had to oversee certain alterations they had decided to make on the top of the stairs and the balcony of Casa Coraggio. MacDonald had left detailed instructions with Bernard as to what was to be done, not anticipating that he would leave suddenly to spend the summer in the Alps. Now he had to detail them by letter to Lilia, who tried faithfully to make Giovanelli, the Italian architect, understand and bend his intentions to MacDonald's desires. The house, Lilia told Janie Cobden, was filled with "a bevy of masons, carpenters, house-painters, bellmen, gas-men and companions to look on," all of whom were "enraptured—and most ecstatic" when they overheard her and Irene singing duets.[11]

The summer, however, was not without its traumas. An outbreak of cholera caused great consternation, especially across southern Europe, and many cities were quarantined. Bordighera was spared a serious outbreak, but even so the cart passed through the streets three times each night, the crier tolling a bell and mournfully calling, "Bring out your dead." Horror stories were rife, such as families casting afflicted members outside towns nearby, stripping them of their clothing, and leaving them to die. Naples reported one thousand new cases on a single day. Lilia, in writing to her mother, bravely attempted to put the best face on her fears by veiling them in humorous exaggeration:

> We take *every* precaution—Barrels of chloride of lime at the front door—Carbolized sheets hung up before every door in

the house—every mason and painter disinfected every time he enters the house—barrels of gunpowder in the cellars, so that we can blow up the house directly as a case approaches to our door, and we hold handkerchiefs soaked in [word?] every time we saunter forth to breath the pestilential air. We hardly eat a thing and no figs or peaches (oh dear no) for fear of germs. . . . Our hair is turned white with fear, and our palsied and enfeebled knees knock together, and our teeth (all loose from agitation) chatter, when we hear the dreaded cart and bell. . . . I shouldn't wonder if you find us all emigrated to Australia when you get home. . . . Really, we are glad you are not coming very soon as the railway carriages are said to be very infectious.[12]

She was genuinely relieved to learn that her parents were not planning to return until well into October at the earliest.

When the travelers returned to Casa Coraggio in the autumn of 1884, MacDonald had ready for publication both his study of *The Tragedie of Hamlet, Prince of Denmarke,* and a new volume of *Unspoken Sermons* (second series). He was also well into a new novel. Now sixty years of age, he was monitoring his powers of mind, wondering when they might begin to fail. He remarked to Charlotte that he found his brain no "worse than it was," observing that he seemed to be able to retain things from his reading better than formerly. "I may forget the word for a meaning, but I do not forget the meaning of a word," he added.[13]

He also published during this year his preface to a new translation of *Letters from Hell,* an anonymous work by a Danish author that had first appeared in 1866. The work had been very popular throughout Europe, having gone through, for instance, twelve editions in Germany in the course of one year. MacDonald, who saw in it imaginative energy and the power of truth, offered to write a commendatory statement for a new translation to appear in England. He was, he explained, most impressed by the imaginative depiction of the

awful verity, that we make our fate in unmaking ourselves; that men, in defacing the image of God in themselves, construct for themselves a world of horror and dismay; that of the *outer darkness* our own deeds and character are the informing or inwardly creating cause; that if a man will not have God, he never can be rid of his weary and hateful self.[14]

In his preface MacDonald makes clear that hell is an awesome reality. He had not changed his thinking on the eternality of damnation discussed earlier, but he was loath to be misunderstood. Lest anyone feel that he had dismissed the necessity for the wicked to receive the just consequences of their sins, he was careful to underscore that such was not the case.

He dedicated the second series of *Unspoken Sermons,* as he had the first, to Louisa: "These also after eighteen years, to my wife." Less abstract than their predecessors, these meditations are more devoted to the practical dimensions of the life of the spirit: self-denial, the nature of prayer, the necessity of forgiving of others. In the sermon "Life" he makes clear his view of the Atonement[15] and the nature of eternal life. Eleven sermons are built on New Testament texts; the twelfth is on Job. Beneath the title appears a quotation from Isaiah 40: "Comfort ye, comfort ye my people." The one idea tying all the sermons together is stated in "Self-Denial": "The good Father made his children to be joyful; only, ere they can enter into his joy, they must be like himself, ready to sacrifice joy to truth."[16]

The novel he was working on during the winter of 1884–1885, inspired by his trip to northern Scotland, he ironically titled *What's Mine's Mine*. Like the sermons he had just completed, the emphasis of the novel is on the practical aspects of the spiritual life. In the sermons he is concerned more with the personal dimensions of growth; in the novel he undertakes to clarify the experiential steps of coming to spiritual commitment and the nature of the everyday conflict between good and evil.

Set in the Highlands of northern Scotland, the story concerns the tensions between two families: the Palmers—London worshipers of rank and mammon who have purchased an estate in the

Highlands to hunt the stag, and the native Macruadhs—proud,[17] virtuous, and impoverished, whose eldest son Alister is the chief of a "sore-frayed, fast-vanishing" clan. His brother Ian, modeled on MacDonald's brother John, epitomizes Christian wisdom and virtue. Their widowed mother, whom both boys greatly revere, clings to that type of Christianity which fears rather than trusts, overly solicitous of the faith of others while not possessed of inner peace. She exhibits the shortcomings of a certain Christian mental-ity MacDonald never tired of exposing.

The story presents two themes: the successive steps in spiritual conversion as the Macruadh men impart spiritual truths to Palm-er's two daughters and the nature of Christian virtue as the Macru-adh's respond to Palmer's crass and unjust demands on the clan. Ian is the spokesman for MacDonald's interpretation of Christian realities. He helps his mother, brother, and the Palmer girls to un-derstand the truths each needs. Through him his mother comes to a more mature understanding of the significance of Christ's death. Alister sees that as long as a Christian stands on his rights instead of leaving them in God's hands, or loves property as possession, he cannot know spiritual freedom; Christina and Mercy Palmer hunger after a true relationship to God.

The girls' most prominent need is to be jolted out of their self-centered world of facade and privilege and properly oriented to the physical world of sacramental grace. Speaking of Christina, after Ian has rescued her from drowning, MacDonald writes:

> How was it that, now first in danger, self came less to the front with her than usual? It was that now first she was face to face with reality. Until this moment her life had been an affair of unrealities. Her selfishness had thinned, as it were vaporized, every reality that approached her. Solidity is not enough to teach some natures reality; they must hurt themselves against the solid ere they realize its solidity. . . . It is when we are most aware of the factitude of things, that we are most aware of our need of God, and most able to trust him. . . . It is not the

hysterical alone for whom the great dash of cold water is good. All who dream life instead of living it, require some similar shock. Of the kind is every disappointment, every reverse, every tragedy of life.[18]

To be rightly related to things as they are is to begin to perceive the God whose hand MacDonald saw present in all aspects of life. He expressed the idea in his first novel, *David Elginbrod*, and again in *Donal Grant*: "To make things real to us, is the end and the battle-cause of life."[19] This becomes a dominating idea in the later fiction and accounts for a certain diminution of overt preaching.

MacDonald drew Ian with imaginative strength, in part because of his fond memories of his brother John, and in part because, his spiritual wisdom notwithstanding, he is as well an earnest seeker and doubter:

Ian . . . doubted most about the things he loved best, while he devoted the energies of a mind whose keenness almost masked its power, to discover possible ways of believing them. To the wise his doubts would have been his credentials; they were worth tenfold the faith of most. It was truth, the higher truth, he was always seeking.[20]

Here is MacDonald's apology for his brother John, as he remembered the singular strength of his probing mind and his moments of doubt. Ian also incarnates many of MacDonald's struggles.

Ian's character as a wise and earnest doubter is in part a result of MacDonald's finishing his study *The Tragedie of Hamlet—with a study of the text of the Folio of 1623* while he was working on the early phases of *What's Mine's Mine*. Hamlet, as MacDonald understood him, also vacillates between faith and doubt as he considers the validity of the supernatural communication that comes to him from his father's ghost at the very beginning of the play. MacDonald took stern issue with the more traditional interpretation of Hamlet as a man of inaction, paralyzed by too much thinking. He saw him, rather, as a man of keen moral sense and firm resolution. Once Hamlet satisfies himself as to the correct course of action, he performs it; the play concerns the steps by which he comes into a conviction of what that action should be. MacDonald saw *Hamlet* containing a theme very like any of a number of his novels: life consists in discovering one's highest duty and performing it.

MacDonald dedicated his book on Shakespeare's great tragedy to his stepmother's brother in Edinburgh, Alexander Stewart MacColl, to whom, he said, he owed "the true understanding" of Hamlet's "To be, or not to be . . ." soliloquy. MacDonald argued that Hamlet is not in this speech considering suicide but rather he is contemplating the "metaphysics of existence" and posing the question "which is nobler—to endure evil fortune, or to oppose it *a' outrance;* to bear in passivity, or to resist where resistance is hopeless —resist to the last—to the death which is its unavoidable end."[21] In many ways MacDonald saw in Hamlet an analogy to his own moments of uncertainty and struggle with his faith and with the course of his life's work. "To my mind, he is the grandest hero in fiction—absolutely human—so troubled, yet so true," he affirms.[22]

MacDonald's volume on *Hamlet* represented the final form of a lecture he had given many times, for a fixed honorarium of five guineas, over some twenty years. He was careful in his preface not to represent himself as a scholar of Shakespeare, but rather as one who desired simply "to bring out the most important—chiefly moral, partly artistic—points of the play."

THIRTY-SIX

Utter Honesty

*But now, dear friend, let me, in this case . . . go into the
whole thing as between ourselves. I feel driven to it for the
sake of that honesty without which we are not saved . . .*
—MacDonald to Mrs. Fanshawe, Christmas 1883.

Several incidents from the decade illustrate how adamantly
MacDonald tried to maintain his principles and adhere to the
highest ethical standards. He was extremely earnest in his intention that his life manifest the high standard of practical Christian
living that his sermons defined. The constant effort was not without difficulties.

While keenly aware of his ethical and spiritual responsibilities,
he at the same time opposed excessive self-examination, not wanting to paralyze his life by too much self-scrutiny. He observed in
The Marquis of Lossie:

> I suspect that self-examination is seldom the most profitable,
> certainly it is sometimes the most unpleasant, and always the
> most difficult of moral actions—that is, to perform in a genuine
> fashion. I am certain that a good deal of the energy spent by
> some devout and upright people on trying to understand
> themselves and their own motives, would be expended to bet-
> ter purpose, and with far fuller attainment even in regard to
> that object itself, in the endeavour to understand God, and
> what he would have us to do.[1]

His focus was perennially on trying to be actively obedient. He
believed the effort involved discouragement enough without morbidly dwelling on his failures.

Incidents from his life illustrate his earnestness. On a lecture tour along the Riviera in 1888, addressing English-speaking communities, he was on a train passing through Monaco. A young gambler fresh from the casinos at Monte Carlo sat down beside him and showed an inclination to talk. Discovering he was a nephew of someone MacDonald knew, they soon established common ground.

But MacDonald was not willing that their seemingly chance meeting consist simply in an exchange of pleasantries; he sought in honesty to do the young man some spiritual good. Feeling the place to start was to arouse his conscience, MacDonald told him that he could not understand how a gentleman could be content to better himself through other people's losses, that money gotten without value given was defiled, and that the young man had too much money. Surprisingly, the man did not take the reprimand unkindly, and they parted friends. MacDonald was quite willing to risk incurring the man's indignation and wrath, for he believed eternal destinies were at stake.

A similar instance of MacDonald's willingness to sacrifice— this time immediate momentary gain, together with a person's good opinion—for the truth's sake occurred with a person who wanted to be one of his benefactors. Mrs. Fanshawe, who had urged them to move to Bordighera and helped them find the site for Casa Corragio, was a self-appointed empress of the English community there. An ebullient personality whose enthusiasms were contagious, she was socially esteemed as the person to know. She was quick to seize opportunities to help people but not without a view to her own advantage.

She was also something of a gossip. Somewhat too free with her remarks concerning others, she was known to have indulged in joking at others' expense. When in 1883 she noticed that the MacDonalds could use some financial help to accomplish their many charities, she sent them a sum of money at Christmas. MacDonald quickly refused it, returning on Christmas Day the check together with a lengthy typed letter of careful explanation.

It seems that MacDonald had learned that she had on an

occasion spoken disparagingly of him, calling him a "shuffler," and, while he remonstrated that he was quite willing to let time reverse or confirm the validity of the remark, he wrote he could not put himself under any obligation to her. The incident had not, he affirmed, qualified his love for her, but nevertheless it had a bearing on the matter

> Since then, and after knowing of it, I have kissed you—*and heartily meant it:* but when it comes to the matter of taking a gift of money from you, I feel I must beware:—I do not know you well enough, and you do not know me well enough, to justify it. . . . If you say, I was right in the epithet I used, for so I regard your line of conduct, I answer, that confirms my objection: can I accept anything of earthly value from one who so judges me—rightly or wrongly? Would it not be a mean thing, and confirm such a judgment?

Knowing her to be a voluble and elusive person, he was careful in the letter to allow her no refuge and at the same time give her no reason to doubt his Christian love for her. To accept the money would confirm her belittling remark. He closed the letter by appealing to the vantage point of eternity:

> But, come what may of this, I look up, and see the fields of eternity stretching away and away in the sunlight of the Father's presence: and in those fields I see us all playing like blessed little boys and girls of God's kingdom, sometimes looking back with wondering smile that we could have cared so much down here about this and that trifle—only we hardly knew how trifling it was.

One can never be certain what proportion temporal events may take in terms of eternity. The true significance of obedience is not determined by a human estimate of it.

> I am a profound believer in a destiny from which we cannot escape, and that destiny is obedience and bliss. I shall reach it one day, through the ever present help of my Lord and my God; and every time I learn to be more fair, or to love one

better, I come one little step nearer to that bliss. . . . This of all days is the one of which to remember the unity. . . . So I tell you here, and say it for my wife, who will read this before I send it, that we love you, and mean to love you, and I hope nothing I have been driven to say will hurt you more than it must hurt you.[2]

The incident reveals much about MacDonald: his meticulous honesty, his determination to strive for utter rectitude in human relationships, his unhesitating willingness to incur another person's offense in the pursuit of his interpretation of that person's larger spiritual good, and his keenness to see all facets of life in the light of the opportunities they afforded him to work out his religious convictions.

MacDonald's attitude toward another woman in whom he took offense further illustrates the extremes he was willing to take. On this occasion the woman was back in England, an acquaintace of Georgina Cowper-Temple. What she had been guilty of is not clear, but to MacDonald's mind she had committed a sin of the deepest die, the nature of which was generally known. Evidently she thereafter gave a public display of repentance and subsequently attempted to reposition herself in society among her former friends, but MacDonald doubted her sincerity. Georgina wrote him trying to intercede on her behalf: he should forgive her, accept her repentance, and receive her as a friend; but he refused.

He explained he had nothing to forgive her for; the offense was not against him personally. But he interpreted her actions as an attempt to gain reinstatement in society, rather than a genuine loathing of what she had done and a desire to become otherwise. Detailing his judgment of the matter to Georgina, he began by even allowing that her repentance might have been sincere. The issue as he saw it was that he not act falsely himself.

She may have seen her own vileness and repented, God only knows, but even then he cannot require of me to act as if I had his insight and knowledge. That he will restore her at last,

I believe, but I see nothing that he requires of me to do in the matter.

If I were to go to see her, or to receive her, I should be false, as I must and deeply suspect her to be—so false that she does not yet see the utter horror of her wicked selfishness. Things cannot be smoothed over. God himself could not and never will do that. If she knows that he has forgiven her, that ought to content her till it be possible that others should know it. She ought to be content to bear her shame. Nothing can remove that but the lifting of her up into a region where sin is no more possible because she loathes it. While she cares for the judgment of society, her worship of which demon-idol cast her into the gulf, she can rise above nothing.[3]

He was not asking Georgina to abide by his view of the matter, but the doubt in his mind about the genuineness of her contrition was too large for him to give her the benefit. To accept her as if it were genuine might be to confirm her in her falsity. He saw his course as the right way for him to serve righteousness; therefore, he would be unwavering.

He was, however, unstinting in trying to meet any need in others. When, in November of 1886, an impoverished writer in London appealed to him for the loan of a small sum of money, he responded sympathetically, but confessed he had not a sovereign in the bank. Even so, he sent the petitioner a penned note addressed to A. P. Watt, his agent in London, directing the latter to advance him a guinea and to recommend him work if he could.[4]

Given the nature of his convictions and the challenges he consistently posed in his writings to prevalent attitudes among professing Christians, he was often asked to defend himself. He had, on the one hand, a huge following of avid devotees but on the other, an appreciable number who disdained his positions. Many from among the latter were of strict orthodox persuasion, whose approach to truth and reality tended to be unemotional and rationalist and who felt that their creeds contained and defined truth.

MacDonald found encounters with such people trying and distasteful and avoided them when he could do so without compromising his vision of truth. Argument was, after all, rather futile, especially with people of such mentality. Argument was confined within the limited perimeters of their rationality, within which they were concerned only with being intellectually right. MacDonald saw it as deflecting attention from the central issue of achieving a vital personal union with God through Christ and obeying him. But he would never slight someone who was earnestly seeking truth. Sometimes he found he must reply.

One such occasion occurred in 1885, after he stayed in the home of an acquaintance who persisted in commending a doctrinal position that was thoroughly rationalist and precisely conceived. Afterward, the host wrote MacDonald an extended letter, summarizing this position and asking MacDonald specifically to show him where it was deficient. MacDonald was moved to respond. What he wrote shows how he handled such situations and how he depreciated the value of argument while at the same time making his position clear. The letter deserves to be presented in its entirety. It is, among his short documents, perhaps the clearest statement of his thinking on the dangers inherent in cold theological recitations of Christian doctrine:

Bordighera
31 Jan. 1886

Dear W_____,

When I had the pleasure of being your guest I entered with you into a conversation such as I am in general far from favourable to, believing it not at all conducive to profit. Had you been a stranger, I should have avoided or declined the argument. But in answer to your letter, I reply thus far, that your presentation of your opinions, which are the same as from childhood I was familiar with, I refuse entirely as the truth, holding them as the merest invention of the human intellect in the attempt to explain things which the spirit of the Son of Man alone can make any man understand for his salvation.

If however any man ask me, as you do in your letter, to give in its stead the attempt of my intellect to explain the same things, I answer, far be it from me to do so! I am not going to replace in the same kind in dried and petrified form, what I see of the truth, favouring thus the idea that anything else whatever than a vital union with Christ, as of the members with the body, as of the branches of the vine, is of any avail to the well-being of a man. It is in no sense what we believe about Christ, or what way we would explain his work, that constitutes or can be the object of faith. No belief in the atonement, for instance, whether that atonement be explained or understood right or wrong, no belief in what the theologians call the merits of Christ, is in the smallest degree or approximation what the Lord or his apostles meant by faith in him. It is to take him as our Lord and Master, obey his words, be prepared to die for him; it is to take on us the yoke his father laid on him and regard the will of God as the one thing worthy of a man's care and endeavour—as indeed our very life— that, and nothing less than that, is faith in the Son of God.

Then as to all things that are necessary for our growth in the Divine life, that is, for growing like to him in whose image we are made, he promises to teach us by his spirit everything. Nor even if a man could, which is impossible, know with his understanding the deepest mysteries, would these avail him the least, that would not constitute the knowledge of them after the true fashion: they must be spiritually discerned—in a way that no man can by any possibility teach his neighbour, but which only the Spirit of God can teach. I think and believe that the mischief done to the kingdom of Christ by teaching of what is called doctrine by theologians, and calling that teaching the Gospel, instead of presenting Christ as he presented himself, and took a whole life of labour to present himself, is enormous, and the cause of a huge part of the infidelity in the world. Let us follow the Lord, studying the mind of him, and not what the scribes and the elders teach about him.

If any man come to me with theological questions, if I find that they are troubling him, and keeping him from giving himself to God, I do my best to remove any such obstructions as are the result of man's handling of the eternal things: what I count false, I will not spare. But if the man come to me only for the sake of conference on the matter, I will hold none. Let him get what teaching he is capable of receiving from his knowledge of Christ, and the spirit given him. If he is satisfied with the theology he has learned, I should give myself no trouble to alter his opinion. I should do him no good either by success or failure in the attempt. I have other things altogether to do. I have to take up my cross and follow the master first, and then persuade him who will be persuaded to come with me. He is the atonement, and through him, through knowing him and being every day, every hour, every moment taught by him, I shall become pure in heart, and shall at length see God. No doctrine shall come between me and him. Nor will he come between anyone and God save to lead him home to the father. The whole mischief has come of people setting themselves to understand rather than to do, to arrange God's business for him, and tell other people what the Father meant, instead of doing what the father tells them, and then teaching others to do the same.

If I am told that I am not definite—that something more definite is needed, I say your definiteness is one that God does not care about, for he has given no such system as you desire. But, I ask, is not the living man, the human God, after his 3 and 30 years on earth, poor and scanty as are the records of him, a definite enough object of faith for your turn? He is not, I grant you, for the kind of definiteness you would have, which is to reduce the infinite within the bounds of a legal document; but for life, for the joy of deliverance, for the glory of real creation, for the partakings of the divine nature, for the gaining

*of a faith that shall remove mountains, and for deliverance
from all the crushing commonplaces of would-be teachers of
religion, who present us with a God so poor and small that to
believe in him is an insult to him who created the human
heart—the story of the eternal Son of God, who knew and loved
his father so that he delighted to die in the manifestation of
him to his brothers and sisters, is enough, triumphantly
enough. To have to believe in the God of the Calvinist would
drive me to madness or atheism; to believe in the God of our
Lord Jesus Christ, is to feel that, if such God there be, all is
well, he may do with me as he pleases. I am blest.*

*Thus, or somehow thus, I would answer any man who
pressed me to be more definite. Not that I could not give what
seemed to me the best of reasons why the Lord should die, but if
I set them out, it shall be in a vital fashion, and not in a*
hortus siccus *of heavenly flowers.*[5]

*So far, my dear sir, I have answered, so far I have declined
to answer your letter. I have other reasons also, the result of a
long life's experience in these regions, for doing as I have done.
But the day will come for saying anything. May we be of those
who walking the streets of the New Jerusalem hold sweet counsel
together without danger of being misunderstood.*[6]

That MacDonald thought precisely and consistently on matters of Christian doctrine is abundantly clear from his writings, especially from *Unspoken Sermons*. But in any contact with an individual he was convinced help lay in addressing the heart not the head. Mere intellectually held opinions were spiritually dangerous.

He was determined not to be misunderstood or misrepresented. He had long been interested in hymn writing and openly encouraged his musically inclined friends to set some of his poems to music.[7] But he was infuriated when he learned of an attempt on the part of certain people to set to music the lyric from *Phantastes*, "Alas, how easily things go wrong,"[8] as he did not want people remarking, "As George MacDonald says," and then quoting it. It is positioned dramatically in that fantasy as a description of the experience of a character of low spiritual development; he did not want it used to convey a false impression of his view of life. So deeply did he feel on the matter that he sought the help of lawyers and was willing to go to court to prevent it happening.

Music was an important part of family life. Louisa returned from England to Bordighera in the fall of 1885, two weeks ahead of her husband, to oversee the installing of the new organ at All Saint's. She took great delight in the prospect of having free access to a large instrument of such quality and spent a great deal of time with it, practicing sometimes five and six hours a day. In addition to giving family concerts, she and her daughters participated in community musical events. Her playing provided an important emotional outlet as well, as the children steadily grew up and one by one left home.

MacDonald was extremely fond of Louisa's singing and playing, although he could not read music or carry a tune. He remarked on one occasion that all he understood about music is that "some comes in and some stays outside." When Louisa and the girls played and sang in the parlor, he often paused in his study simply to listen.

Through the 1880s the activities and interests of the children continued to take considerable attention, putting steady demands on the family purse. In the summer of 1884, Greville sought to begin a practice in Florence, that cultural mecca of great charm and beauty, to be nearer his parents. His father not being able to advance him sufficient money, he borrowed two hundred fifty pounds from his rich uncle Joshua Sing and located at 5 Via Rondinelli. Lily went in the fall to help him get situated in his new quarters, his practice being located in his residence. The venture, however, did not succeed; he had but two or three patients during the year he was there. His deafness, together with his difficulty with the language, no doubt were in large part responsible for the failure.

During the middle of 1885 he moved back to London and began rooming with Robert. Then, his fortune took a decided turn for the better: he was able to secure the position of Assistant Demonstrator of Anatomy at King's College, London. The following year he was elected resident medical officer to the Hospital for Diseases of the Throat and Nose in Golden Square. In addition, following his father's example, he began composing and delivering public lectures on various subjects, such as on the artistic principles pertaining to the anatomy of the human body. He also wrote a novel but was unsuccessful in interesting any publisher.

The family had long been concerned about Greville's inability to manage prudently his affairs and to complete the projects he would begin (weaknesses the children in general faulted themselves for having). Irene declared that he needed nothing so much as an efficient, well-organized wife, and the family generally agreed, wondering when he would discover the right girl. In March 1888, however, when he announced he was about to marry a nurse, Phoebe Winn, the family was horrified. She was matron of the Throat Hospital where Greville had been elected surgeon. Greville described her to his mother as "powerfully built, gentle as any woman need be in spite of a rather defiant mouth, sensible on every practical subject, devoid of sentimentality."[9] "What a woman for any gentleman to marry!" MacDonald exclaimed to Louisa and then consoled himself: "Well, this world and all its beginnings will pass on into something better."[10]

But Louisa, less quickly resigned to the prospect, left with Lilia immediately for London to prevent the union, in spite of the facts that MacDonald was at the time on a lecture tour along the Riviera and that Europe was experiencing a severe winter storm. Her valiant effort failed; the marriage took place that March. But Phoebe, devoted to Greville's care, proved to be the companion he needed, not only by nursing him through his many ear problems and, in 1891, a serious bout with blood poisoning, but also by bringing a practical organization to bear on his life. MacDonald and Louisa both came in time to appreciate her.

Ronald, engaged to an American girl, Louise Vivenda Blandy, was also married in 1888, on July 7. They began their life together at Casa Coraggio, with everyone quickly becoming quite fond of Vivenda. Both MacKay and Bernard were enrolled at Cambridge, MacDonald barely able to meet the expense of keeping them there.

MacDonald's health, however, continued to be good through the decade. He remarked in 1887 that he felt better than he had for forty years. One consequence was that he lectured a good deal each year, making extended tours of England and Scotland and also taking engagements along the Riviera. He tended to push himself to his limits on these tours, arranging tight schedules and maintaining a hectic pace, sometimes for three- and four-month periods. He knew he was overdoing, he said, when the plainest words would not come or "the thoughts go ahead of the words, and the words are not ready."[11]

Even at such times he was surprised to see how avidly the people were listening. He did not fail to draw crowds of a thousand or more in the larger cities. He even considered making another lecture tour of America, a project he had entertained with varying degrees of strength since the tour of 1872–1873. He was lecturing more now on such plays as *Julius Ceasar, Macbeth,* and *The Merchant of Venice,* and increasingly on Dante. His mastery of Italian was leading him into a larger appreciation for the poetic skill and deeper insights of the great Florentine. His love of language also led him to take up the study of Spanish.

THIRTY-SEVEN

Themes Old and New

The only triumph the truth can ever have is its recognition by the heart of the liar.—"The Final Unmasking," Unspoken Sermons, Series Three

To a casual observer near the end of the decade, MacDonald appeared more prosperous and healthy than he had ever been. But the truth was he still faced the constant need of making money. Therefore, in addition to maintaining a strenuous lecture schedule he forced himself to keep writing novels, although he was clearly becoming tired of story telling. It is an interesting paradox that he produced his weakest novels when his health was at its best and, physically, he was suffering the least. Because he was convinced of the value of suffering, his afflictions seemed to arouse him to do his best imaginative work.

While his novels from the last part of the decade were among his weakest, his expository work may be the strongest. In *Unspoken Sermons, Series Three* MacDonald undertook to define the foundational concepts of Christianity, attempting to make firm his philosophical base.

A strong earthquake hit early on the morning of February 23, 1887, rudely shaking people out of their beds and frightening everyone. It leveled many houses, and several people were killed. Since the quake occurred on Ash Wednesday, the natives were unwilling to begin cleanup until the following day. The series of aftershocks kept them camping along the high street, under the olive trees or in carriages along the roadsides, for some time. Because a particularly raucous street carnival had just preceded the event, some were sure it was a sign they had danced too much, to God's displeasure. Louisa, practicing the organ at All Saint's the next day when an especially strong aftershock struck, pulled out all the stops and played the "Hallelujah Chorus," refusing to be moved from her seat.[1] The quake was to her an inspiring display of God's almighty power.

Casa Coraggio, sturdily built of stone, survived for the most part quite intact, with the exception of some cracked plaster. But its stucco tower—a feature the family had really never cared for— was declared unsafe and had to be dismantled. Household items from shelves and cupboards were generally strewn across the floor, with many vases and dishes broken. The family noted, however, that a small figure of Christ atop one of the bookshelves remained upright and in place, although all around it had fallen.[2] The Mac-Donalds opened their doors to their homeless neighbors, but since most preferred to remain in the open until the aftershocks subsided, only one family accepted their invitation. Everyone remained apprehensive for some time. MacDonald later told his cousin James that such things as a passing train or a footfall overhead instantly aroused the fear that another earthquake was coming.

MacDonald's books were all disshelved and in heaps. In picking them up he found in a biography of Johann Lavater, Swiss theologian and poet whose aphorisms were esteemed by many (including William Blake), a pronouncement of Lavater's that reads: "Act according to thy faith in Christ, and thy faith will soon become sight." In the middle of making a similar point in writing his novel *Home Again,* he was so struck by the coincidence he could not refrain from recounting it in a footnote.

Early in the writing of this novel, he confessed to Winnie that he seemed unable to generate zest for the story, and shortly before the work appeared, he remarked to his cousin James: "When it pleases God that I stop writing stories, I shall be glad, for I never *feel* that it is my calling by nature, though it is, I hope, by a yet higher command."[3] The shortness of the work and the general flatness of the story itself attest to his sense of drudgery, but the work is not without merit.

In its slight plot, built on the archetypal pattern of the parable of the prodigal son (a pattern that appears in so much of his work), MacDonald again drew the image of the ideal father, one that had been fairly muted in his writings since *Warlock O' Glenwarlock*. Its basic theme is another version of one occurring in *What's Mine's Mine*—that spiritual health depends first of all on finding a solid orientation to things as they are in the world God has made. In this novel the threat to that orientation is the pursuing of illusions, abstracted realities that distort the real or attempt to obscure it altogether. While the plot is slight and the characters rather wooden, the novel does contain in passages of author monologue direct and compelling expressions of the ideas gripping him at the time, written in prose less convoluted than that in some of the longer works.

The Elect Lady, which MacDonald wrote immediately after finishing *Home Again*, is a still less satisfying performance, although several of the characters have moments when they assume a greater reality than those in *Home Again*. The various elements of the plot have a potential for a dramatically successful story, but MacDonald uses them only as a rack on which to place various homilies, a persistent characteristic of his work at its weakest. This work presents an amalgam of themes better expressed in the other novels. They are not well interrelated, so that it is difficult to discern a main theme in the story. Even the most avid devotee of MacDonald's thought must weary of the mere repetition of these ideas.

In *Unspoken Sermons, Series Three,* however, as MacDonald undertook to explore several of the more foundational concepts of Christianity, he achieved his most profound and in some respects his freshest expression of his ideas. An understanding of them is necessary to a good working understanding of his final novels and his crowning fantasy *Lilith*. The presentation of his ideas has its foundation in the first sermon, "The Creation in Christ," so that this volume is more unified than series one and two. He concerns himself with ultimate spiritual realities, insisting that the spiritual relationship between the Father and the Son is the central cohering force in the universe. He defines truth, freedom, justice, righteousness, and the Christian hope in terms of this reality.

His entire understanding of Christianity always derived from his perception of the relationship between the Father and Son, and in his first sermon he makes very clear why he saw this relationship as so important: the interaction between the self-effacing love of the Son and the self-giving love of the Father reveals that love is the only good in the universe, and selfishness the basic evil.

As MacDonald developed the concepts that issue from this core, he was quite conscious of the degree to which he was departing from widely held popular concepts in theology. In the sermon on justice he maintains that the prevalent concept of the justice of God is such that, were it attributed to any human ruler, he would be identified as the worst of tyrants. For it holds that unredeemed people, born with impulses to sin and having never had a true view of God's nature and grace, are hopelessly condemned to punishment by horrible suffering for eternity.

After depicting this moral nightmare he again details his theory of the nature of punishment, giving it definitive expression: God's punishment is unfailingly remedial; there is no opposition between punishment and forgiveness; and God in justice is bound to destroy sin by saving people from their sins. The only true atonement for sin is practical: the complete repentance of sinners, their making full restitution, and their practicing righteousness thereafter. This is the work Christ has begun and is accomplishing within people, not for them. Only this theological position satisfied MacDonald's sense of justice and mercy. Within its confines he could contemplate with equanimity that God would not be niggardly in bestowing on people all the suffering necessary to the destruction of all sin. At stake was humanity's ultimate welfare.

MacDonald was careful to acknowledge that some good people he loved and honored held to the view of the Atonement that he was opposing, and, so long as they remained satisfied with their view, he did not want to disturb them. He certainly was not interested in argument. He was quite confident that the time would come as they grew in their union with God that they would see otherwise. Rather, he was writing to people who, having encountered this teaching, were morally repulsed by it and had either turned from accepting Christianity or had accepted it joylessly. They trusted in the "merits of Christ" for salvation from the wrath of God and the just consequences of their sin, not unlike people who had found a foolproof insurance policy.

MacDonald affirmed in his sermon "The Truth" that he believed that every fact in nature is a revelation of God. Further, he said he suspected all the facts of nature were such that "we learn God unconsciously." The degree to which this idea is present in the novels since *What's Mine's Mine* attests to the strength with which he held it. The relative sparsity of direct references to God in some of his later works—a fact that has afforded some scholars cause for remark—may well be understood in terms of this principle:[4] Nature was constantly revealing God.

In the novel he started after completing *Unspoken Sermons, Series Three,* he gave this conviction the most complete expression yet. He paradoxically combined this idea with the Christian perception that the physical world will be destroyed that the spiritual world may emerge triumphant. An earthquake, much on his mind since the one that occurred in 1887, becomes the informing metaphor of the story.[5]

Titling it *A Rough Shaking,* MacDonald told the story of Clare Skymers growing up. Like *Ranald Bannerman's Boyhood* and *Gutta Percha Willie,* it is a book more for children than for adults. Clare is another of MacDonald's idyllic children, such as Diamond in *At the Back of the North Wind,* but his experiences do not intermingle the realistic with the fantastic.

He is a good boy seemingly unaware of God and does not

consciously rely on God's care. Divine Providence, nevertheless, sustains him, so that he secures his basic needs, though generally in conjunction with considerable suffering at the hands of callous and miserly people. The emphasis falls on the individual's obligation to be good and accept responsibility for his life, rather than on consciously depending on God to provide. In Clare's case God did provide but in response to Clare's perseverance and undaunted resourcefulness rather than to his conscious faith.

The Flight of the Shadow, another slight novel MacDonald was writing at the turn of the decade, is more directly an imaginative depiction of some of the dominant themes of *Unspoken Sermons, Series Three*. Many of its themes and images strongly anticipate those of *Lilith*, forming an imaginative link between the sermons and the final fantasy. The realities at the heart of things—the loving relationship between Father and Son in the Godhead and Christ's atonement for all things—reveal by contrast how evil are such attitudes as vicious selfishness and love of power, exemplified in *The Flight of the Shadow* by Lady Cairnedge. MacDonald insists that the one principle of hell is, "I am my own."

THIRTY-EIGHT

The Keenest Loss

*I told some congregation lately that every good father with
good children knew in a dim way the very joy of God
himself.*—MacDonald to Louisa, October 14, 1890

As the decade passed into the nineties MacDonald's pace
hardly slackened: lecuturing, writing, keeping up with his children's expanding activities. His health, the inevitable deteriora-
tions of body notwithstanding, continued quite strong, his mind
alert. But extreme difficulties and trials lay ahead for him.

Emerging advances in technology impressed him with their
use; he was delighted with them. He remarked in 1888 of talking
to his host on the telephone at the latter's business some eight
miles away as though he were in the same room. By this time he
was regularly using a typewriter, and even Louisa began to type
much of her correspondence, all in capital letters.

He began to suffer deafness in 1889. Greville examined him
and told him that one ear was quite bad, but Greville was able
to strengthen his hearing in the other. Otherwise, his health was
remarkably robust for his age. Encouraged by his vigor and the
large demand for his lectures, he spent a good amount of time
during the last years of the decade on the lecture circuit.

He spent much of 1889 lecturing, touring Scotland with
Robert in the autumn. His fellow Scots greeted him with fervor,
urging him to return the following year with the "pilgrims," a
prospect that the family seriously entertained for a time, but it did
not materialize. They had done little with the troupe since Grace's
death. The family did, however, continue throughout the decade
to have Christmas nativity tableaux, with Bernard specializing in

the lighting. Most of the characters were played by the children Louisa and the girls tutored. The annual event was generally viewed in Bordighera as the highlight of the year's community activities.

The MacDonald family now included three young women, all of whom were especially close to Lily: Louise Vivenda, Ronald's wife; Belinda ("Linda") Bird, who had become engaged to Bernard in 1884[1] and who together with her mother spent most of her time at Casa Coraggio; and Eva Pym, daughter of an English family the MacDonalds had long known, who came to Casa Coraggio for her health.

Ronald, who had graduated from Oxford with a concentration in history, began in the spring of 1889 to consider emigrating to the United States to take a position in a school in Alabama. MacDonald met the prospect with dismay: both the climate and the society would be uncongenial. He much preferred the thought of establishing his son in a school of his own in England and talked of trying to raise five hundred pounds for this purpose. Greville expressed his willingness to insure his life to raise a like amount in order to launch the venture. But Ronald, not finding the idea appealing, took a position at Hill School in Pottstown, Pennsylvania, and left for America that summer with his wife. After a term there he became headmaster of Ravenscroft School, an Episcopal institution in Asheville, North Carolina.

Vivenda, however, did not take well to America, became hysterical and delirious, and would not allow Ronald out of her sight. Crushed by seeing his formerly vivacious and sweet-spirited bride so broken and ill, he was further burdened by having to care for their baby Ozella and to study only when Vivenda was asleep. MacDonald, deeply moved by his son's plight, determined during the summer of 1890 to go to Asheville, but then the family decided Lily's going would be more helpful to Ronald.

Consequently, Lily boarded an ocean liner bound for New York early in September, in order to be with her brother by the time his school opened. She remarked that her enforced leisure on ship afforded her a curious sensation, as no one wanted her or "cared a rap" what she did. It seems that her long-standing habit of being unstintingly at the service of others issued in their, however unconsciously, presuming on her.

Russell Gilder met her at New York and helped her on her way to North Carolina. She was intending to bring Vivenda back to Bordighera, if Ronald was agreeable and his wife at all able to travel. But Vivenda's health was worse than Lily had anticipated, and she died shortly after her arrival. Ronald, all but overcome with fatigue, was seized with near despair. Lily's presence and strength of spirit were a great comfort, seeing him through a most difficult trial.

Eighteen-ninety was a year of strange contrasts for the MacDonalds. Ronald's trauma was balanced by the joy of Bernard's marriage to Belinda, which took place on September 4, while Lily was en route to America. The MacDonalds would have preferred to have the wedding in July. They had been in England during May and June for MacDonald's lecturing and had stayed to see MacKay graduate from Cambridge in early July.[2] But Belinda's mother had died shortly before, and propriety dictated they wait at least until September. As it was, George and Louisa took a chalet in Switzerland to rest during the heat of August.

While on the road that spring and summer, MacDonald had with him the proofs of his last three-volume novel, *There and Back,* correcting them in his spare time. In it MacDonald again reworked familiar themes but with an energy and freshness that render it as impressive as any of his novels. He dedicated the novel to Ronald, "in the sure hope of ever lasting brotherhood," identifying him as "my son and friend, my pupil, fellow-student, and fellow-workman." The date of dedication, February 1891, places it in the winter after the passing of Vivenda, at a time when MacDonald's sympathetic concern for Ronald, alone in a foreign land, was especially strong.

But the character of the novel itself suggests another reason for the dedication. In a biographical essay written as a tribute to his father after his death, Ronald tells of a conversation in which he had asked his father why he never undertook to write a novel of "mere human passion and artistic plot":

> He replied that he would like to write it. I asked him then further whether his highest literary quality was not in a measure injured by what must to many seem the monotony of his theme—referring to the novels alone. He admitted that this was possible; and went on to tell me that, having begun to do his work as a Congregational minister, and having been driven . . . into giving up that professional pulpit, he was no less impelled than compelled to use unceasingly the new platform whence he had found that his voice could carry so far.[3]

This conversation no doubt lingered in MacDonald's mind and influenced him. In interesting contrast to most of his works, this one exists as pure story for the first quarter of its length before religious concerns are introduced.

Apparently, he determined to present a larger quantity of "mere human passion and artistic plot" before introducing his typical interests. MacDonald confessed to his cousin James in April 1887 that he had a long novel one-third written, and he was at a loss to know how to work it out.[4] He was also, he told his cousin, anticipating the day when he could quit writing stories. *There and Back* was, therefore, on a back burner while he had been writing his two "short stories," as he called them, *Home Again* and *The Elect Lady*, with their strong and direct religious intentions expressed throughout. Perhaps his perplexity concerned how to integrate his Christian themes into *There and Back* in order to produce a more unified whole.[5]

A variation of the *Bildungsroman* structure, the story concerns a foundling, Richard Lestrange, who discovers his true parentage and inheritance as the novel closes. The separate quests for God of Richard and his love interest, Barbara, form the matrix of the novel. Richard's quest begins radically; he reacts with earnest unbelief against the evangelical God-in-a-box of the woman he as a child supposes to be his mother. Barbara's quest is quite different. Her parents are antagonistic to Christianity, and she, in her open and sweet-spirited manner, is looking for the God behind nature. Typical to MacDonald's thought, the characters develop Christian faith not from ponderings over scripture passages but from human longings and moral realities carefully and shrewdly considered.

When *There and Back* finally appeared in April 1891, The *Athenaeum* observed the author's purpose was "Miltonic, as ever; nothing less than to 'justify the ways of God to men,'" and felt it would therefore be distasteful to many readers.[6] Curiously, the reviewer chose to commend MacDonald's portraits of several of the minor characters as the most noteworthy and thus, by silence, reflected adversely on the major ones. But Richard and Barbara, because they are shown as developing into MacDonald's ideal, rather than possessing it before the story begins, may be viewed as among the most real and convincing he drew over his long career. His not introducing the religious themes until the story is well underway also gives the imagination time to become acquainted with the characters before attention is called to the religious argument.

In September 1890, MacDonald was back in Britain on another lecture tour, speaking almost every day throughout a seven-week period. He was introduced on one occasion as the man who had done more than anyone else to "Christianize Christianity," and crowds at times were "almost foolishly enthusiastic."[7] In the larger cities he consistently drew large audiences: a thousand at Glasgow (where he sat for his picture) and fifteen hundred at Nottingham, although it was the off-season for lecturing. But he worried about what he detected as a general decline in the moral tone of his country, with selfishness, greed, and dishonesty on the rise. The presence of certain other lecturers, however, such as Lady Mary Murray, holding forth on socialism and temperance, were "indications of something deeper—the scattering of the fallen leaves as the footsteps of the Son of Man draws near them" and were thus a source of encouragement.[8]

In Aberdeen, William Geddes lunched with him to talk about his poetry, bestowing high praise. The following March Geddes's article appeared in *Blackwoods Magazine,* lauding MacDonald for perpetuating in his poetry, together with Tennyson, the legacy of Wordsworth in his ability "to reveal to us . . . the glory of the visible world as the symbol of a divine and invisible omnipresence."[9] He further suggested that the present Laureate, Tennyson, might recognize in MacDonald a younger brother carrying on the "true procession." It was evidently his intention to suggest that MacDonald be appointed Laureate in the event of Tennyson's death. The aging Tennyson did in fact die the following year, but the cloak did not fall to MacDonald, perhaps because of the degree to which his repeated theological insistences had come to repulse some of the literary authorities of the time.

MacDonald's health was good, with the exception of such ailments as an annoying tooth, which he had been told he must have out in London. "We shall see," he remarked, for it would be the first of his lost teeth he had not extracted himself. The task of pulling it himself proving to be too difficult, however, he allowed a London dentist to do it, refusing the gas he offered, and then engaged him to make a set of false teeth. He philosophized that although the "outer man" was decaying, he was feeling "the inner, the thing that trusts in the perfect creative life," growing stronger.[10]

His sense of humor, never lacking, remained strong. He penned a joke to his wife: " 'Has your husband been overworking himself?' he asked a lady whose husband is out of his mind. 'Oh, dear, no! We belong to the landed gentry,' was her reply."[11] Occasionally, he would forget a word, and his rheumatic knees made rising to approach the lectern increasingly difficult; nevertheless, he affirmed that he was "wonderfully well." Greville told him a man was as old as his arteries, and MacDonald's were good for another fifteen or twenty years.

At last, near the middle of November, with his new teeth making his mouth feel, he said, as though it were filled with "thirteen gravestones" and rendering him unwilling to eat, he left 85 Harley Street (Greville's residence) for the trek back to Bordighera. His baggage, as he described it to Louisa in a letter, shows that he was taking considerably more than his clothes. It consisted of four great parcels, one of which contained a heavy garden fork for his gardener, a banjo, two large brass fittings of a hanging lamp, his dressing gown, and his Italian cloak. Another had two great glass shades done up in straw and paper; a third was filled with chimneys for house lamps, a copper vase, and nearly seven pounds of bacon, together with miscellaneous items; and a fourth contained a new typewriter.[12]

In January 1891, very close to the time when *There and Back* appeared, MacDonald also published a pocket anthology of excerpts from the writings of the Renaissance author Sir Philip Sidney, a tribute to "one of the noblest of Englishmen." He gave it the lengthy title: *A Cabinet of Gems, cut and polished by Sir Philip Sidney; now, for the more radiance, presented without their setting by George MacDonald*. Sidney was to MacDonald not unlike what he was to W. B. Yeats, a name synonymous with the ideal, "our perfect man."[13] His writings, together with the legend for nobleness of action that had grown up around him, had long inspired MacDonald as epitomizing the ideal of moral and spiritual man. Sidney's epigrammatic style had also influenced MacDonald's.

The year 1891, however, brought several painful trials to the MacDonalds. In late February, nine-year-old Octavia died, another victim of tuberculous. As her fever was intermittent she did not seem in immediate danger, but she was seized with convulsions and died in a half hour. In effect raised by Louisa she had been so close to her grandmother that Lily remarked to Winifred that she feared her mother would never care for anything again. Louisa did, however, come to accept the tragedy, so that, before Lily returned from America in May, she was able to write to her firstborn about their loss. But a yet more painful one would follow.

That May, MacDonald began his final season of lecturing with a series of six talks in Belfast. He was under stress because, en route to Belfast, he lost his portmanteau, which contained, he lamented to Louisa, his annotated copy of Tennyson's *In Memoriam,* his annotated Milton, his bonnet with St. George's brooch, and his fur jacket with an almandine brooch. Nevertheless, in a hall reputed to be acoustically difficult, no one's voice had ever filled the auditorium as had his. His lecture on Burns drew a crowd of over fifteen hundred.

His extended tour over northern Britain lasted through the summer. In mid-July, Louisa came to Stock Rectory, Billericay, to rest and await her husband. He was then in Huntly, delighting to be there at the time of year when in clear weather there is no night. The atmosphere was just right for him to complete his *Scotch Songs and Ballads,*[14] a collection of thirty-eight poems in Scots dialect. On this visit he was invited to preach in the parish church, as well as the independent chapel of his family. One day his cousin James took him in "a carriage and pair" to the churchyard where all his family were buried. He took solace in the undulating fields of grass with bare hills all about and the air full of the sweet odor of white clover under a serene sky. "I get little bits of dreamy pleasure sometimes," he told Louisa, "but none without the future to set things right. 'What is it all for?' I should constantly be saying with Tolstoi, but for the hope of the glory of God."[15]

In his spare time he was working hard to finish still another volume of sermons. He remarked while composing this series that writing sermons was the hardest kind of writing that he ever did. Since his publisher wanted a title other than *Unspoken Sermons, Series Four,* MacDonald at first proposed *Study Sermons* and then chose *The Hope of the Gospel.* Consisting of twelve sermons on New Testament texts and published in 1892, the volume offers a compact, comprehensive introduction to MacDonald's thought. In the final sermon, "The Hope of the Universe," he offered his vision for the immortality of animals, a conviction that had grown as he aged.

Lily had returned from America peremptorily in May, prompted by the news that Eva Pym, who had also contracted tuberculosis, was rapidly deteriorating. MacDonald hoped that "her evening" would be "like a Scotch midsummer one—a gradual fading into the morning—no night at all," but it was not to be.[16] She died an agonizing death. Louisa was hurt that Eva refused her ministration, accepting only Lily's, who was constantly at her bedside. Her demise was quick but her suffering intense; she died midsummer. Lily's unreserved nursing of her friend was, however, at a terrible price: she soon began to cough and spit blood.

Greville was consulted at once and found tuberculous in her lungs and larynx. Lily, impatient with herself, agreed to spend a week at sea with complete rest. They were determined to spare no expense to provide the best care for her, borrowing against Casa Coraggio if necessary. But Lily's condition steadily deteriorated. She was seized with periods of histrionics—sometimes exaggerated expressions of affection, at others extreme irritability and a self-absorption uncharacteristic of her. The family was deeply distressed.

In September she told her mother that she felt there was someone else inside her making her do these things. While she talked she had an expression on her face so like Eva Pym's that Louisa believed that Eva's spirit had returned to rest on her. Winifred, Irene, and Louisa, together with a nurse, gave themselves to caring for Lily, taking her in a bath chair to a nearby hillside covered with pines to breathe the clear air whenever she felt up to making the effort. But, as the fall passed, her appetite waned, her convulsive coughs ended in nausea, and her temperature soared.

MacDonald counseled Louisa to remember "we are only in a sort of passing vision here, and . . . the real life lies beyond us. If Lily goes now, how much the sooner you and I may find her again. Life is waiting us. We have to awake—or die—which you will—to reach it."[17] He was still in England, extending his lecture tour well into November because of their sore need of money. During that summer Louisa had lost what was left of her legacy from her father, some two thousand pounds. The English Bank of the River Plate, where it was deposited, had failed. "There's a nut for us to crack without any kernel," she wryly commented to her husband.[18]

His engagements at last concluded, MacDonald returned to Casa Coraggio the second week of November. Apprehensive but not without hope, he assumed a share of the care of his firstborn, faithfully entering her room through the night to keep the fire burning. But she did not improve and died peacefully in her father's arms on November 22. "I think I'm going, Mammy, to the others, you know, to join them," she said, as she quietly departed. She had been an emotional center of family life since she was a child and had endeared herself to all who knew her by her jolly, sweet-spirited nature. Her passing created an emotional chasm in the family that was impossible to fill.

Lily was buried beside Grace in the Stranger's Cemetery in Bordighera. Ironically, William J. Matheson, who had long been deeply attached to her, was buried in England the same hour. Although Lily's funeral was held in the rain, Greville recalls Mac-Donald was loath to leave the grave, twice returning after the others had left, and was at last led away with difficulty.[19] Perhaps the place his firstborn occupied in his emotional life may best be measured by the birthday letter he wrote to her at the beginning of 1891, when she was in Asheville with Ronald.

C. C. B.
Jan. 4, 1891.

Dearest Child,

I could say so much to you, and yet I am constantly surrounded by a sort of cactus-hedge that seems to make adequate utterance impossible. It is so much easier to write romance, where you cannot easily lie, than to say the commonest things where you may go wrong any moment. Even this is not the kind of way I meant to write to you. It is all wrong. I can only tell you I love you with true heart fervently, and love you far more because you are God's child than because you are mine.

I don't thank you for coming to us, for you could not help it, but the whole universe is "tented" with love, and you hold one of the corners of the great love-canopy for your mother and me. I don't think I am very ambitious, except the strong desire "to go where I am" be ambition; and I know I take small satisfaction in looking on my past, but I do live expecting great things in the life that is ripening for me and all mine—when we shall all have the universe for our own, and be good merry helpful children in the great house of our father. I think then we shall be able to pass into and through each others very souls as we please, knowing each other's thought and being, along with our own, and so being like God. When we are all just as loving and unselfish as Jesus; when like him, our one thought of delight is that God is, and is what he is; when the fact that a being is just another person from ourselves, is enough to make that being precious—then, darling, you and I and all will have the grand liberty wherewith Christ makes free—opening his hand to send us out like white doves to range the universe.

Have I not shown that the attempt to speak what you mean is the same kind of failure that walking is—a mere, constantly recurring, recovery from falling. . . .

Tell Ronald from me that Novalis says: "This world is not a dream, but it may, and perhaps ought to become one." Anyhow, it will pass—to make way for the world God has hidden in our hearts.

Darling, I wish you life eternal. I daresay the birthdays will still be sparks in its glory. May I one day see that mould in God out of which you came.

Your loving Father

At the time he had no hint that this would be the last birthday letter he would write her.

THIRTY-NINE

Out-Issues of the Soul

I lean to a wild one [story], into which one can put so much more.—MacDonald to R. W. Gilder, May 15, 1875.

In the early fall of 1891, MacDonald wrote Louisa about writing another fantasy: "God will help my brains to make sure of it, for they feel tired of inventing within mere human laws."[1]

Such writing provided an imaginative release for him, allowing him a freedom that more realistic stories did not. During the prior winter, no doubt while he was working on *There and Back* and chafing under the demands of a story that he was uncertain how to resolve, he might have laid it momentarily aside and turned to write the first version of his final fantasy, *Lilith*. In the compelling strength of its imagery and the poignant charm of its enigmatic conversations, the story evidences his exhilaration in being free from the demands and restraints of realistic writing. It is the crowning achievement of his life's work.

The manuscript of the first version of *Lilith,* dated March 29, 1890, and written in free-flowing hand with remarkably few deletions and corrections, suggests that the initial narrative came to him completely and quickly. However, this version was extensively and painstakingly reworked over a period of five years. Eight different manuscripts of *Lilith* exist in the British Library, where Greville and Winifred, the last two of the children to survive, agreed before Greville's death in 1944 to reposit them. The final three are printer's copies, the revisions on them concerning mechanical errors and minor adjustments. The many basic reworkings of the text reveal a careful and elaborate evolution of the story to its final form. The first text is handwritten with few revisions; the next four are typed, and the deletions and emendations are extensive. When MacDonald typed the second copy from the first, he made extensive changes as well, so that there are five revisions.[2]

The relative lack of alterations in the first manuscript, dated March 29, 1890, suggests a confident and energetic approach to his task. But during the evolution of the story, Lily died, and her passing had profound effects on him, no doubt accounting for the more somber tone. When Mary and Maurice had died, MacDonald worked through his grief in composing *A Book of Strife in the form of the diary of an old soul;* now, his profound sense of loss intensified yet more his imaginative explorations of the spiritual world, as he tried to find solace in completing his vision of the life immortal. The situation forms yet another instance in which his best work came out of periods of trial and suffering.

As the story evolved the process of completing it became increasingly exhausting. In the letters he wrote from the later part of the period he often spoke of being tired. He was always a meticulous workman, assiduously trying to achieve as great a perfection as he was able in his writing, and now, working on the final and crowning imaginative presentation of his vision, he worked even harder for a perfect completeness. "I am a little tired," he told Winifred during the summer of 1893, "having been hard at work cutting and killing and re-embodying and shifting, and trying generally to restore or order, and draw out hidden meanings from their holes."[3]

His doctors, fearing for the effects of the strain, limited him to working but four hours per day. When finally he sent the completed manuscript to the publishers, he was quite exhausted and did nothing for several months afterward, which was most unusual for him. He was seized with a severe attack of influenza, which so incapacitated him that the family spent the summer of 1894 in the mountains above Florence, where the temperature was reputed never to rise above eighty-two degrees.

When the proofs came that fall, he was able to slowly work through them. It was, he felt, the last book he would write. "I am working at the proofs of a book which I hope to send you by and by," he told Helen. "But the many touches necessary to finish it tire me much. I'm growin' some auld!"[4]

He also was aware that his work might not be well received. He told Georgina, for instance, that he feared she would not like it.[5]

His apprehension increased when Louisa read the manuscript. She was distressed that she could not understand it, and her inability alarmed him. Perhaps his powers were indeed waning, or the intricacies of his vision were too obscure. Greville, whom MacDonald felt of all his children understood him the best now that Lily was gone, agreed to read the fantasy and render a verdict. When he enthusiastically pronounced it "The Revelation of St. George," both his parents were relieved, and plans for publication went forward.[6]

MacDonald's first purpose in *Lilith* is similar to that in his initial fantasy, *Phantastes*. Colin Manlove rightly observes that in a sense the two may be seen to compose a single fantasy.[7]

In both MacDonald wants to impress on his readers the existence of the realm of spirit with its higher realities. He became as he grew older increasingly dismayed with the growth of materialist and commercialist attitudes and with the strictly rational and empirical approaches to experience that increasingly ignored or denied these realities. A similar mentality had deeply offended him during his seminary days, and it seemed to have steadily increased during his lifetime.

So he made a strong point at the beginning of the tale concerning the spiritual nature of the realm in which his protagonist inadvertently finds himself. The story concerns the experiences of the protagonist, Mr. Vane, who stumbles into the realm of "seven dimensions"—a world that contains unexpected revelations and intensified moral principles. The extra four dimensions are those of spiritual reality.[8]

Vane comes into this higher realm before he is ready to experience it. A student fresh out of Oxford, he is intellectually curious, wanting to advance human knowledge by noting analogies between the physical and the "metaphysical," his misapplied term for the spiritual world. The realm of the metaphysical is to him arcane and curious; he probably would not have distinguished it from the occult. One day, browsing in the library of his ancestral home, he follows an elusive old librarian who flees upstairs into the garret and disappears through a mysterious mirror. Vane follows and finds himself in the world of seven dimensions. In this altered world the old librarian is a wise Raven who acts as Vane's guide in the several adventures that follow. He is also Adam, who, together with his wife Eve, is invested with the charge of being caretaker of souls, effecting their transition into eternity by means of their "sleeping"—or spiritually dying into newness of life.

The world of *Lilith* is, therefore, MacDonald's rendition of the world of spiritual reality that good people enjoy to some measure in this life and all will enter after death. MacDonald's version is singularly shaped by his concepts and theological perceptions. He avoided referring to this world as Faerie, as he did in *Phantastes,* because he wanted to avoid conveying the slightest impression that it had only a fanciful reality; the reality of this realm is appreciably more certain.

While MacDonald's vision was thoroughly derived from his understanding of Scripture, based on his earnest scrutinizing of the Greek texts ever since his days at King's College, he did not directly appeal to Scripture as its authoritative source but rather to revelation as it occurs within the human heart. Extremely impatient with the practice that offered biblical proof-texts as authority for any system of idea, he was most careful to avoid even the slightest suggestion of such an attitude. By his use of many scriptural images he communicated his high respect for the Bible; his understanding of Scripture was the fountainhead of his vision. He always felt keenly that the key question was what does scriptural imagery really indicate? He concluded that the sense of mercy and justice resident deep within the consciousness of a good, spiritually mature person was the final determiner of true biblical meaning. The understanding of Scripture that is most satisfying to such a heart is most correct.[9]

Greville, in telling of his father's writing of *Lilith*, remarked that MacDonald felt that he had a mandate directly from God to write it and adduced the compact and free-flowing nature of the first version of the fantasy as evidence.[10]

MacDonald would have been loath to claim publicly any inspiration similar to that of the biblical writers; that would have been inconsistent with his nature. But neither would he have completed a book without a sense of divine sanction. Throughout his career, whenever he felt at all thwarted in the production of a story, he took it as a sign that he was not exercising sufficient dependence on God. Each of his stories answers to his vision of what he believed Scripture revealed. Roderick McGillis sees the relative lack of overt references to God in *Lilith* as a reason for reading it as other than a Christian document.[11] Seeing no direct references to God in the final version of *Lilith*, as in the other fantasies and fairy tales, he feels this "releases these works from religious doctrine and opens them up to wider interpretation. . . . This is important since it encourages us not to read *Lilith* as a Christian document." But this feature may be explained in terms of the strength of MacDonald's conviction that to see anything truly is to see God in it, a prevalent theme in his later novels.

During his writing of *Lilith*, G. P. Putnam's Sons of New York asked him for a preface to a fresh edition of his fairy tales, titled simply *The Light Princess and other fairy tales*, which appeared in 1893. MacDonald obliged with his essay "The Fantastic Imagination," which is an important statement of his view of the nature and significance of fantasy. In it he refused to discuss the meanings of his stories—"so long as I think my dog can bark, I will not sit up and bark for him," he explained—but he encouraged his readers to find their own meanings. The reader's interpretation was better than his because the reader who is a true person will imagine true things, and the truth that a person sees is precisely the truth needed at the time. Therefore, to MacDonald's mind, an array of differing interpretations was possible, each possessing its own validity in terms of the respective reader's spiritual state. MacDonald felt the type of fantasies he wrote could minister to spiritual growth, and he trusted that they would accomplish this within each reader.

The reviewers of *Lilith,* however, were generally mystified and dismayed by its contents, and some were unsparing in their remarks. The writer in the *Athenaeum,* who professed to remember with fondness such characters as David Elginbrod and Robert Falconer, announced his confusion: "It is not less than grievous to find the sweet bells jangled, and the imagination, once lofty and penetrating, declined to the incoherent and grotesque." He stated he had earnestly tried to follow the narrative and enter into "the strange games with Adam and Eve," but "a regard for the preservation of sanity prevented us from dwelling on the shifting phases of nightmare" of the story. "That some high purpose pervades this strange mystical farrago we are willing to believe," he concluded, "but its method of presentment seems to be neither lucid nor edifying."[12]

Similarly, the reviewer in *The Critic* regretted having been lead on "a wild goose chase from the Here into the Nowhere," and further complained he had never read a book "so full of striking resemblances to the works of other authors," professing to see parallels to Marie Corelli's recently published *Soul of Lilith,* Swift, Dante, Browning, and the book of Revelation.[13]

The general reaction to his fantasy no doubt prompted MacDonald to worry even more about the impairment of his abilities with age.

Katharine Parson Woods wrote a kinder review in *The Bookman,* commending the scene of the "punition" of Lilith in Mara's House of Bitterness, although she complained about the "undignified" transition from this world to that of the seven dimensions. She was confident that some "true souls" would understand it but that it would be "to the wise of this world sound signifying nothing," a rather accurate assessment.[14]

After the initial reviews a general silence and neglect set in.

The most gratifying commendation from individuals must have come when MacDonald sent a copy of *Lilith* as a gift to H. G. Wells, whose science fiction fantasies began appearing that same year. He responded warmly:

> I have been reading your *Lilith* with exceptional interest. Curiously enough, I have been at work on a book based on essentially the same idea, namely that, assuming more than three dimensions, it follows that there must be wonderful worlds nearer us than breathing and closer than hands and feet. I have wanted to get into such kindred worlds for the purposes of romance for several years, but I've been bothered by the way. Your polarization and mirror business struck me as neat in the extreme.[15]

FORTY

Trials Yet Await Thee

All my life I had wanted I knew not what, and now the thing I wanted but knew not was about to be given me.— Lilith (A)

The passing of Lily left a vacuum in her parents' lives that was never filled. Though they took pleasure and solace in the loving attention of the children left to them, their minds persistently dwelt on the contrast between the joy they had known before Mary's death, when the family was complete, and the absence they now felt, with four of their children gone. Life was now, by comparison, incomplete.

In addition their physical ills were increasing. "I think we feel . . . as if we were getting ready to go," MacDonald confided to Helen. "The world is very different since Lily went, and we shall be glad when our time comes to go after our children."[1]

In April 1892, Bernard's wife Linda gave birth to their third grandchild, and MacDonald was gratified they chose to name him Maurice. Also, Ronald had returned from America, bringing his daughter Ozella, whom MacDonald described as the "quaintest darling of a child, odd and pretty, like her name."[2]

Deciding against going to England that summer, they took instead a villa in the Swiss Alps, at Arth-am-see, on Lake Zug, there to rest and work on the collected edition of his poetic works, which appeared in 1893. He told Carey Davies that putting his poems into final form was "very troublesome, but one cannot let wrongness of any kind willingly pass."[3]

Consisting of four hundred and thirty-eight poems, the two-volume edition, although it does not include his *A Book of Strife, in the form of the diary of an old soul* and other scattered poems, is a fairly complete presentation of his life's poetic endeavor.

Before they went to Switzerland he had finished the manuscript for his next novel, *Heather and Snow*. Evidence suggests he began it after Lily's death and completed it early that June.[4]

When he had returned in November 1891 from his extensive lecturing, he was encouraged by the many commendations he had received on *There and Back*—Davies had told him it was his best English story—and he even considered attempting another three-volume work. He confessed to Louisa, however, that he did not know when he had felt so imaginatively barren, and he decided he would attempt another only if "it please God to give . . . things to write about."[5]

The story he did write fell considerably short of three volumes in length, being one of his shorter novels. *Heather and Snow* has, nevertheless, considerable imaginative strength. The main theme concerns the spiritual growth into full personhood of the main character, Francis ("Francie") Gordon, the young Scottish laird who grows up with Kristy and desires her hand. "Ye'll please me best by no wantin to please me; and ye'll please God best by duin what he's putten intil yer hert as the richt thing, and the bonny thing, and the true thing, though ye suld dee i' the duin o' 't,"[6] she tells him, refusing her consent until he becomes a man according to MacDonald's ideal of moral and spiritual maturity.

The novel contains some of MacDonald's most imaginatively vivid descriptions and memorable characters. That death was much on his mind is evident in the prominence given it in the story, and his handling of the subject attests to his full acceptance of it. A snowstorm, powerfully described, takes the lives of two of the main characters. "No story, however, ends in this world," MacDonald observed, and he invests the scene with a sense of peace concerning death and immortality. This novel, together with his intense depiction of the afterlife in *Lilith*, helped him come to terms with Lily's passing.

MacDonald had been obsessed with the specter of losing his

mental powers for some time, and now increasingly he found himself unable to remember things. Writing to Helen in 1894, he corrected a reference she had made in a prior letter and confided: "Oh, don't I understand the interfering tricks of age! How often I swear at myself for an old fool!"[7]

With increasing evidences of senility MacDonald's personal anxieties began to mount. Evidences of some of these may be found in the scene near the end of *Lilith* in which Vane passes through a series of dreams before he comes to the end of his sanctifying sleep. In one of these dreams the Raven tells him, "Trials yet await thee, heavy, of a nature thou knowest not now." A graphic statement of MacDonald's apprehension, it stands as a sort of prophecy of what was ahead.

MacDonald's aging was perhaps the greatest trial he underwent. The moods that had continually beset him through the years, and about which he had poetically remarked, "Such differing moods can scarce to one belong," now came on him with double strength, and his spirit oscillated between the "low," which he felt came from the "mere man," to the "grand," which came from God.[8]

By 1895, periods of mental confusion became more frequent, especially aggravated by traveling, and he feared becoming utterly dependent on his family. At times he felt desolate, haunted with the groundless dread that his loved ones would all leave him. At still other times he felt forsaken by God. But then his mood would shift, and moments of euphoric confidence would come in which he was certain that "what will be well is even now well," and his hope was as vibrant as ever. "My wife and I are somewhat tired now by life, but not tired of it," he told a friend in 1896.[9]

Convinced that the way to strengthen his failing mind was to exercise it, he undertook the writing of yet another story. In 1896, when a request came from the *Glasgow Weekly Mail* for a story for serialization, he drove himself to undertake the task.

Titling it *Salted with Fire,* MacDonald demonstrates that he had not yet lost his narrative powers. Thematically it reworks ideas present in *Lilith:* that God's view of what is significant in human life is quite different from humankind's, that those who live by the wisdom of humankind must come sooner or later to repentance, and that it is through the agonizing of an awakened conscience that one comes to perceive the real. The different forms these themes assume within a realistic story keeps them from being merely repetition, and the fervency with which MacDonald held them invests the story with a measure of strength.

Salted with Fire appeared in the *Glasgow Mail* from January 9 to May 1, 1897, and then was published in America in book form by Dodd, Mead and Company. That Hurst and Blackett in London did not bring it out until 1900 offers evidence that MacDonald's reputation in England had lost its former strength. The ideas and issues with which he was concerned during the last part of his career did not capture the public imagination like the ones he had emphasized earlier, when he had boldly opposed prevalent ideas of the nature of God and popular concepts concerning eternal punishment.

The sense that his popularity was waning in England no doubt saddened him, though he could not but take heart from the continuing sales of his earlier works. During the final decade of the century, no fewer than twenty-seven of his novels and stories appeared in fresh editions, some of them, such as *Annals of a Quiet Neighbourhood,* in more than one. Further, he was now finally relieved of all financial worries. In addition to his royalties, Greville, recently become financially secure, undertook in 1893, as a tribute to his parents, to match his father's income annually, thus doubling it. This gesture of filial love and esteem was, however, not a source of undiluted pleasure to his father. MacDonald, who disdained the accumulation of money, feared that his son had come to pursue wealth for its own sake at the expense of his spiritual welfare, and he and Louisa agonized over the possibility.

Also, Casa Coraggio, its stately Scotch firs in front now quite tall, had begun to yield them less pleasure. The holding of weekly open house, for instance, was becoming increasingly burdensome.

MacDonald sensed that people frequently came from great distances out of curiosity just to see the revered prophet perform. So long as he had felt these occasions were sources of genuine help, he gladly held them, even when he was little inclined. But he was asked with annoying frequency why he did not include something lighter in tone, so that he had continually to respond: "I don't in the least care to amuse people; I only want to help them."[10]

Frivolous attitudes came to annoy him deeply. On one of these occasions, while he was speaking with an earnest visitor in a corner of the room, an influx of chattering people prompted him to confess, "I want to go on talking to you, but I can't stand this." He then left the room, returning only when he had regained his composure. "Bordighera keeps advancing in the loss of its virtues and repose," MacDonald lamented to Greville. "We shall be compelled, I fear, to open our doors only half-way before long."[11]

In addition to his mental discomforts, MacDonald was beset with the agonies of eczema. He had long been annoyed by this affliction of the skin, but in the latter part of this decade the problem increased dramatically, giving him as great physical distress as anything he had suffered. He had always been able to sleep easily, but now the itching rashes and oozing blisters prevented his sleeping. At times he neared complete collapse but doggedly tried to carry on, setting for himself yet more rigorous reading programs.

It was during such physical torments that the family's physician and MacDonald's good friend, Dr. John A. Goodchild, became embroiled in a court trial, accused of having libeled another doctor. Several of the MacDonald family were involved in the case. MacDonald, summoned as a witness, took the stand in behalf of his friend, allowing his fiery Celtic spirit full expression. He defended Goodchild so eloquently that Greville, in recounting the incident, credits his father with being responsible for the case being withdrawn.[12]

In spite of his sufferings MacDonald commanded the energy and the discipline to write yet one more story. A slight work titled *Far Above Rubies,* it is of singular interest because the main character, Hector MacIntosh, is a thinly disguised portrait of MacDonald as a struggling young author. As an aged man MacDonald's memory was dwelling on his past career. In painting Hector he described much of his own nature and many of its tendencies, and thus he indicates how he saw himself when he was younger.

Like his creator, Hector is a twenty-five-year-old poet whose characteristics are thoroughly Celtic. He has "a strong tendency to regard only the ideal, and turn away from authority derived from an inferior source." A dedicated poet, he is preoccupied with writing only verse that embodies the ideal. He loves the Celtic myths, fascinated by their "vaguely showing symbolism," and his mind is constantly "haunted with imaginary forms of loveliness." Further, he has a keen conscience, one "ready to give him warning of the least tendency to overstep any line of prohibition," and he never consciously refuses to heed such warnings. A final comment on Hector's career depicts the aged MacDonald's view of his own:

> Now he has an audience on which he can depend to welcome whatever he writes. That he has enemies as well goes without saying, but they are rather scorners than revilers, and they have not yet caused him to retaliate once by criticizing any work of theirs. Neither, I believe, has he ever failed to recognize what of genuine and good work most of them have produced. One of the best results to himself of his constant endeavor to avoid jealousy is that he is still able to write verse, and continues to take more pleasure in it than in telling his tales. And still his own test of the success of any of his books is the degree to which he enjoyed it himself while writing it.

When MacDonald contemplated his career, he was modestly satisfied. The degree to which officials in the literary establishment disdained his work rankled him, but he found some basis for self-congratulation in the purity of his responses. His awareness of a large audience of appreciative readers gratified him, and his story telling, although it had grown wearisome, had on balance yielded him personal enjoyment.

Not only does the portrait of Hector suggest himself, but Annie, in her self-effacing, buoyant spirit and dedicated encouragement of her husband, suggests Louisa. The title is, of course, an allusion to the description of the ideal wife in the final chapter of the book of Proverbs. The little story appeared in 1898 in the Christmas number of the *Sketch,* and Dodd, Mead later published it as a pocket-sized book.

It was his final effort. Senility rendered him still more emotionally unstable, and he became steadily more taciturn. Occasionally he would break out in a cry of despair or loneliness, saying he feared all would leave him and he would be left alone in a strange house. When such spells occurred, Louisa's playing or Irene's singing a favorite hymn would transform his mood to one of peace and wonder, and his large blue eyes assumed the air of waiting for something to come.

To his often-posed question of whether he was losing his wits, Louisa would patiently comfort him with no, they were only "ben the hoose" (within the house). But, although she was determined to nurse him to the end, she was nevertheless failing physically herself. Long having suffered from an enlarged thyroid, living in Italy had exacerbated her problem so that her breathing was now restricted. She tried to keep her difficulties from her husband, and Irene and Winifred took turns ministering to him. But Winifred was married to her cousin, C. Edward Troup (son of Robert Troup and Margaret MacDonald), on January 2, 1897, and the burden became too great for Irene and her mother.[13]

A specially trained man and woman were engaged to be MacDonald's constant attendants, and he seemed quietly grateful for their ministrations. Even when the suffering from eczema was intense, he tried to write verse, although his scribbling was extremely difficult for anyone to decipher. Some that Greville managed to read show his mind echoing the cry of Isaiah, "O that thou wouldst rend the heavens, that thou wouldst come down" (Isaiah 64:1):

Come through the gloom of clouded skies,
The slow dim rain and fog athwart,
Through East winds keen and wrong and lies,
Come and make strong my hopeless heart.
Come through the sickness and the pain,
The sore unrest that tosses still
The aching dark that hides the gain—
Come and arouse my fainting will.[14]

Then suddenly, after his agonies had become intense in the extreme, he reached a turning point. His eczema, with all its torments, left him, his skin became smooth, and he was again able to sleep peacefully. At the same time he became completely silent, so that for the final five years of his life he made hardly a sound. He may have suffered a stroke, but it was as if he determined to wait patiently in silence until the end came.

In 1899 the children decided their parents needed a permanent home in England in which to spend their summers. Greville financed and Robert planned a retirement home for them on a three-acre plot of land near Haslemere, southwest of London, in Surrey. Named St. George's Wood, it was beautifully situated amid large copper beech trees and a large, well-kept garden. They spent the summer of 1900 there. When the weather permitted, MacDonald was taken for daily drives, dressed in a white serge suit, a red cloak, and a gray felt hat.[15]

The following year, on June 8, the family gathered there to celebrate with him and Louisa their fiftieth wedding anniversary. Throughout the well-wishing of a great many nieces and nephews, together with that of a few old friends still remaining, such as Octavia Hill, MacDonald sat mute but glad, taking care that Louisa was never out of his sight.

Louisa's health, still tolerably good for her age, began to decline rapidly after this occasion. In her final letter to Greville she assured him, "Dear, don't think I am miserable about the dying part of it—that is all right."[16]

When she died on January 13, the following year, the daughters feared to tell their father. When they did, he abandoned himself to weeping.

He remained for three and a half more years, spending most of the time in bed, his two daughters caring for him. Irene became the bride of Cecil Brewer, an architect, on May 25, 1904. Consequently, MacDonald was in Winifred's care at Ashtead, Surrey, when the moment came for which he had so long yearned, on September 18, 1905.

At his privately held funeral the coffin, with his Scottish plaid of the MacDonald tartan draped over one end, was borne by his sons. Kingsbury Jameson had the chief part of the service. Among the mourners was Mr. Alphaeus Smith, who had been a member of the Trinity Congregational Church in Arundel, where MacDonald had held his pastorate over fifty years earlier. The body was cremated at Woking so that the ashes could be returned to Bordighera, to reside in the Stranger's Cemetery by the bodies of Louisa, Grace, and Lily.

Near the end of the century, during that time when MacDonald had known periods of near despair because of his sufferings and his sense of being forsaken by God, Professor Collins, a Christian teacher in Bordighera, had made a special effort to befriend him. He had been greatly influenced by MacDonald's writings in his Christian pilgrimage; now he would in turn try to serve his mentor. Louisa recounted to Winifred how, on one occasion when MacDonald seemed especially depressed in spirit, lying prone and silent on his couch, Collins, who was kneeling beside him, counseled, "It's all right, it's coming all right to you." MacDonald sighed. Collins continued, quoting Christ:[17] "What I do thou knowest not now, but thou shalt know hereafter. It will be all right. You will see it so." MacDonald looked up at him, his whole frame trembled, and he murmured, "And that triumphantly," kissing Collins's hand. The visit concluded with MacDonald placing his hand on Collins's head and silently blessing him.[18]

He was tenacious in his faith to the end. A verse from the book of Job that he quoted near the conclusion of *Lilith* epitomizes his attitude: "All the days of my appointed time will I wait tell my change come."[19]

FORTY-ONE

After a Hundred Years

It is, indeed, blessed to be human beings, with Jesus Christ for the center of humanity.—The Seaboard Parish, Chapter 3

Almost one hundred years have passed since George Mac-Donald's prolific writing career ended. He preferred his "outer life" be forgotten; only truths worth knowing from his "inner life" should endure.[1]

But his outer life is an inspiring story of his struggle to incarnate truth, strengthening our respect for the man and helping us understand his significance to our times. George MacDonald is most important because he achieved such stimulating imaginative presentations of his Christian convictions. He is the forerunner of such later writers of religious fantasy as G. K. Chesterton, Charles Williams, J. R. R. Tolkien, C. S. Lewis, and Madeleine L'Engle. He is a commendable novelist and a significant theologian, but his strongest imaginative talent lies in writing literary fantasies that are mythic, that is, that contain themes, incidents, and characters which seem to answer to the reader's deepest nature and desires, portraying enduring truths of the human spirit. He is the original master in wielding the imaginative power these later writers also possess.

In being an author who wrote such a large and diverse body of imaginative writing—realistic novels, romances, fairy tales, fantasies for adults, and poetry—with the primary purpose of serving his vision of Christian truth, he may justly be viewed as the father of all such contemporary writers. Given the interest of a large read-ing public in such materials, together with the number of contem-porary authors who view imaginative writing primarily as a vehicle to convey Christian concepts, his influence is quite large.

This is not to ignore the literature of such predecessors as John Bunyan and William Blake, writers MacDonald held in high es-teem. But he differs from them in his discovery of the power of symbolism over allegory. "A fairytale is not an allegory," he writes in "The Fantastic Imagination." "There may be allegory in it, but it is not an allegory. He must be an artist indeed who can, in any mode, produce a strict allegory that is not a weariness to the spirit." MacDonald's symbolism is largely impervious to the intel-lectual analysis that allegory demands, possessing rather an open-ended imaginative appeal that defies easy interpretation and yet seems to convey so intensely truths for which the human spirit yearns. "A fairytale, like a butterfly or a bee, helps itself on all sides, sips at every wholesome flower, and spoils not one," he explains. It is "very like the sonata" because its metaphors are "sufficiently loose" and present themselves with "suitable vagueness."

In MacDonald's work, therefore, there is a happy blending of substance of thought with felicity of expression. Christian read-ers tend to venerate him for the former, while many literary schol-ars respect him for the latter. He needs to be saluted for both.

George MacDonald's Christian convictions were hard earned. He continually struggled with a weak constitution, many illnesses, and almost constant poverty. His emotions swung from elation to depression. He was deeply grieved by the deaths of four of his children in young adulthood. Several in the established religious and literary communities of his day scorned him for the gist of his thought. But within this context of struggle and adversity he knew the deep love of a completely dedicated wife, the joy of a large family of loyal, obedient, and highly talented children, the gladness of a large group of dedicated friends, and the assurance that his writings were considered immensely helpful by a very large number of the contemporary laity both in the United Kingdom and in America.

Perhaps the best way to summarize briefly MacDonald's ideas as a Christian thinker is to note the themes in *Lilith*. Central to his thought is his vision of a glorious destiny for mankind. Corollary ideas are his views of the nature of the self, the need for each person's spirit to awaken and grow, the subjective nature of hell, and the centrality of paradox in truth.

Deeply grounded in his study of the Bible, his vision affirms a human destiny grand beyond the power of the imagination to encompass. He enjoyed countering the objection that his expectations for the eternity of mankind were too good to be true by saying they were so good they had to be true. In the concluding chapter of *Lilith*, Vane suggests that his vision must have come from God and not simply from his own mind, for it seems to be true on the deepest level of human desire. People desire beauty to be, and beauty is, because God has given it; since good people desire truth more deeply than they do beauty, can it be that the truth they desire will have no realization? If the dream is from God, God will fulfill it. Vane concludes he is content to wait until in death he comes to see and know.

MacDonald's vision of human destiny, like that of Paul in Ephesians, is that in the fullness of time all things will be united in Christ. He understood this to mean that people will become true and righteous in thought and act. Whatever suffering may be necessary to this end will be experienced.

MacDonald imaginatively makes this point in the experience of both Vane and Lilith. At the beginning of the story Vane is what his name implies: proud and self-assured, and his approach to knowledge is futile. Lilith epitomizes self-centeredness, the central evil of the universe. Immediately after he prematurely enters the Realm of Seven Dimensions, Vane meets Mr. Raven, who seeks to take him to Eve's house to sleep. When Vane refuses, the adventures that follow bring him to see how inaccurate are his sense perceptions, how vain his theorizings, and how futile the activity that springs from his best intentions. Lilith is brought to see herself as God sees her, a moral horror. Both come in the end to accept the sleep that sanctifies.

MacDonald proceeds in *Lilith* to give definitive expression to his doctrine of the self. Selves exist as possibilities in people; each person must nurture the growth of his true, higher self, which is the image of God, the essential fire of Life that, however obscured, is within all persons. The lower selves, which are the various masks people adopt to suit inferior purposes, must be denied. This is accomplished not by self-reform but by willingly accepting sleep in Eve's house, during which the individual becomes spiritually perfected.[2]

The self-centered like Lilith must suffer disintegration in the Evil Wood until at last they come to Mara's house, a symbol of the bitterness of repentance. Lilith's and Vane's experiences provide a paradigm for all lost souls.

The necessity of sleeping suggests the central reality of Christian conversion, that of dying into life. Each genuinely good deed done in this life vaguely foreshadows the dying to self. During the final sleep, the individual dreams, passing through phases of consciousness in which he makes atonement for all offenses and injuries inflicted in life. Once he awakes from sleep, all dying is over; such persons are constantly infused with pure life from God, the Life, and are now able to live with all their "blessed might." They in joy proceed to meet their "father and brother," the Father and the Son, who as immanent and sacrificing Spirits have been covertly working throughout all of life and experience to complete creation by bringing all beings "home." They are, therefore, not overtly present in the main narrative for theological reasons; the moon, however, acts as a symbol for their ministering presence.

The Evil Wood is MacDonald's version of hell, its terrain determined by the consciousness of each individual who travels through it. The seen world, MacDonald observed, is a person's mind turned inside out.[3]

Because the monsters and the horrors of the eternal world are the products of the mind that produces them (seemingly arising from the subconscious of the individual), they are uniquely suited to the spiritual condition of that mind. In the Evil Wood those unwilling to repent and die to their inferior selves must "die many times, die constantly, keep dying deeper, never have done dying." People must live through their various spiritual errors, experiencing all their consequences, until they come to the end of themselves and, broken, accept sleep.

MacDonald's insistence on the paradoxical nature of truth occurs throughout the fantasy. A prime instance is his handling of the biblical statement that woman shall be saved in childbearing.[4] In the Region of Seven Dimensions an ancient prophecy holds that Lilith's child shall be her death, but Mr. Raven affirms that she shall be saved by her childbearing. In the narrative both are true.

His working out the paradox affirms his view of the nature of salvation. In the myth of *Lilith*, which MacDonald drew from the cabala, a system of Jewish mythology, Lilith's pride is kindled when she bears Adam a child, supposing she has created it. In the fantasy MacDonald names the child Lona and makes her primarily responsible for the final defeat of Lilith. Later, in their both succumbing to sleep, they are atoned. Thus, Lilith is both "slain" and saved by her child. Lona, who symbolizes the sacrificial nature of redemptive love, is slain in expressing her love to Lilith, only to awake later in Eve's house to fullness of life. MacDonald's understanding of truth affirmed many such paradoxes. Divine vengeance is the divine love that brings people to the destruction of their false selves that their true selves may emerge.

MacDonald undertook in his final fantasy, therefore, to give mythic expression to the essential Christian convictions he had been expressing throughout his long ministry. He had always opposed the sectarian spirit that pervades Christianity mainly because it detracts attention from central Christian realities: God is Father of all; in Christ he suffers to bring people to himself; divine love, the ultimate power in the universe, is eternal and will not be defeated. Humanity's destiny is to awaken and develop as spiritual beings in righteousness: their true home is in God.

> Many a wrong, and its curing song;
> Many a road, and many an inn;
> Room to roam, but only one home
> For all the world to win.[5]

Endnotes

PREFACE

1. 8 August 1879, The Huntington.
2. Greville MacDonald, *George MacDonald and His Wife* (London: Allen & Unwin, 1924). Hereafter cited as *GMDW*. Joseph Johnson, *George Mac-Donald* (London: Pitman, 1906), is a "tribute of love and respect" written in an idealized tone and containing little that is helpful.
3. Greville MacDonald, *Reminiscences of a Specialist* (London: Allen & Unwin, 1932). Hereafter cited as *ROS*.
4. Michael R. Phillips, *George MacDonald: Scotland's Beloved Storyteller* (Minneapolis: Bethany, 1987); William Raeper, *George MacDonald* (Tring, Herts: Lion, 1987); Elizabeth Saintsbury, *George MacDonald: A Short Life* (Edinburgh: Canongate, 1987); Kathy Triggs, *The Stars and the Stillness* (Cambridge: Lutterworth, 1986).
5. "The George MacDonald Collection," *Yale University Library Gazette*, 51(1976): 74–85. This is an excellent description of the letters in this collection.

INTRODUCTION

1. 23 May 1853, The Beinecke.
2. Much critical material has been written on the nature of literary myth and fantasy. Among the most helpful works are Northrop Frye, *The Secular Scripture: A Study of the Structure of Romance,* (Cambridge, MA: Harvard University Press, 1976); J. R. R. Tolkien, "On Fairy Stories," *The Tolkien Reader* (New York: Ballantine Books, 1966): 3–84; C. N. Manlove, *Modern Fantasy: Five Studies* (Cambridge: Cambridge University Press, 1975); Eric Rabkin, *The Fantastic in Literature* (Princeton, NJ: Princeton University Press, 1976); Roger C. Schlobin, ed., *The Aesthetics of Fantasy Literature and Art* (Notre Dame, IN: The University of Nortre Dame Press, 1982).
3. *Victorian Fantasy* (Bloomington, IN: Indiana University Press), 9.
4. G. K. Chesterton, "Introduction," *GMDW,* 9–15; C. S. Lewis, "Preface," *George MacDonald: An Anthology* (New York: Macmillan, 1948): 10–22; W. H. Auden, "Introduction," *The Visionary Novels of George MacDonald,* Anne Fremantle, ed. (New York: Noonday, n.d.), v–x. For a study of MacDonald's influence on the images of Eliot's later poetry, see Kathryn Walls, "George MacDonald's *Lilith* and the Later Poetry of T. S. Eliot," *English Language Notes* 16 (1978): 47–51.
5. Marion Lochhead, *Renaissance of Wonder: The Fantasy Worlds of J. R. R. Tol-

kien, C. S. Lewis, George MacDonald, E. Nesbit, and Others (San Francisco: Harper & Row, 1977): 1–2.

6. Some small evangelical publishers have discovered a large market for MacDonald's novels and have issued most all of them in retitled, abridged paperback editions. Bethany House Publishers, Minneapolis, with Michael Phillips as their editor, has abridged and reissued the following (The titles they use are in parenthesis): *Alec Forbes of Howglen* (*The Maiden's Bequest,* 1985); *David Elginbrod* (*The Tutor's First Love,* 1984); *Donal Grant* (The Shepherd's Castle, 1983); *Paul Faber, Surgeon* (*The Lady's Confession,* 1986); *Malcolm* (*The Fisherman's Lady,* 1982); *The Marquis of Lossie* (*The Marquis's Secret,* 1982); *Robert Falconer,* (*The Musician's Quest,* 1984); *Sir Gibbie* (*The Baronet's Song,* 1983); *There and Back* (*The Baron's Apprenticeship,* 1986); *Thomas Wingfold, Curate* (*The Curate's Awakening,* 1985); *Warlock O'Glenwarlock* (*The Laird's Inheritance,* 1987); *Weighed and Wanting* (*The Gentlewoman's Choice,* 1987); and *What's Mine's Mine* (*The Highlander's Last Song,* 1986).

   Victor Books, with Dan Hamilton as editor, has brought out abridged editions of *Guild Court* (*The Prodigal Apprentice,* 1986); *Mary Marston* (*The Shopkeeper's Daughter,* 1986); *A Quiet Neighborhood* (1985); *St. George and St. Michael* (1986); *The Seaboard Parish* (1985); and *The Vicar's Daughter* (1985).

   Sunrise Publishers of Eureka, California, has recently issued the following novels in their original, unedited form, as collector's items: *Alec Forbes of Howglen, David Elginbrod, Donal Grant, The Elect Lady, Malcolm, Robert Falconer, Salted with Fire, Sir Gibbie,* and *Thomas Wingfold,* together with editions of MacDonald's sermons and poems. More are forthcoming. Many general trade publishers offer the fairy tales and fantasies in complete editions.

   Johannesen Printing and Publishing of Whitethorn, California, is reproducing all of MacDonald's work in their original forms.

7. George McCrie, *The Religion of our Literature* (London, 1875), and Samuel Law Wilson, *The Theology of Modern Literature* (London, 1899), find him doctrinally unsound. The reviewer of *There and Back* (The *Atheneum* 3313 [25 April 1891]: 532–533), assails MacDonald for his "Miltonic" purpose.

8. See David Holbrook, "George MacDonald and Dreams of the Other World," *Seven: An Anglo-American Literary Review* (1983):4, 27–37; Roderick F. McGillis, "George MacDonald—The *Lilith* Manuscripts," *Scottish Literary Journal* (December 1977): 2, 40–57; Joseph Sigman, "Death's Ecstasies: Transformation and Rebirth in George MacDonald's *Phantastes, English Studies in Canada* (Summer 1976): 2, 203–226; Edmund Cusick, "MacDonald and Jung," *The Gold Thread: Essays on George MacDonald,* William Reaper, ed. (Edinburgh University Press, 1990): 56–86.

9. Rabkin, *The Fantastic in Literature,* 105.

10. MacNeice, *Varieties of Parable* (Cambridge: Cambridge University Press, 1963): 96.
11. Frye, *The Secular Scripture*, 6, 43.
12. Rabkin, 99.
13. George to William Mount-Temple, 13 January 1879, The National Library of Scotland.
14. Instead of speaking of soul and spirit, MacDonald tends to refer to the "self," which is beset by false selves, and the "deeper self," which needs to be awakened in each person and is one with the divine.

CHAPTER 1

1. As an adult George MacDonald kept in one of his desk drawers an assortment of family mementos. Among them was a lock of his mother's hair, a little silver-set seal she gave her husband on the occasion of their wedding, and some remains of her writing, chiefly a letter to her mother-in-law Isobel MacDonald. In the letter she remarks that she had weaned her son George before the customary three months were up, her husband and friends having insisted she do so because of her health (*GMDW*, 32–33). Robert Lee Woolf, who attempts to develop a Freudian interpretation of MacDonald's writings in his *The Golden Key* (New Haven: Yale University Press, 1961), contends that this circumstance (which is not that unusual in itself) left indelible psychological scars on MacDonald. He then dubiously undertakes to analyze his later writings on this assumption.
2. *A Book of Strife, in the form of the diary of an old soul* (London, 1880). Henceforth, *DOS*.
3. 10 May 1849, The Beinecke.
4. *Robert Falconer*, Chapter 10.
5. *Alec Forbes of Howglen*, Chapter 26.
6. Sir C. Edward Troup, "Notes on George MacDonald's Boyhood in Huntly," *The Deeside Field* (n.d.): 62–63.
7. Portsoy, 15 August 1833, The Beinecke.
8. N.d., The Beinecke.
9. 1 August 1834, The Beinecke.
10. 3 June 1853, The Beinecke.
11. *Alec Forbes of Howglen*, Chapter 12.

CHAPTER 2

1. Sir William Robertson, "Dr. George MacDonald," *British Weekly* XXXVIII (21 September 1905), 349–350.
2. *Alec Forbes of Howglen*, Chapter 59.
3. Cosmo Innes, ed., *Fasti Aberdonenses: Selections from the Records of the University and King's College of Aberdeen 1494–1854* (Aberdeen, 1854).
4. 5 January 1841, The Beinecke.

5. Troup, "Notes."
6. October 1841, The Bienecke.
7. Some writers have suggested that MacDonald secured a position sometime during his 1842–1843 term cataloging a library in one of the castles in the north of Scotland. It is true that the area immediately west of Aberdeen boasts some of the most impressive castles in Scotland, and such an undertaking would have been quite appropriate for an Aberdeen scholar. Greville, in his biography of his father, supposes such to have been the case but admits that he was unable to find any records authenticating the story. He resorts to speculating that a scene in the novel *Alec Forbes of Howglen,* in which Cupples refers to being employed in a library in the north of Scotland, is autobiographically significant, but this is pure suppostion and in actuality begs the question. He also assumes MacDonald's father must have had some acquaintance with the proprietor of Thurso Castle, inasmuch as he used his name in advertising flour from his mill (*GMDW,* 73), but this too proves nothing concerning George MacDonald's ever having been there.

Rev. Robert Troup, a fellow student who became acquainted with MacDonald in 1844 and was his lifelong friend, in some handwritten "Notes" on George MacDonald's life, writes: "After his second year, he missed the session of 1842–1843, and spent a year in a nobleman's house in one of the most northern counties of Scotland, partly perhaps in tutorial work, but chiefly I believe in arranging and cataloguing the large library of the mansion. So I have been told, but I do not recollect by whom." That his statement rests by his own admission on hearsay seriously calls into question its validity. Muriel Hutton rightly observes that there is in the Yale collection of letters "nothing to confirm Robert Troup's statement" (p. 75). Further, two pieces of evidence strongly argue against MacDonald's ever having had such an experience. The one is that, when in 1853 he applied for the position of librarian at Owens College, Manchester, he never referred in his credentials to any such cataloging experience. At the time he very much needed the position and would most certainly have listed such experience had he had it. The second item of evidence is that, in discussing in a letter to Helen Powell in 1883 the inspiration for his novel *Castle Warlock,* he confesses that his imagination had been inspired by a drawing of a castle. Then he confides to her that in reality he had seen few castles and states: "Aberdeen, Banff, Cullen, and Huntly are the *only* places I knew when I left [Scotland] at the age of twenty." (24 December, The Beinecke. Italics his.)
8. Troup, "Notes."
9. *Ibid.*
10. 19 August 1865, The Beinecke.

CHAPTER 3

1. *Malcolm,* Chapter 30.
2. Ian Bradley, *The Call to Seriousness* (New York: Macmillan, 1976): 41, 52, 63.
3. *Ibid.,* 177, 182.
4. 8 November 1845, The Beinecke.
5. 10 February 1846, The Beinecke.
6. To his father, 10 February 1846. The Beinecke.
7. To his father, 8 November 1845, The Beinecke.
8. To his father, 13 March 1846, The Beinecke.
9. To his father, 11 April 1847; The Beinecke.
10. 8 November 1845, The Beinecke.
11. To his father, 12 January 1847, The Beinecke.
12. To his father, 12 January 1847, The Beinecke.
13. Undated fragment, The Beinecke.

CHAPTER 4

1. Powell's present marriage to Phoebe Sharman was his second. His first wife, who had died earlier in the century, had borne him five children—one son and four daughters. I am indebted to Freda Levson for compiling a family genealogy.
2. Undated fragment, The Beinecke.
3. 31 May 1849, The Beinecke.
4. N.d., The Beinecke.
5. 12 May 1849, The Beinecke.
6. 28 October 1848, The Beinecke.
7. See Charles Williams, *The Figure of Beatrice* (London, 1943), for a helpful discussion of the nature and extent of this spiritual paradigm.
8. N.d., The Beinecke.

CHAPTER 5

1. For much of the information on Highbury College throughout this chapter, I am indebted to Prof. Michael Nicholls of Spurgeon's College, London, who graciously gave me access to his extensive research into the history of Highbury and New College.
2. N.d., The Beinecke.
3. Arminianism derives from the theology of Jacobus Arminius (1560–1609), a Dutch Reformed theologian who questioned the determinism of Calvinist thought. He insisted that divine sovereignty did not violate the freedom of the human will, that Christ died for all, and that the teaching of predestination was unbiblical.
4. *The Minute Book of the College Committee* for 1848. I am indebted to Mr.

John Creasey, Librarian of Dr. Williams's Library, 14 Gordon Square, London, for his information.

5. N.d., The Beinecke.
6. 15 May 1849, The Beinecke.
7. *The Prelude*, Book Sixth, ll. 111–113.
8. "The Fantastic Imagination," *Dealings with the Fairies* (New York, 1893). The essay was first written for this edition of his often-reprinted fairy tales. It was also added the same year to a fresh edition of *Orts* published by Sampson Low, Marston & Co.
9. 15 May 1849, The Beinecke.
10. 13 October 1849, The Beinecke.
11. To A. J. Scott, *The Poetical Works of George MacDonald in Two Volumes* (London, 1893). vol. I, 271.
12. An entry in *The Minute Book of the College Committee* for 14 December 1849 notes that five pounds were allotted to MacDonald "to cover the expenses of some Lectures on Chemistry, which he is delivering to his brother Students." I am indebted to Mr. John Creasey, librarian, Dr. Williams's library, for this information.
13. 5 October 1849, The Beinecke.
14. F. Hal Broome, "The Scientific Basis for George MacDonald's Dream-Frame," Raeper, *The Gold Thread*, 87–108. Broome's is a thorough and carefully documented study of MacDonald's knowledge of contemporary science.
15. Owen Chadwick, *The Victorian Church: An Ecclesiastical History of England, Part I* (New York: Oxford, 1966): 391, 396.
16. 20 May 1853, The Beinecke.
17. 3 August 1849, The Beinecke.
18. 15 May 1849, The Beinecke.
19. 1 October 1849, The Beinecke.
20. N.d., The Beinecke.
21. 27 April 1850, The Beinecke.

CHAPTER 6

1. 25 July 1849, The Beinecke.
2. 7 August 1849, The Beinecke.
3. 7 August 1849, The Beinecke.
4. 23 February 1850, The Beinecke.
5. 19 March 1850, The Beinecke.
6. 16 April 1850, The Beinecke.
7. 23 April 1850, The Beinecke.
8. The printed *Report of the Committee of Highbury College,* for 1850, read to the Annual Meeting of Subscribers on 18 June 1850, contains the following entry: "Mr George MacDonald, who had graduated at the University

of Aberdeen, and obtained his Master's degree before he entered Highbury, has completed his theological course in this Institution. Though he has not, at present, any pastorate in prospect, the Committee hope he will soon find some suitable sphere of ministerial labour, in which he may be employed with satisfaction to himself and with advantage to the church." I am indebted to Mr. John Creasey, librarian, Dr. Williams's Library, 14 Gordon Square, London, for this research.

CHAPTER 7

1. 17 June 1850, The Beinecke.
2. 17 June 1850, The Beinecke.
3. 19 January 1853, The Beinecke.
4. 23 September 1850, The Beinecke.
5. N.d., The Beinecke.
6. 30 August 1850, The Beinecke.
7. Briggs, 189. The average annual *per capita* income of the total population at that time was approximately forty pounds.
8. 4 October 1850, The Beinecke.
9. 17 December 1850, The Beinecke.
10. 16 October 1850, The Beinecke.

CHAPTER 8

1. 13 January 1851, The Beinecke.
2. *GMDW,* 125, 140.
3. 1 February 1851, The Beinecke.
4. 19 February 1851, The Beinecke.
5. Troup, "Notes."
6. 12 January 1852, The Beinecke.
7. 17 May 1852, The Beinecke.

CHAPTER 9

1. 15 April 1851, The Beinecke.
2. 27 July 1852, The Beinecke.
3. 27 July 1852, The Beinecke.
4. 5 April 1853, The Beinecke.
5. 29 April 1853, The Beinecke.
6. 24 June 1853, The Beinecke.
7. 3 June 1853, The Beinecke.
8. 19 February 1851, The Beinecke.

CHAPTER 10

1. 1 July 1853, The Beinecke.
2. 4 or 5 July 1853, The Beinecke.
3. 4 July 1853, The Beinecke.
4. 20 May 1853, The Beinecke.
5. 4 or 5 July 1853, The Beinecke.
6. 27 June 1853, The Beinecke.
7. 21 December 1850, The Beinecke.
8. 4 August 1853, The Beinecke.
9. 21 March 1853, The Beinecke.

CHAPTER 11

1. 21 December 1853, The Beinecke.
2. 21 December 1853, The Beinecke.
3. N.d., The Beinecke.
4. Chadwick, 400.
5. 23 October 1853, The Beinecke.
6. 6 December 1853, The Beinecke.
7. N.d., The Beinecke.
8. 6 February 1854, The Beinecke.
9. N.d., The Beinecke.
10. 4 May 1854, The Beinecke.
11. N.d., The Beinecke.
12. 26 June 1854, The Beinecke.
13. 17 September 1854, The Beinecke.
14. 21 December 1854, The Beinecke.
15. Chadwick, 545–550.
16. 14 December 1854, The Beinecke.
17. 30 May 1854, The Beinecke.

CHAPTER 12

1. 8 February 1855, The Beinecke.
2. N.d., The Beinecke.
3. N.d., The Beinecke.
4. N.d., The Beinecke.
5. N.d., The Beinecke.
6. 7 July 1855, 783.
7. 27 September 1855, The Beinecke.

CHAPTER 13

1. *DOS,* January 27–28.
2. 2 January 1856, The Beinecke.

3. 2 January 1856, The Beinecke.
4. Alexander Gilchrist, *Life of William Blake* (London, 1863) 1:123. Blake engraved and published his work, but he never printed these poems in the commercial press.
5. "Death's Door," engraving for Robert Blair, *The Grave,* 1808.
6. 8 August 1856, The Trustees of the National Library of Scotland.
7. 16 July 1856, The Huntington Library.

CHAPTER 14

1. March 1856, The Beinecke.
2. 8 November 1856, The Beinecke.
3. 28 November 1856, The Beinecke.
4. "An Invalid's Winter in Algeria," *Good Words for 1864,* 5:795.
5. *Ibid.,* 797.
6. *Ibid.,* 796.
7. 18 March 1857, The Beinecke.

CHAPTER 15

1. 2 January 1858, The Beinecke.
2. 8 September 1857, The Beinecke.
3. N.d., The Beinecke.
4. Ethel Colburn Mayne, *The Life and Letters of Anne Isabella, Lady Noel Byron* (London, 1929): 392. Italics Lady Byron's.
5. N.d., The Beinecke.
6. 12 August 1857. Quoted in *GMDW,* 280–281.
7. To Flora Sing, 11 December 1857, The Beinecke.
8. N.d., The Beinecke.
9. Thomas Carlyle, *German Romances,* 4 vols., 1827; Charles Dickens, *A Christmas Carol,* 1843; William Makepeace Thackeray, *The Rose and the Ring,* 1853; Hans Andersen, *Wonderful Stories for Children,* 1847. See Prickett, *Victorian Fantasy,* on the rising popularity of fantasy during this period, and "Fictions and Metafictions: 'Phantastes,' 'Wilhelm Meister,' and the Idea of the 'Bildungsroman,' Raeper, *The Gold Thread,* 109–125, on the influence of Goethe on *Phantastes.*
10. 2 January 1858, The Beinecke.
11. Reed-Nancarrow, *Remythologizing the Bible,* provocatively discusses the revelatory character of *Phantastes,* especially as regards acts of reading and interpretation. See especially Chapter 3. John Pennington, "*Phantastes* as Metafiction: George MacDonald's Self-Reflexive Myth," *Mythlore,* (Spring 1988) 3, 26–29, discusses the remarkable extent to which *Phantastes* anticipates modern metafictional techniques.
12. Keith Wilson, "The Quest for 'The Truth': A Reading of George MacDonald's *Phantastes,*" *Etudes Anglaises,* (1981): 2, 140–152, points out that

scholars who see Anodos's journey as composed of random and arbitrary events need to acquire a closer familiarity with MacDonald's thought. He discusses *Phantastes* in terms of MacDonald's sermon, "The Truth," from *Unspoken Sermons: Third Series*.

13. *DOS*, 5 April.
14. 18 April 1858, The Beinecke.
15. 17 May 1858, The Huntington Library.
16. 18 April 1858, The Beinecke.
17. 20 May 1858, The Beinecke.
18. 24 August 1858, The Beinecke.

CHAPTER 16

1. *Athenaeum*, No. 1619 (6 November 1858): 580.
2. N.d., The Beinecke.
3. N.d., The Beinecke.
4. *GMDW*, 319–320.
5. See David S. Robb, *George MacDonald* (Edinburgh:Scottish Academic Press, 1987); *God's Fiction* (Eureka, CA: Sunrise Books, 1989).
6. *GMDW*, 313.
7. 4 January 1860, The Beinecke.
8. *Orts*, 281.
9. Henry Crabb Robinson, *Diary* (New York, 1877): 495.
10. Mark Twain, *Autobiography* vol. 2 (New York: Harper, 1959).
11. Derek Hudson, *Lewis Carroll* (London: Constable, 1954): 112–113.
12. *GMDW*, 313.
13. N.d., The Beinecke.
14. N.d., The Beinecke.
15. N.d., The Beinecke.
16. N.d., The Beinecke.
17. N.d., The Beinecke.
18. N.d., The Beinecke.
19. R. B. Shaberman, "George MacDonald and Lewis Carroll, *North Wind: Journal of the George MacDonald Society*, No. 1 (1982): 10–30. Shaberman argues that Carroll was influenced in his Alice books by *Phantastes* and notes many similarities between the fantasy writings of MacDonald and Carroll.

CHAPTER 17

1. N.d., The Beinecke.
2. N.d., The Beinecke.
3. J. M. Bulloch, *Aberdeen University Review* (November 1924): xii, 40–43, presents several versions of this legendary epitaph.
4. N.d., The Beinecke.
5. Robb, *MacDonald*, is fulsome in his praise of MacDonald's ability to repro-

duce Scots speech: "For both the quantity and quality of his Scots prose, MacDonald deserves a secure place in our picture of Scottish fiction. Its excellence is not merely the result of his knowing the words and pronunciations but arises, as is true of all such linguistic mastery, because his mind and personality are inward with the characteristic outlook of the society which used them. . . . His evident, and explicit, love for the Scots tongue is a facet of his feelings for the country which formed him" (p. 37).

6. For a discussion of MacDonald's fictional use of his mother-tongue, see Roderick McGillis, "The Abyss of His Mother-Tongue: Scotch Dialect in Novels by George MacDonald," *Seven: An Anglo-American Literary Review*, No. 2 (1981): 44–56.

7. *GMDW*, 302.

8. Robb, *MacDonald*, 14–15, surmises that MacDonald's interest in spiritism, or "animal magnetism," derived in part from William Gregory, a professor of chemistry at the University of Edinburgh, who had a deep interest in this subject.

9. *David Elginbrod*, Book 3, Chapter 12.

10. *The Scottish Novel: A Critical Survey* (London: John Murray, 1978): 101, 109.

11. 17 January 1863.

12. John Malcolm Bulloch, *A Centennial Bibliography of George MacDonald* (Aberdeen: The University Press; 1925), reprinted in Mary Nance Jordan, *George MacDonald: A Bibliographical Catalog and Record* (privately published for The Marion E. Wade Collection, Wheaton College, Wheaton, IL, in Fairfax, VA, 1984), 16. Mary Jordan's meticulous work is an invaluable tool for anyone interested in MacDonald bibliography. The existence of pirated American editions without dates makes it difficult to give exact numbers. Raphael B. Shaberman, *George MacDonald: A bibliographical study* (London: St. Paul's Bibliographies; 1990) is also a comprehensive and very helpful work.

13. 3 February 1863, The Beinecke.

14. In later editions of *Adela Cathcart* MacDonald deleted these three, publishing them elsewhere, and added others.

15. Bulloch, 10.

16. Edith Lazaros Honig, *Breaking the Angelic Image: Woman Power in Victorian Children's Fantasy* (New York: Greenwood Press, 1988), praises MacDonald's grandmother figure in the fantasies and his creation of women characters in general in the novels. She writes that in the creation of Tangle (in "The Golden Key") MacDonald "resoundingly proclaimed the equality of the sexes . . . with the creation of a truly courageous, nonstereotypical heroine for the first time in a very serious work of fantasy" (p. 92).

17. N.d., The Huntington Library.

18. 29 March 1864, The Huntington Library.

19. Van Akin Burd, *John Ruskin and Rose La Touche: Her Unpublished Diaries of 1861 and 1867* (Oxford: Clarendon Press, 1979): 92.
20. 19 November 1868, The Beinecke.
21. N.d., The Beinecke.

CHAPTER 18

1. N.d., The Huntington Library.
2. Derrick Leon, *Ruskin: The Great Victorian* (London, 1949): 355.
3. N.d., The Beinecke.
4. N.d., The Beinecke.
5. N.d., The Beinecke.
6. N.d., The Beinecke.
7. N.d., The Beinecke.
8. N.d., The Beinecke.
9. N.d., The Beinecke.
10. N.d., The Beinecke.
11. N.d., The Beinecke.
12. N.d., The Beinecke.
13. See, for instance, his references to Carlyle in his essay, "The Imagination: Its Functions and Its Culture," in *Orts*.
14. 14 August 1865, The Beinecke.
15. 18 August 1865, The Beinecke.
16. N.d., The Beinecke.
17. N.d., The Beinecke.
18. 5 November 1865, The National Library of Scotland.
19. N.d., The Beinecke.

CHAPTER 19

1. 21 February 1866, The Beinecke.
2. 1 December 1866, The Beinecke.
3. 13 December 1866, The Beinecke.
4. N.d., The Beinecke.
5. *Athenaeum*, No. 1964, 810.
6. *Athenaeum*, No. 2123 (4 July 1868).
7. *Fortnightly Review*, IV (July 1868): 115–116.
8. *Robert Falconer*, Chapter 10.
9. 9 February 1866, The Huntington.

CHAPTER 20

1. 21 February 1866, The Beinecke.
2. 5 October 1866, The Beinecke.
3. N.d., The Beinecke.

4. 21 July 1865, The Beinecke.
5. *GMDW,* 362*ff; ROS,* the early chapters.
6. 2 April 1867, The Beinecke.
7. 17 April 1868, The Beinecke.
8. ROS, 30.
9. Fagging refers to the long-established practice in British public schools of the younger boys serving the older ones. The shortcomings of the system are exposed in such novels as Thomas Hughes's, *Tom Brown's School Days* (1857) and several of the novels of Dickens.
10. N.d., The Beinecke.
11. *GMDW,* 369–370.
12. N.d., The Beinecke.
13. Roderick F. McGillis, "Language and Secret Knowledge in *At the Back of the North Wind,*" *The Durham University Journal,* LXXIII (June 1981): 191–198. McGillis opposes Colin Manlove's view that MacDonald so separates supernatural episodes from natural ones that "the whole book is the result of two quite separate imaginative acts." (*Modern Fantasy,* 80).
14. *At the Back of the North Wind,* Chapter 37.
15. 30 September 1867, The Beinecke.

CHAPTER 21

1. 22 July 1868, The Beinecke. Gas lighting had been introduced into the London theatre in 1817; electric lighting was widely used by 1868. Tom Driver, *History of the Modern Theatre* (New York: Delacorte Press, 1970), 61–62.
2. *GMDW,* 386.
3. N.d., The Beinecke.
4. *GMDW,* 384.
5. 22 July 1868, The Beinecke.
6. *ROS,* 34–35.
7. 8 December 1868, The Beinecke.
8. Leon, 345.
9. Part III, Chapter 11.
10. 24 June 1868, The Beinecke. This letter offers an example of Greville's rather cavalier handling of the correspondence he quotes in his biography. Occasionally he will simply omit material without giving any indication he has done so, and he will also make alterations. When he quotes this letter (*GMDW,* 381), he omits the entire paragraph: "I also have to regret that I talked conceitedly to you. But you will forgive me, and I shall be cured of it in time." He then takes the liberty to alter his father's "But you will forgive me" to read "But you will forgive us," and adds it to the paragraph to which it does not belong, without using ellipses. Other instances of such alterations could be noted. And, of course, when students of MacDonald's

life quote from Greville in their work, instead of consulting the extant letters themselves, such errors are perpetuated.

11. *GMDW,* 381.
12. To Jelf, 27 March 1868, King's College, London. I am indebted to Michael Page, Archives Assistant at King's, for this information.
13. 18 December 1868, The Beinecke.
14. 11 February 1868, The Beinecke.
15. Anon., "George MacDonald," *Book News,* CXXVII (March 1893): 303–304.
16. N.d., The Beinecke.
17. 13 April 1868, The Beinecke.
18. N.d., The Beinecke.
19. December 1867, The Beinecke.
20. January of 1868, The Beinecke.
21. The correspondence contains his exact schedule: Coatbridge on the 5th, Glasgow the 6th and 7th, Haddington the 8th, Glasgow the 9th, Stirling the 11th, Edinburgh the 12th, Dunfermline the 13th, Portobello the 14th, Edinburgh the 15th, Galashiels the 19th, Alexandria the 20th, Dumbarton the 21st, Helensburgh the 22nd, Dundee the 23, 24, and 25, Montrose the 26th, Breehin the 27th, Perth the 28th, Aberdeen the 29th and Feb. 1, Peterhead the 2nd, Fraserburgh the 3rd, Aberdeen the 4th, and Newcastle the 8th, Huntly the last two days of January.
22. 7 January 1869, The Beinecke.

CHAPTER 22

1. N.d., The Beinecke.
2. 11 June 1869, The Beinecke.
3. N.d., The Beinecke.
4. 22 July 1869, The Beinecke.
5. 22 July 1869, The Beinecke.
6. 22 July 1869, The Beinecke.
7. 22 July 1869, The Beinecke.
8. 8 July 1869, The Beinecke.
9. Bulloch, *Bibliography,* 50.
10. *Wilfrid Cumbermede,* Chapter 59.
11. *Wilfrid Cumbermede,* Chapter 15.
12. See Burd. Greville, in *ROS,* presents helpful material on this affair.
13. 18 September 1870, The Beinecke.

CHAPTER 23

1. J. Knight, Critical Notice, iv (July 1868): 115–116.
2. *Guild Court,* Chapter 31.

3. John Dyer, "The New Novelist," *The Penn Monthly* (June 1870): 221–225.
4. 16 November 1868, The Beinecke.
5. 28 December 1871, The Beinecke.
6. 3 August 1869, The Beinecke.
7. 14 April 1870, The Beinecke.
8. 6 July 1869, The Beinecke.
9. 3 November 1869, The Huntington Library.
10. 3 November 1869, The Huntington Library.
11. The extant copies of the correspondence to R. W. Gilder, contained in the Beinecke Collection, are typed. This may indicate that typed copies of originals were made later, since the other correspondence of this period is in longhand. Nevertheless, MacDonald did come to use a typewriter during his lifetime. The typewriter was being perfected in America at about this time. S. W. Soule, of Milwaukee, Wisconsin, patented the first practical typewriter in 1867; Remington placed a machine on the market in 1874.
12. N.d., The Beinecke. G. K. Chesterton wrote of *The Princess and the Goblin* in 1924: "'Of all the stories I have read, including even all the novels of the same novelist, it remains the most real, the most realistic, in the exact sense of the phrase the most like life" (Introduction, *GMDW,* 9).
13. 27 July 1871, The Beinecke.
14. *George MacDonald* (New York: Twayne, 1972): 81–82. Students of MacDonald have variously identified the grandmother. Roderick McGillis, "'If You Call Me Grandmother, That Will Do,'" *Mythlore* 21 (Summer, 1979): 27–28, lists various interpretations, seeing her as a force reconciling opposites. Nancy Willard, "Goddess in the Belfry," *Parabola* 3 (1981): 90–94, notes possible pagan sources. Lesley Willis, "'Born Again': The Metamorphosis of Irene in George MacDonald's *The Princess and the Goblin,*" *Scottish Literary Journal,* 1 (May 1985): 24–38, sees her as "Jesus, the perfect self in whom all possibility of fulfillment is to be found," and discerns many biblical principles in her behavior. See my *The Harmony Within: The Spiritual Vision of George MacDonald* (Grand Rapids, MI: Eerdmans, 1982; Eureka, CA: Sunrise, 1989): 29–36 for a fuller discussion of how she embodies MacDonald's thought.
15. 15 August 1871, The Beinecke.
16. 30 April 1872, The Beinecke.

CHAPTER 24

1. Robert E. Spiller, *et. al., Literary History of the United States,* third ed., rev., (New York: Macmillan, 1963): 800.
2. 29 January 1872, The Beinecke.
3. 18 June 1869, The Beinecke.
4. 11 September 1872, The Huntington Library.

5. 5 October 1872, The Beinecke.
6. 3 October 1872, The Beinecke.
7. 29 October 1872, The Beinecke.
8. 3 October 1872, The Beinecke.
9. *Lady Byron Vindicated*, 1870. MacDonald's view is presented in his character Lady Bernard in *The Vicar's Daughter.*
10. George MacDonald: His First Appearance in America, *The Boston Journal,* 10 October 1872.
11. *GMDW,* 425.
12. 21 October 1872, The Beinecke.
13. Unidentified newspaper clipping, The Beinecke.
14. 3 November 1872, The Beinecke.
15. 29 October 1872, The Beinecke.

CHAPTER 25

1. Unidentified newspaper clipping, The Beinecke.
2. N.d., The Beinecke.
3. 6 November 1872, The Beinecke.
4. 14 November 1872, The Beinecke.
5. Greville (*GMDW,* 428) speaks of a lecture in Philadelphia during this time, but, as we noted in the prior chapter, it is sufficiently clear from Louisa's letters and the newspaper clippings that the event of which he speaks had taken place on 21 October.
6. 5 December 1872, The Beinecke.
7. N.d., The Beinecke.
8. Tuesday 26 November 1872
9. 22 November 1872
10. 6 December 1872, The Beinecke.
11. Unidentified newspaper clipping. The MacDonald Collection, The Beinecke. *GMDW,* 428–429.
12. 19 December 1872, The Beinecke.
13. 22 December 1872, The Beinecke.
14. 22 December 1872, The Beinecke.
15. 22 December 1872, The Beinecke.
16. *The Newark Morning Register,* 27 December 1872.
17. 26 January 1873, The Beinecke.
18. *GMDW,* 441.
19. 27 January 1873, The Beinecke.
20. 2 February 1873, The Beinecke.
21. 7 February 1873, The Beinecke.
22. "MacDonald," *The Liberal Christian,* 23 November 1872. The same writer described MacDonald's physical appearance: "His forehead, though marked with prominent perceptive organs, retreats a little too swiftly for

the highest intellectual effect. His strong and generous nose is full of character and humanity—of courage and will and benevolence. His mouth is too much hidden by a full mustache and beard to tell its story very plainly, but it suggests rather an Irish than a Scotch humor. He has a full figure, not tending to the least grossness; delicate feet, daintily shod; and exquisitely white hands, tapered and ringed with a signet, of which he makes the most eloquent use. He is evidently a lover of color."

23. 20 March 1873, The Beinecke.
24. 16 February 1873, The Beinecke.

CHAPTER 26

1. 6 March 1873, The Beinecke.
2. 25 March 1873, The Beinecke. In this letter to Mary, Louisa listed their commitments: "Wed. the 26—Homer, N.Y.—the 27, Oswego, N.Y., Friday Buffalo—no lecture till Niagara either Sat. or Sunday. Monday, Hamilton, Canada—Shall like to be in our own dominions—Tuesday April 1st Toronto, Canada. Wednesday Ann Arbor., Mich., Where the Spence's mother lives—Friday, Chicago, Ill. about 900 miles from New York. Decatur Davenport and Milwaukee come in and some other not known, then back to Ann Arbor on Friday 13th April. April 23 Montreal, Sat. April 26 Boston. Last lecture there a matinee. Then to New York and Hurray a few more lectures and the torture of the sea on the 24th May and then my heaven if we get to our Haven."
3. 25 March 1873, The Beinecke.
4. Louisa MacDonald to Bob, note written on dinner menu, 31 March 1873, The Beinecke.
5. 1 April 1873, The Beinecke.
6. 12 April 1873, The Houghton.
7. *GMDW,* 455.
8. 5 April 1873, The Beinecke.
9. 21 April 1873, The Beinecke. "There is a sweet old lady who was my grandfathers first cousin: then she has a daughter who married a Methodist clergyman," Greville explained to Mrs. Cunningham. "It is so delightful to see the old lady and Father together, talking over old people, times and places. There are many things about his family that she is able to tell him which he did not know, and of course she wants to know everything about her relations in the old country."
10. 4 May 1873, The Beinecke.
11. 6 May 1873, The Beinecke.
12. Unidentified newspaper clipping, The Beinecke.
13. *GMDW,* 459.
14. Unidentified newspaper clipping, The Beinecke.
15. Unidentified newspaper clipping, The Beinecke.

CHAPTER 27

1. 13 May 1873, The Beinecke.
2. 22 June 1873, The Huntington Library.
3. *Ibid.*
4. Bulloch, *Bibliography,* 29.
5. Chapter 38. For a defense of MacDonald's using his own speaking voice in his fiction, see Robb, *MacDonald,* 39–41.
6. Bulloch, *Bibliography,* 29, lists an 1871 edition but that obviously is an error, as Jordan observes (p. 73).
7. Toronto, vii (April 1875): 367–368.
8. Letter to "Friends," Christmas Eve 1873, The Huntington Library.
9. 24 September 1873, The Beinecke.
10. Published in 1865, the story had appeared in more than one hundred editions by 1895 and had been translated into six languages.
11. The Scottish poet James Macpherson published in 1762 what he said was a translation of an epic in Gaelic by the ancient poet Ossian. Scholars later demonstrated quite satisfactorily that his work was his own fabrication. Nevertheless, many scholars were taken by its charm, wanting to believe in its authenticity. MacDonald wrote that Tennyson "had never believed Ossian was a reality, but seemed a good deal more ready to believe in him when he had read a few lines, with which he was delighted." (To Helen Powell, 24 March 1875, The Beinecke.) The issue of the poem's historical reality seems not to have been a crucial one to MacDonald, who was quite ready to appreciate the poem's strengths apart from this controversy.
12. 13 August 1874, The Huntington Library.
13. *GMDW,* 46.
14. 17 April 1875, The Beinecke.
15. 21 April 1875, The Beinecke.
16. N.d., The Beinecke.
17. N.d., The Beinecke.
18. Also titled *The Wise Woman* and *The Lost Princess.* Dodd, Mead, and Company of New York paid him one hundred dollars for the rights to publish it.
19. *St. George and St. Michael,* Chapter 17.
20. Saint George is the patron saint of England; hence, he stands for the Royalists. Saint Michael, the archangel, for whom the feast of Michaelmas is held on September 29, is considered to extend special help to individuals in combat, whether in war or in spiritual conflict with the devil or at the hour of death. This emphasis on individuality makes him an apt symbol for the Puritan cause.
21. Bulloch, *Bibliography,* 42.

CHAPTER 28

1. Owned by Lord Mountbatten from 1939 to 1979, Broadlands was opened to the public at the time of his death and may be visited today.

2. They had first met in the early 1860s: "A young tutor in our family lay in a dying state in our house in Curzon Street. Mr. Davies came with a young brother of his own (also in a consumption) and administered the Communion to him, and brought also to the young sick man a fellow countryman, (for he was Scotch) to read 'Saul' to him. It was the blessed George Mac-Donald; and from that time he has been one of our dearest friends and teachers." *Memorials of Lord Mount-Temple* (Printed for Private Circulation, 1890): 106.

3. He was "an ardent advocate of such diverse movements as the introduction of flowers into parks, allotments for labourers, the preservation of commons, the formation of Bands of Mercy, the protection of women and children, the prevention of cruelty to animals, temperance, the admission of women into the medical profession, and of universal education" (Leon, 356–357).

4. Van Akin Burd, *Ruskin, Lady Mount-Temple and the Spiritualists,* (published for the Guild of St. George by Brentham Press, 1982), 6, quotes Cowper's mother as remarking of him: "He runs to Church and runs back. He runs before breakfast and runs after. . . . He is a very sincerely religious man but partly believes in Mahomed, Vishna, Buddha, the Pope, the Patriarch, at least he has a large charity for them all. He loves high, low and Broad Church."

5. Burd, *Spiritualists,* 27, quotes her as saying of herself in 1878: "I have not yet got to be a Christian. I only see it . . . far off . . . & sit myself in darkness."

6. *Memorials,* 107. Burd, *Spiritualists,* gives a carefully documented account of various seances held at Broadlands. Interest in spiritualism was rather widespread during the latter half of the nineteenth century, affecting several literati, such as Elizabeth Barrett Browning, Sir Arthur Conan Doyle, and William Butler Yeats.

7. 30 May 1875, The Beinecke. MacDonald's letter of condolence to Ruskin shows something of how earnestly he tried to minister to his need:

> My very dear Ruskin, I want just to speak a word in your ear. I do not know what it shall be, I only want you to know it is my voice. Do not turn your head to look at me, or stop what you are doing to think a moment about me. Go on. But the Psyche is aloft, and her wings are broad and white, and the world of flowers is under her, and the sea of sunny air is around her, and the empty chrysalis—what of that?
>
> Now we are all but Psyches half awake, who see the uni-

verse in great measure only by reflection from the dull coffin lid over us. But I hope, I hope, I hope infinitely. And ever the longer I live and try to live, and think, and long to live perfectly, I see the scheme of things grow more orderly and more intelligible, and am more and more convinced that all is on the way to be well with a wellness to which there was no other road than just this whereon we are walking.

Let us then call a word now and then through the darkness as we go. There is a great sunrise behind the hill. But that hill Death alone can carry us over. I look to God to satisfy us all. It cannot be but that he will satisfy you to your heart's content. You have fought a better fight, I think, than you yourself know, and his gentleness will make you great in the kingdom of love.

For Rose, is there anything fitting but gladness? The growing weight is gone; the gravestone heaved from off her; the fight with that which was and yet was not herself is over. It may be she haunts you now with ministrations. Any how the living God does. Richter says it is only in God that two souls can meet. I am sure it is true.

My wife's heart is with yours in your loss. She sends her love. If we could do anything for you! Your friend ever, GMD

8. 21 December 1875, The Beinecke. Greville, in quoting this letter (*GMDW,* 472), omits the last sentence, thus leaving the impression that MacDonald was more taken with Mrs. Acworth than what actually was the case. Writers who rely on Greville's accuracy have made the same omission.

9. Burd, *Spiritualists,* asserts Annie Munro believed herself "gifted with second sight" (p. 25).

10. After her father's death MacDonald wrote of Dorothy Drake: As her father's form receded from her, his spirit drew nigh. I mean no phantom out of Hades—no consciousness of local presence: such things may be—I think *sometimes* they are; but I would rather know my friend better through his death, than only be aware of his presence about me; that will one day follow—how much the more precious that the absence will have doubled its revelations, its nearness!" (*Paul Faber, Surgeon,* Chapter 49, italics his).

11. N.d., The Beinecke.

12. MacDonald used this anagram on his bookplate, adding it to Blake's etching titled *Death's Door.* He used it throughout his library.

13. 27 October 1875, The Beinecke.

14. N.d., The Beinecke.

15. In *Thomas Wingfold, Curate* Helen's ponies are named Zephyr and Zoe.

16. 23 April 1877, The Trustees of the National Library of Scotland.

17. 25 April 1876, The Beinecke.

18. The *Athenaeum* (11 November 1876): 622. *The Fortnightly Review*, xxvii (January 1877): 93–96.
19. George McCrie, *The Religion of Our Literature*, 287. See pp. 294–314 for his analysis of *Alec Forbes of Howglen* and *David Elginbrod*.
20. *Cf. The Princess and Curdie* for the most vivid imaginative rendition of this idea.
21. *Thomas Wingfold, Curate*. Chapter 75.
22. *Thomas Wingfold, Curate*. Chapter 83.
23. N.d., The Beinecke.
24. 24 July 1875, The Beinecke.
25. 7 September 1875, The Beinecke.

CHAPTER 29

1. 1 April 1877, The Beinecke.
2. 7 May 1876, The Beinecke.
3. *GMDW*, 470. The text was published by Oxford University Press, 1925, titled *Dramatic Illustrations of Passages from the Second Part of The Pilgrim's Progress by John Bunyan*, Arranged in the year 1877 by Mrs. George MacDonald.
4. These, together with MacDonald's robe, are presently in the possession of Freda Levson of London.
5. "Notes Referring to Family Letters," The Beinecke.
6. 10 December 1876, The Beinecke.
7. *The Marquis of Lossie*, Chapter 42. *Stickit* suggests one who has failed in the ministry.
8. Bulloch, 29.
9. "These Conferences were established by those who felt that, amidst all the Conferences and public meetings for discussion and for public worship, something still was wanting. Each religious community has had its special public worship, some as a development of the worship of the Temple at Jerusalem, some as of the meetings in the Upper Chamber of the Church in the House. . . . But something still was wanting, something akin to the spirit of the meeting on the day of Pentecost, when people were gathered together of one accord, in one place, to seek the outpouring of the Spirit directly on the individual, without the intermediate agency of Ceremonies, or Office-Bearers; a tongue of fire on each head, and these anointed and consecrated individuals making up the unity of the whole. A meeting, not of sectional, but of universal character, all speaking as the Spirit moved them, not of doctrines or of systems, but of the wonderful things of God. In 1874, a few persons were led together on this new basis. It was a meeting not for the promulgation of any new system, nor for the combined execution of any organized plan; it was one of grateful, loving hearts, united through the attraction that drew them all to their common centre, and

through their participation in the same desire to lead a higher and deeper Christian life" (*Memorials*, 116).

10. "When many or most were able to say that they took Christ to be their Saviour, not only from the guilt but from the power and practice of sin, we were led on to see that the Scripture command, 'Be *filled* with the Spirit,' was our immediate privilege, and that Pentecost was but a sample of that dispensation of the Spirit, which was the gift of God to the Church in all generations. As we waited and prayed 'with one accord,' there came upon the company such a sense of the presence and power of God as filled most hearts full, unspeakably full of the realization of the Father, Son, and Holy Spirit. 'The Communion of the Saints' never meant so much to us before. The great truths we had believed and taught were illuminated as with the sun, and many felt the power of the Spirit for service as never before.

"After this, in all the meetings, we were able to fix our minds on Christ Himself, and to dwell on the closer union to which in His love He was calling us; Himself living in these tabernacles a supernatural life, the great heart and head vitalizing and guiding the 'members of his Body.' It was no new teaching, but a new and soul-inspiring, satisfying *realization* of old lessons learned in the head, and now experienced in the life" (*Memorials*, 125, quoting Mrs. Russell Gurney's description of the 1874 Conference).

11. "At several meetings, Dr. George MacDonald seemed to be entrusted for us with special messages, not poetic alone, as his cannot fail to be, but, above all, eminently practical, in for ever pressing upon his hearers the fact that willingness to do the will of the Father leads to knowledge of his doctrine; and as the tender filial communings of his mind with God were revealed, we recognized that we also of the nineteenth century had our George Herbert" (*Memorials*, 130).

12. Greville lists as contributors H.R.H. the Princess Alice of Hesse, the Earl and Countess of Ducie, Lord and Lady Darnley, the Cowper-Temples, the Russell Gurneys, Lord Lawrence, the Charringtons, the Mathesons, the Baroness Paul Ralli, the Miss Hills, Mr. and Mrs. C. Edmund Maurice, and "a host of relatives and other friends, even old servants" (*GMDW*, 506).

13. 1 April 1877, The Trustees of The National Library of Scotland.

14. 2 August 1877, The Beinecke.

CHAPTER 30

1. 17 February 1878, The Trustees of the National Library of Scotland.

2. N.d., The Beinecke.

3. N.d., The Beinecke.

4. N.d., The Beinecke.

5. 14 October 1877, The Beinecke.
6. 5 October 1877, The Beinecke.
7. 14 October 1877, The Beinecke.
8. 31 October 1877, The Beinecke.
9. N.d., The Beinecke.
10. N.d., The Beinecke.
11. 29 October 1877, The Beinecke.
12. MacDonald had been introduced to Princess Alice, "whom he found very simple and charming," a year earlier at Buckingham Palace by Dean Stanley of Westminster (*GMDW*, 479).
13. 4 November 1877, The Beinecke.
14. 31 October 1877, The Beinecke.
15. To Cowper-Temple, n.d., The Trustees of the National Library of Scotland.

CHAPTER 31

1. 6 January 1878, The Trustess of the National Library of Scotland.
2. *Ibid.*
3. 7 April 1878, The Trustees of the National Library of Scotland.
4. *GMDW*, 485.
5. Leon, 441, 511–514.
6. 17 February 1878, The Trustees of the National Library of Scotland.
7. *GMDW*, 487.
8. *Paul Faber, Surgeon,* Chapter 54, italics his.
9. 13 January 1879, The Trustees of the National Library of Scotland.
10. The MacDonalds' good friend, Sir Edward Burne-Jones, was a designer of tapestry and stained glass for Morris's firm, which produced furniture (the Morris chair), wallpaper, and printed textiles as well, for the uplifting of public taste. Morris was motivated by the Christian Socialist movement and the teachings of John Ruskin.
11. Greatly expanded in the twentieth century, it became a resort hotel named Hotel Splendido. Today it stands as one of the most elegant of the resort hotels in the area.
12. Professor Giorgio Spina of the 'Universita' di Genova Istituto di Lingue e Letterature Straniere, wrote in answer to my query: "The Florentine young lady was named Verita (Truth) according to the historical climate. In fact, during and after the Italian Risorgimento, families were accustomed—especially in Tuscany—to christen their sons and daughters Verita (Truth), Liberta (Freedom), Libero (Free), and so on."
13. 6 January 1878, The Trustees of the National Library of Scotland.
14. He found Tischendorf's various editions of the Greek New Testament, published between 1841 and 1869, very helpful, and was intensely interested in the significance of Tischendorf's recent discovery of the Codex

Sinaiticus, a manuscript of the Greek New Testament dating back to the fourth century. MacDonald referred to it simply as the "Sinaitic."

15. N.d., The Beinecke.
16. *Paul Faber, Surgeon, Cf.* chapter 35.
17. 7 April 1878, The Trustees of the National Library of Scotland.
18. 7 February 1879, The Beinecke.
19. Introduction, Everyman's Library Edition by Dent, 1914, as quoted by Bulloch, *Bibliography,* 43.
20. *Sir Gibbie,* Chapter 24.
21. *Sir Gibbie,* Chapter 31.
22. 21 December 1878: 801.
23. *Anthenaeum,* (June 1879): 755–756.
24. *British Quarterly Review; Paul Faber, Surgeon,* lxix (January 1879): 237; *Sir Gibbie,* lxx (October 1879): 535–536.

CHAPTER 32

1. *GMDW,* 489. This may have been a sign of his having tuberculosis, but it was unrecognized as such.
2. 21 August 1879, The Houghton.
3. 7 February 1879, The Beinecke.
4. 21 August 1879, The Houghton.
5. *GMDW,* 505.
6. To Georgina Cowper-Temple, 26 January 1880. The Trustees of the National Library of Scotland.
7. 6 May 1898, The Beinecke.
8. Bulloch, *Bibliography,* 13.
9. 26 January 1880, The Trustees of the National Library of Scotland.
10. *DOS,* 27 October.
11. *Mary Marston,* Chapter 54.
12. *Mary Marston,* Chapter 5.
13. *Thomas Wingfold, Curate,* Chapter 8.
14. The original title, under which it was published by Harper's in New York and Lothrop in Boston in 1881. The London edition, published in 1882 by Sampson Low, Marston, Searle and Rivington, was titled *Castle Warlock.* Confusion between the two titles has persisted. See Bulloch, *Bibliography,* 15.
15. *Warlock O' Glenwarlock,* Chapter 45.
16. *Warlock O' Glenwarlock,* Chapter 8.
17. He probably meant Tilguhillie.
18. Robert would soon become an apprentice with I. I. Stevenson, a London architect.
19. 24 December 1883, The Beinecke.
20. Joseph Johnson, *George MacDonald* (London:Pitman,1906): 239.

CHAPTER 33

1. *Weighed and Wanting,* Chapter 31.
2. *GMDW,* 506.
3. Ronald entered Trinity College, Oxford, in 1882, and Robert became apprentice in the firm of architect I. I. Stevenson in London the same fall.
4. *DOS* 27–29 November.
5. 17 August 1879, The Beinecke.
6. 9 January 1881, The Beinecke.
7. *Weighed and Wanting,* Chapter 35.
8. *Lilith,* Chapter 29.
9. Manlove, *Modern Fantasy,* depicting MacDonald's thought, summarizes: "It is a case of 'You may as well come quietly'" (p. 62).
10. Bulloch, *Bibliography,* 31–32, lists the various sources of the reprints. After adopting the title, which commonly means "worthless scraps of food," MacDonald had second thoughts concerning its aptness and appended a small preface in which he explained that he meant to convey, not the idea that he felt his work was worthless, for indeed it had cost him considerable thought and labor, but rather that the essays were "but fragmentary presentments of larger meditation." The choice of title was no doubt prompted by an initial humility, which, he later saw, was open to misinterpretation.
11. It had appeared serially in *Good Things,* January–June, 1877.
12. Woolf, *The Golden Key,* sees a "choking, pessimistic gloom" in the story's conclusion, commenting that MacDonald "wrote like a man in despair . . . angry with an anger he felt to be futile" (pp. 178–179). But the triumph of evil is momentary; evil people are sent to the "animal country" where they are "ruled with a rod of iron" until they "learn what freedom is, and love and seek it" (Chapter 34).
13. *The Princess and Curdie,* Chapter 7. Such passages as Psalms 18:24–26 and 50:16–21 define the biblical principle MacDonald is depicting.

CHAPTER 34

1. Today, remodeled with a fifth story and terraces added, it is a modern apartment complex containing nearly forty units.
2. *GMDW,* 501. Greville appears to be incorrect in giving the date of their being "adopted" into the family as 1881. Family correspondence indicates it was 1880.
3. *GMDW,* 510. The listing that Greville gives of the separate scenes, as though they were given by Lily as a part of a letter that she wrote to Jane Cobden Unwin (9 January 1881), do not in fact appear in that letter, which is now contained in The Beinecke Collection. This is another example of Greville's altering letters without indicating he is doing so, presumably in

accordance with his own recollections. He was generally with the family for Christmases, and this practice became a tradition with them. Georgina Cowper-Temple records: "On Christmas Eve [1883], we were dining in our little room looking on the olive wood, and we heard the sound of many voices, and looking out, lamps glimmered among the trees, and figures carrying lanterns and sheets of music. Who should they be but the dear MacDonald family visiting the houses of all the invalids in the place, to sing them carols and bring them the glad tidings of Christmas. The next day they had the most beautiful tableaux ever seen of the Annunciation, the stable, the Angels, and the Shepherds, ending up with the San Sisto, in their wonderful room in the Coraggio, and had invited the peasants to come and enjoy this, for them, novel representation of the event of the blessed Christmastide. That house, Coraggio, is the very heart of Bordighera, the rich core of it, always raying out to all around, and gathering them to itself" (*Memorials*, 83–84).

4. Anonymous, "George MacDonald at Bordighera," *The Critic and Good Literature*, V (2 February 1884): 54–55. From *The London World*.

5. 14 January 1882, The Beinecke.

6. 14 January 1882, The Beinecke.

7. *Donal Grant*, Chapter 29.

8. *Donal Grant*, Chapter 42.

9. 13 October 1877, The Beinecke.

10. *Athenaeum*, (29 April 1882): 537.

11. *Donal Grant*, Chapter 1.

12. *Athenaeum*, (29 April 1882): 537.

CHAPTER 35

1. *Memorials*, 83.

2. 13 January 1883, The Beinecke.

3. 24 December 1883, The Beinecke.

4. James Linton Bogle, *The Meanderings of a Medico* (Printed for Private Circulation, 1928): 138–139. Bogle moved into Casa Grazia in 1901. Speaking of Grace Jameson, he remarks: "Her father, George Macdonald, poet, novelist and divine, lived in Casa Coraggio, a house a few doors away, and it was he that made Bordighera such an attractive place to so many English visitors."

5. 8 May 1884, The Beinecke.

6. Georgina Mount-Temple wrote concerning Grace's death: "They all acted on their principle, '*we deny dying*' they did not murmur or allow themselves to think it a sad event, but tried and contrived to be glad for her. Dolly wrote to me that 'she never knew people so act up to their theories' " (*Memorials*, 85).

7. 30 July 1884, The Beinecke.

8. N.d., The Beinecke.
9. 20 August 1884, The Beinecke.
10. N.d., The Beinecke.
11. 7 September 1884, The Beinecke.
12. N.d., The Beinecke.
13. Last Sunday of 1884, The Beinecke.
14. Preface to *Letters from Hell* (Anon.): vi, vii. italics his.
15. *Unspoken Sermon, Second Series,* "What Jesus did, was what the Father is always doing; the suffering he endured was that of the Father from the foundation of the world, reaching its climax in the person of his Son. God provides the sacrifice; the sacrifice is himself. He is always and has ever been, sacrificing himself to and for his creatures. It lies in the very essence of his creation of them. The worst heresy, next to that of dividing religion and righteousness, is to divide the Father from the Son—in thought or feeling or action or intent; to represent the Son as doing that which the Father does not himself do" (pp. 142–143).
16. *Unspoken Sermon, Second Series,* 226.
17. "It was a human and not a devilish pride. I would not be misunderstood as defending pride, or even excusing it in any shape; it is a thing that must be got rid of at all costs; but even for evil we must speak the truth; and the pride of a good man, evil as it is, and in him more evil than in an evil man, yet cannot be in itself such a bad thing as the pride of a bad man" (chapter 5).
18. *What's Mine's Mine,* Chapter 30.
19. *Donal Grant,* Chapter 1.
20. Chapter 9.
21. *The Tragedie of Hamlet—with a study of the text of the folio of 1623,* 124.
22. *Donal Grant,* 277.

CHAPTER 36

1. *The Marquis of Lossie,* Chapter 43
2. Christmas Day, The Beinecke.
3. 30 September 1888, The Trustees of the National Library of Scotland.
4. 4 November 1886, The Houghton.
5. A dried garden.
6. 31 January 1886, The Beinecke.
7. When he had been in Manchester, MacDonald apparently helped edit and publish a collection of hymns, described as "songs suitable for children to express their worship and . . . for elder Christians to give mature expression to their faith." Hymns and Sacred Songs for Sunday Schools and Social Worship, ed., G. B. Bubier (Fletcher and Tubbs, 1855). Succeeding editions appeared in 1856 and 1866. The catalogue entry in The British Library reads: "In fact edited by G. B. Bubier, G. MacDonald, and the

latter's brother." MacDonald also wrote a series of articles, "Luther the Singer," *Sunday Magazine* (December 1866 through September 1867), in which he translated a large number of Luther's hymns and discussed Luther's faith and poetic abilities.

8. Alas, how easily things go wrong!
A sigh too much, or a kiss too long,
And there follows a mist and a weeping rain,
And life is never the same again.

Alas, how hardly things go right!
'Tis hard to watch in a summer night,
For the sigh will come, and the kiss will stay,
And the summer night is a winter day. (*Phantastes*, Chapter 19)

9. *ROS*, 221.
10. 5 March 1888, The Beinecke.
11. 4 October 1889, The Beinecke.

CHAPTER 37

1. *GMDW*, 515.
2. *GMDW*, 515.
3. 12 April 1887, The Beinecke.
4. See, for instance, McGillis, "The *Lilith* Manuscripts," 56.
5. No doubt he had in mind Hebrews 12:25–29, in which the writer affirms that God will shake heaven and earth in order that only unshakeable realities may remain. The idea is developed from one found in Haggai 2:6–7.

CHAPTER 38

1. "Bernard leaves us tonight," Lily wrote to her Aunt Charlotte in January 1888, "so Linda is rather solemn. They have been engaged for four years now, and are almost like married people in their ways to each other. They are perfectly suited to each other, and we get fonder and fonder of Linda" (The Beinecke).
2. Upon graduation, MacKay entered Christ's College as a medical student.
3. "George MacDonald: A Personal Memoir," *From a Northern Window* (London, 1911), pp. 66–67.
4. April, 1887, The Beinecke.
5. The plot of *There and Back* shows MacDonald had considerable knowledge of the craft of bookbinding. There is some slight evidence that he did some bookbinding on the side, as a sort of hobby. He could well have learned the craft earlier from his father-in-law, who had it as a hobby. In 1889, in writing to Charlotte, he told Godwin that he had arranged the gospels "exactly in the chronological order he [Godwin] has given the story of our

Lord; that is, I have cut out two copies of the Greek and pasted them on paper, and am now binding the sheets, that I may be able to use the book constantly for study and comparison of gospels" (15 Jan.; The Beinecke). But earlier the Cowper-Temples had had a similar project in the Greek text bound for him. Given the demands of his writing and lecturing schedule, he would have had little time to spend developing a hobby.

6. 25 April 1891: 532.
7. To Louisa, 23 Oct. 90; The Beinecke.
8. To Louisa, 19 May 90; The Beinecke.
9. "George MacDonald as Poet," CXLIX: 361–370.
10. To Louisa, 5 Nov. 90; The Beinecke.
11. 13 October 91; The Beinecke.
12. To Louisa, n.d.; The Beinecke.
13. "In Memory of Major Robert Gregory."
14. Aberdeen: John Rae Smith, 1893.
15. To Louisa, 13 July 1891, The Beinecke.
16. To Louisa, 27 May 91; The Beinecke.
17. 31 October 91; The Beinecke.
18. N.d.; The Beinecke.
19. *GMDW,* 526.

CHAPTER 39

1. 18 October 1891, The Beinecke.
2. McGillis, "The Lilith Manuscripts," undertakes a comparative study.
3. 14 June 1893, The Beinecke.
4. 13 January 1895, The Beinecke.
5. 28 December 1894, The Trustees of the National Library of Scotland.
6. GMDW, p. 548.
7. The Impulse of Fantasy Literature (Kent, Ohio: The Kent State University Press, 1983): 75. Manlove offers a comparison of the fantasy elements of each. See also Reed-Nancarrow, *Remythologizing.*
8. In Lilith A the dimensions are four; they become seven in Lilith B. For a discussion of this idea, see my The Harmony Within, pp. 86–88. Reed-Nancarrow, *Remythologizing,* presents the view that the world of *Phantastes* is "our own world, truly and imaginatively perceived," whereas the world of *Lilith* is "a world beyond our ordinarily parochial experience, which allows us to place that experience in a universal context" (p. 148).
9. MacDonald clarified his view of the nature of the inspiration of Scripture in his sermon, "The Knowing of the Son": "When the disciples became, by the divine presence in their hearts, capable of understanding the Lord, they remembered things he had said which they had forgotten; possibly the very words in which he said them returned to their memories; but must we believe the evangelists always precisely recorded his words? The

little differences between their records is answer enough. The gospel of John is the outcome of years and years of remembering, recalling, and pondering the words of the Master, one thing understood recalling another. We cannot tell of how much the memory, in best condition—that is, with God in the man—may not be capable; but I do not believe that John would have always given us the very words of the Lord, even if, as I do not think he did, he had spoken them in Greek. God has not cared that we should anywhere have assurance of his very words; and that not merely, perhaps, because of the tendency in his children to word-worship, false logic, and corruption of the truth, but because he would not have them oppressed by words, seeing that words, being human, therefore but partially capable, could not absolutely contain or express what the Lord meant, and that even he must depend for being understood upon the spirit of his disciple. Seeing it could not give life, the letter should not be throned with power to kill; it should be but the handmaid to open the door of the truth to the mind that was of the truth. *Unspoken Sermons, Series Three;* pp. 26–27.

10. GMDW, p. 548.
11. "Lilith Manuscripts," 56.
12. *Athenaeum,* Vol. 106 (9 Nov. 1895), p. 639.
13. *The Critic,* Vol. 28 (25 Jan. 1896), p. 58. Roderick F. McGillis, "George MacDonald and the *Lilith* Legend in XIXth Century," *Mythlore,* 6 (Winter 1979): 3–11, gives an account of the history of this legend. Jeanne Murray Walker, "The Demoness and the Grail: Deciphering MacDonald's Lilith," in Robert A. Collins and Howard D. Pearce, eds., *The Scope of the Fantastic—Culture, Biography, Themes, Children's Literature* (Westport, CT: Greenwood Press, 1985): 179–190, discusses how MacDonald blends the *Lilith* myth with the form of the grail quest.
14. *The Bookman,* Vol. 2 (Oct. 1895), pp. 133–35.
15. Dated September 24, 1895. *ROS,* 323.

CHAPTER 40

1. 16 April 1892, The Beinecke.
2. To Helen, 16 April 1892. Ronald remarried, on 6 June 1904. His bride was Mary St. Johnston, a widow.
3. Bulloch, *Bibliography,* 34.
4. *Ibid.,* 25.
5. 13 October 1891, The Beinecke.
6. *Heather and Snow,* Chapter 37.
7. 4 March 1894, The Beinecke.
8. *DOS,* September 3, 4.
9. *GMDW,* 539.
10. Frances M. Brookfield, "George MacDonald at Bordighera," *Sunday Magazine* (London), XXXIV (April 1905): 401–405.

11. *ROS*, 312.
12. *GMDW*, 557–558.
13. MacKay also married Blanche Bird that year, on 10 November.
14. *GMDW*, 559.
15. *GMDW*, 560.
16. *ROS*, 357.
17. John 13:7.
18. N. d., The Beinecke.
19. Job 14:14.

CHAPTER 41

1. MacDonald to James T. Fields, 8 August 1879, The Huntington Library.
2. For the sleep metaphor, see Ephesians 5:14 and Isaiah 26:19.
3. "The Imagination: Its Functions and Its Culture," Orts, (London, 1882): 5.
4. *Lilith*, Chapter 30.
5. 1 Timothy 2:15.
6. *Phantastes*, Chapter 22.

Bibliography

Anderson, Hans. *Wonderful Stories for Children*. 1847.

Bogle, James Linton. *The Meanderings of a Medico*. Printed for Private Circulation, 1928.

Bradley, Ian. *The Call to Seriousness*. New York: Macmillan, 1976.

Briggs, Asa. *A Social History of England*. New York: The Viking Press, 1983.

Brookfield, Frances M. "George MacDonald at Bordighera." *Sunday Magazine*. (London) 34 (April 1905): 401–405.

Bubier, G. B. *Hymns and Sacred Songs for Sunday Schools and Social Worship*. London, 1855.

Bulloch, J. M. *Aberdeen University Review* 12 (November 1924): 40–43.

————. *A Centennial Bibliography of George MacDonald*. Aberdeen: Aberdeen UP, 1925.

Burd, Van Akin. *John Ruskin and Rose La Touche: Her Unpublished Diaries of 1861 and 1867*. Oxford: Clarendon Press, 1979.

————. *Ruskin, Lady Mount-Temple and the Spritualists*. Published for the Guild of St. George by Brentham Press, 1982.

Carlyle, Thomas. *German Romances*. 4 vols. London, 1827.

Chadwick, Owen. *The Victorian Church: An Ecclesiastical History of England*. London: Black, 1972.

Driver, Tom. *History of the Modern Theatre*. New York: Delacorte Press, 1970.

Dyer, John. "The New Novelist." *The Penn Monthly* (June 1870): 221–225.

Freemantle, Anne, ed. *The Visionary Novels of George MacDonald*. New York: Noonday, n.d.

Frye, Northrop. *The Secular Scripture: A Study of the Structure of Romance*. Cambridge, MA: Harvard UP, 1976.

Geddes, William. "George MacDonald as Poet." *Blackwood's Magazine* 149 (March 1891): 361–370.

"George MacDonald." *Book News*. 127 (March 1893): 303–304.

"Rev. George MacDonald." The Montreal *Daily Witness* 29 April 1873. Four o'clock edition.

"George MacDonald at Bordighera." *The Critic and Good Literature*. 2 (February 1884): 54—55. From *The London World*.

"George MacDonald: The English Novelist at the Tabernacle." *The American Standard* (Jersey City, NJ): 26 November 1872.

"Rev. George MacDonald's Lecture on Hood." The Montreal *Daily Witness* 30 April 1873. Four o'clock edition.

Gilchrist, Alexander. *Life of William Blake*. 2 vols. London, 1863.

Gill, Stephen, ed. *The Oxford Authors: William Wordsworth*. Oxford: Oxford UP, 1984.

Hart, Francis Russell. *The Scottish Novel: A Critical Survey*. London: John Murray, 1978.

Hein, Rolland. *The Harmony Within: The Spiritual Vision of George MacDonald*. 1982. Eureka, CA: Sunrise, 1989.

Holbrook, David. "George MacDonald and Dreams of the Other World." *Seven: An Anglo-American Literary Review* 4 (1983): 27–37.

Honig, Edith Lazaros. *Breaking the Angelic Image: Woman Power in Victorian Children's Fantasy*. New York: Greenwood, 1988.

Hudson, Derek. *Lewis Carroll*. London: Constable, 1954.

Hughes, Thomas. *Tom Brown's School Days*. London, 1857.

Hutton, Muriel. "The George MacDonald Collection." *Yale University Library*. 51 (1976): 74–85.

Innes, Cosmo, ed. *Fasti Aberdonenses: Selections from the Records of the University and King's College of Aberdeen 1494–1854*. Aberdeen, 1854.

Johnson, Joseph. *George MacDonald*. London: Pitman, 1906.

Jordan, Mary Nance. *George MacDonald: A Bibliographical Catalog and Record*. Privately published for the Marion E. Wade Collection, Wheaton College, Wheaton, IL, in Fairfax, VA, 1984.

Knight, J. "Critical Notice." Rev. of *Robert Falconer* by George MacDonald. The Fortnightly Review 4 (July 1868): 115–116.

Lang, A. "Three New Novels." *The Fortnightly Review* 27 (January 1877): 93–96.

Leon, Derrick. *Ruskin: The Great Victorian*. London: Routledge, 1949.

Letters from Hell. 1884. London: Macmillan, 1911.

Lewis, C. S. *George MacDonald: An Anthology*. New York: Macmillan, 1948.

Review of *Lilith*. *The Critic* 28 (25 January 1896): 58.

Lochhead, Marion. *Renaissance of Wonder: The Fantasy Worlds of J. R. R. Tolkien, C. S. Lewis, George MacDonald, E. Nesbit, and Others*. San Francisco: Harper & Row, 1977.

"*Malcolm*. A Romance. By George MacDonald." *The Canadian Monthly* 7 (April 1875): 367–368.

Mayne, Ethel Colburn. *The Life and Letters of Anne Isabella, Lady Noel Byron*. London: Constable, 1929.

McCrie, George. *The Religion of our Literature*. London, 1875.

MacDonald, Greville. *George MacDonald and his Wife*. London: Allen & Unwin, 1924.

_____. *Reminiscences of a Specialist*. London: Allen & Unwin, 1932.

"MacDonald." *The Liberal Christian* 23 November 1872.

"MacDonald on Burns." *Newark Morning Register* 27 December 1872.

MacDonald, Ronald. "George MacDonald: A Personal Memoir." *From a Northern Window*. 1911. Eureka, CA: Sunrise, 1989.

McGillis, Roderick F. "The Abyss of His Mother-Tongue: Scotch Dialect in Novels by George MacDonald." *Seven: An Anglo-American Literary Review* 2 (1981): 44–56.

_____. " 'If You Call Me Grandmother, That Will Do.' " *Mythlore* 6 (Summer, 1979): 21ff.

_____. "George MacDonald and the Lilith Legend in XIXth Century." *Mythlore* 6 (Winter 1979): 3–11.

_____. "George MacDonald—The *Lilith* Manuscripts." *Scottish Literary Journal* 4 (Dec. 1977): 40–57.

_____. "Language and Secret Knowledge in *At the Back of the North Wind*. *The Durham University Journal* 73 (June 1981): 191–198.

MacNeice, Louis. *Varieties of Parable*. Cambridge: Cambridge UP, 1963.

Manlove, C[olin]. N. *Modern Fantasy: Five Studies*. Cambridge: Cambridge UP, 1975.

_____. *The Impulse of Fantasy Literature*. Kent, Ohio: Kent UP, 1983.

_____. "The Circle of the Imagination: George MacDonald's *Phantastes* and *Lilith*." *Studies in Scottish Literature* 17 (1982): 55–80.

Memorials of Lord Mount-Temple. Printed for Private Circulation, 1890.

Mendelson, Michael. "George MacDonald's *Lilith* and the Conventions of Ascent." *Studies in Scottish Literature* 20 (1985): 197–218.

The Minute Book of the College Committee for 1848 and 1849. Dr. William's Library, London.

"New Novels." Review of *Alec Forbes of Howglen* by George MacDonald. The *Athenaeum* (17 June 1865): 810.

"New Novels." Review of *Robert Falconer* by George MacDonald. The *Athenaeum* (4 July 1868): 12.

"New Novels." Review of *Thomas Wingfold*. The *Athenaeum* (11 November 1876): 622.

Nicholls, Michael. Unpublished Notes on the History of Highbury and New College.

"Novels of the Quarter." Review of *Paul Faber, Surgeon. The British Quarterly Review* 69 (January 1879): 237.

"Novels of the Quarter." Review of *Sir Gibbie. The British Quarterly Review* 70 (October 1879): 535–536.

"Novels of the Week." Review of *Gifts of the Child Christ, and other Tales.* The *Athenaeum* (29 April 1982): 537.

"Novels of the Week." Review of *Lilith.* The *Athenaeum* (9 November 1895): 639.

"Novels of the Week." Review of *Paul Faber.* The *Athenaeum* (21 December 1878): 801.

"Novels of the Week." Review of *Sir Gibbie.* The *Athenaeum* (14 June 1879): 755–756.

"Novels of the Week." Review of *There and Back.* The *Athenaeum* 3313 (25 April 1891): 532–533.

Pennington, John. "*Phantastes* as Metafiction: George MacDonald's Self-Reflexive Myth." *Mythlore 3* (Spring 1988): 26–29.

Phillips, Michael R. *George MacDonald: Scotland's Beloved Storyteller.* Minneapolis: Bethany, 1987.

Plumb, J. H., *et. al. The English Heritage.* St. Louis, MO: The Forum Press, 1978.

Prickett, Stephen. *Victorian Fantasy.* Bloomington, IN: Indiana UP, 1979.

Rabkin, Eric. *The Fantastic in Literature.* Princeton, NJ: Princeton UP, 1976.

Raeper, William. *George MacDonald.* Tring, Herts: Lion, 1987.

———, ed. *The Gold Thread: Essays on George MacDonald.* Edinburgh University Press, 1990.

Reed-Nancarrow, Paula Elizabeth. "Remythologizing the Bible: Fantasy and the Revelatory Hermeneutic of George MacDonald." Dissertation Univ. of Minnesota, 1988.

"Report of the Committee of Highbury College for 1850." Dr. William's Library, London.

Ries, Richard. *George MacDonald.* 1972. Eureka, CA: Sunrise, 1989.

Robb, David. *George MacDonald.* 1987. Eureka, CA: Sunrise, 1989.

"Robert Burns: Mr. George MacDonald's Lecture on the Scottish Poet." *Cincinnati Enquirer* 7 February 1873.

Robertson, Sir William. "Dr. George MacDonald." *British Weekly.* XXXVIII (21 September 1905): 349–350.

Shaberman, Raphael B. *George MacDonald: A bibliographical study.* London: St. Paul's Bibliographies, 1990.

_____. "George MacDonald and Lewis Carroll." *North Wind: Journal of the George MacDonald Society,* 1 (1982): 10–30.

Sigman, Joseph. "Death's Ecstasies: Transformation and Rebirth in George MacDonald's *Phantastes.*" *English Studies in Canada.* 2 (Summer 1976): 203–226.

Saintsbury, Elizabeth. *George MacDonald: A Short Life.* Edinburgh: Cannongate, 1987.

Spiller, Robert E., *et. al. Literary History of the United States.* 3rd rev. ed. New York: Macmillan, 1963.

Stowe, Harriet Beecher. *Lady Byron Vindicated.* 1870.

Thackeray, William Makepeace. *The Rose and the Ring.* London, 1853.

Tolkien, J. R. R. "On Fairy Stories." *The Tolkien Reader.* New York: Ballantine Books, 1966, 3–84.

Triggs, Kathy. *The Stars and the Stillness.* Cambridge: Lutterworth, 1986.

Troup, Sir C. Edward. "Notes on George MacDonald's Boyhood in Huntly." *The Deeside Field* n.d.: 62—63.

Unsigned editorial. *Every Evening* [Wilmington, DE] 22 November 1872.

Walker, Jeanne Murray. "The Demoness and the Grail: Deciphering MacDonald's *Lilith.*" Robert A. Collins and Howard D. Pearce (eds.), *The Scope of the Fantastic—Culture, Biography, Themes, Children's Literature.* Westport, CT: Greenwood, 1985.

Wall, Kathryn. "George MacDonald's Lilith and the Later Poetry of T. S. Eliot." *English Language Notes* 16 (1978): 47–51.

Willard, Nancy. "Goddess in the Belfry." *Parabola* 3 (1981): 90–94.

Williams, Charles. *The Figure of Beatrice.* 1943. New York: Noonday, 1961.

Willis, Lesley. " 'Born Again': The Metamorphosis of Irene in George MacDonald's *The Princess and the Goblin.*" *Scottish Literary Journal* 1 (May 1984): 24–38.

Wilson, Keith. "The Quest for 'The Truth': A Reading of George MacDonald's *Phantastes.*" *Etudes Anglaises.* 2 (1981): 140–152.

Wilson, Samuel Law. *The Theology of Modern Literature.* London, 1875.

Woods, Katherine Ann. Review of *Lilith. The Bookman* 2 (Oct. 1895): 133–35.

Woolf, Robert Lee. *The Golden Key.* New Haven: Yale UP, 1961.

Yeats, W. B. *The Collected Poems of W. B. Yeats.* New York: Macmillan, 1956.

Index